Ukrainian Political Economy

Ukrainian Political Economy

The First Ten Years

Robert S. Kravchuk

palgrave
macmillan

First published 2002 by
PALGRAVE MACMILLAN™
175 Fifth Avenue, New York, N.Y. 10010 and
Houndmills, Basingstoke, Hampshire, England RG21 6XS.
Companies and representatives throughout the world.

PALGRAVE MACMILLAN is the global academic imprint of the Palgrave Macmillan division of St. Martin's Press, LLC and of Palgrave Macmillan Ltd. Macmillan® is a registered trademark in the United States, United Kingdom and other countries. Palgrave is a registered trademark in the European Union and other countries.

ISBN 0–312-21034–5 hardback

Library of Congress Cataloging-in-Publication Data

Kravchuk, Robert S., 1955-
Ukrainian political economy : the first ten years / by Robert Kravchuk.
p. cm.
Includes bibliographical references and index.
ISBN 0–312-21034–5
1. Ukraine—Economic conditions—1991- 2. Ukraine—Economic policy—1991-
I. Title.

HC340.19.K7 2002
330.9477'086—dc21

2002029242

A catalogue record for this book is available from the British Library.

Design by Autobookcomp.

First edition: December 2002
10 9 8 7 6 5 4 3 2 1

Printed in the United States of America.

Contents

For Natalie, Elisa, and Timothy

Acknowledgments

This book is the result of a series of happy career accidents in the early 1990s that have continued throughout the ensuing decade. In late 1992, less than a year after Ukraine's December 1991 referendum on independence, while serving in the Connecticut state budget agency in the administration of then-Governor Lowell P Weicker, Jr., I was asked to participate in the U.S. Treasury Department's program of technical assistance to governments of the former Soviet Union. Naturally, I pressed hard to serve as a resident budget advisor in Ukraine, the birthplace of my paternal grandfather. My efforts were rewarded with success, and my family and I moved to Kyiv in early 1993.

Consequently, my first word of thanks must extend to former Deputy Treasury Secretary for International Affairs David Lipton, himself a veteran advisor to the Polish Solidarity government of the 1980s. David provided me with my first opportunity to know Ukraine. As busy as he was, David always served as a valuable sounding board for my reform ideas during my service in Kyiv. Critical supporting roles were played by other Treasury Department officials, notably Mark Sobel, Vic Miller, and Bob Banqué. Further, Treasury's chief central bank advisor, Dr. Len Lapidus, read the chapter on monetary reform and provided valuable suggestions that resulted in much improvement. Warm thanks to one and all.

My involvement in Ukrainian affairs has continued in the form of a series of subsequent U.S. Treasury missions, study visits, funded travel, and ancillary advisory projects. My activities have brought me into extensive contact with an array of political and economic experts and authorities who have helped me to gather data and to form my thinking. Consequently, they have influenced the analysis and approach that this book has taken. Alone in the first rank of this group is Dr. Taras Kuzio, currently working at the Centre for Russian and East European Studies at the University of Toronto. A tireless colleague and Ukraine-watcher, Taras not only read every page of the manuscript, he also made several excellent suggestions for improvement. Over the years, he has supplied me with a steady stream of data and research materials. He always knows exactly what I need and where to find it. In an important sense, he may be regarded as the book's "godfather." I honestly could not have achieved the depth and level of rigor displayed here without his support. My debt to Taras is considerable.

I have been fortunate to have had so many excellent teachers over the years, and especially so in the decade since completing my graduate work. My time in Kyiv proved to be an effective "post-doctorate" period of study in the emerging field of transition economics. I learned much about the dynamics of inflation from Daniel Kaufmann, former chief of the World Bank Mission in Kyiv; Simon Johnson, who now teaches in the Alfred P. Sloan School at MIT; and Alexander Yastremskiy, deputy rector of the University of Kyiv-Mohyla Academy. I learned much about Ukrainian fiscal policy from Professor Ivan Rozpoutenko, head of the economics and finance faculty at the Ukrainian Academy of Public Administration. Ihor Shpak, former director of the fiscal analysis unit of the Ukrainian parliament, generously provided revenue and expenditure data on the central government and Ukraine's regions. Dr. Volodymyr Yatesnko, currently with the United States Agency for International Development, visited me at the University of Connecticut in 1995 and lectured to my classes there on labor market developments in Ukraine. Academician Dr. Valeriy Hayets, of the Institute of Economics of the Ukrainian Academy of Sciences, provided me with a deeper understanding of the structure of the Ukrainian economy. Hayets's colleague, Inna Lunina, generously shared her work on the evolving pattern of Ukraine's intergovernmental fiscal flows.

Other Ukrainian experts to whom I am indebted include Ilko Kucheriv, of the Democratic Initiatives Fund, who, together with his friend and collaborator, Dr. Yevhen Holovaka, of the Ukrainian Institute of Sociology, shared their extensive knowledge of the changing structure of Ukrainian public opinion regarding economic reforms. While the present text does not contain a rigorous analysis of public opinion, their support was essential to the proper interpretation of public attitudes during the 1990s.

During my service in the Ministry of Finance in Kyiv, the kindness and warmth of many officials there made my stay so much more comfortable than it might have been, especially in the crisis years of 1993–94. Among the many to whom I am indebted, special mention goes to Ivan G. Dmitriev, who laid the early foundation for Ukraine's state treasury, and Anatoliy Maksiuta, head of the department for the formulation and execution of Ukraine's state budget and a former student from my days teaching at the Ukrainian Academy of Public Administration.

Encouragement to complete this book was provided by several expatriates in Kyiv, whom it has been my pleasure to know. These include: Natalie Jaresko, former economics section chief in the U.S. Embassy in Kyiv, and later President of the Western NIS Fund; Peter Sochan, an experienced Canadian banker, formerly with the Import-Export Bank of Ukraine and the Citizen's Network for Foreign Affairs; Michael Zienchuk, a Canadian advisor to the economics minister; Professor Glenn Wright of the Ukrainian Academy of Public Administration and the Central European University in Budapest; and Professor Hugh Hinton of the University of Toldeo, whom I met while he was serving on a Fulbright Fellowship in Kyiv. All have shared generously their ideas, information, contacts, and warm hospitality. I have, indeed, been blessed to have such friends and colleagues.

Insofar as I am among the newcomers to Ukrainian economics, I have learned from the efforts of others who have recently begun to labor in this field, including: Paul D'Anieri of the University of Kansas; Trevor Brown of the Ohio State University; Jim Clem of the Harvard Ukrainian Research Institute and the Davis Russian Research Center; and Dr. Volodymyr Pigenko, field manager for Charles Wise's Indiana University Parliamentary Development Project in Kyiv. Last but not least, my thanks go to John Mikesell, my colleague at Indiana University, who has always been the voice of wisdom whenever I found myself confronted with a seemingly imponderable problem, as is so often the case when laboring in the post-Soviet world.

No book is ever the sole product of the author's efforts; rather, it is embedded in a larger stream of work that preceded it, and of which it is a piece. In the present instance, this book has benefited from the work of several scholars who I greatly respect and admire, and who collectively provided the inspiration for this work. They are: Dr. Oleh Havrylyshyn of the International Monetary Fund; Bohdan Krawchenko, formerly with the Canadian Institute of Ukrainian Studies and currently serving as deputy rector of the Ukrainian Academy of Public Administration; Rudolf Tökes, Professor Emeritus of Political Science at the University of Connecticut; Robert W. Campbell, Professor Emeritus of Economics at Indiana University; Anders Åslund, of the Carnegie Endowment; and Charles Wise, my colleague in the School of Public and Environmental Affairs. They may never fully appreciate how much they have inspired me.

Finally, I must thank my friends, Tanya and Viktor Petlovaniy, who opened both their hearts and their home to me so many times during my frequent visits to Kyiv. I also owe a considerable debt of gratitude to Dean Astrid E. Merget and colleagues at the Indiana University School of Public and Environmental Affairs, whose support for international and comparative research has been invaluable in so many ways. As always, any and all errors and omissions are the sole responsibility of the author.

Robert S. Kravchuk
Saratov, Russia
May 29, 2002

[*Note*: In the interest of space, many supporting tables and graphs have been omitted from the text. The author will make these available to readers upon request in the form of a "Statistical Appendix." Interested readers should contact the author at Indiana University.]

Transition, Economics, and Reform in Ukraine's "Quadruple Transition"

Taras Kuzio
Resident fellow, Centre for Russian and East European Studies, University of Toronto

This volume is the work of many years of painstaking research by Robert S. Kravchuk in a field so sorely neglected by contemporary Ukrainian studies. Until now there were few solid academic studies of what has been a missing segment of the all-embracing "quadruple transition" under way in post-Soviet Ukraine of marketization, democratisation, state-, and nation-building.

Ukrainian economics, society, post-communist transition, and governmental reform are all areas that have long been inadequately dealt with by Western students of contemporary Ukraine. This is hardly surprising insofar as Ukrainian studies was not represented in political science or Soviet (area) studies during the Soviet era, and for obvious reasons. In the post-Soviet era, Ukrainian studies has emerged as a serious field, but the majority of academics have been more concerned with democratisation, elections, nationalism, identity, and language than with the political economy of reform.

This has been the case in the United States, where only a small number of scholars work explicitly on Ukrainian economics. British scholars rank second in terms of work on Ukraine, and Canadian academics appear to be largely uninterested in contemporary Ukraine (which is surprising given the large proportion of Canadians of Ukrainian descent). In any case, academics who study Ukraine in the English-speaking world tend to be more focused on culture and history. Only a very small number, of which Robert Kravchuk is a leading scholar, have moved into economics. This volume is therefore a highly welcome contribution to a very sparse field.

The Ukrainian economy has been in freefall since the late 1980s, and only in 2000 did it recover from a decade-long recession that was deeper and lasted longer than the Great Depression of the west in the 1930s.

Ukraine's "quadruple transition" was therefore significantly hampered by a severe socioeconomic crisis that affected all other areas of policy reform, including democratic consolidation and reform of the state sector.

The poor socioeconomic situation engendered electoral support for the anti-reform Left. This, in turn, affected the potential survivability of the Ukrainian state, insofar as Ukraine's communists never abandoned the goal of Ukraine going backward to Soviet Ukrainian statehood. During the 1990s, a strong communist presence in parliament ruled out the introduction of a fully proportionate election system. This was based on fears that a true system of proportional representation would work to the Communists' advantage. These fears appeared justified when between the 1994–98 and 1998–2002 parliaments, the Communist faction grew by 50 percent.

This situation also propelled the executive to press for a presidential republic, rather than a parliamentary one, or one where parliament elects the president. Such a system exists in Moldova, where a communist majority in parliament in 2001 led to a communist president in 2001. It is not completely coincidental in the case of Ukraine that, with two years of economic growth preceding the 2002 elections, the Communist Party lost half of its seats in parliament.

The economic crisis also affected Ukraine's social system and demographics. In the last decade Ukraine's population has declined as birth rates have fallen and mortality rates—especially among elderly males—have risen substantially. The social crisis was exacerbated by the shortage of funds available for health care and social welfare. Young males were increasingly unfit for military service, which reduced the military effectiveness of the Ukrainian armed forces. Several months (and, in some cases, years) of arrears in wage and pension payments could only be repaid in 2000, when Ukraine's first reformist government, led by Prime Minister Viktor Yushchenko, benefited from an improving economy.

The lack of budgetary funds necessitated large-scale international financial assistance from bodies such as the International Monetary Fund and World Bank. Reliance on these international institutions meant that Ukraine's sovereignty was in many ways restricted, because funds were loaned on condition that certain policies were undertaken. This had a positive effect on Ukraine in educating its leaders in sound economic and financial policy, lessons that were badly needed, when we recall Ukraine's tragic experience with hyperinflation in 1993.

Finally, the socioeconomic crisis affected Ukraine's foreign policy. Energy dependence on Russia militated against Ukraine adopting a more confrontational approach in its relations with Moscow. In the midst of a severe socioeconomic crisis, and with few budgetary funds at its disposal, Ukraine's leaders have had few cards to play in Moscow.

Robert Kravchuk's book covers a very impressive range of important areas within Ukrainian economics and reform and it is for this that we will be grateful to him. The volume will be highly useful to scholars, governments, policymakers, and students interested in Ukrainian economics, reform, and post-Soviet transition.

Chapter 1

Economic Crisis, Change, and Reform in the Ukrainian Context

Ukraine: An Interesting Case of "Non-Reform"

In the wake of the collapse of the USSR, Ukraine's strategic significance has become of particular interest to policy makers and scholars in western countries. This "newly discovered" nation of some 50 million souls is significant, not only due to its large population but also due to its land mass (it is the largest nation entirely within continental Europe—slightly larger than France), its geographic position, and its enormous economic potential. If these reasons were not enough, Ukraine is crucial to the West precisely because it was the "prized possession" of the former Soviet Union. In fact, as former U.S. National Security Advisor Zbigniew Brzezinski has put matters, "it cannot be stressed strongly enough that without Ukraine, Russia ceases to be an empire, but with Ukraine suborned and then subordinated, Russia automatically becomes an empire."[1] The maintenance of Ukraine's independence is crucial to the stability of the whole of Europe and to the political maturation of Russia as well.[2]

Historically dominated by its larger, stronger northern neighbor, Ukraine has seen little independence in over 400 years.[3] Following the fall of the Romanov dynasty and dissolution of Imperial Russia during World War I, the Ukrainian Republic was proclaimed on December 25,

1917, but was effectively established only in December 1919. Following a bloody civil war, on December 30, 1922, Ukraine joined with Russia, Bielorussia (now Belarus), and the Transcaucasus to found the Union of Soviet Socialist Republics (USSR). Although formally a signatory to the union treaty, Ukraine was, in fact, subjected to a damaging economic colonization during the years of Soviet rule.[4]

A process of "Russification" of the people and culture began under Josef Stalin, Soviet leader from 1924–53.[5] Stalin resorted to the most extreme measures to subdue Ukraine, including precipitating the infamous terror famine of 1933–34, which inaugurated the forced collectivization of Ukrainian agriculture.[6] There is broad agreement that, during 70 years of Soviet rule, Ukraine was the most thoroughly repressed republic of the former union. A uniquely Ukrainian sense of national identity was preserved in the regions of western Ukraine, however, which was to remain robust under Austrian, then Polish administration, until after World War II. To this day, western Ukraine remains a bastion of intense nationalistic sentiment, and—with the city of Kyiv—is a vital center of Ukrainian nationalism.

Immediately following the failed Moscow coup of August 1991, Ukraine seized the opportunity to secede from the former Soviet Union, declaring its independence on August 24, 1991.[7] A nationwide referendum on December 1, 1991, ratified Ukraine's independence, with 90 percent of those voting in favor. The results were unambiguous: Voter turnout exceeded 84 percent.[8] More than 70 percent of Ukrainians voted for independence. At the same time, Ukraine chose its first-ever popularly elected president, Leonid M. Kravchuk, the former ideology chief of the Communist Party of Ukraine, who campaigned on a strong platform of national sovereignty and independence.

Public opinion polls and anecdotal evidence at the time indicated that the lop-sided vote for independence was prompted by widespread dissatisfaction with Moscow's economic policies and hopes for a better life as an independent state.[9] But political independence has brought only economic decline and untold hardships for many Ukrainians. The highly fragmented structure of Soviet industry, and especially its geographic dispersion, has prevented politically independent Ukraine from immediately achieving genuine economic independence. Clearly, the most perplexing aspect of Ukraine's post-Soviet experience has been its rather mixed economic record, which combines stunning successes with remarkable policy failures. The ironic outcome has been that, despite its vast economic potential, Ukraine has lagged behind most other former Soviet countries in its transition to a market economy.

Such laggard performance has not gone unnoticed. For instance, in 1996, the World Bank categorized Ukraine as among the slowest reforming countries.[10] In 1998, the Heritage Foundation-Wall Street Journal *Index of Economic Freedom* ranked Ukraine 125th out of 156 countries, labeling Ukraine as among the "mostly unfree" economies of the world. In 2000, the Freedom House *Nations in Transit* report ranked Ukraine's economic reforms at 4.58 on a 7.00-point scale (with 1.00 being the best), behind most other Central and East European states.[11] In 2001, the World Economic Forum ranked Ukraine 60th of 75 countries overall in its *Global Competitiveness Report* (ranking it lower than many developing and third-world countries).[12] In April 2001, the World Bank placed Ukraine on its list of the "world's poorest countries," having an annual per capita income of less than $750 (along with countries like Pakistan, Rwanda, and Nicaragua).[13] This is a remarkably poor record for a country so rich in human and material resources, and after ten years of independence.

Ukraine displays many of the common macroeconomic features on the World Bank's profile of a typical "country in crisis," including[14]:

- large and persistent fiscal deficits in the 5–13 percent range (Ukraine's ranged 5–27 percent from 1991–97);
- real GDP growth declines of 1–3 percent per year (Ukraine's real GDP fell by over 60 percent from 1991–98);
- surging inflation of at least 10 percent per year (Ukraine's inflation has ranged from a high of about 10,250 percent in 1993, to a low of 10 percent in 1997);
- high and volatile current account deficits of between 4.5 and 15 percent of GDP (Ukraine's was better at between 2.3 and 3.1 percent);
- low levels of private investment of 10–19 percent of GDP (Ukraine's has been falling since 1993, to around 14 percent by 1999).

Ukraine's record is therefore an abysmal one, which raises many serious questions concerning the economic reform process in Ukraine. Among them: Why, after ten years of independence, have Ukraine's economic reform efforts failed to produce the much-anticipated turnaround? Why, until 2000, has the Ukrainian economy apparently refused to grow?[15] What have been the missing elements in Ukraine's economic policies? What domestic and international political and economic forces have prevented forward progress on reforms? In order to address these and other questions, it is useful to summarize the essential tasks of post-socialist economic reform.

The Essential Features of Economic Transition

The strategy of economic transition in the formerly socialist countries of Eastern Europe and the former Soviet Union has been described as a "table standing on four legs."[16] Given the near-religious fervor with which some economic reformers have advanced their views, these strategic elements constitute what may be termed the "canon of reform":

(1) Stabilization;
(2) Liberalization;
(3) Privatization; and
(4) Institutionalization

Stabilization of the macroeconomy is a necessary precondition for market transition. This includes a program of government expenditure control and budget deficit reduction; cessation of subsidies to large, loss-making state-owned enterprises; monetary discipline to curb inflation; reduction of external trade deficits; restriction of foreign debt to manageable levels; and an effort to reach full currency convertibility. Some degree of economic imbalance may be expected (that is, output falls, fiscal deficits, inflation, and concomitant pressures for currency devaluation); however, these factors must be anticipated in the formulation and implementation of a rigorous stabilization program.

Liberalization of prices and decontrol of interest rates and hard currency transactions should be accompanied by any necessary currency devaluation, deregulation of labor markets, and removal of barriers to foreign trade and investment. Prices and markets simply cannot perform their signaling and resource allocation functions in the presence of controls and other administrative impediments. Successful transition to the market, therefore, involves substantial liberalization along a broad front.

Privatization is the sine qua non of economic transition. It is the key feature and defining characteristic of the overall reform effort. Other components of the reform program vitally depend upon it. The hardships imposed on the population by economic stabilization measures and liberalization of prices make sense only when accompanied by significant privatization of the economy. Small- and medium-sized privatization can pave the way to absorb the millions of workers who may expect to lose their jobs from privatization of large-scale enterprises, many of which may not survive the sudden "jolt" of market competition. Effective transition cannot be achieved unless incentives for proper management of enterprise capital are in place. In other words, private ownership is the very foundation of market reform.

Institutionalization concerns the establishment of legal, political, and administrative mechanisms that provide structure for nurturing and developing private enterprise and that facilitate the accomplishment of stabilization, liberalization, and privatization of the economy. (In this respect, market transition is really more of a "three-legged stool" standing on a firm foundation of market-enabling institutions.) Unfortunately, the policy dimension of reform has tended to eclipse the institutional dimension, which, while so critical to successful reform, has only recently begun to receive the attention which it deserves.[17]

Rapid institutionalization is vital. Transition to the market can be very much of a race against time. There are limits to the public's patience with the hardships that accompany reforms—even in relatively quiescent Ukraine. In the absence of apparent improvements in the material conditions of life for ordinary citizens, the hardships imposed by the transition process threaten to generate political opposition to the reforms. This can threaten to undercut the entire transition process.

In its essence, then, noted Hungarian economist János Kornai defines post-socialist reform as "a substantive change," where at least one of the pillars of the centrally planned economy is rapidly and decisively eliminated:

(1) Dominant influence of official ideology;
(2) Dominant position of state and quasistate ownership; and/or
(3) Preponderance of bureaucratic coordination.[18]

It almost does not matter where the initial steps toward terminating the administrative-command economy take place; dismantling any one of these building blocks of socialism effectively brings the others down as well. According to this understanding of reform, then, in 2001 Ukraine was still very much of a "reforming economy": The central planning regime no longer coordinated the economy; bureaucratic intrusion, significant in the 1991–94 time frame, was declining; and state ownership of enterprises had been relinquished for small- and medium-sized firms (albeit much more slowly for large-scale and so-called "strategic" enterprises). However, despite considerable progress, after ten years of sovereign existence, Ukraine has much more to accomplish in order to complete the transition to market.

The Ukrainian Reform Paradox

What Has Been Achieved?

The key economic achievements of the early independence period include establishing Ukrainian economic sovereignty, substantially completing privatization, commencing (but not finishing) industrial restructuring, and liberalizing prices and trade. Progress was much slower in other significant areas, such as eliminating direct and indirect state subsidies to loss-making enterprises; seriously reducing credit emissions from the banking system; establishing control over government spending, especially for its overly generous social programs; and stabilizing the currency. The main economic achievement of independent Ukraine came in September 1996, with the introduction of a new national currency, the hryvnia, which coincided with the successful liquidation of Ukraine's chronic five-year inflation problem. All this has been to the good.

Yet, paradoxically, Ukraine in 2002 remains very much stuck in between the plan and the market. Unable to return to Soviet-era planning, Ukraine seems nonetheless unable to move forward to fully embrace market reforms. The most significant policy failures have been in the areas of large-scale privatization, corporate restructuring, enterprise governance, agricultural reform (especially private ownership of land), and creation of an "investor friendly" business climate. As noted above, these constitute the essence of economic transition, and their neglect has effectively prevented attracting necessary volumes of industrial investment. Questioning Ukraine's commitment to reforms, foreign firms have been reluctant to invest in Ukraine. This will hinder future growth in productivity, output, and real incomes. In the meantime, Ukraine has only been able to achieve and maintain macroeconomic stability by relying upon massive periodic infusions of capital from the International Monetary Fund and World Bank. Having emerged from the Soviet period without significant amounts of foreign debt, Ukraine after 1992 took on such large amounts of new debt that international credit ratings agencies expressed serious concern that Ukraine may be unable to meet its scheduled year 2000 loan payments.[19]

The ultimate paradox is that Ukraine has fulfilled many requirements under the "canon of reform" but has still managed to avoid a genuine transition to the market. As Daniel Kaufmann, the former World Bank mission head in Kyiv, observed, "Ukraine's continuing output collapse in the face of substantial macroeconomic stabilization suggests that, at least in Ukraine's case, macro-stabilization is not a sufficient condition to enable growth to occur."[20] Kaufmann points to a panoply of institutional factors that account for Ukraine's abysmal growth record, including: lack of coherent commercial, tax, and land codes; a labyrinthine tax system; arbitrary enforcement of laws and regulations; inadequate bankruptcy laws; high corporate and payroll tax rates combined with significant tax privileges; excessive controls on hard currency transactions; and lack of enterprise reform, especially in the agricultural sector. All of this implies that Ukraine's laggard economic performance is more the result of government policy failure rather than unfavorable terms of trade, energy dependency on Russia, or what Ukrainian elites refer to as Ukraine's "unique historical experience."

Economic Shock, but No Therapy

Ukraine's early commitment to rapid economic reform eroded rather quickly in the early 1990s. Despite its apparent success in Poland (and perhaps elsewhere) "shock therapy"—the so-called "big bang" approach—is not easy to achieve. There are several key elements of a radical reform program, all of which need to be implemented simultaneously[21]: liberalizing prices[22], freezing wages and salaries to prevent wage-pull inflation, reducing government expenditures, raising taxes to reduce budget deficits, tightening bank credit in order to help stabilize the currency, and liberalizing external trade.[23] Studies have shown that countries that have initiated revolutionary economic change—with the notable exception of Russia until 2000—have generally raised living standards more rapidly than countries that embraced gradualism.[24] The question of whether Ukraine should pursue a rapid transition to a market economy (shock therapy), or pursue a more evolutionary approach (gradualism) has been settled in favor of the latter. Why has Ukraine chosen to forego rapid reform? Did policymakers really have a choice?

Ukrainian leaders have preferred to search for a middle road between the plan and the market in an effort to create the elusive objective of the former regime: a "socially-oriented market economy." But as early as 1995, there seemed little doubt that the search for a "third way" in Ukraine would prove futile. After nearly ten years of economic decline, Ukraine's experience raises the possibility that a country in transition might reach equilibrium conditions in a semipermanent state of "near-transition." This would be, in many respects, the worst possible outcome.

The success of transition appears to depend on the fourth essential element in the canon of reform: institutionalization. The avowed purpose of the "big bang" approach is rapidly to tear down the institutional apparatus of the former socialist regime.[25] This can be done rather quickly, but few would agree that the state should be entirely torn down overnight.[26] Indeed, economist Robert Skidelsky observes that, in the case of shock therapy, "the crucial requirement for success is also the most difficult: a strong and legitimate state."[27] It is now clear that the institutional framework appropriate to a functioning market economy takes considerable time and effort to develop. This argues for a more gradualistic approach, an iterative process of: building a network of market institutions and firms[28]; proper sequencing of reforms, rather than simultaneous implementation[29]; and building market institutions based on the specific circumstances of individual countries.[30] Also important to recognize is the cushioning effect that gradualism can have on the economic dislocations that transition imposes on ordinary citizens. There are real, concrete, political limits to the hardships that citizens are willing to endure in the name of reform.

This is not to argue that gradualism cannot be painful. As Polish finance minister Leszek Balcerowicz has pointed out, "the experience in reform-resistant Ukraine shows that slower change isn't necessarily kinder and gentler."[31] Given sufficient time, coalitions will tend to form around the pre-existing socialist institutions, with the danger that they are maintained long past their practical usefulness. Unfortunately, there does not appear to be a formula for determining under what conditions a transition economy should opt for shock therapy, as opposed to gradualism, and vice versa.

Swedish economist Anders Åslund observes that there were enormous differences among the experiences of countries during the early transition process.[32] After almost a decade's experience with the former Soviet countries, we can now say that market transition is a decidedly "path-dependent" process. Outcomes can vary broadly due to conditions that may be quite country specific, such as: initial economic conditions; resource endowments; the policies implemented; access to foreign markets; and the preferences of political leaders. Sharp differences among post-socialist countries have, in many cases, overshadowed the countries' similarities.[33]

In fact, it can be argued that, in the case of Ukraine, its inherited industrial structure militates against rapid reform. For one thing, the economy on the eve of independence was highly concentrated. Some

30–40 percent of industrial output of the former USSR—Ukraine included—was produced by single-firm industries (that is, monopolies).[34] For another, efficiency based on the rigors of comparative advantage was not an objective of the command economy. With few exceptions, Ukrainian industries are not competitive in foreign markets. The result has been that Ukraine and other Soviet successor states must deal with the challenge of developing a new composition of trade. In addition, Soviet geographic specialization of industry led to an unfortunate degree of economic interdependence between what are now independent countries. Finally, the entire edifice was built on a foundation of cheap, plentiful energy. But Ukraine imports over 40 percent of its fossil fuel and has paid world market prices for several years now. A major reconfiguration of the capital base and much new investment are called for, both of which will take considerable time to bear fruit.

Consequently, a panoply of economic experts have criticized the very concept of shock therapy for its lack of completeness. For instance, Michael Ellman argues that the "debate over the correct policy—'shock therapy versus gradualism'—is largely irrelevant."[35] Similarly, Jozef van Brabant observes that, "the debate between advocates of shock therapy and gradualism has to some degree been a waste of energy, a pointless exercise in semantics that has unfortunately had calamitous consequences for . . . economies in transition."[36] James R. Millar puts it more bluntly: Where it has been attempted, "shock therapy destroyed the old system, but could not create a new one."[37] That requires a long-term program of institution-building, which is impossible to accomplish in a few short years.[38]

In Ukraine, as elsewhere, political support for reforms is a critical factor. Economist John Williamson's study of 13 cases of radical economic change concluded that effective reformers had to develop and nurture a strong political base.[39] Political scientist Paul Kubicek has observed that the slow pace of Ukrainian reforms can be largely attributed to the difficulty of mobilizing a constituency that supports such reforms.[40] Social support for reform in Ukraine has from the start been highly tenuous. A mid-1998 survey conducted by SOCIS-Gallup, Kyiv, for the International Foundation for Electoral Systems (IFES) found that a plurality of citizens would prefer a centrally planned economy: Over 33 percent would favor a return to central planning, while just 25 percent favored a market economy (down from 39 percent in 1997).[41] At the same time, some 29 percent favored a stream of small, steady reforms over rapid reform (favored by 22 percent), and 24 percent did not wish market reforms to take place at all. It turns out that

1996–97 had been the most promising time to pursue reforms, with 43 percent favoring rapid reforms. The IFES report concluded that, by the end of 1998, proponents of a market economy were losing the battle for public support. The crisis had persisted far too long.

In this environment, new firms and the emerging commercial class are struggling to find their voice but have found few champions to plead their case. Even worse, due to lagging industrial restructuring, key industries remain heavily reliant on remnants of the former state planning apparatus to ensure access to factor markets, provide tax privileges and other subsidies, and conduct business with the state on a concessionary basis. Established interest groups tend to be very conservative (that is, "Red").[42] This supports Alexander J. Motyl's observation that "the structural legacy of the USSR's collapse, in particular, the kinds of elite Ukraine inherited and its resource endowment, has kept Ukraine on the path of evolutionary change."[43] He concludes that Ukraine seems destined to "muddle along" a gradualistic path to reform. Due to the absence of appropriate enabling conditions, then, the gradual approach has been preferred over the more revolutionary, big bang, or shock therapy.

"Tinkering" with Reforms in Ukraine

The Ukrainian economic reforms did not start out as a fully developed and coherent reform package. Neither has there been a wholesale abandonment of the many familiar socialist institutions that governed the economy for so long. Due to a severely fractionated and contentious parliament, Ukrainian reformers have pursued a "blended" or "third way" between the plan and the market. The presence of inertial tendencies held over from the former Soviet regime meant that Ukraine's reforms have tended to be largely incremental, or "piecemeal," in nature.

Economic reform in the early independence period was therefore very much a process of "tinkering with the system," rather than one of substantive change. In the former USSR, such tinkering began under Khrushchev, was extended under Brezhnev, and broadened (greatly) under Gorbachev.[44] Tinkering continued in independent Ukraine, albeit in a dramatically altered political environment.

The process of tinkering is, by now, quite familiar: decentralizing some decisions; substituting price signals for direct commands in some sectors; providing economic incentives to influence enterprise behavior; moving administered prices closer to "market" prices; formation of new economic structures, such as "cooperatives"; leasing property; and privatizing smaller firms only. But such efforts at creating "administered markets" (an oxymoron) are to no real avail; they cannot substitute for market discipline. In order to genuinely reform the socialist economy, a radical break with the past is required. The principal features of the old system must be abandoned and eventually will be. This entails making market institutions the defining basis of the economic system. Ukraine is yet a long way from establishing this new system of market institutions.

Due to the politics of reform, Ukraine has reached a kind of "half-way house" between the old command economy and the market-driven, price-regulated, private property–based economic system. It is what economist Robert Campbell has described as a "semi-reformed" economy.[45] Based on the Eastern European history with such experiences prior to 1990, this kind of economy is not very stable.[46] It does not go far enough in subjecting firms to the kind of direct competition that they need to dramatically improve their performance. Indeed, this "hybrid" system creates problems of its own, including: a decrease in output with no attendant benefits of asset reallocation; an increase in budget deficits; a tendency toward rampant inflation and currency devaluation; and social unrest. Each of these problems was evident in Ukraine in the 1990s.

In order to overcome these difficulties, Ukraine will have to abandon the policy of tinkering, in order to create a solid institutional foundation for the market economy. Building new market institutions will require: privatization of large-scale industry (including agriculture); dissolution of inefficient, loss-making enterprises; break-up of state-owned monopoly enterprises (to promote equity and dampen inflationary tendencies); development of a new banking system and other financial institutions; establishment of an efficient stock market; and creation of governmental fiscal management procedures and controls that meet modern international standards.

The important task is to draw a clear line of demarcation between the government and enterprise sectors, on the one hand, and between the state and the private, free market economy, on the other. By 2001, there was a panoply of laws that purported to move in this direction but that contained such levels of incoherence and inconsistency that they interjected mostly uncertainty and confusion into economic affairs. A degree of consistency must be achieved.

Ukraine's Problems: Understandable, Analyzable, and Correctible

Frequently changing policies; weak, ambiguous, and mutually contradictory laws; selective enforcement of existing laws and regulations; and unclear jurisdictional boundaries among government ministries have contributed to the perception of instability in Ukraine's business climate. Under these conditions, a big bang approach would have resulted in short-term rapid price escalation, acute output deterioration, and massive budget deficits, without generating the desired supply-side response. But Ukraine's more gradual approach was not able to escape this fate, either. The resulting popular frustration has generated a strong temptation to return to direct administrative controls in the attempt, as Ukrainian newspapers frequently put it, to "restore order" in the economic sphere. In fact, examination of Ukraine's first ten years' experience with reforms reveals a record of oscillation between piecemeal reforms, half-measures, and periodic efforts to reassert administrative control over key economic variables. That record is examined in the chapters that follow.

First, we must more thoroughly examine Ukraine's macroeconomic record since the country achieved independence in late 1991. That is the subject of chapter two. Subsequent chapters will describe and analyze the causes of Ukraine's dismal economic performance. The book argues against those who believe that Ukraine's current problems are somehow unique and require special, or in some sense "non-standard," solutions. That is the essence of the search for the "Ukrainian third way" to market transition. This author takes issue with this point of view.

The analyses, arguments, and policy prescriptions contained within these covers are based on the author's firm conviction that Ukraine's problems—as difficult and intractable as they may appear—are understandable, analyzable, and correctible. As such, despite the unprecedented scale of the economic and political transition underway on the territory of the former Soviet Union, there is much that Western political and economic analysis can contribute to resolution of the crisis. To that end, this book is devoted.

Chapter 2

The Ukrainian Economy in the 1990s

Economic Crisis and the Output Collapse

Most economic indicators for Ukraine in the 1990s were overwhelmingly negative. From the data in table 2.1 it can be calculated that, from 1991–98, Ukraine's real GDP declined by a cumulative 62.1 percent. By comparison, Russia's fell by less—just over 40 percent; average in the Commonwealth of Independent States (CIS) was a 50 percent decline.[1] Industrial output and capital investment fell by similarly large magnitudes: nearly 59 and 81 percent, respectively. No sector or industry was spared, with the steepest declines coming in heavy industry and raw materials extraction. Table 2.1 also indicates that the industrial collapse has shown few signs of reversal, until 1999–2000. In 2001 there was a recorded growth of 9.0 percent in real GDP.[2] Only time will tell if this growth record can be sustained. The central point for present purposes is that Ukraine's economic free-fall of the 1990s raises questions about the nature of the collapse and its relation to the essential features of economic transition.

Some experts have questioned the inevitability of the industrial collapse experienced by former socialist economies.[3] Such questioning seems strangely out of place. For it is now quite clear that, in the 25 years immediately preceding the collapse of the USSR, there were serious misallocations of capital and labor throughout the entire Soviet economy.[4] The record shows that the period leading up to and including the perestroika era witnessed a steady decline in productivity.[5]

Table 2.1
Basic Economic Indicators of Ukraine, 1991-2000

	1991	1992	1993	1994	1995	1996	1997	1998	1999	2000	Cumulative Pct. Change 1991-98	Cumulative Pct. Change 1991-99
Output and Income				(Percent Change from Previous Period)								
Real GDP	-8.7	-9.9	-14.2	-22.9	-12.2	-10.0	-3.0	-1.9	-0.3	6.0	-62.1	-43.6
Gross Industrial Output	-4.8	-6.8	-8.0	-27.3	-12.0	-5.1	-0.3	-1.0	4.0	n.a.	-58.7	-49.1
Employment	-1.7	-4.0	-2.3	-5.4	n.a.	-2.1	-2.5	-1.0	-2.0	n.a.	-19.8	-20.8
Capital Investment	-7.1	-36.9	-10.3	-22.5	-20.5	-22.0	-8.6	-0.6	-4.0	n.a.	-81.0	-77.9
Prices and Wages				(Percent Change from Previous Period)								
Consumer Price Index	261	2830	10255	501	182	40	10	20	19	26		
Wholesale Price Index	263	3928	9767	655	281	17	5	35	16	n.a.		
Average Nominal Wages	240	2304	3948	418	261	22	9	-1	24	n.a.		
Government Finances				(Percent of GDP)								
Consolidated Budget Revenues	36.5	32.8	40.0	49.1	40.1	38.6	42.4	39.8	37.0	40.5		
Consolidated Budget Expenditures	50.6	45.0	46.5	59.7	48.0	43.2	49.6	41.9	38.4	38.2		
Consolidated Budget Deficit	-14.1	-12.2	-6.5	-10.5	-7.9	-4.6	-7.1	-2.1	-1.4	2.4		
Directed Credits	13.6	12.8	8.0	4.2	3.2	1.0	0.0	0.0	0.0	0.0		
Extrabudgetary Funds Balance (1998 Est.)	0.5	3.5	0.5	0.4	0.4	0.4	0.5	0.4	0.0	0.0		
General Government Balance	-27.2	-21.5	-14.0	-13.4	-10.7	-5.2	-6.6	-1.7	-1.4	2.4		
External Sector												
Gross Foreign Debt ($US billion)	n.a.	n.a.	1.4	7.2	8.2	8.8	9.6	11.5	12.8	n.a.		
Exchange Rate (HRV/$, Average for Period)	n.a.	0.00208	0.04539	0.317	1.47307	1.8295	1.867	2.4495	4.1	5.44023		
Current Account Balance (% GDP)	n.a.	n.a.	-2.3	-3.1	-3.1	-2.7	-2.7	-3.1	2.7	n.a.		
Memorandum: Nominal GDP												
Billions of Karbovanets:	299	5168	142016	1079200	5083601							
Millions of Hryvna:					50836	81519	93365	102,593	127,126	175,010 (preliminary)		

Sources: Ministry of Finance of Ukraine; IMF country studies on Ukraine (various issues, 1993-2001); European Expert Service, "Ukraine in Numbers," *Ukrainian Legal and Economic Bulletin* (various issues); European Expert Service, Centre for Macroeconomic Analysis of Ukraine, *Ukrainian Economic Trends* (various issues); and the author's calculations.

Stagnation led to decline, so that all post-socialist countries in the 1990s experienced a deep economic depression. Only Albania, Poland, and the former German Democratic Republic had begun to recover by 1994. (To be fair, most of these economies also began their reform programs earlier than CIS countries, the German economy is soft, and Albania has since suffered a serious relapse.) By the end of 1995, the Czech Republic, Hungary, and some of the smaller newly independent states of the former USSR had also begun to show positive real growth rates.[6] But it has taken Ukraine over ten years to turn the corner.

The official data can be notoriously imprecise and may in fact overstate the scale of the output decline. But it is widely accepted that Ukraine experienced a dramatic real output fall. Reasons for Ukraine's chronic recession were apparently not the result of a continuation of what János Kornai has termed the socialist "shortage economy," nor did it derive from general insufficient demand.[7] Rather, the root causes may be traced directly to the circumstances of the transition from socialism and the simultaneous unleashing of unfettered market forces. The problem is that these forces were loosed in the institutional vacuum left by a receding state that lacked the means to regulate the emerging market economy. Consequently, there are no clear "rules of the game."

The output collapse is therefore symptomatic of the unregulated transition from what was a general shortage economy, in which supply constraints predominated, to a freer, but demand constrained economy.[8] Ten years of inconsistent policy measures got Ukraine "stuck in the middle," as it were. After a decade of partial transition, it exhibits characteristics of an economy subject to both supply-side and demand-side constraints. It has developed into economist Robert Campbell's "semi-reformed economy."[9] It finds itself in a kind of "half-Keynesian state," where demand factors play a considerable role in determining output but where doctrinaire Keynesianism is not an appropriate guide to macroeconomic policy.[10] The development of effective macroeconomic policy instruments must therefore await transformation of the real structure of the economy, which calls for substantial progress on privatization, land reform, demonopolization of industry, development of commercial law, and reform of enterprise governance.

Demand-side management of the semi-reformed economy is not possible where large amounts of state ownership of industry persist. Further, indirect management of demand does not suit the authorities' instinctive preferences for administrative, supply-side controls. The slow pace of privatization and enterprise governance reform accounts for much of the ineffectiveness of Ukrainian economic policy. Effective ownership of property is necessary in order for enterprise managers to seek new markets and to squeeze inefficiencies out of their firms. This is impossible without considerable privatization, corporate governance reform, capital market development, industrial restructuring and meaningful bankruptcy law.[11]

But Ukrainian policymakers tend to view the output collapse as *the problem* rather than as a symptom of deep-rooted inefficiencies held over from the former regime. The government's focus on stemming the output fall has pit two sets of economic objectives against each other. In the short run, reorganization and restructuring of the real sector works against maintaining employment levels, as firms can be expected to shed excess labor and reduce demand for other factor inputs. In the long run, efficiency and growth are promoted through reallocation of productive resources, reduction of state subsidies, and imposition of a hard budget constraint (that is, enterprises must become self-financing). A further problem is that these reforms work against the short-run objectives of maintaining social stability during the difficult transition period. The effort to steer a course between stemming the fall in output and promoting long-run growth has at times led to contradictory policy measures. This explains some of the apparent "zig-zags" that economic reform has taken since 1991.

In addition, disruption of state coordination of the economy has left an enormous void. The command-administrative system has withdrawn, but the emerging market institutions are not fully developed.[12] Also, backwardness in the financial sector, insolvency of banks, and considerable amounts of financial repression (that is, governmental direction of capital allocation) all militate against reversal of the chronic decline in output and dwindling real investment. The government's seeming inability to cleanse the banking system of bad loans and establish appropriate regulatory procedures is clearly to blame for much of the sluggish investment activity. Capital mobilization on the scale that is required will be impossible in the face of Ukraine's poorly functioning financial institutions. Consequently, the transformational recession persisted long after it was reversed in other post-socialist countries.

Capital Investment Trends

Throughout most of Ukraine's Soviet years, gross fixed investment averaged around 30 percent of national income, which is quite high by almost any standard. However, according to British economist David

Dyker, "Ukraine [had] been a consistent exporter of capital to the rest of the Soviet Union," which meant that a proportionately lower rate of aggregate fixed capital investment took place in Ukraine than in the rest of the USSR.[13] Soviet investment levels, though high, were not based on any rational calculation of returns but on development strategies that had been adopted to meet other criteria. Much investment was aimed at "patching-up old obsolete production capacities, as organizations at all levels . . . tried to fulfill exacting output targets."[14] Serious problems emerged as inefficient projects were adopted. Cost and time overruns were common, as initial starts typically were followed by months (and sometimes years) of delay and inaction.

The Soviet economy was able to grow rapidly during its early years, mainly due to its reliance on extensive (as opposed to intensive) investment, based on an abundance of cheap labor, raw materials, and energy. Little concern with relative investment efficiency in the face of capital scarcity was present. Ironically, the trend in Soviet capital productivity from the very beginning of central planning was almost uniformly downward, despite its—at times—rapid economic growth.[15] As with so many other economic problems lurking beneath the surface of the former Soviet economy, in 2001 gross investment in Ukraine continued to be in a state of collapse.

The real percentage change in investment has been negative since 1991, with an accumulated aggregate 78 percent fall through the end of 1999. To place this in perspective, it must be understood that much of Ukraine's fixed capital already is superannuated, subject to frequent breakdown, and increasingly difficult to maintain. In 1990, some 24 percent of total fixed capital was obsolete. (By Ukrainian standards, this means more than 34 years old!) It is estimated that 75 percent of fixed assets will be over 20 years old by 2010.[16] It is obvious that much of the capital stock has been kept in service well beyond its efficient economic life. This is an ominous development. In Dyker's words, "it condemns the economy to in-built obsolescence."[17] Writing in 1992, Dyker did not foresee the Ukrainian capital stock arriving at a technologically satisfactory level before the early part of the next century. The timetable has become much more attenuated since then.

Prevalence of the "Shadow Sector"

Coinciding with the collapse of official output has been the increasing prevalence of shadow activity as a significant feature of Ukraine's economy. The "unofficial" (that is, unregistered and untaxed) economy was estimated to comprise some 60 percent of total economic activity by early 1996.[18] Exclusion of shadow activity from the official statistics, therefore, greatly overstates the estimated economic decline.[19] The shadow sector, however, is nothing new. From 1960–89, the unofficial economy grew in the former USSR by an estimated 3,000 percent, accounting for more than 20 percent of income.[20] Shadow activity has grown exponentially in the post-Soviet period. For instance, in 1992, a survey of 223 private firms determined that 54 percent of aggregate profits were derived from shadow activities.[21] In 1994, a poll of 200 companies operating with foreign capital revealed that 55 percent of their revenues came from the shadow sector.[22] Further, approximately 57 percent of all currency from 1997–98 circulated outside of the banking system. It seems safe to conclude that a significant proportion of the work force has come to be partially or fully employed in shadow activities.[23]

Shadow activities are not strictly criminal in nature. To be sure, there is a certain criminal layer of illicit activity, which accounts for some 33–50 percent of it. But most shadow activity consists of ordinary people meeting their personal needs. They operate more or less in the open; however, most of it is unmonitored by state authorities and hence escapes taxation. As I have observed elsewhere, "it results from individuals and firms protecting themselves from excessive regulation, confiscatory taxation, and rampant corruption."[24] Shadow activity is, almost by definition, untaxed. A particularly abundant source of "shadow profits" derives from barter transactions. The government estimates that barter deals accounted for over 42 percent of total sales volumes in both 1997 and 1998.[25] This effectively removes some 50–60 percent of all economic activity from the tax base, thereby threatening fiscal instability. The government thus has strong incentives to pursue shadow operators.

At the same time, the availability of a more or less free market "in the shadows" has helped to ease conditions among the general population during the transition period. Razumkov, et al. estimate that at least two-thirds of Ukrainians have participated in the shadow sector.[26] Taras Kuzio puts the figure at 75 percent.[27] Former Deputy Prime Minister Viktor M. Pynzenyk believes that the benefit to ordinary citizens has been substantial. In a speech before parliament in January 1996, Pynzenyk estimated that the average level of consumption by citizens of Ukraine exceeded their average monthly incomes by some 2.5 times.[28] However, a particularly pathological aspect of the shadow economy is that it greatly compromises the government's macroeconomic policies. To date, the government has essentially avoided any real effort to curtail shadow activity. In 2001, it remains, at one and the same time, both a blessing to the Ukrainian people and a curse to government policymakers.[29]

Fiscal and Monetary Policy Achievements

The Inflationary Impulse

One of the most intriguing issues in Ukraine's recent economic history was the two-year slide into hyperinflation in 1992–93, followed by the long drive to monetary stabilization, which was effectively achieved in September 1996. There have been other challenges since then, particularly avoiding financial chaos during the Russian crisis of 1998, but the groundwork for Ukraine's monetary policy was laid by 1996. It is now clear that serious expenditure control problems, coupled with lavish amounts of budget subsidies and directed credits to state enterprises and agricultural concerns combined to trigger a tragic bout with inflation in 1991–95.[30] Without an effective domestic debt financing capability, inflation broke out into the open in 1991–92. As predicted by economic theory, Ukraine's price inflation was accompanied by rapid increases in the money supply.[31] The period of greatest expansion was 1992–94, which was followed by a dramatic reduction, starting in mid-1994. Stabilization was accomplished at the same time that Ukraine's permanent national currency, the hryvnia was introduced, in September 1996.

Fiscal Deficits

Ukraine's inflation was the direct result of lax budgetary discipline. Real revenues and expenditures were remarkably robust in the face of annual falls in real GDP, and, therefore, largely unrelated to the rampant price inflation. This suggests that political factors played a greater role in fiscal policy than did macroeconomic considerations.[32] Especially in the credit emissions to the enterprise sector, there was a direct link between government outlays and the inflationary impulse.

The overall level of public expenditure is high in Ukraine, relative to most market economies, since independence, running at between 40–60 percent of GDP. That is some 20–30 percentage points higher than the average for the vastly wealthier European Union countries. Even though Ukraine lacks the fiscal resources to afford the overly generous social programs it inherited from the USSR, as an aging society some 25 percent of the population qualifies for pension and other benefits.[33] The social safety net is therefore quite burdensome. Reducing the fiscal expenditure has been difficult in the face of such near-universal social commitments.

Although the situation slowly is improving, establishing fiscal transparency, spending control, and accountability remains an important government objective. With social attitudes favoring wide dispersal of benefits, the government has been unable to target programs on only the neediest groups. Budget and expenditure systems have not been geared toward spending control, so that ministries and state enterprises have not been subject to a hard budget constraint. This has meant that the availability of cheap bank credits and off-budget subsidies considerably eroded enterprise incentives to seek improvements in efficiency. At mid-1999, the lack of a fully functioning state treasury prevented effective tracking of cash outlays and government spending commitments.

On the revenue side, a serious problem has been that tax collection rates are inadequate. Frequent and dramatic tax rate and base changes, combined with high marginal rates, selective enforcement, and gratuitous tax concessions have eroded perceptions of fairness. Tax evasion is widespread. A further erosion of the tax base has occurred due to the expanding shadow economy. It has been estimated that approximately 32,000 enterprises avoid paying taxes.[34] Further, revenues actually reaching the central government are less than collections, since regional and district tax offices have routinely siphoned tax receipts without reporting the same to the state treasury. The array of taxes, rates, bases, and means of administration in Ukraine are incompatible with the needs of a market economy. The challenge for tax reform is to restore fairness while at the same time reducing disincentives to work and produce. And this must be done without increasing the fiscal deficit and while avoiding a return to inflation. Tax reform has proved elusive, however. A presidentially sponsored comprehensive tax reform failed in 1997, when parliament enacted the president's "Economic Growth '97" tax package on a piecemeal basis, leaving out its more substantive features.

Financing Budget Deficits

Unless Ukraine is able to increase tax collections or dramatically reduce expenditure pressures, fiscal deficits will persist. Noninflationary financing of deficits via issuance of state domestic debt was slow to establish in Ukraine. This meant that, well into 1996, the National Bank of Ukraine played the dominant role in deficit financing, via credit expansion. Ukraine issued its first domestic state bonds in the first quarter of 1995, but Ukraine's domestic debt market has not been able to fully finance budget deficits. As late as 1998, foreign borrowing was being used to cover over 60 percent of the total deficit. Further development and maturity of the domestic public debt market will remain a critical fiscal policy objective.

Privatization and Enterprise Restructuring

What Was the Extent of Privatization?

Privatization of the state sector is the essence of market transition. True privatization involves a permanent transfer of ownership and control of an enterprise from the state to private investors and/or managers. Privatization is not an end in itself but a means toward the more efficient management of productive assets. It should induce a permanent shift in enterprise behavior toward consideration of economic rates of return and market risk-taking. Rapid privatization should bring with it the benefits of a shrinking state sector, reduced subsidies to loss-making enterprises, an expanded tax base, reduced opportunities for corruption, and more rapid economic growth. No other dimension of the economic reform package is capable of sustaining the transition to market; only private property will suffice.

Ukraine's experience with privatization was quite mixed before 1995; however, small-scale privatization, which started slowly, accelerated in 1995–96. It was virtually completed in 1998. On the other hand, medium- and large-scale privatization has lagged, grinding to a near standstill in 1996. It has proceeded at a snail's pace since then. "Scale" is defined under Ukrainian law on the basis of an enterprise's book value of assets. Small-scale privatization involved mainly shops, boutiques, restaurants, and small service establishments. Over 95 percent of the estimated stock of 55,000 small enterprises in Ukraine had been privatized by year-end 1998, mainly going to existing managers and employee groups.[35] To put this achievement in proper perspective, these enterprises collectively account for a mere 2 percent of industrial output. Ukrainian industry remains highly concentrated in large, monopolistic enterprises, which have been resistant to privatization efforts.

By mid-1997 only 9,649 of the over 18,000 medium- and large-scale firms had entered the corporatization stage (pre-privatization).[36] Some 5,087 of these had transferred more than 70 percent of their shares to private hands.[37] An additional 3,328 enterprises either entered corporatization or transferred less than 70 percent to the private sector. The slow progress on large-scale privatization largely reflects ongoing parliamentary resistance to development of the Ukrainian private sector. This manifested itself sharply in the 1994–95 moratorium on privatization.[38] The ban was lifted only when parliament compiled a standing list of what it considered to be "strategically important" enterprises that were to be excluded from privatization.[39] According to the government, by the end of 1999, privatized enterprises accounted for approximately 71 percent of industrial output and more than 50 percent of industrial employment.

The Special Problem of Agriculture

Substantial progress has been made in agro-industrial privatization, but not in land reform or in the effective decollectivization of farming. Of the approximately 6,000 medium-to-large agro-industrial complex (AIC) enterprises that had entered the mass privatization program by early 1999, over 5,600 had begun selling shares.[40] But the slow pace of reforms, especially parliament's foot-dragging on land ownership and the development of an effective real estate market, has hindered further progress.

President Leonid M. Kuchma has made agricultural reform a priority of his administration. But agricultural reforms sputtered out dramatically in the wake of the March 1998 parliamentary elections, and governments at all levels routinely interfere in AIC enterprise decision making. A law permitting leasing of land enacted in September 1998 has yet to have any significant effect on land-use decisions. Land—including private farm plots—can not be sold or pledged as collateral for farm loans. This severely restricts availability of financing for purchases of seed, fertilizer, and equipment. At year-end 1999, only some 14 percent of arable land was farmed privately. This means that the bulk of private farming activity is still conducted on small household plots, many of which were started back in the perestroika period.[41] These 11.5 million small plots accounted for more than half of all livestock and the bulk of potatoes, vegetables, and fruits grown in Ukraine.[42] By this measure, continuing state ownership of farm land is disastrous for Ukraine.

The Desired Behavioral Change Has Not Been Forthcoming

Unfortunately, privatization has thus far produced little real change in the behavior of the typical enterprise.[43] Around 85 percent of all shares have gone to incumbent managers and employee groups through preferred allocations during the initial, closed subscription phase of privatization. For small enterprises, some 56 percent of all entities were transferred to collective ownership at mid-1997 (another 2 percent remained in state hands). Consequently, there has been little substantive behavioral modification, especially in most large enterprises. Enterprises purchased and controlled by insiders are unlikely to seek new markets, control costs, or eliminate redundant labor.

In the post-privatization firm, investment tends to fall, and the wage bill increases.[44] Big, inefficient, and overburdened with much unnecessary fixed investment (that is, obsolete equipment, employee housing, vacation sanitariums and resorts, etc.), most large enterprises are highly illiquid. Many have resorted to informal means of financing, such as delaying wage payments or deliberately running up large amounts of unpaid bills. By May 1999, overdue accounts payable among firms had reached the extraordinary level of 80 percent of GDP.[45] Perpetually strapped for cash, many enterprises continue seeking budgetary and credit subsidies, tax privileges, and state contracts. Estimates of continuing direct subsidies to enterprises placed the figure at 3.1 percent of GDP in 1998 (and 19.4 percent, including estimated implicit subsidies).[46] Economists Paul Hare, Mohammed Ishaq, and Saul Estrin have concluded that this is due to the exclusionary nature of the privatization process in Ukraine.[47] Lack of a behavioral response is rooted in the perverse incentive structure of the former regime. Larger enterprises find that there is still more to be gained from government subsidies and tax privileges than from increasing operating efficiency. The direct result has been that the number of loss-making enterprises, and net economic losses, continued to increase throughout the 1990s. In 1998, 54 percent of enterprises were money losers, with their average losses fluctuating between 15 and 30 percent throughout the 1990s.

Limited Demonopolization Progress.
The IMF estimates that some 30 to 40 percent of industrial output in the former USSR was produced by monopolies.[48] Due to the Soviet affection for enormous enterprises, Ukraine in 1991 inherited many single-firm industries. A large proportion of Ukrainian output is still produced by industry associations and so-called "financial-industrial groups" (FIGs), which are a species of the vertically integrated entities that were long ago outlawed in most Western economies. Over 98 percent of industrial output is produced by the estimated 18,000 firms classified as either medium- or large-scale. The trend also seems to favor continuance of large-scale enterprises. In fact, monopolists grew in number by 36 percent in 1993 alone, from 795 to 1,078. As late as February 1998, the 200 largest enterprises in Ukraine accounted for 90 percent of

industrial output.[49] Monopoly enterprises vary broadly by sector, and substantial progress has been made in reducing their number in some industries, notably heavy industry, construction, and cement production.

The law "On Containing Monopolization and Preventing Unfair Competition" was enacted in February 1992, and the Anti-Monopoly Committee was established in November 1993 in order to identify and monitor enterprises in concentrated industries that are to be subject to regulation. The threshold was set very high, however, at 35 percent of the market for certain goods and services, including the national and regional levels.[50] Unfortunately, the high threshold level means that, of the more than 700 markets that are affected by monopolies, only around 30 percent will be regulated. The power to regulate monopolies was initially exercised through the now defunct "system of state orders and state contract," by setting prices and tariffs directly on the output of monopolists. To prevent the creation of new monopolies, and the further accumulation of market share, the Anti-Monopoly Committee cooperates with the State Property Fund (SPF) to clear all such proposed purchases.[51] In addition, a January 1997 law protects against unauthorized usage of one firm's name by another and protects service marks, advertising, packing materials, general appearance of goods, etc.[52] These laws establish criminal penalties for the harming of another's business reputation or tie-in sales, unfair state discrimination against businesses, and coercive contracts. The law was further tightened in March 1998.[53]

An Unfriendly Business Climate.

The business environment in Ukraine is generally subject to overregulation, and there is much unwarranted state intrusion in business operations. An enormous amount of activity is required for accomplishing even the most routine tasks, such as business registration, on-site inspections, audits, and meetings with officials at government office buildings. Rules, requirements, and regulations burden commerce with delay, introduce uncertainty, and provide opportunities for corrupt officials to exact bribes. The State Committee on Problems of Development of Business Enterprise in late 1997 reported that some 1,050 types of commercial activity had been subject to licensing by law, edict, or regulation.[54] Further, it was reported that 25 government departments and agencies possess legal authority to audit businesses. For the average firm, the number of such annual checks by 1998 had risen to 296. Surveys of small businesses consistently indicate that the two most painful legal problems are registration and government audits.[55] It is estimated that Ukrainian enterprises spend the equivalent of 3 percent of GDP on regulatory compliance each year, an enormous drag on the economy.

In a spring 1993 survey of western firms operating in Ukraine, "constantly changing laws and regulations" and the "unclear distribution of functions among government organs" were cited by almost three-quarters of the respondents as obstacles to doing business.[56] In 1996, Kyiv-based attorney Myron Rabij reported that the most serious legal impediment to doing business in Ukraine was that tax laws, customs regulations, and licensing procedures were "cumbersome and often ambiguous," leading to "arbitrary or inconsistent implementation of regulations or corruption."[57] The state remains quite intrusive. In 1997, the two "most painful" legal problems reported by small businesses were the arcane licensing procedures and frequent on-site check-ups on businesses' operations by governmental bodies.[58]

Reducing government regulation has been a major emphasis of President Kuchma since February 1998, when the president issued a decree ordering significant deregulation.[59] A deadline of April 1, 1998, was set to simplify business registration, reduce the number of activities that require registration, shorten the review time necessary for licensing, limit the number of audits and inspections of businesses, and establish a fixed tax for small businesses. The decree established the State Committee on Entrepreneurship Development, which was given power to implement changes in regulations of governments at all levels that may hinder commercial development.

Kuchma's intent was to draw the approximately 1.5 million "shadow sector" firms into the official economy. This would literally swell the number of registered businesses in Ukraine from the current number of around 90,000. As a further simplification, in early July 1998, Kuchma issued a decree that simplified accounting procedures and tax filings for small business. In late July, a second decree placed restrictions on both announced and unannounced inspections of business premises. Inspections were limited to one a year, and at least ten days advance notice had to be given. To limit the inconvenience, inspections by all government agencies had to be conducted on the same day.[60] Little additional progress was made on deregulation throughout 1998–99, however. The administration also encountered considerable bureaucratic resistance to the decree, especially from the State Tax Administration (STA), which was seeking to increase tax compliance via intensive audits of malingering firms.

Other serious problems consistently cited by business leaders include high tax rates and the general inadequacy of the banking system.[61] In addition, the commercial code is underdeveloped, and there remains great uncertainty as to the security of ownership rights. Protection of intellectual property is especially lacking. All of this has placed private firms at a disadvantage to state-owned and -operated entities. In summary, it seems that Ukraine will only slowly evolve in the direction of a market economy and will encounter much resistance along the way.

Employment and Wages

Increasing Joblessness

The former USSR guaranteed jobs to workers at regulated wages. Benefits were universally provided, both by the state and by enterprises (which provided, among other things: vacation retreats, job training, kindergarten, child care, and often housing). Some of the paternalism that characterized the former regime has continued in post-Soviet Ukraine, but many of the benefits have been reduced or eliminated. Unemployment has officially run at levels that are deceptively low. In mid-1994, however, serious increases in unemployment were reported for the first time, and they have accelerated. Official registered joblessness was barely 6,800 at the time of independence. But this figure had climbed to over 1 million by the end of 1998. Rising unemployment has produced severe dislocations in the lives of many workers and carries with it increased levels of anxiety and social tension.

Hidden Unemployment and Underemployment Are Widespread

Official unemployment rates ran at around 5 percent at year-end 2000, but this does not completely reflect the employment picture. The number of full-time employed workers fell from nearly 4 million in early 1994 to under 2.3 million at mid-1999.[62] This 1999 number is but a small fraction of the nearly 20 million workers reportedly employed.[63] Many workers have been placed on administrative leave, or are officially registered as employed but are paid part time, or not at all. As evidence of this, the average number of days actually worked as a percent of all work days fell steadily from 86 percent in 1994 to 78 percent in 1999.[64] "Hidden unemployment" has therefore become quite pervasive in Ukraine. Many workers prefer to remain "formally employed" even though they are not paid regularly, if at all. In the late 1990s, enterprises continued to assume responsibility for many social services that have naught to do with their business missions (including kindergartens and schools, job training, housing, and health care) and that workers would lose altogether if they were let go. Firms, too, have incentives to hoard labor: Workers must be given three months' notice to be laid off. Their employers therefore prefer to place them on "unpaid leave" rather than pay what amounts to three months' severance.

In March 1993, on the basis of inspections of 6,900 enterprises, the State Center of Employment reported that nearly 572,000 of the 3.9 million workers employed, or 14.6 percent of the total, were on long-term leave.[65] That was reportedly twice more than the number in 1992. In certain regions of Ukraine, levels of hidden unemployment reached 58 percent. In March 1995, the International Labor Organization (ILO) estimated that some 44.5 percent of all factories had some workers on short-term leave.[66] Recent estimates place the number of hidden unemployed at close to 3.5 million. Many of these workers are now at least partially engaged in shadow activities.[67]

Hidden unemployment may be expected to decline, since enterprise-provided benefits are shrinking and the time period for registration for unemployment benefits has been shortened (from three months to seven days).[68] Consistent with these developments, registered unemployment has risen dramatically since the end of 1995. Despite such growth in the jobless ranks, the official unemployment rate stood at just 3.7 percent in December 1998. The ILO, however, estimated actual unemployment levels at closer to 9.8 percent, or two to three times the official rate. The annual October household survey confirmed the rate in unemployment to be nearly 9 percent in late 1997 (with a distinct bias toward underestimation, since elderly are considered ineligible for employment). In April 1999, the World Bank estimated the real unemployment rate to be 30 percent in Ukraine (and 50 percent in Crimea).[69] Joblessness greatly exceeds new job creation. In Ivano-Frankivsk Oblast, for instance, there were more than 227 applicants for each job vacancy; in Volynska Oblast, 88; and in Zakarpattska Oblast, 83.[70]

Three-quarters of the unemployed are women, and over half have completed a degree of higher education. Despite the industrial vacancies that still exist, their higher skill levels will make many of them more difficult to place in factory jobs. The result is that labor market turnover has reflected more "quits" than "hires." Almost every ninth worker quit their job in the first half of 1999, but only one in twelve was hired within the same period. Natural levels of mobility (mainly retirements and young people entering the work force) would imply that turnover should ordinarily run at around 3 percent, even though this may be high in light of Ukraine's depopulation during the 1990s. This means that Ukraine has extremely high *gross* rates of turnover, while there have been relatively small *net* changes in the overall labor force. A great deal of jockeying is therefore taking place, with workers competing for a dwindling number of better jobs. At January 1, 1998, there were still only 37,600 official vacancies, reflecting low levels of job creation in the highly privatized small- and medium-size enterprise sectors. In any case, these firms employ only around 5 percent of the labor force.[71] At the close of the 1990s, therefore, Ukraine still had severe unemployment problems and great numbers of underemployed workers.

Eroding Real Wage Levels

Real wage levels, which were highly volatile in 1991–92, have stabilized at a small fraction of their pre-independence level. There is no doubt that the government's policy of indexing official monthly incomes whenever the official CPI index rises by 5 percent or more in a given month has had the effect of dampening further deterioration in real wage levels.[72] Falling inflation levels from year-end 1994 were also extraordinarily beneficial. Despite real growth in wages of 3 percent in 2000, they are still at but a fraction of their 1990 levels. Government data reflects only wage schedules, however, not actual wage payments, which have been held up, in some cases, for many months. This problem is quite pervasive: The government reports that some 45.6 percent of workers are not paid on time. At December 31, 1999, some UAH 6,462 million (around $1.3 billion) in wages arrears had accumulated, up from 4,908 million at year-end 1997.

Payments in kind are not included in the official statistics. Some 12–15 percent of wages have been paid in the form of finished product. In 1998, for, instance, in-kind wage payments exceeded UAH 2.7 billion, and now run at over UAH 500 million per month, or some 12–13 percent of paid wages. In agricultural enterprises, the value of output paid as wages exceeded 53 percent of actual cash payments made.[73] The low wages available in Ukraine have not proved sufficient to attract foreign investment. One reason is that wages tend to bear little relationship to labor productivity levels, which vary broadly. In any case, labor productivity rates in Ukrainian industry have been falling since 1991, and by 1997 were but 70–75 percent of their 1990 levels.[74] (And less than half of their 1990 levels in construction materials, light industry, and food processing.) As such, Ukraine has not been able to take advantage of its relatively low-cost, well-educated work force.

External Trade and Investment

It is clear that Ukraine's reform economic efforts were significantly hampered from the start by an unfavorable international economic environment. Collapse of the economic space of the former USSR, and of the Council for Mutual Economic Assistance (CMEA, more commonly known as COMECON), dramatically altered Ukraine's former trading patterns. In the 1990s, Western economies, weakened by recession, were unable to replace the trade Ukraine had lost. Some economists estimate that between 50–80 percent of the decline in Ukraine's output in 1992–93 resulted from the collapse in trade.[75] Foreign markets were glutted with commodities from former Soviet countries, which suffered severely deteriorating terms of trade. (Witness: the collapse in world aluminum prices.) Further, input prices rose significantly, especially for energy products. Coupled with Ukraine's generally laggard domestic policy performance, these developments only compounded Ukraine's problems.[76]

Patterns of Trade

From 1991–97, Ukraine's trading patterns favored Russia and other CIS countries. Roughly 53 percent of Ukraine's 1997 foreign trade turnover of $35.5 billion was with CIS countries, about $18.9 billion, of which, 33 percent, or $11.8 billion, was with Russia. The dependence on Russian trade was far reaching. Economist Alex Granberg estimated that some 67 percent of Ukraine's final product in 1993 was accounted for by inputs from Russia.[77] Ukraine's other major CIS trading partners are Belarus, Moldova, Turkmenistan, and Uzbekistan.[78] Ukraine has run overall trade deficits with CIS countries, however, totaling $2.50 billion in 1997, but falling to $1.47 billion by 2000.[79] These are due mainly to Ukraine's appetite for imported energy. Fuel, oil, and oil products accounted for 40 percent of the total value of imports in 1998. The overall pattern is changing somewhat, however. According to the State Customs Committee, in 1998 imports fell 17.3 percent to $13.9 billion, with a 26.5 percent decline in trade with CIS countries. Exports also fell, by 13.9 percent, with exports to CIS countries falling 27.8 percent. Exports to Asia fell 24 percent but grew by 30.3 percent to North and South America, 6.3 percent to Europe, and 19.2 percent to Africa.[80]

Ukraine has offset the CIS trade deficit somewhat with surpluses from trade with the rest of the world. Through the third quarter of 2000, Ukraine actually ran a foreign trade surplus, with trade outside the former Soviet Union completely offsetting the deficit with CIS countries. Diversification of trade away from Russia and the CIS dampens Ukraine's reliance on its former Soviet trading partners. A damaging trade war with Russia in 1996–97 dramatically reduced trade with the CIS overall, falling from a high of over 58 percent in 1994 to some 44 percent by 1998.[81] It has fallen further since then, albeit more steadily.

Russia triggered the dispute by imposing quotas and customs and excise duties on imported Ukrainian agricultural and other products. Since Ukraine depends upon sales of foodstuffs and industrial equipment to Russia in order to partially offset imports of Russian energy products, this was potentially very damaging to Ukraine's trade position. Throughout the post-independence period, Russia has remained Ukraine's most important supplier of petroleum (100 percent), gas (81 percent), and raw materials (50 percent).[82] However, Ukraine is working hard to reduce its dependence on Russian energy by increasing oil imports from Azerbaijan and gas from Turkmenistan. Some 30 percent of exports to Russia and the CIS and 20 percent of CIS imports are conducted on a barter basis.[83] By 1997, barter trade had fallen by three-quarters from its 1994 levels as a result of the Russian-Ukrainian trade dispute. Barter trade with G-7 nations remains a fairly modest 1.8 percent of exports.

The commodity structure of Ukraine's foreign trade is heavily weighted toward mineral resources, chemicals, raw materials, and unfinished products (including salt, cement, iron ore, fertilizers, ferrous and nonferrous metals, and metal products).[84] These are largely low-value-added items that are sensitive to changes in global commodities prices. Ukraine has been unable to upgrade the technological content of its trade toward higher value-added products and services.[85] This places the country at an obvious strategic disadvantage to Russia and the western industrialized countries. The low earnings on commodity exports also tend to perpetuate Ukraine's dependence on Russian oil and energy products.

Over the five-year period from 1994–98, the contribution of exports to Ukraine's GDP increased from 26 percent to over 40 percent.[86] Due to strengthening commodities prices on global markets, during most of 2000, exports accounted for some 60 percent of Ukrainian GDP.[87] The primary export markets are in Russia (19.2 percent of the total in 1999); China (5.9 percent of total); Turkey (5.4 percent); Germany (4.5 percent); and the United States (3.5 percent). Exports to CIS countries—excluding Russia—accounted for 13.6 percent of the total.[88] Ukraine has sought to reduce its trade dependence on Russia by shifting it to other republics and to the West. But economic interdependence between Russia and Ukraine has been asymmetrical. As Ukraine expert Paul D'Anieri observes, "[it] is much easier for Russia to find substitutes for Ukrainian grain than for Ukraine to find substitutes for Russian oil."[89] Ukraine has therefore also sought to diversify its exports in search of hard currency earnings to pay for Russian energy products. In the effort, Ukraine has significantly increased its arms exports since 1994, from $20 million to over $1 billion at the end of 1996.[90] In that year, Ukraine merged three major arms export firms into a single company, Ukrspetsexport, in order to increase the effectiveness of what had become the fastest-growing source of foreign exchange.

Ukraine has consistently maintained its interest in bilateral trade relations with Russia and the CIS but has been careful to avoid any larger political or security linkages. Jealously guarding its sovereignty, Ukraine has rejected all attempts to transform the CIS into a supranational body. Consequently, Ukraine has only initialed certain CIS treaties as an "Associate" member. In addition, Ukraine has refused to join the Russia-Belarus Union, the CIS Customs Union (renamed the Eurasian Economic Union in 2001),[91] and the Payments Union. However, in March 1998, Ukraine and Russia concluded an Interstate Economic Treaty, formalizing previous agreements to drop the value-added tax (VAT) and other trade barriers between the two countries. These measures alone were expected to permit expansion of trade between the two countries by some 10–15 percent, especially for agricultural products.

Foreign Direct Investment

Foreign investment is crucial to Ukraine's future, especially in light of the dearth of domestic investment capital. However, compared to other Eastern European and former Soviet countries, Ukraine has enjoyed relatively little foreign direct investment (FDI). In 1999, investment volumes boomed in most countries of Eastern Europe—doubling in Slovenia, tripling in the first quarter in the Czech Republic, and up 13 and 23 percent in Poland and Hungary, respectively.[92] Accumulated per capita FDI in Ukraine totaled barely $49 at the end of 1998, compared to $1,745 in Hungary, $822 in the Czech Republic, $595 in Poland, and $102 in the much larger Russia.[93] Ukraine had accumulated FDI of just $2.43 billion by January 1, 1999.[94] Even tiny countries like Moldova, Turkmenistan, and the Kyrgyz Republic had higher cumulative FDI. Additionally, Ukraine was all but totally eclipsed by the Baltic states.[95] In terms of total investment, Poland and Hungary garnered 25 percent and 19 percent, respectively, of total foreign investment between 1989–98. Russia came in third, with 16 percent of the total. Ukraine barely took 2.6 percent of foreign investment, even though it accounts for 12.6 percent of the population of the region.

The government has repeatedly affirmed that it wishes to attract FDI. Laws and regulations are enacted to protect investment inflows, but corruption, ineptitude, and ex post facto changes to the law have imposed hardships on investors. Foreign investors cite many impediments to investment in Ukraine. In 1998, foreign firms reported that the most serious obstacles included: legal uncertainty (100 percent reporting), unsatisfactory transportation infrastructure (97.5 percent), state failure to fulfill its commitments (90 percent), influence of the state and residual effects of central planning (80 percent), poor telecommunications infrastructure (80 percent), corruption (75 percent), and lack of support on the part of state bodies (75 percent).[96] These findings are broadly consistent with a survey taken two years earlier by the British government–sponsored organization, Technical Assistance to the CIS (TACIS).[97] Many investors simply hold back. The government therefore has yet to permit investors to begin the necessary work of renewing the capital base.

Of consequence to Ukraine's regions has been the uneven distribution of FDI across the geography of Ukraine. Foreign investment in Ukrainian companies totaled $1.8 billion in late 1997, going to some 6,247 firms. The highest concentration of investment—30.8 percent of the total—went to 2,586 firms in Kyiv Oblast. By contrast, Ukrainian firms invested barely $137.8 million abroad. (Of this, $52.2 million went to other former Soviet republics.)[98] FDI through July 1998 was highly concentrated in the center-north regions of Ukraine. This indicates that certain regions benefit more than others from FDI. Recent growth rates have been higher in eastern Ukraine, however, which may reflect the discovery by foreigners of that region's vast economic potential.

"Capital Flight": How Much Has Escaped Abroad?

A problem related to the scarcity of investment capital is the large volume of capital that has been spirited out of Ukraine during the 1990s. Although capital transactions have been subject to strict controls, capital has fled the country through ordinary import-export trade, much of which has been conducted on a barter basis, providing opportunities for "hidden profits" in foreign currency. Independent estimates placed the amount of Ukrainian capital abroad in 1996 at between $25 and $50 billion.[99] The government officially claimed that only some $1 billion was on deposit in foreign banks, a figure that certainly grossly understates the true amount.[100] Capital flight is therefore largely unmonitored.[101] There were indications that capital flight was falling from 1994–98, however. The difference in value between the import and export sides of barter trade has been falling, especially in trade with Russia. However, the Russian and Ukrainian customs services report vastly different data concerning the value of exports and imports to and from one another.

Accumulation of Foreign Debt

In 1992, Ukraine had no foreign debt outstanding.[102] This provided the country's most significant inherited economic resource: an enormous amount of debt capacity. As might be expected, Ukraine's foreign debts steadily increased over the 1990s. Ukraine's principle creditors are Russia, the IMF, the World Bank, and various commercial banks. From an estimated $1.4 billion in late 1992, Ukraine's indebtedness grew to over $12.1 billion by early 2000.[103] That figure is $9.635 billion net of IMF credits. By March 1, 2001, that figure had climbed to $14.07 billion, including $10.03 owed abroad.[104] Ukraine's external debt is still regarded as affordable by international standards but gradually is becoming much more burdensome. The debt-to-GDP ratio stood at between 15–20 percent in 1998 but rose to over 40 percent in 1999. GDP growth in 2000 resulting from favorable commodities market prices reduced this ratio somewhat, to around 34 percent. Total debt as a percent of exports has also risen, climbing from 43–48 percent in 1994–97, to 65–77 percent in 1998–2000. Likewise, the debt service-to-export ratio climbed dramatically since 1997. Affordability had therefore become an issue at the close of the 1990s.

Ukraine's foreign debts mounted after the country placed two- and three-year Eurobonds worth DM 1 billion and ECU 500 million in 1998. Some $375 million in IMF loans and another $330 million from the World Bank also were recorded that year. Additionally, over $155 million of Ukraine's indebtedness to foreign holders of its treasury bonds (domestically-issued debt), which were converted to two-year Eurobonds in 1998, came due in 2000.[105] In 1999, Ukraine had to pay $1.2 billion in debt service, plus $670 million owed by the National Bank to the IMF. A shortage of foreign currency reserves meant that Ukraine failed to make its scheduled principal and interest payments on its outstanding U.S. dollar–denominated bonds issued through Chase Manhattan Bank Luxembourg, S.A. These very same bonds had been rescheduled just 18 months earlier, and for the same reasons.[106]

In 2000 and 2001 Ukraine faced payments of around $3.28 billion and $2.3 billion to service its nearly $12.1 billion foreign debt. In 2000, Ukraine had to transfer to the IMF another 570 million SDRs (about $785 million) to repay principal and up to 60 million SDRs ($80 million) in interest. But at the end of 1999, Ukraine had foreign currency reserves of just $1.25 billion. The hope was that fresh IMF credits would cover these payments.[107] But to no avail. The debt situation reached crisis proportions in January 2000. On January 5, Moody's Investors Service lowered Ukraine's long-term country ceiling for foreign currency bonds and notes, from a B3 rating to Caa1, with a "negative outlook." The downgrading reflected the government's intention to reschedule its foreign currency bonds and notes by the end of January 2000.[108] On January 20 the government announced it would seek rescheduling of its Paris Club debt (Eurobonds). The deal would exchange Eurobonds worth $1.9 billion maturing in 2000 and 2001 for new securities in order to relieve the debt burden on the economy.[109] Although Ukraine halted its payments to Paris Club–member countries in January 2000, in April 2001, it was still awaiting a reply. Despite its increased export earnings, at mid-year 2001, Ukraine was able to meet only 55 percent of its debt service target.

Ukraine has lost much credibility in international capital markets. Moody's has signaled the possibility of further downgrading, pending the outcome of negotiations between Ukraine and its creditors. (Ukrainian debt already is considered very risky; Ukrainian T-bill rates ranged from 69.8 to 74.9 percent per year on the Frankfurt Exchange in mid-April 2001.) In the meantime, Ukraine's debts continue to mount. Together with state domestic debt (which is denominated in hryvnia, but much of which is held by foreigners), the consolidated national debt (including private debts) reached almost $22 billion at the start of 1999. The truly unfortunate point is that Ukraine's debt accumulation purchased much valuable time for industrial restructuring in 1995–2000, which was squandered. The result is that Ukraine now has much less flexibility to accomplish that end. Its debts are coming due.

Conclusion: Is Economic (Re-)Integration the Answer?

It has become clear after ten years of decline that the primary threat to Ukrainian security lies in the domestic economic realm, as opposed to external military threat.[110] Ukraine's enormous trade interdependence with Russia is a reality that, for the foreseeable future, must be lived with. But, as Paul D'Anieri has observed, "It is not so easy to protect Ukrainian independence while cooperating economically with Russia."[111] The problem is that Ukraine's trade with Russia is asymmetrical: It is relatively easy for Russia to inflict harm on its neighbors' economies at much less cost to itself. Oil and energy products are the main resources that Ukraine needs from Russia.

Ironically enough for Russia, as world oil prices climbed in the late 1990s, the share of export earnings in Russian GDP rose from 20–25 percent in 1994–97 to over 50 percent in 2000.[112] This makes Russian economic recovery ever more dependent on energy exports to countries like Ukraine, which Moscow is coming to view as important customers. Be that as it may, Russia has taken advantage of the leverage afforded by Ukraine's $4.1 billion energy debt, swapping debt for equity shares in Ukrainian state-owned enterprises. The debt burden already has forced Kyiv to agree to unification of the Russian and Ukrainian electric power grids. More of the same kind of pressure can be expected, unless Ukraine increases dramatically its export earnings or develops abundant alternative energy sources. Ukraine's problem is therefore how to benefit from economic exchange with Russia while maintaining as much of its precious sovereignty as possible. It is a difficult balance.

Ukraine has been relatively successful in building linkages to the West in attempts to counterbalance somewhat its trade dependence on Russia. For instance, the Treaty on Partnership and Cooperation between Ukraine and the European Union went into effect on March 1, 1998. Since then, Ukraine has taken the first steps toward harmonization of its laws with the legislation of the European Union.[113] Further, Ukraine is among 15 states that are conducting negotiations for membership in the 152-member World Trade Organization (WTO).[114]

These efforts will amount to little more than a chimera, however, unless fresh sources of energy are developed. In the short-to-medium run, that means dealing with Russia as a fact of life. In the long run, Ukraine's independence depends on its ability to thoroughly reform the economy. This is something that international economic integration cannot accomplish. Ukraine must do this on its own. The following chapters explore in some detail the reasons that this has proved to be so very difficult to achieve.

Chapter 3

Establishing Economic Sovereignty, 1991–94

Presidential Leadership in Economic Reforms

The former economic advisor to the Ukrainian president, Anders Åslund, has observed that, "at the foundation of a nation, the nature of the leader is of great significance."[1] In a similar vein, Vice Rector of the Ukrainian Academy of Public Administration Bohdan Krawchenko focuses on the entire cadre of political leaders, arguing that elites play the critical role in nation-building.[2] Finally, Alexander Motyl stresses the primacy of the state in the development of nationalism, in that the state is a powerful instrument of social control and regulation over the lives of citizens.[3] Building on both Krawchenko and Motyl, with specific reference to Ukraine, Taras Kuzio and Andrew Wilson see the achievement of Ukrainian independence as the work of two elites, operating jointly: (1) the cultural intelligentsia; and (2) those members of the Communist Party *apparat* who embraced the idea of Ukrainian independence (commonly referred to as "national communists").[4]

The intelligentsia was too weak and disorganized to take power or to universalize its program. The main mouthpiece of the national movement in the 1980s, the Popular Front for Perestroika in Ukraine or Rukh, therefore effectively surrendered its nation-building program to an elite-led *nomenklatura,* in a Faustian bargain that brought independence at the expense of economic and political reforms. As Wilson points out, "the historical weaknesses of the Ukrainian national movement made it necessary for nationalists to seek a historic compromise with the former ruling elite."[5] For better or for worse, then, the backgrounds, careers, personal characteristics, and policy preferences of Ukraine's first two presidents—and of their most powerful supporters—are reflected in Ukraine's economic development during the 1990s.

The presidency of Leonid M. Kravchuk (December 1991–July 1994) effectively postponed economic and political reform in favor of the necessary tasks of nation-building. The confused and contradictory policies emanating from Kyiv during his presidency must be seen against the political uncertainties that Kravchuk faced. This was a particularly dangerous period for Ukraine. The president was required to muster all of his skill, and the resources of the state, simply in order to keep a lid on the country. Former U.S. president Richard M. Nixon, a shrewd judge of leadership, after meeting Kravchuk, concluded that the Ukrainian president was a very astute politician. And indeed he is. For he managed to establish Ukraine's sovereignty and maintain peace and order with a minimum of violence and almost no ethnic conflict. It is impossible to overestimate the importance of this accomplishment. However, a particularly worrisome aspect of President Kravchuk was that, at certain crucial times, there was little correlation between what he said and what he did. For instance, he would call for reform even as he was strengthening the hold of the former communist *apparat* over the state and the economy.

Kravchuk's preference for the old communist network in his appointments to elite positions in government quieted potential opposition to independence from the *nomenklatura,* but it also guaranteed key economic management posts for powerful state enterprise directors from eastern Ukraine. As economist Volodymyr Zviglyanich has put it, "under pretext of moving toward liberal democracy, rule of law and . . . a market economy, a revamped collectivist elite entrenched itself in power, with Mr. Kravchuk as its leader and symbol."[6] This imposed an unfortunate trade-off between domestic order and economic reform. It stymied progress on industrial restructuring, reduction of credit emissions to enterprises and agriculture, and liberalization of prices and trade. No less an astute observer of Ukrainian politics than Dr. Bohdan Havrylyshyn commented that the relative peace was bought at the purchase of economic reforms.[7] During Ukraine's early formative period, would-be reformers were at odds with one another over whether it would even be possible to have the one without the other.

In another study, this author wrote that, "the twin sagas of . . . Kravchuk's management of the economy were massive emissions of cheap credit and budget subsidies to industry, paired with the imposition of administrative controls over prices and exchange rates."[8] The upshot was a vain attempt to reduce the very inflationary pressures that his policies had unleashed—and it was unsuccessful. Large, state-owned enterprises and powerful sectoral lobbies actively petitioned Kyiv for ample amounts of "soft credits" (loans never to be repaid), presumably in order to halt the output fall. Kravchuk himself seems to have mistakenly believed that Ukraine's rapid price inflation was the result of a serious imbalance between goods and money, so that increasing liquidity of enterprises would cause production to increase, thereby putting a brake on inflation. As we will learn in chapter 7 of this volume, however, the availability of cheap credit and budget subsidies frustrated the necessary steps toward monetary stabilization and structural reform. Tragically, in 1992–94, everyone but the Ukrainian authorities seemed to understand this.[9]

Leonid D. Kuchma succeeded Kravchuk as Ukraine's president in July 1994, after a hard-fought campaign. Kuchma's election signaled a dramatic shift in Ukraine's economic reform agenda. Under Kuchma, Ukraine would pursue international economic integration, by seeking GATT membership, a seat on the Council of Europe, and eventual EU membership. These are steps that Kravchuk never overtly advocated. However, like Kravchuk, Kuchma had always insisted that he was in favor of evolutionary, gradual reform. Also like Kravchuk, Kuchma's presidency has seen fairly continuous conflict with parliament over control of the executive branch and determination of the powers of local governing bodies. Kuchma's first term was also preoccupied in 1995–96 with ratification of a new constitution. To one degree or another, then, the struggle over economic reform has been captive of struggles to define the institutional structure of government.

Presidential leadership in economic reform, however skillful, is contingent to at least some extent upon starting conditions, factor and resource endowments, and the path laid down by past decisions. Therefore, in order to place in proper perspective the opportunities, constraints, and choices confronting Ukraine's presidents during the 1990s—and to fully appreciate the economic potential that has been squandered—one must begin with the sort of economy that Ukraine inherited from the USSR. The basic "economic instincts" of the Ukrainian post-Soviet elites, their mentality and modus operandi, were also formed by the Soviet experience. It is to this topic that we must now briefly turn.

The Ukrainian Economy at the Time of Independence

Legacy of the Command-Administrative Economy

Ukraine had no economic sovereignty under the Soviet regime. It was obliged to accept decisions made at the center in Moscow (that is, Gosplan dictates). Kyiv was therefore unable to tailor its economy to the needs and desires of its own citizens. Moscow determined production priorities, schedules, means, and quantities according to the logic of central planning.[10] Decisions taken by Gosplan emphasized almost exclusively quantitative goals (that is, units of output, volumes, or tonnage). Prices were fairly rigid and set administratively. These were not "market prices" in the classical sense, insofar as they did not reflect opportunity costs or relative scarcities. They were employed mainly as means to regulate distribution and consumption patterns.

State-owned enterprises (SOEs) were evaluated on how well they met quantitative targets (in terms of material product), not on profits. The industrial incentive structure was set in order to maximize output. There were also advantages to "over-fulfilling" plans, but there was little incentive for minimizing costs or using resources efficiently. Investment capital was viewed largely as a "free good" and allocated according to noneconomic criteria. Consequently, interest rates were set at artificially low levels and were therefore essentially meaningless. Accounting procedures were designed to facilitate and monitor plan implementation, control SOEs, and evaluate progress. Transactions between SOEs consisted mainly of accounting adjustments made in centralized state bank accounts; money often did not change hands. SOE investments, savings, and cash were coordinated in state budget accounts. All SOE residual income accrued to the state budget. Households were an exception, however; individuals could accumulate surprisingly ample amounts, often placed in savings accounts.

Fiscal policy favored subsidies for rapid industrialization and extensive (versus intensive) absorption of labor and material resources in SOEs (40–60 percent of outlays, or 20–30 percent of GDP); generous provision of social benefits (20–30 percent of outlays, and 10–15 percent of GDP); and an egalitarian distribution of income.

The budgetary emphasis was on the allocative and redistributive functions of government; there was little or no concern with economic stabilization. Inflationary pressures were contained primarily via tight budgetary control but also through "forced savings" (that is, chronic scarcities of consumer goods) and a largely closed external trade sector.

Piecemeal Soviet Economic Reforms, 1965–89

Soviet economic failures in the early 1960s resulted in dwindling crop yields, increasing food prices, and the need to employ gold and hard currency reserves to import grain.[11] Increasing citizen demands for consumer goods also pressured the state at this time. Consequently, in 1965, the USSR implemented a number of measures designed to improve economic performance. The so-called "Kosygin Reforms" included increasing agricultural investment and emphasizing consumer goods output over capital goods. An attempt was also made to reform the central planning process by shifting greater decision-making responsibility to SOEs.[12] Prices remained under strict administrative control, however, constraining the effectiveness of the reforms.

The limited effects of the 1965 reforms were exhausted by around 1970. Command methods of economic management were increasingly ineffective, due to continuation of the underlying stagnation and overdevelopment of the capital goods sector. Oil price increases in the 1970s temporarily "masked over" these negative trends, as Soviet exports earned hard cash. But the consumer goods sector as a proportion of industrial output fell further, as the government continued to shift the internal terms of trade away from the household sector. Performance continued to lag during the 1970s and into the 1980s, however, which became known as the "period of stagnation" *(period zastoy)*.

In March 1985, Mikhail Gorbachev was made General Secretary of the Communist Party of the Soviet Union.[13] The new leader emphasized the need for reduced rigidity in the economic system in order to revive performance. To this end, he began to experiment with what, initially, were limited reforms. The basic motivation of his reforms was the continuing fall of productivity growth rates, despite high investment levels. His initial attempts were aimed at intensified use of labor and material resources, increased discipline in the labor force, and enhanced coordination. It was not until June 30, 1987, that the first step toward a more radical restructuring, or perestroika, was taken, through enactment of the Law on State Enterprises.[14] The centerpiece of Gorbachev's industrial reform program, the law emphasized greater autonomy for enterprises and their "self-financing" (that is, covering costs out of operating revenues). Collective farms were permitted to sell their entire product to nonstate buyers. But most of the essential functions of central planning were retained.

In March 1989, in a move that would begin the unraveling of the Soviet system, Gorbachev devolved greater economic autonomy to the regions, giving the republics an average 36 percent jurisdiction over all-union industrial production, versus 5 percent previously. (Ukraine gained republican control over 42 percent.)[15] But, as Robert Skidelsky has observed, these moves inadvertently fueled separatism in many republics: "By decentralizing management tasks from the government to the enterprises, Gorbachev found he had shifted political power to the republics."[16] Nagging economic problems, labor unrest, and stiffening opposition to reforms resulted in the reintroduction of detailed quantitative planning in December 1989 (for all consumer goods and infrastructure construction), introduction of rationing in some areas, new price and wage controls, increased taxes, and prohibitions on strikes by workers. In addition, throughout the perestroika period, fuel, metallurgy, machine building, and most chemical industry branches remained controlled by Moscow ministries. This "piecemeal exceptionalism" was a critical shortcoming in Gorbachev's reforms.

Another critical problem was the failure to eliminate the soft budget constraint on SOEs, whose directors continued to rely upon budget subsidies to finance their inefficient operations. The basic unprofitability of many sectors, therefore, remained unexposed. Further, the overvalued ruble required large and growing export subsidies. The "shortage economy" that had characterized classical central planning only intensified, as SOEs and households began to hoard increasingly scarce inputs and consumer goods. Individuals and enterprises built up large inventories of badly needed items. Consequently, as demand for many of these items fell, finished goods output fell further, and with it, enterprise profits and state tax revenues. Curiously, household savings rose dramatically, but this was largely involuntary, the result of deepening consumer goods shortages.

The Effects of Soviet Stagnation on Ukraine

The Ukrainian economy leading up to the Soviet break-up reflected the adverse trends discussed immediately above. Table 3.1 presents changes in selected economic indicators for the period 1966–89. The data in this table indicate a steady decline in the growth of gross social product

(GSP),[17] national income, industrial output, and fixed productive assets.[18] The observed increase in enterprise profits, investment, and new fixed assets is fully accounted for by rising price levels and costs of construction. Thus, these are more a result of suppressed inflationary pressures than a real increase. Living standards also fell in real terms, starting in the mid-1960s.[19]

By 1988, the economy was plagued by severe disproportions in the system of wholesale and retail pricing. Cost recovery levels far exceeded pricing levels for nearly all of Ukrainian industry. This implies that very serious misallocations of productive resources were rampant in the system. State budget subsidies were used to compensate SOEs for these price distortions. Large subsidies caused the poorly performing firms to escape detection, due to a "leveling off" of reported performance of both the efficient and inefficient enterprises and workers' collectives. This obviously destroyed any incentive to cut costs or otherwise improve. State subsidies simply prevented the worst SOEs from being shut down.

Regional Structure of Trade and Transfers

As late as 1989, Ukraine had only limited access to foreign markets outside of the USSR. In that year, fully 84 percent of Ukrainian exports went to other Soviet republics.[20] The remainder went to CMEA members or to third-world countries—usually other socialist countries, such as Cuba. Trade within the Soviet Union was dominated by transactions with Russia. In 1991, over 20 percent of Ukrainian national income was spent on imports from Russia (measured in terms of world market prices), and nearly the same proportion was earned on exports to Russia.[21] Such trade was lop-sided, however; Russian imports from and exports to Ukraine amounted to only around 4–5 percent of Russian GNP.[22]

Despite the history of internal economic colonization of Ukraine by Russia dating back to czarist times, at the time of the Soviet collapse, Ukraine was not being exploited economically by Russia.[23] Quite to the contrary, Ukraine was in fact a net recipient of transfers and subsidies from Moscow, most notably in the energy sector.[24] As indicated by the data in Table 3.2, indirect transfers amounted to an estimated 3.61 percent of GDP (and larger for some other republics).[25] Further, Russian net subsidization of Ukraine was steadily increasing (that is, Ukrainian transfers to Russia were falling) throughout the 1980s, a trend that has continued in Russian-Ukrainian trade throughout the 1990s.[26] Immediately prior to independence, then, and especially with the jump to world market prices for energy products, Ukrainian trade

Table 3.1
Selected Indicators for the Ukrainian Economy, 1966-89
(Percent change)

	1966-70	1971-75	1976-80	1981-85	1986-89
Gross Social Product (GSP)	6.7	5.6	3.4	3.3	2.6
National Income (NI) Produced	6.7	4.6	3.4	3.4	3.0
Fixed Productive Assets	6.9	8.0	6.4	5.3	3.5
Industrial Output	8.5	7.2	3.9	3.4	3.8
Agricultural Output	2.5	3.0	1.6	0.5	2.0
Construction and Installation of New Fixed Assets	8.0	5.7	1.9	2.7	4.1
Capital Investments	6.7	6.4	2.1	3.1	5.3
Profits of Enterprises	n.a.	8.9	1.0	5.3	11.5
Real Income Per Capita	5.9	3.8	3.2	2.7	2.0 *

* 1986-88. Unavailable since 1989.

Source: Various issues of *Narkhoz Ukrayiny*. As reported in Ivan Lukinov, "Radical Reconstruction of the Ukrainian Economy: Reasons, Reforms, Outlook," in I. S. Koropeckyj, ed., *The Ukrainian Economy: Achievements, Problems, Challenges* (Cambridge: Harvard University Press, 1992), pp. 21-43. The data are from Figure 2-1 on p. 43.

with Russia went into a chronic deficit position. This was a problem that would haunt the Ukrainian leadership well into the next decade and beyond.

Indicators of Ukraine's Economic Potential

Ukraine's economic potential at the time of independence cannot be assessed properly without consideration of the territorial division of labor within the former USSR. Despite having a population amounting to just 18 percent of the Soviet population and possessing 15.8 percent of its productive capital and just 2.7 percent of Soviet territory, Ukraine produced vast amounts of key industrial and agricultural products, including over 45 percent of iron ore, 41 percent of pig iron, 35 percent of steel products, and 25 percent of machinery. Note, however, that there was an overemphasis on extractive industry, manufacture of productive assets, and armaments.

Defense-related industries had priority in Ukraine, absorbing almost two-thirds of all scientific-technical resources. The emphasis on defense production meant that there was systematic underinvestment in the modernization of the more profitable branches of industry, such as light industry, food processing, and forestry.[27] During perestroika, for instance, only one-tenth of industrial investment was allocated to food processing and light industry. Over three-quarters was allocated to

Table 3.2

Regional Structure of Indirect Transfers, 1990

(Millions of Current Rubles)

Country	Transfer Donor Through: Underpriced Exports of Oil and Gas	Transfer Donor Through: Overpriced Imports of Non-Oil and Gas	Transfer Recipient Through: Overpriced Exports of Non-Oil and Gas	Transfer Recipient Through: Underpriced Imports of Oil and Gas	Net Transfer as % of GDP
Russia	15,811	13,867	4,071	3,166	3.67
Ukraine	430	3,500	780	6,979	-3.61
Belarus	1,564	1,281	2,745	3,699	-8.91
Uzbekistan	833	2,274	2,113	1,403	-1.26
Kazakhstan	1,672	1,748	1,666	1,984	-0.50
Georgia	5	917	2,877	432	-16.02
Azerbaijan	936	845	2,465	906	-10.09
Lithuania	285	333	1,479	1,480	-17.09
Moldova	0	577	3,148	-532	-24.05
Latvia	7	397	1,096	559	-10.43
Kyrgyzstan	24	605	516	336	-2.72
Tajikistan	22	617	756	339	-6.08
Armenia	0	910	1,439	350	-9.16
Turkmenistan	963	583	659	98	10.81
Estonia	0	329	948	287	-12.08

Source: Lucjan T. Orlowski, "Indirect Transfers in Trade Among Former Soviet Union Republics," *Europe-Asia Studies* 45, no. 6 (1993): 1001-102.

machine-building (Gorbachev's fixation), the fuel-energy complex, and metallurgy. The consumer goods sector was progressively de-emphasized during the Soviet period. By 1970 Ukrainian industrial output was dominated by heavy industry and remained so until independence. The result was chronic shortages of consumer goods.

The overall picture is one of a lop-sided industrial structure, with an overinvestment of capital in heavy industry but with a great opportunity in the consumer goods sector. The low value-added content of Ukraine's main export goods—grain, mineral extraction, heavy machinery, and chemicals—militated against generating ample hard currency earnings, however, which argues in favor of attracting foreign loans and investment to Ukraine. Despite some serious economic reform challenges, of all the newly independent states of the former USSR, Ukraine was regarded with the most optimism. Indeed, in 1990, Deutsche Bank ranked Ukraine as first among the former Soviet republics with the greatest potential for integration with western European markets.[28] The World Bank went even further, asserting that Ukraine had potential to become one of "the richest countries of the world."[29]

The Political Economy of Independence, 1989–91

As Gorbachev's reforms apparently spun out of his control, the center in Moscow grew visibly weaker. Ukrainian nationalists—always possessing vast latent potential—became more politically active. However, as Kuzio and Wilson rightly observe, even though the parliamentary elections of 1990 signaled an end to the communists' monopoly on political life in Ukraine, it revealed that "support for the national opposition was confined to 25–33 percent of the electorate."[30] (This was confirmed a year later in the March 1991 referendum on Gorbachev's new union treaty.[31]) However, the main vehicle for the expression of Ukraine's national sentiment, Rukh, received a boost from the elections, becoming ever more insistent on separating from Moscow.

Rukh saw itself as the vehicle to implement perestroika in Ukraine, the primary goal being establishment of a humane, democratic society. Rukh was much less concerned with economic issues. Its program from the start emphasized development of the Ukrainian state and language (supported by 73 percent of delegates to its inaugural congress) rather than the solution of pressing economic problems (supported by just 46 percent).[32] Kuzio and Wilson argue that, in 1990–91, the Communist Party of Ukraine (CPU) *apparat* would have to seek common ground with Rukh precisely in order to preserve a sense of legitimacy.[33] They further observe that "the CPU believed [that] declaring sovereignty was a step towards adopting a new Union treaty." The Declaration of Sovereignty was overwhelmingly adopted in parliament by a margin of 355 to 4 on July 16, 1990.

Insufficiently strong to take power in their own right, the nationalist opposition made a more or less implicit deal with the former communist elite to leave the system basically unreformed as long as they would get what they desired most: an independent Ukraine.[34] The visible leader of the "communists-turned-democrats," Leonid M. Kravchuk, began as early as September 1989 to embrace Rukh's principles and program.[35] In a speech to Rukh's inaugural congress, he expressed a desire to have Rukh as an ally in restructuring Ukraine.[36] Thus began an "unholy alliance" between the *nomenklatura* and the opposition, whose shared goal—independence—obscured momentarily the vast ideological differences between them.

In his study of Ukrainian nationalism, Andrew Wilson observes of this period that "in 1989–91, it was an almost universal theme in nationalist propaganda that Ukraine would benefit economically by withdrawing from the USSR."[37] Specific industrial interests also were engaged, insofar as the more Russified eastern oblasts favored independence as the means to move control of SOEs from Moscow to Kyiv, closer to home and more susceptible to being influenced. The opportunity to assert Ukrainian independence came with the failure of the Moscow coup attempt of August 19–21, 1991.

During the attempted coup, Leonid Kravchuk vacillated somewhat. In the face of what might be a fait accompli, rather than voice support for Yeltsin, as had so many other republican leaders, Kravchuk urged caution.[38] In the aftermath of the coup's failure, however, Kravchuk led the CPU to join the democratic opposition on August 24, to adopt Ukraine's Declaration of Independence by a vote of 346 to 1. At the same time, Kravchuk redeemed himself by resigning from the CPU and CPSU. As Kuzio and Wilson observe, "the Declaration of Independence . . . was clearly an attempt by the CPU to hold onto power in an independent state."[39] Independence was to be ratified in a national referendum on December 1, 1991. At the same time, Ukraine's first popularly elected president was to be decided. During the campaign, Leonid Kravchuk, the former communist functionary, would transform himself into a living symbol of Ukrainian nationalism by appropriating the Rukh program on a wholesale basis.

Kravchuk's 1991 electoral program stressed the economic advantages of independence, with broadly shared benefits for all Ukrainians.[40] Although independence was the key issue of the campaign, the question of Ukraine's future relations with Russia remained a central concern that each candidate had to address. In October 1991, Kravchuk stated that, "for us, the Union with Russia is the cornerstone of Ukraine's policy . . . Contacts with Russia are our long-term and far-sighted policy. This is our history, our roots, and we have to take this into account."[41] Kravchuk's continuing advocacy of economic ties with Russia was clarified somewhat in November 1991, when he stated that he meant "mutually profitable trade and cooperation with other sovereign states" and not a single market, in which "absolutely everything is unified and identical."[42] Kravchuk thus succeeded in linking his election as president to the question of Ukrainian independence. He would become in the process the personal embodiment of the new Ukrainian state, winning decisively, with 61.6 percent of the popular vote in a six-way contest.

Kravchuk's victory marked the *nomenklatura*'s success in retaining their position of power, social status, and privilege. Basically, "the state had usurped the intelligentsia's national ideology to fill the vacuum left by the collapse of communism, and promoted it [the ideology] with a vengeance."[43] Ukraine was now independent, but members of the former CPU (now outlawed) were still very much ensconced in the halls of power.[44] Kravchuk's ties to the former communist elite were to hamper his effectiveness as an economic reformer, however, as would become increasingly clear over 1992–93.

Establishing Economic Sovereignty Over Ukraine

Kravchuk's Halting Efforts at Reform

The immediate problem in the wake of achieving political independence was to establish economic sovereignty over Ukraine, and not market reform per se. This was only partly begun during the Gorbachev years, when the various republics had been granted substantial rights over the all-union enterprises on their respective territories. In 1989–90 Ukraine had also taken some initial steps in the direction of reform that were oriented toward this goal.[45] Upon passage of the Declaration of State Sovereignty on July 16, 1990, Prime Minister Vitold Fokin collaborated with the chairman of the Parliamentary Commission on Economic Reform, Volodymyr Pylypchuk, in the development of Ukraine's first program of economic reforms. (Fokin himself was the former head of the Ukrainian branch of Gosplan.) Basically reflecting Pylypchuk's thinking, this first program was designed mainly to permit Ukraine to exert greater control over its own economy rather than to facilitate a genuine transition to the market.[46]

The main objective of these early reforms was to withdraw from the USSR in an orderly fashion. The cornerstone of the program was a series of measures to prevent consumer goods from being diverted to Russia due to the higher prices to be found there. This was accomplished by issuing ration coupons for certain critical goods along with the payment of salaries. These coupons were to be used in parallel with rubles. The program also called for disentangling trade and monetary policies from those of Russia and other former Soviet countries. Thus, as a further means to avoid shortages from goods leaving the country, on April 10, 1991, a system of export licensing was put in place for all consumer goods. Coordinating monetary policy with Russia was extremely difficult, since the former Soviet ruble continued to circulate as legal tender in Ukraine throughout 1992.

In the immediate aftermath of the August coup, and the August 24, 1991, Declaration of Independence, a plethora of reform programs and proposals were advanced, from sources inside and outside of officialdom. After his initial collaboration with Pylypchuk, Fokin himself presented at least two further detailed reform programs to parliament.[47] The first was entitled "Fundamentals of Ukraine's National Economic Policy Under Conditions of Independence," which parliament failed to adopt in fall 1991. The second was more successful, being adopted at a closed session of parliament on March 24, 1992, entitled, "Fundamentals of National Economic Policy." This program had been authored—at Kravchuk's specific request—by the chairman of the president's "State Council" (or Duma), Oleksander Yemelyanov, a former high-ranking official in the Ukrainian branch of Gosplan.

Yemelyanov's plan reflected Kravchuk's nationalist sentiments, blaming virtually all of Ukraine's economic problems on Russia. Its main provisions called for an immediate exit from the "ruble zone" and the introduction of a new Ukrainian currency, the hryvnia. Yemelyanov's program was sharply criticized by economics minister Volodymyr Lanoviy on the basis that it would frustrate market reforms and install a new command economy in Ukraine. Ultimately, the lack of specific details in the plan dampened the enthusiasm of parliament, which approved the program anyway, after it was reconsidered in committee.

The same month, Lanoviy unveiled his own "Plan for Economic Policy and Market Reforms." Lanoviy's program, in principle, embraced monetary stabilization, sharp reductions in budget expenditures (especially for enterprise and consumer subsidies), tax system improvements, reduced budget deficits, price liberalization, rapid privatization, and the freeing of external trade. Lanoviy submitted his reform program to the International Monetary Fund (IMF), along with other necessary documentation for membership. The IMF subsequently admitted Ukraine to membership on March 3, 1992, mainly on the strength of Lanoviy's personal credibility. Membership in the World Bank followed later that year. Both multilateral lenders would provide badly needed capital during Ukraine's critical early transition period (though not without setbacks).

Acute goods shortages resulted from price differentials between Russian and Ukrainian goods, which were largely a consequence of the failure of the Central Bank of Russia to supply sufficient quantities of banknotes to countries still in the Ruble zone. Substantial quantities of goods were gravitating toward Russia, and the situation was threatening to reach crisis proportions. In response to shortages of critical consumer goods (for example, sugar, table salt, and butter), Ukraine already had issued multi-use rationing scrip in June 1991, which circulated as a parallel currency to the Russian ruble. However, continuing shortages of banknotes prompted Ukraine in January 1992 to issue a non-cash counterpart to the ruble, the karbovanets, or "kupon," which initially was good for use only in state stores. On January 2, 1992, the Russian government under Prime Minister Yegor Gaidar liberalized prices broadly, which forced Ukraine to do the same in order to maintain supplies of critical goods. During that month, prices were raised an average of 435 percent. The government really had little choice, even though such a rapid price rise obviously imposed a severe hardship on ordinary Ukrainians.

In Kravchuk's first address to parliament following his election as president, he stated flatly that the integration of Ukraine's economy with those of the other former Soviet republics was a top priority.[48] However, when disputes arose with Russia in early 1992 over coordination of reform policy, Kravchuk understood the need to cut economic ties, at least in the near term. In a speech in spring 1992, he stated that, "our dependence on Russia is dependence on the ruble . . . The ruble zone forces us to move away from Russia."[49] Thereafter, Ukraine entered a period where it pursued a policy of economic isolation, or rather "insulation," from Russia.

The turn away from Russia was supported by three otherwise conflicted groups: the *nomenklatura,* nationalists, and national communists. Their common focus was centered on preserving Ukraine's sovereignty in the face of their fearsome northern neighbor.[50] During this period, Russia and Ukraine both eschewed cooperation, each choosing instead to act unilaterally to establish their economic sovereignty. The pattern for the politics of economic reforms was being set at this time, for a significant cross-section of Ukrainian nationalists, former communists, government officials, and the public opposed reforms but supported severing political and economic ties to Russia. The critical question for the future would be whether Ukrainian independence could be sustained in the absence of fundamental market reforms. At this time, apparently, most influential policymakers did not perceive a necessary connection between the two.

There were further price increases for major food items on July 1, 1992, causing waves of panic buying in Kyiv. Parliament and the public were sharply critical of these harsh measures.[51] The problem clearly was Ukraine's continuing vulnerability to shifts in Russian monetary policy. Therefore, in order to "normalize trade" with Russia, on the advice of the IMF, Ukraine formally exited the ruble zone on November 12, 1992. The karbovanets became legal tender for all transactions on that date. Departure from the ruble zone was generally smooth and orderly.

Ukraine was now free to steer its own course in the monetary realm. But full monetary independence also removed the last remaining restriction on issuance of credits to Ukrainian industry, paving the way for Ukraine's tragic bout with hyperinflation in 1993–94. In order to assert control over its own money supply, parliament subsequently established a National Bank of Ukraine on the basis of the Kyiv branch of Gosbank. Parliament also enacted measures extending sovereignty over all Soviet enterprises located in Ukraine and established a legal basis for levying taxes. The main thrust of measures at this time, again, was aimed at achieving control rather than reform.[52]

The central figure in Ukrainian politics at this time was President Leonid Kravchuk. The president saw himself in many respects as a bridge between factions, able to rise above conflict to build a consensus. A reflection of his consensus-building approach was the creation in spring 1992 of a presidential advisory council, or Duma, that contained dozens of advisors to the president on such matters as humanitarian, scientific, legal, and economic reform.[53] All state organs were obliged to consider decisions taken by the Duma.[54] The practical result of his preference for conflict avoidance was that Kravchuk failed to use his rather sweeping powers of decree—and enormous moral authority—to reform the economy. Any hope that he would do so were dashed in July 1992, when he dismissed the reform-minded Lanoviy, replacing him with Valentyn Symonenko, an avowed communist and former party official from Odessa. This move was a reflection of Kravchuk's reluctance to use "shock therapy," and its abruptness reduced substantially the credibility of Kravchuk's commitment to marketization.

The president had dismissed Lanoviy over discontent generated by the July 1992 price increases. At the same time, Prime Minister Fokin was given until September to propose changes in the structure of government, with an eye toward filling key cabinet posts with "experts."[55] Fokin was kept on by Kravchuk even though his government narrowly avoided dismissal in a 139 to 135 vote of no confidence in July.[56] Fokin's government fell on September 30, 1992, however, prompting a complete change in government.[57] After two years in office—and with little positive accomplishment in the economic sphere—Kravchuk chose to replace Fokin with Leonid D. Kuchma, former director of the world's largest missile factory, Pivdenmash, located in Dnipropetrovsk.

"Kuchma I": Prime Minister Kuchma Pushes Reforms

Nicknamed the "Iron Minister" by his cabinet colleagues, Prime Minister Leonid D. Kuchma was overwhelmingly confirmed by parliament, 316 to 23 (with 24 abstentions). Starting from October 13, 1992, Kuchma was given ten days in which to form a Cabinet of Ministers and devise an economic reform program of his own. Kuchma's appointment, while ostensibly representing change, actually reflected Kravchuk's rather fragile governing coalition—dependent as it was on the good graces of former *apparatchiks*—which more or less confirmed his dependence upon the established elites, especially industrialists from Eastern Ukraine (the so-called "Red Directors"). It is therefore not likely that Kravchuk expected Kuchma to differ substantially from Fokin.

At first, Kuchma seemed to promise little more than a continuation of Fokin's slow and measured approach to reforms. Despite his statements to the effect that "Ukraine is on the verge of collapse," Kuchma initially mixed vague references to market reforms with calls to develop a unique "Ukrainian model" of reform, one based on "evolutionary change." Thus, early in his term, Kuchma advocated "administrative control" over the economy. For instance, Kuchma initially recommended reorganizing large state enterprises into joint-stock companies, but with the government retaining a controlling interest in such "corporatized" concerns.[58]

In a surprise move, however, Kuchma requested that the Duma be dissolved and that the president's "emergency powers" to rule the economy by decree be transferred to him for a six-month period.

Kuchma's new powers were conferred overwhelmingly on November 18, 1992, by a vote of 308 to 8 (with 18 abstentions). His new authority would permit Kuchma to suspend the articles of the constitution until May 21, 1993, giving the legislature and the president rights in passing laws or issuing decrees in the economic sphere. Additionally, he proposed an economic reform program that received broad approval and support from the IMF, World Bank, and other international lenders.[59]

Kuchma immediately started enacting measures aimed at establishing a legislative basis for the rationalization of the budget, improving tax collections, liberalizing trade, and privatizing rapidly. Many of these measures were those that had been previously drafted under President Kravchuk's direction. At a December 29, 1992, meeting of the Cabinet of Ministers, several presidential decrees were considered that were designed to stabilize the financial and economic situation. Six directives were considered that covered wages for SOE and government employees, increases in the minimum wage and pensions, regulations dealing with new export duties, joint ventures, and leases of premises to trade, food, and service concerns.

Under the direction of Kuchma's team of reformers, in December and January 1992–93, dozens of significant laws and decrees were issued by the government and approved by parliament.[60] The basic Law on Privatization was strengthened, budgeted social welfare payments reduced, and the retail trade sector opened to private competition. Other key components of Kuchma's program called for putting an end to collective farms, raising energy prices to world market levels so as to promote conservation, and combating corruption at all levels of government. The "Basic Principles for a National Economic Policy," which Kuchma unveiled on January 20, 1993, thus embraced ending price speculation, eliminating monopoly pricing, strictly limiting monetary emissions, promoting investment by foreigners, and conserving energy. The essential elements of Kuchma's program were as follows:

(1) Reduce runaway spending through enhanced budgetary discipline;
(2) Reduce inflation to a range of just 2–3 percent per month;
(3) Institute forced privatization measures and provide for private ownership of land;
(4) Reform the tax system to be more progressive;
(5) Institute wage and price controls;
(6) Break up monopolies and offer incentives to state enterprises to spur competition;

(7) Place stringent controls on the volume of imported goods;
(8) Control exports of commodities that are badly needed in Ukraine;
(9) Free many restrictions on foreign investment;
(10) Simplify business registration for persons who wish to start small businesses;
(11) Increase numbers of public works projects, especially improvements in transportation infrastructure;
(12) Combat corruption at the highest levels of government and in enterprise management;
(13) Forbid all Ukrainian enterprises to hold assets in foreign bank accounts;
(14) End the state's monopoly on retail trade as a means to increase the supply of consumer goods.[61]

These measures, crude as they were at the time, promised to significantly boost Ukraine's market transition. Parliament ratified Kuchma's program on February 7, by a vote of 283 to 21.[62] This really came as no surprise, given that the program largely mirrored Fokin's March 1992 program, which had also received broad support.

Kuchma's bold moves in the economic arena appear to have outmaneuvered President Kravchuk, whose reluctance to embrace reforms was becoming ever more apparent. Kravchuk had no choice but to endorse Kuchma's program, thereby sharing responsibility for its impact.[63] Kravchuk remained lukewarm, however, attempting to sidestep criticism from the Left for his failure to "reign in" Kuchma. But he was reluctant to publicly denounce reform. For instance, in March 1993, Kravchuk openly admitted that he had misunderstood Ukraine's economic situation, saying that, "we obviously overestimated the potential of our economy. We overlooked the fact that it was structurally incomplete."[64] But Kuchma's bold stance on the economy had earned him Kravchuk's enmity. Taras Kuzio has written of Kravchuk that "there was no indication that he [ever] accepted the inevitability of the introduction of a market economy."[65] In fact, the president grew increasingly critical of Kuchma's management of various aspects of reform, such as the privatization process and his failure to stem the fall in output.[66]

When Kuchma's emergency powers expired May 21, 1993, the prime minister announced his desire to introduce a state of emergency in order to overcome opposition to economic reform. At the same time, he asked for a six-month extension of his special powers.[67] Kuchma believed that his reforms were being undermined by parliament's control over the National Bank of Ukraine and the State Property Fund (which was responsible for the privatization process).[68]

Consequently, he asked for control over these institutions, as well as veto power over parliamentary acts in the economic sphere. Further, Kuchma threatened to resign when parliament refused 354 to 6 to extend his special powers.[69] The premier insisted that success in combating the economic crisis hinged on restructuring the executive power (a theme that would resound throughout the 1990s).[70] The stage was therefore set for a direct confrontation with the president, who saw in Kuchma's proposals a direct threat to his status as chief executive.

President Kravchuk responded to Kuchma's challenge by seeking direct control over the Cabinet of Ministers. When legislation to extend direct presidential control over the government failed, Kravchuk asserted his control with a decree establishing a temporary "Extraordinary Committee of the Cabinet of Ministers" to deal with economic matters.[71] Unfortunately, this meant that throughout mid-1993, economic reform became caught up in the struggle between president and prime minister for control of the executive branch.[72] These events coincided with a crippling ten-day strike by coal miners in the Donbas region of Eastern Ukraine, which threatened the economy with chaos.

The immediate effect of the strike was to prompt Kuchma to issue on June 23 a more detailed and "improved" economic reform program.[73] The five-part program would reform the tax system, seek energy price agreements with Russia, force privatization of all enterprises, promote export trade, and restrict National Bank credits to industry. This is precisely what the leftist majority in parliament wished to avoid. Consequently, in an abrupt about-face, parliament quickly restored Kravchuk's powers to issue decrees and handed him back his appointments power to the Cabinet of Ministers. For his part, Kravchuk rescinded his June 16 decree.

The miners' strike demands for increased wages and enhanced mine safety were coupled with a call for a national referendum of confidence in the president and parliament. Parliament initially met this demand by scheduling a referendum to be held in September but rescinded its decision a few days later, on the basis that there would be insufficient time to prepare for it. In satisfying the miners' demands, Kravchuk would ultimately remove Kuchma and agree to early parliamentary and presidential elections, to be held in 1994.[74] Nodding to the economic muscle of Eastern Ukraine, Kravchuk appointed as First Deputy Prime Minister the former mayor of Donetsk, Yukhym Zviahilskiy, who was also director of the largest coal mine in Ukraine and a leader of the Donbas Strike Committee.[75] (In fact, it was widely understood that Zviahilskiy played a key role in instigating the strike.) In frustration, on August 31, Kuchma tendered his resignation.[76]

Parliament now entered a high-stakes game for control over the government's policy agenda. It had cleverly rejected Kravchuk's bid for direct presidential rule and now also rejected Kuchma's resignation, 212 to 90, thereby playing the one off against the other. Kuchma was having none of it, however. He twice more offered his resignation, on September 9 and 21. Later that month, parliament finally accepted Kuchma's resignation, voting "no confidence" in the Cabinet of Ministers, 294 to 23.[77] Thus came to an end the many months' long struggle for control of the executive.

Kuchma was undone by conservatives within the presidential administration who had quietly sabotaged him by refusing to vigorously implement his reforms.[78] Parliament, too, had deprived Kuchma of the support required to reduce inflation; it had routinely ordered fresh credit emissions. It also interfered directly in the efforts of the State Property Fund to move forward with Kuchma's aggressive privatization campaign. Parliamentary opposition to reforms had remained a major stumbling block for Kuchma throughout his premiership. Despite ostensible support for reforms, the broad consensus among the people's deputies was that Kuchma's policies were "ill-conceived and hasty."[79] The developing stalemate between the executive and legislative branches frustrated Kuchma's team of young reformers, who began to leave the government, starting in March.[80] Kuchma's demise signaled the end of any serious reform efforts until after the elections of 1994.

Zviahilskiy was appointed Acting Prime Minister on September 22, 1993. However, Kravchuk suspended the post of premier on September 28, demoting him to Acting First Deputy Prime Minister. At the same time, Kravchuk appointed himself head of another temporary body, the "Coordinating Committee to Implement Reforms and Overcome the Crisis."[81] Kravchuk further issued a decree to merge the Presidential Administration with the Cabinet of Ministers under his leadership, thereby bringing the entire executive branch under his control.[82] This was apparently a genuine attempt on Kravchuk's part to end the political stalemate and bring some resolution to the economic crisis. Facing strong parliamentary opposition, however, the president explicitly ruled out further "experimentation" with reforms until after the 1994 elections.[83] Instead, he reverted to an old communist tool to deal with the output fall: reestablishment of state production and consumption targets. Unfortunately for him, this gave the impression of indecisiveness and a wavering commitment to reform in the face of worsening economic conditions.[84]

The Late 1993 Attempt to Renew the Command Economy

In the productive sector, Kravchuk in late 1993 took steps to stem the fall in output by re-establishing the former Soviet system of "state orders and state contracts" for certain critical goods and consumer products.[85] A presidential decree ordered firms to gear their production to supply goods ordered by the state at predetermined prices.[86] The decree covered many consumer goods, most military production, and the most crucial agricultural products. The intent of the policy was to stabilize output levels; however, the policy amounted to a rather feeble attempt to resurrect what no longer really existed. The worst part of it was that it only assured a continuing stream of state support for inefficient enterprises. Enterprises fulfilling state orders were to be guaranteed supplies of fuel, raw materials, and other privileges. Additionally, the government listed resources the production and consumption of which were to be tightly controlled, including: electric energy, oil, gasoline, natural gas, coal, coke, nonferrous metals, vegetable oil, cereals, sugar, textiles, and footwear.[87] However, the policy did not entail planning output levels, as was done under the former Soviet system.

The effort to reassert control over state enterprise orders failed miserably. By mid-1994, it was clear that the system of state orders had broken down altogether and could not be resuscitated in this way, for a number of reasons. For one thing, the president's decree dealt with only 9 percent of all prices. For another, there were no administrative sanctions or penalties for noncompliance. Also, despite the persistence of many price controls and numerous regulations, goods shortages declined sharply by the end of 1993. Finally, state enterprises began to price closer to world market levels, in response to a government requirement that firms producing under state contract or state orders secure their own inputs under commercial contracts. This resulted in narrowing price differentials between the state sector and the shadow economy, as firms now had incentives to raise output prices in order to afford necessary inputs. A corollary effect was to reduce pressure for state budget subsidies. Consequently, in 1993 direct budget and credit subsidies for enterprises actually fell as a percent of GDP. Bowing to the inevitable, Kravchuk officially decreed that the system of state orders would be abolished as of January 1,

1995. But by mid-1994, it had already been a dead item for quite a few months.

Conclusion: "Kravchuk the Reformer"?

In retrospect, several observations about the presidency of Leonid Kravchuk appear to be in order. First, more than anyone else on the political scene in 1989–94, he is most deserving of the title "father of the nation." As the second popularly elected president of Ukraine (Myhailo Hrushevsky in 1917 had been elected president by the National Assembly but not the people), Kravchuk deserves enormous credit for bringing Ukraine out of the Soviet Union. He must have been aware that the weight of precedent was upon him, for every action he took would set the mold for future presidents. To have guided the withdrawal of Ukraine from the USSR alone would ensure Kravchuk a place in Ukrainian history. To also have guided Ukraine's transition to a market economy would have secured him a spot in modern European history. But Kravchuk was no economic reformer. To one extent or another, awareness of his unique role played a part in diverting him from the path of aggressive implementation of market reforms.

In this vein, Andrew Wilson refers to "Kravchuk's paradoxical political persona."[88] Explaining that he appears increasingly nationalistic in the period after 1990, Kravchuk is nonetheless unable to move beyond his commitment to the "economic dogmas of the late communist period."[89] Thus, as Åslund observes, Ukraine was unlike several other countries, "notably Estonia and Latvia, [where] market economic reforms were seen as part and parcel of nation-building. In Ukraine . . . nation-building was widely perceived as separate from market reform." He adds that, "many tendencies drove Ukraine in the wrong direction."[90] The disconnect between nation-building and market reform was a critical factor in diverting Ukraine from the path of market reform.

Second, Kravchuk faced different circumstances, and therefore different trade-offs, than would his successor in office, Leonid D. Kuchma. Kravchuk's first priority had to be nation- and state-building. Due to the conceptual disconnect discussed above, economic reform was only a secondary objective. This order of priorities was reflected in the Rukh program, which Kravchuk and his entourage appropriated almost in its entirety. Tragically for their countrymen, the nationalists' attitudes about sacrificing reform to maintain independence coincided with the interests of the *nomenklatura* and the national communists. Both of these groups opposed economic reforms in order to retain their positions of status and privilege in the unreformed system. Further, the years of Kravchuk's presidency were a time of great danger in Ukraine. Thus, the avoidance of conflict, which might have produced unrest and possibly even led to civil war, was a much more critical concern than reducing budget deficits, fighting inflation, or privatizing rapidly. This element of risk should form the backdrop for any effort to evaluate Kravchuk's economic leadership.

Third, Kravchuk was more committed to consensus and compromise than he was to reform. Anders Åslund had ample opportunity to observe Kravchuk personally, observing that, "his yearning for consensus impeded him from making a clear choice on economic strategy."[91] Kravchuk's personal preference for consensus-building accounts for his failure to decisively employ his powers of decree in the economic realm. In fact, his clearest decisions went in the opposite direction; as Wilson puts it, "many of his decrees were in fact anti-market in spirit."[92] The likelihood that economic reforms might have led to unrest in the heavily industrial and Russophone oblasti of Eastern Ukraine—especially in Donbas—accounts for Kravchuk's reluctance to fully implement reforms.[93] Conflict avoidance was very much the rule of the day. However, it is hard to imagine genuine progress on market reforms in the absence of a struggle for the political future of Ukraine.

Kravchuk discerned that the path of least resistance consisted of a middle-of-the-road policy of neither reform nor nonreform. According to Paul D'Anieri, that way, "even if both sides opposed the prevailing policy, neither side could feel like the game was irretrievably lost."[94] Kravchuk was thus able to placate both sides, but only by continuously jockeying between two sides, causing him to vacillate in his policy commitments. However, above all, economic reform took a back seat to political expediency, for Kravchuk's first priority was avoiding major political crisis. Hence, "Kravchuk found that he could keep the country together politically essentially by doing nothing."[95] As a consequence, in the economic sphere, Kravchuk never really challenged the conservative elements in parliament.

Fourth, despite Kravchuk's reluctance to challenge the bureaucracy that supported him, it is still the case that he misunderstood the need for rapid economic reform. In his basic ignorance of economics, he was joined by the large majority of the former communist *nomenklatura,* who retained their positions in the government *apparat.* The economic basis of Ukraine's political independence was never really understood in government circles except by a few, more or less "token" cabinet ministers and deputy prime ministers (such as Viktor Pynzenyk, Roman Shpek, and Volodymyr Lanoviy), who were ineffective in any case. To be fair, this was not entirely their fault, for just as Prime Minister Leonid Kuchma would learn, little could be accomplished without the support of the *nomenklatura.*

Fifth, despite obvious pride in his personal transformation into the democratic leader of a new, independent Ukraine, Kravchuk's leadership continued to reflect the instincts he developed as a career communist. At critical times, he appeared more concerned with guarding his personal prerogatives against potential political rivals (such as Kuchma) than with improving the well-being of the Ukrainian people. This had unfortunate consequences, such as when he interpreted Kuchma's bold moves for reform as a direct challenge. The president resented taking a backseat to his prime minister, leading him to seek direct control over the cabinet and government. But instead of furthering the cause of reform—this time leading the effort—Kravchuk reversed by decree many of Kuchma's market-liberating measures. Further, Kravchuk's political maneuverings in 1993–94 had a certain simplicity and transparency to them. In fact, his effort to force Kuchma's resignation in 1993 would, by 2001, appear amateurish compared to the power play that Ukraine's energy oligarchs would mount against President Kuchma's own prime minister, Viktor Yushchenko in 2000–2001 (to be discussed in chapter 4.)

Finally, Kravchuk's failures paved the way for his successor. By mid-1994, Kravchuk would appear ineffective to some voters and "far too clever by half" to others. Kuchma, who would remain popular with voters even out of office, took advantage of his image as a well-intentioned victim of Kravchuk's ambitions. As the political center of gravity shifted toward Eastern Ukraine throughout 1993–94, Kuchma, the "favorite son" of Dnipropetrovsk, would discover that he had advantages over Kravchuk, the "sly fox" from Western Ukraine. The poor economy was at least part of the reason for Kravchuk's defeat in the 1994 presidential elections.[96] Therefore, as Kuzio argues, "the Kravchuk era should not . . . be regarded as a failure in comparison to the Kuchma era that followed. Without Kravchuk, there would have been no Kuchma."[97]

D'Anieri aptly sums up Kravchuk's dilemma as largely an institutional problem; he could not operate as reformer because the executive powers of government were too diffused, split between a president and a prime minister who were often in conflict with each other as well as parliament. Hence, "because no actor was both able to implement a program and be responsible for it, not only could policies never be made, but issues could never be resolved."[98] Thus, when Kuchma was rejected in September 1993, "no particular set of policies was being rejected, and it was impossible, therefore, to move on."[99] This situation would persist for over one year, from Kravchuk's struggles with Prime Minister Kuchma in summer 1993 until newly elected President Kuchma would unveil his program of radical reforms in October 1994.

Chapter 4

Kuchma as Economic Reformer, 1994–2001

Kuchma's record as economic reformer is not only lengthier than Kravchuk's (he has been elected to two full terms, after all), but it is decidedly more complicated. As Ukraine-watcher Paul D'Anieri observes, "It was Kuchma, the factory director from Dnipropetrovsk in the east, not Kravchuk, a neonationalist from the west, who advocated reform as prime minister and began to implement it as president."[1] Further, Kuchma's record is one of two small steps back for every giant step forward, zigzagging and backtracking on reform measures in response to both domestic and international pressures. Consequently, the present chapter is entirely devoted to Kuchma's economic leadership.

"Kuchma II": Toward Radical Economic Reform, 1994–98

President Versus Prime Minister Kuchma: How Different?

Economic reform received renewed impetus with the election of Leonid D. Kuchma as Ukraine's second president in July 1994. Candidate Kuchma had run on a platform of renewed economic ties to Russia, greater autonomy for Ukraine's regions, and an "evolutionary approach" to reforms. Unlike Kravchuk, however, Kuchma owed nothing to the former *nomenklatura* after his election, and he no longer had to contend with Kravchuk's interference. As president, therefore, Kuchma surprised nearly everyone by immediately setting about developing plans for accelerating Ukraine's transition to the market.[2] The result was the October 11, 1994, release of an ambitious program of reforms, entitled, "Along the Road of Radical Economic Reform."[3] Kuchma's program was overwhelmingly approved in parliament by a vote of 231 to 54 on October 19.[4] The package received immediate support from numerous Western institutions; especially important endorsements came from the IMF, and Group of Seven (G-7) industrialized nations.[5]

The Basic Outline of Kuchma's Program, October 1994

Kuchma's program was comprehensive, embracing the objectives of reducing the budget deficit from 20 percent of GDP to 8 percent in 1995 (and to no more than 4 percent by 1997), stabilizing the currency and introducing the hryvnia; accelerating medium- and large-scale privatization, liberalizing prices, reducing heavy tax burdens; cutting business regulation, and easing foreign currency restrictions.[6] The World Bank predicted that, if Kuchma's reforms were aggressively implemented, Ukraine could expect real economic growth of 6 to 7 percent by 1996.[7]

The sheer ambition of Kuchma's reforms generated widespread opposition in parliament, which almost immediately engaged him in a battle over the authority to implement the reforms. The game appeared to be one of giving Kuchma just enough rope to hang himself. Despite ostensible parliamentary approval for his program, the legislature continuously handicapped his efforts. For instance, in violation of Kuchma's promise not to increase wages before the end of the year, the very day after approving his program, parliament endorsed broad-based wage increases of between four-to-six times, a doubling of monthly pensions, and a tripling of social security payments.[8] This move was certain to lead to further deterioration in value of the karbovanets. Kuchma responded by aggressively pursuing his plans for freeing exchange rates and liberalizing prices, which parliament reluctantly approved 216 to 78 on November 9.[9] A unified exchange rate to be set by the Ukrainian Interbank Currency Exchange (UICE) went into effect on October 28.

These painful reforms would be fruitless unless privatization was accelerated and enterprise governance reformed. Parliament remained obstinate, however, blocking efforts to restructure Ukrainian industry. In the immediate aftermath of Kuchma's election, on July 29, 1994, parliament placed a moratorium on most significant privatization activities.[10] The ban lasted four months and was lifted only after the Cabinet adopted a list of some 6,147 enterprises to be excluded from privatization, owing to their "national significance and value to the state".[11] In this way, parliament effectively removed from consideration the "cream" of Ukrainian industry, the most desirable enterprises.

In its efforts to handicap Kuchma, parliament had a willing ally in Prime Minister Vitaly Masol. Appointed by former president Leonid Kravchuk just nine days before the June presidential election, Masol marked a return to the pre-independence period (he had previously served as Ukraine's Soviet-era premier).[12] He was ideologically opposed to much of Kuchma's program, and opposed reduction of SOE budget subsidies and other requirements that were necessary to qualify for badly needed IMF loans.[13] Frustrated that the Cabinet did not more vigorously promote his reforms, the president forced Masol out of government "for reasons of his advanced age" on March 1, 1995.[14] Kuchma then appointed former KGB general and First Deputy Prime Minister Yevhen Marchuk as Acting Prime Minister.[15] Initially loyal to Kuchma, Marchuk had not yet exhibited the personal ambitions that would later run afoul of the president and his policies. In the immediate present, Kuchma forced the entire Cabinet to resign in July 1995, permitting him to streamline the body itself, reducing the number of deputy prime ministers from nine to five. However, Pynzenyk—who had been brought back into the government after the July 1994 election—was a casualty of the cabinet shake-up. His dismissal confirmed Kuchma's apparent shift in focus away from tight fiscal and monetary policy and toward greater support for industrial restructuring and welfare reform.[16]

Kuchma on "Correcting Reforms," 1995

Early in 1995, Kuchma's commitment to reforms appeared to waiver. He began to speak publicly of the need for a "correction" of reforms. He elaborated in his formal April 4th Economic Report to Parliament, indicating his desire to shift emphasis from achieving stabilization through monetary means to spurring growth in industrial output.[17] The president criticized "blind monetarism," calling instead for the creation of a "socially-oriented market economy."[18] Kuchma's concept of "correction" implied strengthening the state in order to enhance control over the economic process, to be accomplished mainly through the establishment of so-called "financial-industrial groups" (FIGs). These would essentially be "seamless" networks of banking and industrial enterprises, involving a degree of economic integration not seen since Soviet times.

In late January 1995, Kuchma had decreed that the Cabinet of Ministers draft a law to organize entrepreneurial activity into FIGs, patterned after the Russian model decreed two years earlier.[19] These entities were viewed as means to re-establish desirable economic links with Russian enterprises, in recognition of the high degree of interdependence that still existed between some firms in the two countries.[20] FIGs are currently established under Ukrainian law as conglomerates of banks and manufacturers, operating under a single organizational shell. As in Russia, a FIG is a group of companies that band together to share technology and capital in order to improve competitiveness.

Initially lukewarm on the idea, parliament approved the establishment of FIGs on November 21, 1995, after stripping away certain special privileges (including tax concessions and access to credits) from Kuchma's draft bill.[21] Certain parliamentary factions—especially those on the Right—feared that FIGs would constitute a vehicle for Russian domination of key Ukrainian industries. Hence, the law was enacted after amendments that permitted the establishment of FIGs only in "priority industries," designated by parliament alone. Throughout 1995–98, Ukrainian and Russian enterprises employed this law extensively to create interstate FIGs in heavy machinery, defense, metallurgical, and chemical industries, among others.[22]

FIGs can combine both vertical and horizontal integration to such an extent that new monopolies may be formed. While these are obviously subject to the antimonopoly legislation of both countries, the FIG structure militates against domestic competition. Further, the FIG organization "closely corresponds to the ministries to which these manufacturers [previously] belonged" under the former USSR.[23] As such, FIGs appear substantially to recreate in the private sector the same kind of patronage-based economic system that Mikhail Gorbachev expended so much effort to bring down. Creating FIGs reconstructs much of the "ministry system," albeit on a decentralized basis, including more coordinated resource allocation, lax incentives, and sluggish response to markets. Cross-national FIGs also partially recreate pieces of the former supply system of the Soviet economy. Opponents object that they will favor entrenched, powerful economic interests with privileged access to government authorities in both countries. Thus, the basic question remains whether FIGs are a vehicle for "crony capitalism," or a "Trojan horse" for Russian penetration of Ukrainian industry.

These developments were complicated in mid-1995 by the ongoing struggle between president and parliament over adoption of a post-Soviet constitution for Ukraine. In the absence of general agreement on the basic provisions of a new constitution, the struggle over economic reform and exercise of executive powers remained problematical. On May 18, 1995, however, conclusion of a "Constitutional Accord" between president and parliament provided the framework for orderly governance in the face of the daunting task of negotiating a new constitution.[24] But its implementation was delayed owing to the required constitutional amendments that were needed in order to bring it fully into force. The accord would operate as a "*petite* constitution" until a proper constitution could be adopted. It was signed on June 8, but only after Kuchma threatened to call a nationwide referendum of confidence in himself and parliament on June 28.[25]

The "Law on Power," as it was called, gave the president exclusive rights to form the government, issue decrees, and overrule local councils that attempted to block his reforms.[26] The new agreement did not end contention between the executive and legislature, however. Parliament continuously debated legislation on issues that were now formally within the president's competence, refusing even to consider over 100 laws submitted by the president.[27] In 1995, economic reform was still captive to the as yet unresolved institutional rivalry.

Reestablishing Economic Ties with Russia

The new emphasis on FIGs was an important indication that, by 1995, the priority had shifted significantly, from separating economies and delinking policies to maintaining and even reestablishing economic ties with Russia. In his inaugural address, Kuchma reiterated what everyone had accepted as fact: "the normalization of relations with Russia, our strategic partner, is of principal significance."[28] As Kuzio observes, "maintaining economic ties with Russia was never rejected by any Ukrainian presidential candidate."[29] But Kuchma's reputed preference for close ties with Russia appears overblown in the face of his repeated statements as prime minister that, "Russia is trying to bring about a full paralysis of the Ukrainian economy."[30] Thus, "Kuchma's emphasis on ensuring good relations with Russia was always stated in the same breath as good relations with the West."[31] The one, he wanted; the other, he knew that he simply must have.

In July 1995, Kuchma signed an economic union treaty with Russia and Belarus in an effort to reestablish what trade links could be renewed and to overcome the output collapse. The treaty embraced the concept of integration in production, investment, trade, credit, and currency. Kuchma was attacked for his treaty on the basis that it sacrificed too much of Ukraine's economic sovereignty.[32] Throughout 1993–95, the government's foreign economic policy priority was to reestablish economic ties with Russia without compromising Ukrainian sovereignty. Kuchma has pursued improved economic ties with Russia not as an end in itself, but in conjunction with substantive market reforms. He has consistently rejected involving Ukraine in any new super-national entity that would threaten Ukrainian sovereignty, including organs of the Commonwealth of Independent States (CIS).

The Search for a "Ukrainian Model" of Reforms

Kuchma addressed the National Press Club for Market Reform on November 18, 1995, when he both reinforced his commitment to economic reform and elaborated on his views that economic reforms should adhere to Ukraine's unique, rich historical and cultural traditions.[33] Consequently, the "Ukrainian model" incorporates lessons that Ukraine had learned from both its own and world experience. According to Kuzio, the model has the following general attributes[34]:

- Rejection of Western economic models in favor of a "state-regulated" transition to a socially oriented market. The transition to a market economy would come about through state regulation. Both absolutes would be rejected: the reimposition of total state control and/or the complete withering away of the state;
- Social support of the population during the transition to a market economy;
- Protection of the domestic market and producers, especially foodstuffs and light industry;
- Establishment of a mixed economy allowing the conditions for all types of ownership;
- Division of the state sector via creation of joint stock enterprises where the state would retain at least 51 percent of stock;
- Preservation of the monopoly status of certain key enterprises that could help Ukraine enter the world market;
- State control through price levers;
- The need for a "rigid vertical structure" of government, and the strengthening of the executive and administrative authorities.

These attributes were largely reflected in the economic program of Prime Minister Yevhen Marchuk.

Marchuk's Economic Program, October 1995

In a June 8, 1995, decree, Kuchma named Yevhen Marchuk prime minister, announcing the appointment just minutes after signing the constitutional agreement with parliament in a ceremony at Kyiv's beautiful landmark, the Mariyinsky Palace.[35] Marchuk entered the economic reform arena in October 1995, with the presentation of his reform proposals to parliament.[36] The ninth such program to be submitted since August 1991, Marchuk's wide-ranging program embraced Kuchma's concept of "correcting reforms," calling for a more evolutionary approach to economic transition.[37] Though the new program echoed much of Kuchma's October 1994 program, Marchuk's would slow reforms "in recognition of the prolonged and deep crisis afflicting Ukraine." However, the plan is full of measures which would militate against the development of free markets.[38]

The main tenets of the 116-page program were: state-regulated transition to a socially oriented market economy; social protection of the population from the worst excesses of transition; protection of domestic producers from foreign competition; overcoming the payments crisis; corporatization of enterprises (with the state maintaining a controlling interest); boosting of investments; state control of prices; reform of the tax system to spur small business development; and preservation of monopoly status of key enterprises.[39] There were around 60 general state and sectoral programs drawn up to implement Marchuk's overall program throughout the economy.

Parliament approved Marchuk's program 234 to 61 (with 17 abstentions and 11 deputies not voting) on October 11, 1995.[40] Kuchma hailed the decision as "highly positive" and "a source of confidence . . . for the entire nation."[41] The package was designed to appeal to a wide range of interests, and it enjoyed broad support. Deputies from such diverse factions as Reforms, Statehood, Center, Rukh, Unity, the Interregional Bloc, and Agrarians for Reforms supported the program in its entirety. But parliament soon chose to violate certain provisions of the very program it had so recently approved. For instance, a key feature of the program was the elimination of wage-push inflation by strictly limiting the rate of growth in wages and salaries to 80 percent of the growth of industrial output. But the day after enacting the program, parliament endorsed an increase in the minimum wage that resulted in fresh emissions of some KBV 600 trillion, thereby aggravating inflation. At the time, Labor Minister Mykhailo Kaskevych stated that, "this decision by Parliament has actually cancelled the government program of action adopted yesterday."[42] In an all-too-familiar manner, parliament once again publicly supported the reform program but placed itself at odds with the government over its implementation.

Monetary Reform and Fiscal Discipline, 1996

Prime Minister Marchuk vowed to reduce budget expenditures and credit subsidies in 1996.[43] This was consistent with the major theme of Kuchma's "State of the State Address," delivered to parliament on April 2, 1996, when the president reaffirmed the inevitability of economic reforms aimed at stabilizing the situation in Ukraine.[44] In fact, throughout the year the government made serious efforts to reduce subsidies and credits. The unfortunate result was that a dangerous crisis was generated in unpaid wages, pensions, and interenterprise debts. Fears arose that a chain of bankruptcies would be set in motion.[45] Efforts were made throughout the year to clear the arrears but with little success. Wages and salaries lagged significantly behind schedule, often for months.

What seems clear is that the government used the arrears to meet inflation targets negotiated with foreign lenders, notably the IMF. Further, the arrears crisis failed to dissipate, even after introduction in September of Ukraine's permanent national currency, the hryvnia. Passage of an austere budget almost three months late, on March 22, barely satisfied conditions for resumption of installments under a previously suspended IMF Standby Loan agreement, providing around $300 million of immediate fiscal relief.[46] However, the payments crisis intensified throughout the year, reaching UAH 82 trillion by December 31, 1996.[47] The arrears would persist into 1998, considerably aggravating social and political tensions.

A serious rift developed between Kuchma and Marchuk over various aspects of the latter's implementation of economic reform, costing Marchuk the premiership on May 27, 1996. In dismissing him, Kuchma cited inefficiency in the management of the Cabinet, especially lack of structural changes in state enterprises, the payments crisis, and an inability to cooperate with parliament.[48] In reality, Kuchma feared that Marchuk would become a serious political rival, when he publicly opposed the president over a national referendum on the June 1996 constitution. Another factor was Marchuk's apparent rapprochement with the Left on easing the course of economic reforms.[49] Marchuk, the fifth prime minister since 1992, was replaced on May 28 by First Deputy Prime Minister Pavlo Lazarenko, a 43-year-old oil tycoon from Kuchma's native city of Dnipropetrovsk. Parliament approved Lazarenko's nomination 344 to 22 (with 9 abstentions and 17 not voting) on July 10, 1996.[50]

As he fired Marchuk, Kuchma reaffirmed his commitment to economic reforms, stating that, "Ukraine has passed the point of historic return, and there will be no going back."[51] Newly appointed Premier

Lazarenko affirmed his support for Kuchma's reforms.[52] To simplify implementation of reforms, Kuchma extensively reorganized the government by decree in July, streamlining the Cabinet and ordering the layoffs of 20 percent of government employees (some 10,000) as a cost-cutting measure. In fact, this was a direct move against the midlevels of the bureaucracy, the so-called *nomenklatura,* who were widely viewed as blocking reforms. These measures, however, obscured from the public's view preparation for a far more important event, the introduction of Ukraine's permanent currency, the hryvnia, in September.

The currency reform of September 2 was announced with great fanfare on August 24, the fifth anniversary of Ukrainian independence. With few restrictions on currency conversion, the reform was entirely nonconfiscatory, which enhanced acceptability of the hryvnia. The process went so smoothly that an anti-inflationary retail price freeze was lifted after just two weeks, and the period of conversion was extended until mid-October. To the credit of the National Bank of Ukraine (NBU) Governor Victor Yushchenko, the hryvnia-dollar exchange rate remained stable from its inception until Autumn 1998, when effects of the Asian economic crisis reached acute proportions in Ukraine. The currency reform of 1996 stands as the greatest achievement of the decade in Ukraine's economic reform efforts.

Pynzenyk's Reform Program, Late 1996

Under Lazarenko's direction, the task fell to Deputy Prime Minister Viktor M. Pynzenyk to elaborate a comprehensive program for the government. Apparently, six years of economic decline had convinced many in government circles that more profound reforms than had previously been attempted would be necessary.[53] Pynzenyk's program, dubbed "Economic Growth '97," was even more radical and far-reaching than Kuchma's late 1994 program. Addressing most of the major issues, it sought expenditure cuts in nonessential areas; strong cash control through a strengthened treasury function; reduction in the number of taxes and of tax rates; elimination of many tax exemptions and unjustifiable tax privileges; liberalization of the payment system to reduce the arrears and make barter less attractive; broad deregulation of business, especially licensing procedures; and strong regulation of energy monopolies.[54]

Lazarenko presented the 134-page three-year program worked out by Pynzenyk to parliament on October 15, 1996.[55] True to form, parliament quickly approved the overall program, by a 252-to-64 majority, but failed to act on the large package of draft laws that were introduced to give it force. President Kuchma worked hard for the package, but the premier merely gave it lip service.[56] Pynzenyk found that his other colleagues among the Cabinet of Ministers also abandoned him, so that in the end, he was left to fight for the reforms on his own. In mid-December 1996, Pynzenyk took the reforms directly to the people in an aggressive public relations campaign to push the program through parliament.[57] By early 1997, the most critical part of the reform program—the package of tax law changes that promised to transform incentives throughout the Ukrainian economy—were clearly in jeopardy.

Tax Reform Fails, 1997

Under Pynzenyk's influence, the Lazarenko government made its most important reform efforts in the budgetary sphere, proposing a radical reform of the entire tax system. With high marginal tax rates, narrow bases, and hundreds of exemptions, exclusions, and privileges, Ukraine's tax system was in crisis. It is blamed for driving over one-half of the entire economy into the shadow sector. By 1997, it was abundantly clear that the situation had long since become untenable. Pynzenyk's tax proposals would have greatly simplified taxes through a series of seven draft laws that, collectively, would promote growth by cutting overall taxes by 7.3 percent of GDP. The program's centerpiece was to be a cut in the average enterprise tax burden from 7.6 to 4.1 percent of GDP. A key objective was to bring shadow sector businesses into the official economy. The budget package also included deep cuts in social spending, elimination of all subsidies for rents and utilities, and introduction of an actuarial basis for pension fund management.

The fight over tax reform delayed enactment of the budget for almost six months, to June 27, 1997. The delay placed acute pressure on the government when the IMF threatened to temporarily suspend or reduce considerably its promised 1997 funding of more than $1.2 billion.[58] This would severely constrain Ukraine's ability to repay its energy debts to Russia and Turkmenistan. In the end, the tax package was only partially enacted, with minor changes to the VAT and a major amendment to the enterprise profits tax (levying the tax on "net profits"), including withdrawal of tax incentives for foreign investors (of which the IMF did *not* approve). To the great disappointment of reformers, the remaining five bills were shelved indefinitely. Tax reform had abysmally failed. In frustration over parliament's failure to enact reforms, Pynzenyk resigned his post on April 2.[59]

Failure to secure enactment of the tax package meant that Lazarenko also would be removed, less than one year after taking office.[60] Dismissed by Kuchma on June 19, 1997, for "health reasons," pressure for his removal had been building for several months, over both Lazarenko's inability to gain passage for Kuchma's tax reforms as well as his inaction on a major anticorruption package.[61] The prime minister himself was subsequently accused of embezzlement and money laundering.[62] Owing to these factors, Lazarenko was replaced on July 16, 1997, by a Kuchma crony, minister of the Cabinet of Ministers (and former mayor of Dnipropetrovsk), Valeriy Pustovoitenko.[63] Known for his fierce loyalty to the president, Pustovoitenko first came to Kyiv with Kuchma in 1992, when the latter was named premier. Head of the pro-Kuchma National Democratic Party (NDP), unlike his predecessors, he was expected to support his patron unquestioningly.[64]

To a great extent, the economic policies of 1997 were influenced by the political preparation and posturing for the much-anticipated parliamentary elections of March 29, 1998.[65] The election campaign pitted against one another the two main contending "establishment parties": Putovoitenko's NDP (pro-Kuchma) and Lazarenko's Hromada party (anti-Kuchma). Occupying the political center, these "parties" really functioned more as vehicles for competing business-*nomenklatura* alliances. Hromada, for instance, was centered on the interests of a particular company, United Energy Systems, then headed by Lazarenko's business partner, Yulia Tymoshenko (who was to figure so prominently in national politics in 1999–2000), and allied interests in the energy sector. Again, the core constituency of the NDP was pro-Kuchma.

Both parties failed, however, to garner more than the necessary 5 percent of the vote to secure representation in the new parliament in the proportional half of the seats up for grabs. But individual members were elected on the voting district half of the ballot. Of the remaining seats, the communists got around 25 percent, with other left parties (e.g., the Socialists and the Peasant Party) getting around 40 percent. Rukh, a shadow of its former self, received but 10 percent. The elections therefore signaled no clear direction on economic reforms, promising just more of the same. Table 4.1 provides a breakdown of parliament's party-faction membership after the 1998 elections.

Kuchma Veers Further Off Course, 1998

The presence of Kuchma loyalist Pustovoitenko at the helm meant that rivalry between president and premier was at an end, so that responsibility for the government's economic policy now rested squarely with Kuchma. But the 1998 parliamentary elections failed to break the political logjam between president and parliament. The subsequent election of Oleksandr Tkachenko of the leftist Peasant Party as speaker

Table 4.1
Structure of Parliamant after the March 1998 Elections in Ukraine

Political Orientation	Party/Faction/Coalition	Percent of Ballots Received Under Party Lists	Mandates Gained		Total Seats
			Party List	Single-Mandate Districts	
Leftists	Communist Party	24.68	84	38	122
	Socialist Party-Peasant Party Coalition	8.54	29	5	34
	Progressive Socialist Party	4.04	14	2	16
	All-Ukrainian Workers Party	3.86		2	2
	TOTAL		**127**	**47**	**174**
Centrists	Peoples' Democratic Party	4.99	17	11	28
	Agrarian Party	3.67		8	8
	Green Party	5.46	19		19
	Hromada	4.68	16	7	23
	Social-Democratic Party-United	4.02	14	3	17
	Party of Regional Revival of Ukraine	0.91		2	2
	Social-Liberal Bloc (SLON) [Note 1]	0.91		1	1
	Union Party (Soyuz)	0.70		1	1
	Together [Note 2]	1.90		1	1
	TOTAL		**66**	**34**	**100**

Rightists and Right-Centrists	Rukh	9.40	32	13	45
	Reforms and Order	3.13		3	3
	Forward Ukraine! [Note 3]	1.74		2	2
	National-Democratic Parties' Bloc	1.23		2	2
	National Front [Note 4]	2.72		5	5
	"Fewer Words" Bloc [Note 5]	0.57		1	1
	TOTAL		32	26	58
Others	Seven Smaller Parties [Note 6] - **TOTAL**	2.71		2	2
	Non-Party Candidates			111	111
	GRAND TOTAL		225	220	445 [Note 7]

Notes: [1] SLON was comprised of the Inter-regional Bloc of Reforms and the Constitutional Democratic Party.

[2] Together was composed of the Liberal Party and the party of Labor.

[3] Forward Ukraine! consisted of the Ukrainian Christian Democratic Party and the Christian-Peoples Union.

[4] National Front was composed of the Congress of Ukrainian Nationalists, the Ukrainian Republican party, and the Ukrainian Conservative Republican party.

[5] The "Fewer Words" Bloc was composed of the Social National Party and the All Ukrainian Political Union DSU.

[6] This group included the Party of National-Economic Development of Ukraine, All-Ukrainian Party of Women's Initiatives, Social-Democratic Party, Party of Defenders of the Motherland, Party of Moslems of Ukraine, Party of Spiritual, Economic, and Social Progress, and "European Choice."

[7] Totals do not sum to 450 seats due to failure to elect candidates on the first round in several single-mandate districts.

Source : Ukrainian Central Election Commission, Institute of Political and Ethno-national Research, *Parlament Ukrayini: Vibori '98—Dokumenti, Statistiki, Bibliografia* (Kyiv: National Library of the Parliament of Ukraine, 1998).

also placed a serious obstacle in the way of reforms, especially when Tkachenko unveiled his own alternative economic program.

Predictably, the new parliament was as obstructionist as its predecessor, attempting in October to remove Pustovoitenko in a "no confidence" vote (on the basis of the government's compliance with stringent IMF conditions!).[66] Kuchma himself slipped badly in popularity polls, ranking third as a possible 1999 presidential contender, behind the likely socialist and communist candidates, in a November 1998 survey conducted by his own administration. In the midst of what promised to be a divisive presidential campaign, the president veered sharply to the Left.

To be fair, events at this time were working against Ukraine. The Asian financial crisis hit Ukraine in late October 1997 and would reverberate well into 1998. Ukraine's T-bill rates rose sharply, which placed a strain on the debt service line of the state budget. Throughout 1998, Ukraine would find it difficult to roll over its short-term debt held by foreigners. Ukraine's international reserves were strained as the NBU fought to hold the value of the hryvnia. The most serious problem was the sharp devaluation of the Russian ruble, which occurred on August 17, 1998. In the absence of a steep devaluation of the hryvnia, the Russian currency crisis threatened drastic reduction in the competitiveness of Ukrainian products and would increase Russian exports to Ukraine. Further, due to the increased risk (and not a little bit of panic), international investors were withdrawing from former Soviet countries, including Ukraine. This eliminated the possibility of Ukraine's closing the current account deficit without a devaluation.[67]

The result was that by September 1998—a year after the crisis manifested itself in Ukraine—its international reserves amounted to less than $1 billion, or around one month's worth of imports. To make matters worse, due to parliamentary opposition to reforms, most previously agreed-upon IMF targets were not achieved, so that Ukraine was to receive no international financing in the first six months of the year.

In order to break the political deadlock, in a May 12 speech to parliament, Kuchma outlined a new program that he believed would appeal to the new left-leaning parliament.[68] The so-called "Concept of and Strategy for Economic Growth, 1999–2005" took account of the successes previously achieved under the October 1994 program of IMF-approved "radical reforms," updated to the needs of the current situation.[69] Kuchma's 1998 program would increase the regulatory role of the state, reduce foreign and domestic borrowing, increase financial support for industry, and reduce the budget deficit permanently. The objective was to halt the decline in output and actually to increase real growth to 5 percent annually by 2002. Kuchma's objective was to "turn stabilization [gradually] into positive growth."[70] By focusing on the output collapse, however, Kuchma was appealing to populist sentiments in parliament and society that had always viewed the decline in production as *the problem* to be solved. His plan also had the advantage of not antagonizing the parliamentary left wing, whose supporters Kuchma hoped to attract in the upcoming October 1999 presidential elections.

It is easy to understand Kuchma's frustration with the situation in mid-1998. Originally expected to experience positive growth of 1.0 percent in 1997, Ukrainian GDP actually fell 3.2 percent that year, then grew by a modest 0.2 percent in the first nine months of 1998. In Autumn, the Asian crisis sent certain key industries into a tailspin (for example, steel, which declined 22 percent from its September 1997 level). To compound matters, the worldwide crisis also negatively affected government T-bill sales, raising the likelihood that Ukraine would have to resort to printing money to cover the projected budget deficit of 3.7 percent of GDP. While the exchange rate had remained relatively stable for two years, in September the NBU was forced to abandon defense of its "trading band" against the U.S. dollar, which resulted in a devaluation of nearly 60 percent in the hryvnia, compared to its value when Russia announced its devaluation and debt moratorium on August 17, 1998.[71]

Kuchma acted in late summer to reduce the deficit by decree, ordering draconian spending cuts to pare the annual deficit to 2.5 percent of GDP, from 3.7 percent, by year's end.[72] Nominal cuts of an average 19.4 percent were ordered.[73] Despite his efforts, Kuchma was unable to prevent the downgrading in September of Ukrainian currency bonds by Moody's Investors Service, from B2 to B3, with a negative forecast.[74] A decline in gold and hard currency reserves to critically low levels also raised the risk of default on external debt, prompting Standard & Poor's to rate Ukraine's fiscal position as "unreliable."[75]

As a result of these downgradings, Kuchma took the more drastic step of (more or less) forcibly rescheduling Ukraine's debt, effectively postponing the crisis until 2000.[76] In order to meet the government's immediate cash needs, and to prop up industrial production, in a major speech on November 19, Kuchma explicitly rejected the advice of the IMF and western governments and chose instead to follow Russia's lead of combating the financial crisis with Soviet-era tools.[77] He called for strict currency controls, the printing of more money, and new legislation that would strip the NBU of its independence.[78]

Vacillating on reforms, Kuchma now harshly criticized the monetary policies of the NBU for "artificially restricting the hryvnia rate," thereby depriving the economy of money necessary for growth.[79] To increase liquidity in the enterprise sector, Kuchma explicitly reneged on previous agreements with the IMF, reestablishing government control over the NBU and nationalizing the former agro-investment bank, Bank Ukrayina, which had been led into bankruptcy by the government's policy of directing credits to unworthy growers in the agricultural sector. By prior agreement, Ukraine was also to cancel all tax privileges in order to boost revenue flow, but Kuchma now called for agricultural producers to be exempt from all taxes, except pension fund contributions, for three years. Finally, stating that he was against inflationary cash emissions, he nevertheless called for reviving the previous practice of direct NBU crediting of the budget, which would amount to the same thing: renewed inflation.

The reaction of the World Bank and IMF was swift and unambiguous. They announced jointly on December 7 that Ukraine would receive no new loans or installments on existing loans until February 1999, at the earliest.[80] The European Union also froze an ECU 150 million credit line, pending a final decision by the IMF. Hence, a further bailout of Ukraine by western lenders appeared highly unlikely. The amounts at stake were not trivial. Ukraine in autumn had received two IMF tranches worth $335 million and $340 million in loans from the World Bank; a third IMF tranche was suspended. The NBU badly needed the IMF funds to replenish its depleted hard currency reserves. However, without IMF funding, Ukraine would not be able to redeem $860 million in T-bills and another $1.5 billion in external debt that would come due in 1999. Further devaluation of the hryvnia therefore appeared likely in 1999, especially in light of the growing current account deficit. This prospect produced widespread anxiety in government circles.

Prompted by the currency crisis, President Kuchma presented a major economic policy speech before parliament on November 19, 1998.[81] He made no new proposals but expressed dismay that parliament had acted upon only 1 of some 44 economic bills that he had submitted for consideration. Especially distressing to Kuchma was the failure to enact a new "Law on the National Bank of Ukraine," which he believed left the bank unaccountable and beyond effective government control. Backing his words with action, Kuchma in January 1999 directed the Cabinet of Ministers to draft a long-term program, "Ukraine-2010," that would look beyond present-day problems, and develop a program of practical actions to achieve longer-term objectives.[82] This was the first indication of an important shift in the president's thinking toward improving long-term social, health, and living standards and strengthening the economic foundations of Ukraine.

"Kuchma III": The Long-Term Strategy, 1999–2001

The "Ukraine-2010" Program

The "Ukraine-2010" program was based on medium-term (until 2000) and long-term (until 2010) forecasts, sectoral programs, project proposals, and prioritization of investments for restructuring the economy. It represented the first attempt in post-Soviet times to move beyond the endless succession of crises to envision a wholly transformed Ukraine by 2010. Unveiled initially by Minister of the Economy Vasyl Rohoviy, the purpose of the program was to abandon the old (that is, Soviet) management system; to explicitly involve private individuals, government, and enterprises in building consensus as to socioeconomic objectives; and to agree on a timetable for meeting them. The program contained elements that would appeal to both sides of the political spectrum. The major objectives of "Ukraine-2010" were:

(1) Raise the average life expectancy to 69–71 years (from the 67.4 years recorded in 1997);
(2) Increase per capita GDP from $2,000 (1999) to $4,000-$5,000;
(3) Accelerate real GDP growth to 8 percent by 2006–2010;
(4) Improve real wages by 50 percent by 2005, and 133 percent by 2010 (over 1997 levels);
(5) Expand the share of state budget expenditures on health by at least 1.5 times;
(6) Transform the pension system into a true insurance program, thus permitting an increase in benefits to 40–50 percent of an average monthly wage (versus 32 percent in 1998);
(7) Legalize the shadow economy, cutting it by at least 25 percent by 2005, and 70–80 percent by 2010;
(8) Target financial assistance on the truly needy;
(9) Create a full-fledged housing market in Ukraine;
(10) Employ sound project analysis methods to evaluate the merits of privatization and business development proposals;
(11) Strengthen the banking sector in order to mobilize citizens' savings for economic development;
(12) Increase annual capital investment by at least 11–13 percent a year, to no less than UAH 140 billion per year by 2010.[83]

Prime Minister Pustovoitenko presented the program to members of parliament, economists, bankers, and academics at a conference held for this purpose in early March 1999.[84] He was joined by President Kuchma and other government officials in presenting the program at a second conference, on March 10–11.[85] Some analysts saw the 1999 program as a cynical election-year ploy to assure the population that Kuchma would return the economy to normalcy by reimposing economic planning.[86] They argued that the plan's organization into "stages," prioritization of state-directed investments in key sectors, support for "mixed" forms of ownership, protection of domestic industry, and emphasis on the continuing role of the state all smacked of state socialism. Be that as it may, the program embraced several positive aspects.[87] In particular, the admission that popular support of reforms was necessary and the recognition that only a gradual approach can work where the institutions of a market economy remain at a rudimentary stage. Without concrete actions to implement the program, however, laudatory statements of objectives would remain purely rhetorical. Unfortunately, as with so many previous programs, the necessary cooperation from parliament was not to be forthcoming.

Election-Year Economics, 1999

Due to lack of parliamentary action, Kuchma, in his June 28 Constitution Day speech, announced that, under the constitution, he had temporary authority to issue special executive decrees on economic reform and had, in fact, issued 39 decrees during the last ten days of his constitutional right to do so.[88] His expressed rationale was the deadlock in parliament, which had sidetracked consideration of some 700 bills on economic and social matters (including at least 50 bills that dealt with implementation of the constitution, as well as those pertaining to his "Ukraine-2010" program).[89] Some of the decrees increased minimum wages, promoted specific IMF loan requirements, and sought to stimulate small business development. Kuchma's parliamentary opposition saw many of the decrees as election-year ploys to appeal to the growing underground business interests, pensioners, and workers.

Kuchma carried his campaign for reform further still, by elaborating nine principles for the "unification of our society and the consolidation of the branches of power," in his August 23, 1999, Independence Day speech.[90] Briefly, Kuchma envisioned Ukraine's development adhering to the principles of: democracy and market reforms, a rejection of revolutionary change, social accord, a rejection of the Soviet past, an emphasis on individual rights and building civil society, the rule of law, responsible government, administrative reform, and sound center-regional relations. He reaffirmed the goals and objectives of the "Ukraine-2010" program and set out specific policy proposals to achieve them, especially tax reform, structural change, protection of property rights, and fiscal reform.

Kuchma's Independence Day appeal apparently failed to persuade parliament, however, which rejected nearly every outstanding decree of importance that he had issued by July 15.[91] Further, there were continuing attempts by the Communist faction to unseat Prime Minister Pustovoitenko, Kuchma's strongest ally in parliament.[92] In the midst of the late July 1999 parliamentary attempt to oust the premier, certain top members of the cabinet spoke critically about the dramatic shift in official reform policy. The most open critic was First Deputy Prime Minister Volodymyr Kuratchenko, who made a 12-point statement of protest at a July 29 cabinet meeting.[93] Kuratchenko's statement appeared to some of his colleagues as a call to renew the Soviet-era command economy. Two days after his antimarket statements—which, unfortunately, occurred on the eve of arrival of an IMF mission to Kyiv—Kuchma sacked him.[94] He was succeeded by Anatoliy Kinakh, chair of the parliamentary Committee on Industrial Policy (and Kuchma's successor as head of the Ukrainian League of Industrialists and Entrepreneurs).[95] The government quickly reaffirmed its commitment to market reforms.[96]

Kuchma survived the election challenge of five competitors, garnering 36.5 percent of the vote in the October 31 general election, forcing a runoff against Communist Party leader Petro Symonenko on November 14.[97] Kuchma scored a landslide victory in the runoff, with 56.3 percent to Symonenko's 37.8 percent, thereby securing a second five-year term.[98] In his second inaugural address, the president stressed that Ukraine must "never change the course that [it] had chosen eight years ago on December 1, 1991."[99] Kuchma thus promised more of what Ukraine had experienced for the previous eight years.

The Rise of Viktor Yushchenko, 1999

After repeated attempts to remove him, parliament finally ejected Prime Minister Pustovoitenko on December 14, 1999, when it failed to muster the necessary 226 votes to approve his renomination by his recently reelected patron, Kuchma.[100] According to the constitution of Ukraine, the prime minister is to be approved not later than 60 days after resignation of the Cabinet of Ministers. In accordance with the law, the entire cabinet resigned on the date of the presidential inauguration, November 30. Since the law stipulates that the president may submit a candidate only once, the search for a replacement was on.[101] Kuchma's choice was a bold stroke in favor of genuine reform: National Bank governor Viktor Yushchenko.[102]

The architect of Ukraine's highly successful currency reform of September 1996, Yushchenko was immensely popular with the people for swapping the new hryvnia for the interim karbovanets (or "kupon") without confiscating their savings. He was further credited with high professionalism in the avoidance of a financial collapse through an orderly devaluation of the hryvnia during the August 1998 Russian currency crisis. To put it simply, Yushchenko's reform credentials were impeccable.

Though he admitted discussing the premiership with Kuchma several times, the NBU governor apparently was reluctant to take the post, fearing that a parliamentary majority would not materialize to see his program through.[103] Kuchma prevailed in the end, however, nominating the youthful financier on December 20 at the behest of ten right-center parliamentary groups and factions.[104] It is not entirely clear why Yushchenko accepted Kuchma's nomination. Owing to their weak institutional position vis-à-vis the president and parliament, Ukrainian premiers have typically had short, difficult, and largely unsuccessful tenures. For Yushchenko, the likely effects on his future political career might have been judged as more likely negative than positive. The reality of his position, however, probably left him with no alternative. He had served since 1993 as NBU governor in what had become an increasingly politicized role. He had spurned nomination for president in 1999 (and would likely have lost, in any case).

It seems that it would be increasingly difficult for Yushchenko to avoid assuming a more prominent political role. Consequently, despite the apparent risks, Yushchenko agreed to the appointment on two conditions. First, he would be permitted a free hand to appoint his cabinet. Second, President Kuchma would fulfill his long-standing pledge to orchestrate a "presidential majority" in parliament, breaking the political logjam over reforms and enabling Yushchenko to implement a new program.[105]

The Presidential Majority and the "1,000 Days" Program

Yushchenko was confirmed by a vote of 296 to 12 (with 4 abstentions). The largest parliamentary faction, the 112 Communist deputies, refused even to vote. (They had long regarded Yushchenko as an "IMF stooge.") On the belief that reforms would be possible only if supported by a center-right parliamentary majority, Yushchenko joined with

Kuchma in working to unify the ten factions and groups that had supported his candidacy.[106] Hence, on December 24, 1999, ten parliamentary groups and factions formally signed an agreement to band together in a majority coalition against the Left.[107] This isolated the Left—now comprised only of the Communists, Socialists, Progressive Socialists, and Peasant Party—with fewer than 170 votes (of 450 deputies).

Yushchenko did not waste time forming his team. He quickly appointed a cabinet of reformers, including Serhiy Tyhypko as minister of the (enlarged) Economics Ministry; Yuriy Yekhanurov as First Deputy Prime Minister with responsibility for privatization, administrative reform, and economic deregulation; and Yulia Tymoshenko as deputy premier for the fuel and energy sector.[108] Ihor Mitiukov would retain his post as Finance Minister. Second, on January 5, 2000, the new premier recalled some 200 draft laws that the Pustovoitenko government had submitted to parliament, calling them economically groundless. The Draft State Budget for 2000 was also revised and resubmitted, eliminating certain items pertaining to the social sphere worth UAH 6.3 billion (around $1.16 billion). In addition, Yushchenko promised a new cabinet program, consisting of 12 to 13 points, to be called "1,000 Days of Reform in Ukraine."[109]

Developed in consultation with western advisors, the "1,000 Days" program differed substantially from previous reform proposals in two ways: (1) It called for a dramatic retreat of the state from the economic sphere via deregulation and elimination of subsidies and tax privileges; and (2) it elevated to prominence anticorruption measures and administrative reforms.[110] In regards to the latter, the government was to be restructured by eliminating the rampant duplication and overlapping jurisdictions between different ministries and other state bodies. Direct interference by government bodies in the operations of enterprises was to be prohibited in order to create "normal conditions" for business activities.[111] Further, some 80 percent of the program was to be implemented within the "[f]irst 100 days." Indeed, Yushchenko promised results "on the 101st day."[112]

Some of the actions taken in early 2000 to combat corruption were at odds with loosening the state's grip on the economy, however. For instance, Kuchma decreed stronger control over foreign economic activity, designed to prevent illicit transfer of cash and hard currency-denominated securities out of Ukraine and to prevent evasion of taxes on export earnings. This decree was also partly in order to ensure that sufficient amounts of foreign exchange would be on hand to make over $2 billion of international debt service payments in 2000. (This figure presumed that Ukraine successfully negotiated a restructuring of the debt.) Despite these objectives, the decree would also seriously impair the smooth functioning of import-export trade.[113]

The "Ukraine Towards the XXIst Century" and "Reforms for Prosperity" Programs

On February 28, 2000, President Kuchma addressed parliament and the nation in a speech on national television to introduce a new long-term strategy for economic and social policy in 2000–2004, "Ukraine Towards the XXIst Century."[114] Specifically, the strategy envisaged a "regulatory reform of entrepreneurship" that would: replace intrusive regulations with general laws, eliminate administrative barriers to enterprise development, ease the process of starting a business, require the *ex ante* analysis of public policy proposals, and render civil servants accountable for failure to comply with regulations and for violation of proper procedure. Not willing to wait for parliament, the day after his speech, Kuchma signed a decree to give force to the new program.[115] Specific actions ordered by Kuchma included: clearing wage, pension, and social security arrears; accelerating structural reforms; giving broader rights to local executive bodies; and strengthening control over budgetary expenditures.

The promised "1,000 Days of Reform in Ukraine" was fulfilled in the "Ukraine Towards the XXIst Century" program. In a similar vein, the "First 100 Days" was fulfilled in the form of a specific program of actions submitted to parliament on March 3, 2000, entitled, "Reforms for Prosperity."[116] The principle aim of the program was quite new, being "to increase the economic independence of the citizenry and to promote entrepreneurial activity."[117] Harking back to goals and objectives established by the Pustovoitenko government, the new program envisaged a 1.3-to-1.4-times increase in real incomes and an average annual GDP increase of 6.5 percent by 2002.[118] The program was premised on the successful restructuring of Ukraine's foreign commercial debts, however, which then amounted to some $2.6 billion that Ukraine was unable to repay.

In mid-March, the president presented to parliament some 80 draft laws urgently needed to accelerate reforms. The bills included long-awaited drafts of the Tax Code, Land Code, Housing Code, and Criminal Code, as well as the draft laws "On the Cabinet of Ministers," "On State Support for Small Business," "On Debt Relief for Reforming Agrarian Enterprises," and "On Basic Operation of a Wholesale Electricity Market." The entire reform package was considered so important that, on March 20, Minister of the Economy Serhiy Tyhypko indicated that the Yushchenko government would resign if parliament failed to enact the program (including the president's draft laws).[119]

Tyhypko's dramatics appear overplayed in light of the outcome. The parliamentary majority easily passed the program on April 6, voting 261 to 103 for its enactment.[120] In a first indication of cracks appearing in the presidential majority, however, two influential parliamentary factions, the Social Democrats-United and the Regional Revival faction (headed by millionaire businessman Oleksandr Volkov)[121] voiced concerns over certain features of the program, although in the end they supported it (Volkov personally voted "no"). The various factions in the presidential majority proposed over 150 comments and amendments to the program prior to its approval, which Yushchenko considered a positive development insofar as the executive and legislature would share "solidarity responsibility" for implementing the program.[122] For its part, parliament insisted that the government make quarterly reports about implementation of the program.

Despite the considerable accomplishments of the Yushchenko government in the first quarter of 2000, in an April 19 expanded meeting of the Cabinet of Ministers, President Kuchma bitterly criticized the government for "insufficiently active and not always well-thought steps in the pursuit of reform."[123] The president warned against misplaced optimism regarding Ukraine's posted GDP growth in the first quarter of 2000. He noted that there had not been the necessary "deep qualitative changes" in the economy necessary to sustain the growth for long. In fact, the president argued, it was "rather a result of inertial processes, related to substantial devaluation of the hryvnia during the previous period following the Russian crisis and some growth of . . . demand as a result of partial compensation of wage and pension arrears."[124] There is something to this argument. In this case, Kuchma exhibited a deeper understanding of the economic processes at work in Ukraine than he is generally credited with possessing.

Kuchma also criticized the government, and especially Deputy Prime Minister Yulia Tymoshenko, for the rise in Ukraine's energy debts, from UAH 6.4 billion to UAH 7.9 billion for gas, and UAH 6.5 billion to UAH 8.0 billion for fuel as of April 1, 2000. Kuchma's remarks, though poignant, seem a bit out of place insofar as the Yushchenko government could hardly be held responsible for the state of the economy after 120 days in office. Nevertheless, after the April 19 meeting Yushchenko offered Kuchma his resignation, which the president rejected.

Yushchenko turned his attention to repairing Ukraine's image in international credit markets. He began negotiations with the IMF to resume payments under the Extended Fund Facility (EFF) loan, which had been suspended in September 1999. The situation was looking especially bleak since the NBU stood accused of having misused IMF loan funds. The IMF insisted on an international audit of NBU finances, but that would be completed no sooner than June 2000. In the meantime, Ukraine would have to struggle to meet its domestic fiscal obligations without the infusion of IMF cash. Its main hope in this regard was pinned on increased tax revenues resulting from the recent growth in GDP. However, through December 2000, the Yushchenko government would be the only one since 1994 not to receive a single credit tranche from the IMF.

Decline (and Possible Fall) of Yushchenko, 2000–2001

Since assuming the premiership, Yushchenko had scuffled politically on a fairly continuous basis with several lawmakers who had considerable holdings in the energy sector.[125] Particularly troublesome were the prime minister's conflicts with oil barons Hryhoriy Surkis, owner of the Kyiv Dynamo soccer team, and Oleksandr Volkov, head of the Regional Renaissance faction. Both were peoples' deputies and bona fide millionaires. In November 2000, the conflict assumed the form of a struggle over the political survival of Yushchenko's deputy premier for the fuel and energy sector, Yulia Tymoshenko. An oil magnate in her own right, Tymoshenko was the former head of United Energy Systems of Ukraine, and the former business partner of Pavlo Lazarenko, the errant prime minister who was being held in the United States on charges of racketeering, money laundering, and traveling on a false passport.

Tymoshenko had not been entirely successful in renegotiating Ukraine's energy debt with Russia, and in November stood accused of presenting unduly optimistic data to parliament on the state of the fuel and energy sector in Ukraine.[126] She was challenged on this account by both the chairman of the State Tax Administration, Mykola Azarov, and the secretary of the National Security and Defense Council, former prime minister Yevhen Marchuk. Azarov produced enterprise tax data that appeared to directly contradict that of Tymoshenko. In what appeared increasingly to be a coordinated attack, Marchuk then presented the results of a study by a government panel of experts to the effect that Tymoshenko had deliberately deflated the amount of required payments by energy firms to the state budget by around one-half, and further, that she had understated the actual debt of the energy sector by some UAH 5 billion.

It was well known that Marchuk was a close political ally of Surkis and that the attack on Tymoshenko was largely a means to put pressure on Yushchenko to alter his energy policies. While it is certainly true that in the short run Tymoshenko's efforts to increase competition in the energy sector had increased turbulence and uncertainty in the sector, it is also the case that her activities were having their intended effect: Ukraine's "energy barons" were suffering a decline in their illicit profits. President Kuchma's criticism of Tymoshenko was based on his apparent belief that Ukraine would face acute energy shortages in winter 2001. It is also probable that throughout fall 2000, Kuchma was coming to view Yushchenko as a potentially powerful rival for the presidency.

Another Surkis ally, First Deputy Speaker of Parliament Viktor Medvedchuk, indicated that Yushchenko's government had a "one-year grace period" to enact its program, but that in spring 2001, criticism of the government would intensify. Even before then, Marchuk and Azarov publicly declared their opposition to the government. In the face of such opposition, politicians and lawmakers across the political spectrum expressed renewed support for the Yushchenko government and satisfaction with its work.[127] This was in order to counter the obvious pressure that was being applied against Yushchenko by powerful energy interests bent on derailing his reforms and by President Kuchma, who had never fully supported his prime minister's policies.

Much of the criticism started after Tymoshenko concluded a natural gas deal with the government of Turkmenistan that Kuchma renegotiated several weeks later at a slightly reduced price. Yushchenko was unwilling to dismiss Tymoshenko, however, insofar as she was—operationally speaking—his "political *kamikaze* against the energy clans," according to Peoples' Deputy Mykola Syrota.[128] Nevertheless, Tymoshenko was sacked in January 2001 and subsequently investigated for embezzlement. But the pressure on Yushchenko would continue. Powerful clan leaders saw in the demise of Yushchenko the break-up of Kuchma's parliamentary majority. Kuchma was thus caught up in a power play between the energy interests and the government, revealing, perforce, that he was not as able to neutralize their influence as many previously had believed. Indeed, at this time many came to view the president as ineffective.

In March 2001, the prime minister appealed to ordinary Ukrainians to support his reform program, pointing to the real 6.3 percent growth in personal incomes during 2001 and promising more in the future.[129] In an April 17 speech to parliament, he defended his government's record on economic reform and denied that he was in any way involved in the effort to liquidate the parliamentary majority.[130] It is ironic that Yushchenko should be called to defend his government's performance in the wake of a 6 percent annual rise in GDP and a 7.7 growth rate recorded in the first quarter of 2001. It is ironic that his effectiveness should be criticized in the face of a 17.4 percent real increase in industrial output, the repayment of UAH 1.4 billion in wage and pension arrears, as well as the enactment of two zero-deficit budgets, a foreign trade surplus, and the avoidance of default on Ukraine's international loans. It is ironic that none of Kuchma's other prime ministers—six in all—had enjoyed such standing in the public opinion. Nor had they been so closely identified with the idea of an independent, European Ukraine. It is further irony that no other prime minister had received such wide-ranging international support (and even admiration). But no other Ukrainian premier had been subject to such consistently harsh treatment on the part of government functionaries.

Parliament handed Yushchenko a resounding defeat on April 19, enacting a resolution criticizing the work of the Cabinet of Ministers as unsatisfactory by a vote of 283 to 65. Several parties and deputies groups that were formerly members of the presidential majority voted to condemn the government's performance, including the Democratic Council (formerly known as Regional Renaissance, led by Oleksandr Volkov), Labor Ukraine (led by oil baron Viktor Pinchuk), of which Economics Minister Serhiy Tyhypko was a leading member, and Social Democrats-United (led by First Deputy Speaker Viktor Medvedchuk).[131] They were joined by significant numbers of deputies from the Green faction (which by 2001 had, ironically, been penetrated by serious energy distribution interests). Leaders of these factions had promised to bring down the government if Yushchenko would refuse to form a coalition government. They also demanded a significant share in the ministerial portfolio, which would have spelled the end of reforms.[132] For his own part, Yushchenko would not have served as the figurehead of a government that he did not lead. A vote of "no confidence" was scheduled to take place on April 26.

Leonid Kuchma insisted throughout the crisis that he supported Yushchenko, but if parliament wanted to dismiss him, there was little he could do. The truth is that Kuchma himself was embroiled in a murder scandal that had immobilized him politically.[133] In the midst of repeated calls for his own removal, Kuchma apparently came to view Yushchenko's continued presence in the premiership—with the constitutional right of succession—as only increasing political pressure for his own resignation from pro-Yushchenko forces in parliament.[134] Additionally, the prime minister was quickly emerging as the only proreform figure in Ukraine who enjoyed considerable support in the West, which made him a threat to pro-Russian interests in Ukraine. Consequently, the energy clans made common cause against Yushchenko with their ideological nemesis, the Communist Party.[135]

On April 26, Yushchenko was ousted in a censure motion that was carried by a vote of 263 to 69 (with 24 abstaining and 53 not voting).[136] Interestingly, the demise of Ukraine's ninth government in ten years came for the first time ever in a vote of no confidence.[137] The vote signaled a shift in the parliamentary majority from propresidential forces on the right-center to anti-Kuchma forces comprised of the left-center (Communists plus the oligarchs). After the vote, some right-center factions, including the two Rukh factions, Reforms-Congress, Batkivschyna, and Sobor factions, announced that they would henceforth remain in opposition to Kuchma.[138] Yushchenko agreed to stay on for up to 60 days as acting premier, but he would function, in effect, as a caretaker.[139]

Viktor Yushchenko was undone by a Communist Party faction that had long been unhappy with his market reforms and privatization policies and by four "oligarch parties" (Social Democrats-United, Labor Ukraine, Democratic Union, and Regions of Ukraine) that turned against him for his anticorruption policies and efforts to inject more competition into the energy sector. This was a period of great irony in Ukraine's history, for Yushchenko was removed precisely because he was the most professional, most successful, most credible, and most popular of Ukraine's post-Soviet prime ministers.

These ironies were not lost on ordinary Ukrainians, Ukraine's key allies, and investors in the West. In the weeks and months that followed Yushchenko's ouster, his downfall would have the effect of tarnishing Ukraine's standing among its international benefactors (especially the United States), multilateral lenders, and investors—all but dashing Kuchma's hopes for constitutional reforms to strengthen the presidency, and destroying the (admittedly fragile) presidential majority in parliament. In the period leading up to the 2002 parliamentary elections, it appeared certain that the government of newly appointed Prime Minister Anatoliy Kinakh would certainly not push reforms as vigorously as had its predecessor. Kuchma also faced a new parliamentary opposition that was more organized than before.

It would now be more difficult for Kuchma to give the impression that Kyiv was committed to economic reform.[140] In the wake of Yushchenko's dismissal, Kuchma was quick to pledge his continuing adherence to reforms in a speech delivered to the outgoing cabinet.[141] But this was largely viewed as so much damage control. He wanted foreign loans but was no longer as convincing as he had been in the exciting days of fall 1994. Kuchma in mid-2001 found himself caught between two now incommensurate objectives: resuming IMF lending and amending the constitution to give the presidency more power. Here's the rub: To renew multilateral borrowing, Kuchma would have to demonstrate that parliament supported his reform program. For this purpose, the presidential majority in parliament had been quite useful; it had given the impression that Kuchma and Yushchenko were very much in charge. However, to gain public support for his proposed constitutional restructuring, he would have to convince his fellow citizens that parliament lacked the capacity to enact the necessary laws. For this purpose, having Yushchenko at the helm had been a hindrance. The end result, of course, was that Kuchma would have neither a working parliamentary majority nor a vigorous premier.

It thus appeared that Kuchma's balancing act had finally come to an abrupt end. At the time of this writing, it was not clear that the president even would survive the "Kuchmagate" scandal. As the first ten years of Ukraine's independent existence came to a close, then, economic reforms remained very much captive to institutional competition between president and parliament.

Conclusion: Kuchma and the Politics of Reform

Certain critical observations about Kuchma's record on economic reforms may be made from the foregoing examination. First, what comes through clearest is the lack of strong, consistent leadership. The periodic presidential vacillation on the direction of reforms, combined with the frequent turnover of prime ministers (and, in fact, other key ministerial posts), militated against the implementation of a consistent, longer-term program. Not only does it call into doubt Kuchma's understanding and genuine commitment to reform, but the rivalries that developed between the president and his several prime ministers are evidence that the division of the executive power is simply not clear. Consequently, it is not clear who has the lead on economic reform.

Second, the competition between president and parliament over the course of reforms indicates an unhealthy degree of institutional competition that was, unfortunately, not resolved by the constitution of Ukraine, enacted in 1996. Kuchma's argument that a constitutional amendment is necessary on this score, therefore, has merit. Further, at the middle level of the state bureaucracy, the government is plagued by hold-overs, former Soviet *apparatchiks* who lack imagination, drive, or patriotic fervor. The continuation in office of this group is a major obstacle to reforms.

Third, the absence of a reform coalition in parliament is especially problematical. The brief creation of a working majority under Yushchenko was not sufficiently long-lived to be effective. Also, parliamentary reformers tend to be the most fervent nationalists.[142] They have been kept continuously off-balance by a much better organized, more disciplined left-wing coalition of factions, which at every turn questions Ukraine's legitimate existence as an independent state. The reformers' attention thus has tended to be more focused on maintaining Ukrainian sovereignty and building Ukraine's statehood, quite apart from the question of market reforms.

Fourth, the situation in parliament reflects a general lack of consensus among the public, which, in opinion polls throughout the 1990s, expressed decreasing support for market reforms. Independent polling data indicate, if nothing else, that the public is unhappy with the state of the economy. But is not certain what to do about it. The public sees the economy worsen while at the same time, enterprise directors and other elites with preferential access to government enrich themselves at the state's expense. The president, unable or unwilling to confront the corrupt forces that have penetrated the government, by 2001 appeared unwilling or unable to overcome these forces. As evidence of this, when his energetic justice minister, Serhiy Holovatiy, attempted to enforce anticorruption laws in 1997, Kuchma summarily discharged him. It is not hard to imagine the signal that this sends to criminals, the *apparat,* and the public.

Fifth, ironically, it appears that parliamentary leftists may have been the first to recognize that Ukrainian independence depends vitally upon substantive progress on economic reforms. Their strategy of paying lip service to reforms, formally supporting the government's programs but handicapping its efforts at the implementation stage, has proved to be very effective. Further, many government policies have been quite piecemeal in nature and therefore lacking in comprehensive scope. The partial reforms themselves have been the cause of subsequent problems that have been addressed, in their turn, by further piecemeal measures, thereby compounding matters in a never-ending "crisis of crises." In the meantime, Ukraine has managed to survive largely on the basis of foreign loans, which have propped up the country in the face of recurring economic policy failures. The resulting increase in foreign debt has had the effect of rendering Ukraine more susceptible to external economic shocks, as evidenced by Ukraine's suffering the ill-effects of the Russian currency crisis in late 1998.

Finally, some seven years after Kuchma's initial 1994 Program of Radical Reforms, there had been little real structural change, save that of small- and medium-scale privatization, which is reversible in any case. Large-scale privatization has been laggard, necessitating a continuing flow of subsidies and preferential loans to unprofitable enterprises. A labyrinthine tax system, excessively regulated foreign and domestic trade, and low-paid, unfriendly bureaucrats prone to selective enforcement of the laws prevented meaningful development of the business sector. Based on Kuchma's record, Åslund and de Ménil have concluded that "By and large, reform came to a standstill in June 1995, although some important reforms followed even later."[143] Most notably the currency reform of 1996, covered in chapter 7.

Genuine progress on reforms would require fostering an "investor friendly" environment in which private enterprises could develop and prosper. In 2001, unclear and mutually contradictory legal and regulatory provisions still reserved a great deal of discretion to the bureaucracy, especially in the State Tax Administration, where opportunities for corruption prevailed. The failure of privatization policy, excessive regulation, and the consequent burgeoning of the shadow economy have severely constrained growth of the tax base, which has placed great pressure on the state budget. External debts to cover budget deficits and to finance industrial renewal were used to pay for energy imports and government salaries and were not always directed toward their intended purpose. Finally, as Dominique Arel notes, "despite sustained pressure from the IMF, the World Bank, and the United States, this destructive cycle has not been broken."[144] Thus, despite certain successes, notably the currency reform of 1996, Ukraine in many respects seemed in 2001 further from enacting genuine market reforms than it did in 1991.

Chapter 5

The Challenge of Fiscal Reform

The Centrality of Fiscal Reform

The organization and development of the public finance function is at the heart of managing the transition to market.[1] This means building governmental capacity in the critical areas of fiscal management, especially: budget formulation and implementation, cash management and expenditure control, and debt management. Since the collapse of communism, throughout the countries of the former Soviet Union, new financial management institutions have been under development to: perform fiscal policy analysis, provide effective tax collection and expenditure control capabilities, prioritize expenditures, redesign the state accounting system, separate the administration of monetary and fiscal management functions, and accelerate development of the public debt market. Due to their as-yet nascent domestic debt markets, it has been necessary for many former Soviet republics—like Ukraine—to secure access to bilateral and multilateral lending, particularly from the World Bank and International Monetary Fund (IMF).

Under ideal circumstances, reform efforts would be coordinated by the Ministry of Finance; however, Ukraine has failed to establish the primacy of the Finance Ministry at the center of the system of government, the importance of which apparently continues to elude the authorities. One critical obstacle to more rapid fiscal management capacity building has been the poor understanding on the part of government officials of the role of the fiscal management function. The chronic budget deficits that plagued countries like Ukraine in the 1990s are nearly impossible to bring down in the absence of dramatic improvements in the mechanisms of fiscal management.

There is little doubt that building effective fiscal capacity can have large positive impacts. In a far-reaching study of the international experience, Easterly, Rodriguez, and Schmidt-Hebbel demonstrated the centrality of fiscal reform, showing that public sector balances are highly correlated with a range of macroeconomic variables, including: GDP growth, per capita growth, real interest rates, money creation, investment and consumption rates, real exchange rates, and the current account balance.[2] Addressing the deficit is especially important. Excessive fiscal deficits pose a significant threat of runaway inflation and even the collapse of currencies.

Deficits are also associated with low rates of economic growth; deficit reduction generally leads to improved external balances and improved growth. Although it is not the only factor necessary to realize a country's economic potential, in general, growth accelerates as fiscal deficits improve in the long run. It has therefore become axiomatic that good overall macroeconomic performance is associated with strong fiscal adjustment.[3] Successful fiscal adjustment requires a sustained long-term effort. It is well nigh impossible to sustain fiscal adjustment on such a scale without strong and effective fiscal management capabilities.

Fiscal Policy Challenges

By modern international standards, the state of Ukraine's fiscal management capacities during most of the 1990s may be characterized as grossly underdeveloped. Despite improvement, even as late as 2001, fiscal management was yet in the process of transition from being an adjunct of the former economic planning regime to playing a more central role in the process of governance. Important vestiges of the former Soviet system persisted well into the 1990s, including: development of annual "Economic and Social Development Plans" (complete with sectoral real output targets), state procurement orders, indicative budgetary norms, and extensive price controls. These were still in the process of being abandoned as late as 1997. The revenue and expenditure systems in 2000 remained largely inconsistent with the requirements of a market economy. Reforms were necessary that would, at once, provide proper economic incentives, protect the existing revenue base, promote vertical and horizontal equity among taxpayers, facilitate growth of the private sector, allocate investment capital to the most efficient uses, and improve the national infrastructure.

There is nearly universal agreement that Ukraine's difficulty in reforming public finances has been an obstacle to more rapid economic reform in virtually all key areas.[4] In 1992–95 the government had to rely upon fiscal policy alone to pursue economic stabilization objectives. This presented something of a dilemma, insofar as budgetary instruments are crude tools with which to promote stabilization in the face of persistent budget deficits, such as Ukraine experienced during its early formative years. Further, throughout the entire decade of the 1990s, the composition of Ukraine's budgetary revenue and expenditure flows was subject to dramatic change. Table 5.1 provides the changing composition of the consolidated general government budget for 1992–99. As can readily be discerned, each succeeding year has brought new fiscal management challenges with respect to both the tax/revenue mix and expenditure priorities. Consistency has proved to be an elusive objective.

Analysis of Ukraine's fiscal deficit reveals that it has been primarily expenditure driven. Despite substantial annual falls in real GDP, real revenues, expenditures, and deficits remained relatively stable during 1992–2000. See the trends in Graph 5.1. Even during the period of most rapid price inflation (1992–94), when real GDP fell by over 50 percent and prices rose by more than 14,500 percent, real revenues and expenditures rose a modest 10 and 16 percent, respectively. The statistical evidence therefore suggests that political factors, rather than sound fiscal decision making, predominated in budgetary decision making, especially in 1992–95.[5]

The level of public expenditure is higher in Ukraine than in most market economies, from 1992–97 running at between 40–60 percent of GDP, some 20–30 percentage points higher than in the vastly wealthier European Union.[6] A rapid deterioration in budgetary expenditures is apparent from 1991–94, followed by a marked improvement starting in 1995. However, despite this, expenditure pressures may be expected to rise in the future, due to the investment that will be required for industrial restructuring.

Fiscal analysis, control, and accountability have not been firmly established in any governmental body. Administrative capacity to perform cost-benefit analysis of alternative spending programs still is lacking.[7] The former practice of relying upon central plan determination based on certain formula-generated "budgetary norms" has persisted. Further, the central government was massively involved during

Table 5.1
Composition of Consolidated Government Budget, 1992-1999

Budget Item (Pension Fund Included for Purposes of Consistency)	Billions of Nominal karbovanets [Note 1]					Millions of Nominal hryvnia		
	1992	1993	1994	1995	1996	1997	1998	1999
Total Revenues	1795	56826	531381	2044268	3017214	36889.6	37702.1	43826.7
VAT	987	16971	129994	451733	629968	8242.3	7460.1	8399.5
Enterprise Profits Tax	279	14322	142572	483395	545570	5792	5695	6125
Personal Income Tax	150	2883	34027	160071	265250	3296	3571	4436
Excise Taxes	60	2514	16896	40101	66312	1208	1632	1766
Tax on Land	18	776	4119	63460	81383	1002	1105	1095
Oil & Gas Rents	n.a.	n.a.	n.a.	71852	186880	932	62	77
State Customs	3	107	1840	8534	18085	284	286	257
Import Duties	8	2024	25711	42938	39185	713	972	850
Local & Regional Taxes	n.a.	n.a.	917	12502	27128	357	391	441
Chornobyl Fund Revenues	124	2500	24067	102602	147696	1698	1416	283
Pension Fund Revenues [Note 2]	n.a.	n.a.	92229	415988	699294	8455	8930	10804
Other Revenues (Not Included Above)	166	14729	59009	191092	310463	4910.3	6182	9293.2
Total Expenditures	2325	66100	645353	2448594	3379277	43086	39720.4	45523
Social Security	359	18651	70350	336792	388229	3884.4	4227	4123.3
Social-Cultural Sphere	467	13870	133293	611007	739322	9754.6	8867.2	9238.8
State Capital Improvements	n.a.	n.a.	n.a.	76796	101277	618	1661.1	1459.8
National Economy	714	13921	190675	260822	283576	5528	4082.1	2999.7

Defense	111	2766	23549	101657	101277	1954	1419	1562.2
Police, Customs & Tax Inspectorate	65	3013	19424	89484	131660	1753	1551.8	1668.9
Legislative/Executive	n.a.	n.a.	9050	43657	74270	1288	1311.4	1495.5
Foreign Economic Activity	n.a.	n.a.	17067	12979	33759	171	244	252.7
Chornobyl Fund Outlays	115	1939	22675	94907	145164	1747	1420	1445.5
Domestic Debt Service	6	30	5864	17083	54014	930	1663	1250.7
Pension Fund Outlays [Note 2]	n.a.	n.a.	89730	408571	671804	8394	8801	10757
Foreign Debt Service	0	0	13149	226421	199178	803	748	1808.5
Other Expenditures (Not Included Above)	488	11910	50527	168418	455747	6261	3724.8	7460.4
Budgetary Balance	-130	-9275	-113967	-404326	-361700	-6196.4	-2018.3	-1696.3
Directed Credits (1996 Est.)	660	11359	45375	162561	86404	0	0	0
Balance of Extrabudgetary Funds (Est.)	184	765	14321	20332	32204	23.2	12	1230
Pension Fund (1992 & 1993 Only)	147	171	n.a.	n.a.	n.a.	n.a.	n.a.	n.a.
Employment Fund (1994-96 Est.)	17	381	3241	15249	24153	23.2	12	29.7
Social Insurance Fund (1994-96 Est.)	20	213	1080	5083	8051	0	0	1201
General Government Balance	-606	-19869	-145021	-546555	-415900	-6173.2	-2030.3	-466.3
Financing (Estimated):								
NBU and Bank Credits	330	11747	132105	273878	134500	99.1	19.3	n.a.
Government Bond Sales (Net)	n.a.	n.a.	n.a.	20400	157100	4442.8	1262	2049.2
Other Internal Debt	2	12	2346	0	0	0	0	0
Foreign Financing	0	0	10420	79336	124300	1654.4	851.7	-80.9
Errors and Omissions	-276	-8210	-150	-172941	0	23.1	102.7	1502

Table 5.1 (continued)
Composition of Consolidated Government Budget, 1992-1999

Budget Item *(Pension Fund Included for Purposes of Consistency)*	*Percent of GDP*							
	1992	*1993*	*1994*	*1995*	*1996*	*1997*	*1998*	*1999*
Total Revenues	34.4	40.5	49.1	40.2	37.4	39.6	37.2	34.5
VAT	19.1	12.0	12.0	8.9	7.8	8.8	7.3	6.6
Enterprise Profits Tax	5.4	10.1	13.2	9.5	6.8	6.2	5.9	4.8
Personal Income Tax	2.9	2.0	3.1	3.1	3.3	3.5	3.5	3.5
Excise Taxes	1.1	1.8	1.6	0.8	0.8	1.3	1.6	1.4
Tax on Land	0.3	0.5	0.4	1.2	1.0	1.1	1.1	0.9
Oil & Gas Rents	n.a.	n.a.	n.a.	1.4	2.3	1.0	0.1	0.1
State Customs	0.001	0.001	0.2	0.2	0.2	0.3	0.3	0.2
Import Duties	0.001	1.4	2.4	0.8	0.5	0.8	0.9	0.7
Local & Regional Taxes	n.a.	n.a.	0.0	0.2	0.3	0.4	0.4	0.3
Chornobyl Fund Revenues	2.4	1.8	2.2	2.0	1.8	1.8	1.4	0.2
Pension Fund Revenues [Note 2]	n.a.	n.a.	8.5	8.2	8.7	9.1	8.7	8.5
Other Revenues (Not Included Above)	3.2	10.9	5.5	3.9	3.9	5.3	6.0	7.3
Total Expenditures	43.7	46.5	59.7	48.2	42.0	46.3	38.6	35.8
Social Security	5.9	13.1	6.5	6.6	4.8	4.2	4.1	3.2
Social-Cultural Sphere	9.0	9.8	12.3	12.0	9.2	10.4	8.6	7.3
State Capital Improvements	n.a.	n.a	n.a.	1.5	1.3	0.7	1.6	1.1
National Economy	13.8	9.8	17.7	5.1	3.5	5.9	4.0	2.4
Defense	2.1	1.9	2.2	2.0	1.3	2.1	1.4	1.2
Police, Customs & Tax Inspectorate	1.3	2.1	1.8	1.8	1.6	1.9	1.5	1.3
Legislative/Executive	n.a.	n.a	0.8	0.9	0.9	1.4	1.3	1.2
Foreign Economic Activity	n.a.	n.a	1.6	0.3	0.4	0.2	0.2	0.2

Chornobyl Fund Outlays	2.2	1.4	2.1	1.9	1.8	1.9	1.4	1.1
Domestic Debt Service	0.001	0.001	0.5	0.3	0.7	1.0	1.6	1.0
Pension Fund Outlays [Note 2]	n.a.	n.a	8.3	8.0	8.3	9.0	8.6	8.5
Foreign Debt Service	0.0	0.0	1.2	4.5	2.5	0.9	0.7	1.4
Other Expenditures (Not Included Above)	9.4	8.4	4.7	3.3	5.7	6.7	3.6	5.9
Budgetary Balance	-9.9	-6.5	-10.5	-8.0	-4.6	-6.4	-1.4	-1.3
Directed Credits (1996 Est.)	12.8	8.0	4.2	3.2	1.1	0.0	0.0	0.0
Balance of Extrabudgetary Funds (Est.)	3.5	0.5	0.4	0.4	0.4	0.02	0.01	1.0
Pension Fund (1992 & 1993 Only)	2.8	0.1	n.a.	n.a.	n.a.	n.a.	n.a.	n.a.
Employment Fund (1994-96 Est.)	0.3	0.3	0.3	0.3	0.3	0.02	0.01	0.02
Social Insurance Fund (1994-96 Est.)	0.4	0.1	0.1	0.1	0.1	0.0	0.0	1201.0
General Government Balance	-11.7	-14.0	-13.4	-10.8	-5.2	-6.6	-2.0	-0.4
Financing (Estimated):								
NBU and Bank Credits	6.4	8.2	12.2	6.0	1.7	0.1	0.02	n.a.
Government Bond Sales (Net)	n.a.	n.a.	n.a.	0.4	2.0	4.8	1.2	1.6
Other Internal Debt	0.001	0.001	0.2	0.0	0.0	0.0	0.0	0.0
Foreign Financing	0.0	0.0	1.0	1.6	1.5	1.8	0.8	-0.1
Errors and Omissions	-5.3	-5.8	-0.001	-3.4	0.0	0.02	0.1	1.2
	Billions of karbovanets (KBV) [Note 1]				Millions of hryvnia (UAH) [Note 1]			
Memorandum: **Nominal GDP**	5168	141916	1080307	5083061	8051000	93365	102593	127126

Notes: [1] To convert billions of karbovanets (KBV) to millions of hryvnia (UAH), divide by 100.

[2] The Pension Fund was transferred to the Consolidated Budget as of January 1, 1994, and its revenues reformed in 1997. Since April 1997, the Pension Fund is excluded from the budget. It is included here for purposes of consistency.

[3] Columns may not sum precisely due to rounding.

Sources: Ministry of Finance of Ukraine; IMF (1993, 1995); Marcin Luczynski and Oleg Novoselsky, "Ukraine in Numbers," *Ukrainian Legal and Economic Bulletin* (various issues); European Centre for Macroeconomic Analysis of Ukraine, *Ukrainian Economic Trends* (various issues); source documents; author's calculations.

Graph 5.1

Real Revenues, Expenditures, and GDP

(January 1992 - December 2000)

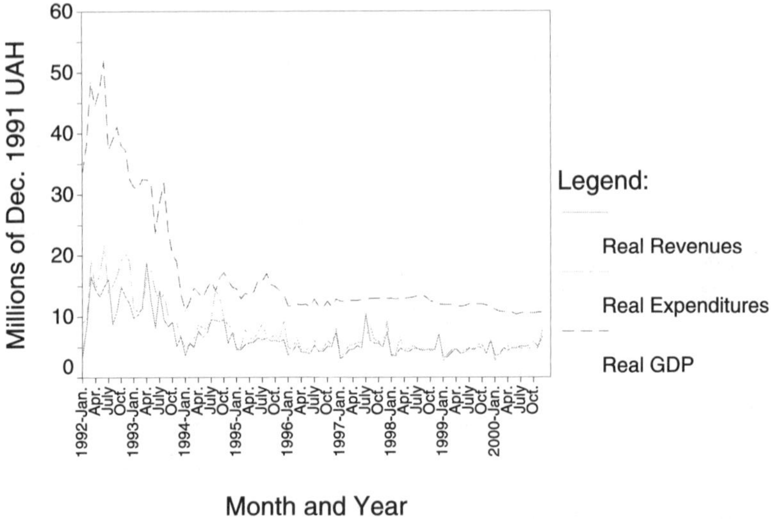

1992–94 in the direct management of the economy, through administration of prices, widespread subsidies, directed credits, and absorption of unfunded pension, disability, and unemployment compensation liabilities. Many of these direct governmental interventions fell away only after 1995, however slowly.[8]

On the revenue side, tax reform in the 1990s took the form of fairly dramatic and frequent experimentation with tax rate and base changes, wreaking havoc on individual financial and business development planning. High marginal rates, extensive concessions to privileged sectors, firms, and individuals, and selective enforcement by tax officials have produced horizontal and vertical tax and income inequities. This has eroded public perceptions of fairness of the tax system, leading to widespread tax evasion. Strengthening tax administration capacities was an essential objective throughout the decade. In the absence of extensive tax administration capacity building, reform of the tax system to support market transition has proven to be exceedingly difficult.[9] Ukraine's "stop 'n go" efforts at tax reform in the first quarter of

1993—changing the tax structure only to repeal reforms as "unworkable" after just three months—graphically illustrate this point, as do the many and frequent revisions of the tax structure since then. (Tax policy reform is treated in chapter 6.)

Though Ukraine's social expenditures have been relatively constant at 30–35 percent of GDP, the country still lacks the fiscal resources to afford the array of social obligations that it inherited from the USSR, even on a reduced basis.[10] Most benefits were overly generous, despite Ukraine's dire financial situation. Having fallen from around 70 percent in 1992, in 2000, nearly 40 percent of citizens were eligible to receive some form of benefit, at a time when only one-third were working in any form of productive activity.[11] Further, over 25 percent of Ukraine's population qualified for pension and other old-age benefits.[12] Ukraine's welfare state was thus quite burdensome by international standards. The situation worsened before improving in 1995–96. But it remained an issue as late as 2001.

In the absence of effective expenditure analysis capabilities, Ukrainian authorities were unable to evaluate social safety net program alternatives, which President Kuchma in 1995 directed to "target" only the neediest citizens. The greatest need was to reduce the universal nature of benefits. This required building capacity to perform the necessary analysis and to execute the budget in accordance with the government's established policies. Budget and expenditure management systems were not geared toward fiscal control, however. Until 1995, spending ministries and state-owned enterprises were not subject to "hard" budget constraints and so had little incentive to exercise fiscal discipline. The availability until then of "instant bank credit" seriously eroded managerial accountability. At year-end 1998, the lack of a functioning State Treasury (that is, cash management system) continued to hinder effective expenditure control.

Throughout 1992–97, the reality of large budget deficits constrained Ukraine's policy options. Soviet Ukraine had little experience with budget deficits. Unfortunately, when deficits mounted after independence, there were few alternatives available for financing them. The government has been slow to establish the capacity to finance deficits in noninflationary ways. Only since the first quarter of 1995 has Ukraine possessed the capacity to employ domestic debt financing, but the domestic financial markets to absorb debt were in 2001 yet at an early stage of development.[13] The unfortunate consequence in 1992–95 was that the National Bank of Ukraine (NBU) was inexorably thrust into the dominant role in deficit financing. Since the Russian currency crisis of 1998, the NBU has once again become the government's largest creditor. This was at the root of Ukraine's tragic bout with hyperinflation in 1993–94, raising the specter of renewed inflation in 1999 and after. (See chapter 7 for a discussion of the link between budget deficits, central bank credits, and price inflation.)

Development of public debt instruments as alternative means of deficit financing had a positive impact on Ukraine's economic stabilization efforts. Ukraine successfully issued its first domestic treasury bills in spring 1995. In the absence of sufficient domestic debt absorption capacity during 1991–95, however, external (foreign) deficit financing was necessary. Domestic debt capacity improved rapidly after 1995, so that, while relatively insignificant amounts of the fiscal deficit were covered through borrowing in 1995–96, by 1997, over 70 percent of Ukraine's deficit was covered through borrowing.

Foreign debt financing of the deficit was again required in 1998, due to softening demand for Ukrainian T-bills. But when international credit markets soured on Ukraine's debt in 1998–2000, the National Bank once again filled the budget deficit financing gap.[14] After the promising developments of the mid-1990s, at the end of the decade budget deficits were still financed through NBU credit (with the ever-present threat of renewed inflation). Owing to election year politics and effects of the Russian currency crisis, Ukraine's reduced access to both domestic and foreign capital in 1998–2000 has placed Ukraine's late budgetary accomplishments in a rather precarious position.

A compounding factor was Ukraine's large and growing domestic liabilities, especially for social benefits. Significant liabilities were added to the government budget via credits extended to inefficient state-owned enterprises, which are essentially substandard loans and not seriously expected to be repaid. These commitments accumulated in 1995–96, together with new debts incurred through budget subsidies, interenterprise arrears, wages and pensions arrears, and enormous amounts of delinquent taxes.

From time to time these debts have been wiped clean by the government through credit emission or legislative edict. This served only to magnify budgetary pressures, however. Starting in 1995, the government tolerated the build-up of significant payments arrears, effectively reneging on many of its old commitments in order to meet the deficit reduction targets required under IMF lending programs. Social policy thus increasingly gave way to Ukraine's acute fiscal imperatives. A key concern is that virtually all of this has occurred on an ad hoc basis, with little long-term fiscal planning or forecasting.

Ukraine's Fiscal Evolution, 1991–2001

The path of fiscal policy reform in Ukraine has followed a course that is by now quite familiar. The authorities followed the path of least resistance, picking off the easy targets first (the proverbial "low-hanging fruit") and turning to more difficult—and politically painful—measures only when and where it has been expedient to do so. By and large, Ukraine's persistent fiscal problems are attributable to the government's genuine desire to cushion the social effects of the economic crisis, particularly on wage earners, families, and pensioners, coupled with parliament's reluctance to embrace comprehensive tax reform.

Budgetary politics have been intensely contentious, resulting in the late adoption of budgets in seven of Ukraine's first ten years. But the lack of priority given to development of the fiscal management function is inexcusable. Financial management reform has occurred in a most haphazard fashion and not as part of a comprehensive program of upgrading and improving capabilities. Ukraine's experience suggests certain fiscal reform initiatives, which will be discussed below.

Ukraine Gains Budgetary Independence

Under the former Soviet regime, fiscal policy had been a passive instrument of economic management. Essential revenue-raising decisions and expenditure priorities were subordinated and subservient to the imperatives of the central economic plan. Major decisions affecting republic- and local-level public finance were made at the center in Moscow. Until the planning process was decentralized somewhat under former Soviet president Mikhail Gorbachev in the mid-1980s, surpluses (if any) generated by state enterprises were transferred directly to the state budget. Such funds were subject to reallocation to other enterprises and industrial sectors by Moscow, pursuant to plan priorities. The entire system was kept in a state of homeostasis through an elaborate management process involving numerous marginal wage, price, output, and tax adjustments.[15] Budgetary balancing was conducted from Moscow throughout Ukraine's Soviet experience. The result was a distinct lack of budget and fiscal management expertise in Kyiv at the time of the Soviet collapse.

During the perestroika period, state enterprises were granted a degree of autonomy, with the subordination of many enterprises transferred to republic-level governments.[16] Under this approach, the constituent republics of the former USSR were permitted to receive an increasing share of revenues. During 1991 the Ukrainian budget was extruded and separated from the all-union budget, with the intent being that Ukraine would partially finance the union government through a system of budgetary transfers to Moscow. Over the course of 1991, however, such transfers were gradually eliminated both for republican budgets and various extrabudgetary funds. Budgetary independence—a key component of securing Ukraine's economic sovereignty—was to bring with it dramatically new fiscal challenges, however.

1991: Fiscal Imbalance Strikes

Ukraine's consolidated budget plunged almost immediately into deficit in 1991, reaching a record of almost 14 percent of GDP that year.[17] This deficit was wholly accounted for by significant increases in expenditure, rather than revenue shortfalls, despite the beginning of what became a nine-year collapse in output. Indeed, revenues actually increased to 36.5 percent of GDP, in the face of a marked decline in enterprise profits tax receipts (that is, GDP was shrinking at a faster rate than tax collections). In 1991, the tax on enterprise profits and the turnover tax each accounted for more than one-third of total revenues, or approximately 10–11 percent of GDP.[18] During the year the government took positive steps to maintain buoyant revenues by retaining proceeds of the payroll tax levied to finance the off-budget Economic Stabilization Fund (abolished at the end of 1991) and by introducing a new 5 percent sales tax.[19] In addition, steadily declining transfers to Moscow during 1991 contributed the equivalent of at least another 5 percent of GDP to the revenue side of the Ukrainian budget.

Expenditures, on the other hand, reached the unprecedented level of 45 percent of GDP, up from 28 percent in 1990.[20] Increases in wages and salaries, continuing price subsidies (for food, energy, housing, and transport), as well as outlays on social safety net programs (mainly for child and family allowances) and support for enterprises in the military-industrial complex were the main culprits. Wages, salaries, and social benefits were subject by law to indexation starting in October 1991, when minimum wages and pensions more than doubled.[21] Increases in wages and salaries also resulted in expenditure increases of approximately 3 percent of GDP on education and health.[22] The resulting increases amounted to nearly 18 percent of GDP, financed entirely through the accommodating monetary policies of the NBU. The inevitable result was an accelerating rate of price inflation.

1992: Fiscal Deterioration Deepens

In order to support the government's price liberalization, monetary control, and private sector development objectives, the 1992 budget was drafted to reestablish near balance between revenues and expenditures. A deficit of merely 2 percent of GDP was targeted for 1992. To achieve this result, a spate of new taxes were introduced on January 1, 1992, including: a 22 percent value-added tax (VAT)[23]; new excise levies on tobacco, alcoholic beverages, furs, and other luxuries; and a broadening of the enterprise income tax base to include the wage bill as well as net profits.[24] Further, a new personal income tax was introduced in July 1991, replacing the tax that applied to the former USSR. As a result of these measures, state revenues were projected to increase by nearly 20 percentage points of GDP, with expenditures rising by no more than 8 percent of GDP.[25]

Rather than achieve budgetary balance, however, 1992 was marked by sharply deteriorating public finances. Massive off-budget subsidies and credits to state enterprises, combined with grossly overestimated receipts from the new VAT drove the budget into deficiency.[26] A significant complicating factor was parliament's substantial delay in adopting the 1992 budget, which occurred only on June 18 (with revised drafts having been rejected in April and May). Until the 1992 budget was adopted, the central government, oblasts, and municipalities operated under a parliamentary decree that permitted continued spending at their inflation-adjusted fourth quarter 1991 levels.

In late April 1992, fears of starting a wage-price spiral propelled parliament to introduce a tax-based "incomes policy" in order to moderate the growth in enterprise wages relative to output. To implement the policy, parliament took a "Decision on Wages in the Productive Sphere," which imposed a statutory obligation to limit wages on enterprises, regardless of sector or form of ownership. Relevant ministries issued instructions to implement the policy, setting maximum limits on total enterprise wage funds for the six-, nine-, and twelve-months of 1992. Taxes on excess wages were imposed, ranging from multiples of 2–5 times the statutory rate, depending on the extent to which wages exceeded the norm.[27] In principle, the policy would have nominal wages growing without excess tax liability, provided that output increased faster than wages.

The 1992 incomes policy did not supersede or replace the October 1991 law on indexation, however, resulting in some confusion and inconsistency in the application of the new instructions under certain circumstances. Further, bonuses paid out of after-tax profits represented a serious loophole in the program that had not been provided for. Further, insofar as the excess tax rates themselves were much lower than similar penalties imposed in Central and Eastern European countries, Ukrainian enterprises did not perceive the policy as a serious one.

According to the IMF, reported revenues from excess wage taxation amounted to a mere KBV 2 billion in the whole of 1992.[28] Finally, the government repeatedly caved in to pressures from various sectoral interests to honor previous agreements on wages and salaries, not to mention parliament's mandate that wages in the budgetary sphere keep pace with those in state enterprises. For all of these reasons, the 1992 experiment in controlling wage growth failed.

Total 1992 government expenditures, including directed credits and off-budget funds, reached nearly 58 percent of GDP, up 8 percentage points from 1991. (Off-budget expenditures as a percentage of GDP increased four-fold.) A measure of fiscal control was achieved in the narrow sphere of the state budget (excluding regional and local budgets), due to consistent efforts to contain expenditures through a system of sequestration, which limited expenditure levels to the actual revenues received. Thus, in the first six months of 1992, the state budget deficit was in a more reasonable range of 2.5–5.5 percent of quarterly GDP.[29]

Expenditures increased sharply in the second half of 1992, however, due to: (1) increases in social safety net outlays, where some 40 percent of the population qualified for some form of cash benefit (the equivalent of nearly 25 percent of GDP); (2) parliament-mandated NBU credits in May-July 1992 to replenish enterprises' working capital, clear interenterprise arrears, and compensate agricultural concerns for losses resulting from price controls and consumer subsidies; and, (3) a December parliamentary decree ordering the Ministry of Finance to obtain further credits for the agricultural and energy sectors directly from the NBU, despite an earlier legislative prohibition on financing deficits through borrowing from the National Bank. Ukraine thus ended 1992 with a consolidated general government budget deficit of around 35 percent of revenues, including off-budget items and directed credits.

1993: Fiscal Consolidation Begins

The consolidated budget deficit was reduced by nearly one-half in 1993, to under 7 percent of GDP (14 percent including extrabudgetary funds and directed credits). Parliament again adopted the state budget late, in April, with a target deficit of 6.2 percent of GDP. To the government's credit, this target was nearly met. A significant revenue effort resulted in consolidated general government revenues increasing by around 7.2 percent, almost all of it coming from heavy increases in enterprise income taxes. In early 1993, wages were reincorporated in the enterprise income tax base (having again been excluded during the first quarter of that year), which approximately doubled the statutory base.[30]

Further, despite increasing inflation, depreciation allowances remained virtually unchanged throughout 1993, effectively resulting in an additional tax on enterprises' capital. This had the unfortunate effect of dampening industrial output. A further problem for enterprises was that, since many prices remained subject to government control, many were unable to pass the VAT on to consumers. Under such conditions, the VAT operated as a second tax on enterprise capital.[31] The deficit had been reduced but at an enormous cost in terms of long-term capital formation and productivity growth.

On the brighter side, state budget expenditures were held relatively constant, even though substantial increases in social security program costs occurred, mainly for consumer subsidies for meat, milk, housing, and communal services. Almost all other items were controlled across the board, with especially sharp reductions in expenditure on the national economy and Chornobyl Fund outlays. Despite these achievements, fiscal policy remained subject to significant pressures from a combination of factors, including:

- Exceedingly high enterprise and individual income tax rates;
- Build-up of considerable internal payments arrears, especially for state sector wages and salaries;
- Increasing external arrears on government debt service (mainly oil and gas debts to Russia and Turkmenistan);
- Sharp increases in producer and consumer subsidies (amounting to some 23 percent of GDP by year's end);
- Ukraine's highly volatile inflationary impulse, especially the outbreak of hyperinflation in the second half of 1993.

Throughout 1993, the government attempted to compensate for the implicit error introduced into its budgetary estimates from high levels of inflation by frequently updating its budget forecasts. But this only served to politicize excessively the budget management process, providing repeated opportunities for enterprise directors and their patrons in government to lobby for increased subsidies and other outlays. Such lobbying became increasingly active in the face of the heavy enterprise tax burdens. Fiscal consolidation was thus initiated in 1993, but the gains were painful and would prove to be politically unsustainable.

1994: Election Year Fantasies and Realities

Fiscal year 1994 saw Ukraine's first post-Soviet elections for both president and parliament. One positive aspect of the campaign season was that, unlike previous years, the 1994 state budget was adopted nearly on time, in early February. An ambitious general government deficit target of a mere 3 percent of GDP was planned. However, revenues were predicted to more than double, to some 86 percent of GDP, which Parliament hoped would permit an across the board *doubling* of expenditures, essentially for increased state sector employment and wages.[32] To accomplish this, the government turned to massive tax increases. The enterprise income tax rate was raised from 18 to 22 percent, the VAT was extended to goods imported from other former Soviet countries, the top marginal personal income tax rate was raised to 90 percent, and sharp excise tax increases were introduced. Finally, nontax revenues in the form of transit fees (for natural gas moved from Russia to Western Europe in pipelines across western Ukraine) were projected to reach levels of some 20 percent of GDP. Unfortunately, the planned revenues from these measures failed to materialize, although both revenues and expenditures did record sharp increases.

The 1994 revenue projections were astonishing in light of the fact that, since 1992, revenue had remained relatively stable as a proportion of Ukraine's recorded GDP. Not surprisingly, both revenues and expenditures ran far below their budgeted levels, barely exceeding 50 percent of their respective targets. Broad VAT exemptions granted early in the year offset most of the impact of the VAT reform, and widespread evasion of the new excise levies (in protest of their high levels) resulted in their gradual reduction through mid-1994.[33] Also, negligible amounts of nontax foreign revenues were generated. Despite an estimated 23 percent fall in real GDP, the ambitious enterprise income tax target actually was met, a result that was to have far-reaching effects on enterprise balance sheets.[34] Tax concessions to alleviate the deleterious effects of price liberalization also occurred late in the year, including suspension of the burdensome 25 percent amortization tax on enterprise assets.

In the face of such disappointing overall revenue performance, the government nonetheless succeeded in containing expenditure growth through "sequestration," forcing nonseasonal expenditures into line with seasonal payments, especially those to the agricultural sector. Elimination of food subsidies, accumulation of significant payments arrears on subsidies and social welfare payments, and a massive one-year turnover of 14 percent in the ranks of the civil service also dampened expenditure pressures. To reduce growth in pensions, in early 1994 indexation of retirement benefits was suspended, permitting erosion of the real value of the minimum pension benefit. This was partially offset, however (despite the government's stated intentions to the contrary), by off-budget government lending of an additional 4.2 percent of GDP, mainly to clear interenterprise arrears.[35]

With the implementation of President Kuchma's Program of Radical Economic Reforms, and the conclusion of an adjustment lending agreement with the IMF in October, a further tightening of expenditures took effect. Subsidies for coal, bread, gas, and communal services were sharply reduced. The combined result of these measures was that the consolidated general government deficit for 1994 exceeded 10 percent of GDP (13 percent including extrabudgetary funds and directed credits), triple the government's original target.

1995: Budgeting Becomes Continuous

Budgetary objectives for 1995 included reforming the tax system so as to more nearly resemble the systems in Western Europe, and reducing the size and scope of the government sector. The 1995 tax reforms included: shifting enterprise income taxes back onto net profits (excluding the wage bill); reducing the basic VAT rate from 28 percent to 20 percent; and restructuring the personal income tax by reducing both the number of brackets and marginal rates, from a maximum of 90 percent to 60 percent. The government's incomes policy, by now limiting the rate of growth of wages to 80 percent of expected inflation, was discontinued in February. Also, enterprises were permitted to adjust upwards their asset balances in order to reflect past inflation (by up to 52 times their balance sheet levels). Collectively, these reforms were expected to reduce substantially governmental revenues. In the face of a shrinking GDP and with rapid price inflation, however, accurate estimates of the precise effects of these dramatic changes proved difficult to develop.

The expected revenue loss was to be partially offset by reductions in exemptions from the enterprise income tax, the base rate of which was also increased from 22 to 30 percent of net income.[36] Royalties were introduced on domestic gas production, land taxes were increased 25-fold, and a presidential decree in May canceled exemptions for the VAT, customs, and excise duties.[37] The net result was to be a deficit target of 7.2 percent of GDP. Enterprise income tax receipts exceeded budgeted levels by some 5 percentage points of GDP, in part from taxation of inflationary gains during the year. The IMF reports that enterprises also increasingly compensated employees "in-kind," rather than with pretax wages, for which the employer would also be required to pay high payroll taxes.[38] The superior performance of enterprise income taxes offset a 3 percent of GDP shortfall in the new energy taxes. The VAT also fell short, slightly, as a result of parliament's failure to enact legislation cancelling the number of exemptions.

The over three-month delay in enacting the 1995 Budget Law threatened the achievement of the 1995 expenditure plan. Household subsidies for energy and communal services continued at their 1994 levels during the first quarter, in the face of decreed increases in domestic gas tariffs, so that sharp increases in domestic and foreign gas payments arrears were recorded. Kyiv assumed these debts, reducing budgeted transfers to regional and local governments in order to pay for them.[39] Government expenditures for coal and agricultural production were reduced, however, reflecting the government's shrinking role in these sectors. Finally, in order to impose tighter discipline in the budgetary sphere, President Kuchma decreed that, for the balance of 1995, the president alone would be empowered to submit to parliament bills that would have the effect of increasing expenditure or decreasing revenues.[40]

Budgeting became a continuous activity during 1995. The Budget Law stipulated that new indices would have to be readopted by parliament with respect to actual results in each quarter of 1995, not later than the twentieth day of the succeeding month. Consequently, a revised budget was adopted in July that reflected laws increasing wages and benefits in the education and health care sectors (by approximately 80 percent of the average Consumer Price Index increase for 1995), increases in capital expenditure, and extended guarantees for payment for imported gas. Expenditures for these items recorded such sharp increases that, in the fourth quarter, Kuchma decreed a 5 percent VAT surcharge and reimposed the 25 percent amortization tax that he had suspended in December 1994. The president also reimposed in September an incomes policy incorporating an excess wages tax of 30 percent for all enterprise sector wages that increased by more than 80 percent of the increase in the CPI index.[41]

In October, the government submitted another revised budget to parliament reflecting the impact of the new tax measures, which would have reduced expenditures along a broad front. But parliament rejected the revised budget and all of the new taxes, excepting the tax on excess wages. Further, in a move that would place enterprises in a significant tax squeeze, parliament doubled the official subsistence wage level and the minimum income amount, which had the effect of ratcheting upward all wages throughout the economy. The effect of these tax changes, expenditure shifts, and adjustments was a budget deficit of some 8 percent of GDP (10.8 percent including directed credits and extrabudgetary funds). However, this figure would have been higher, were it not for the efforts of the government to contain expenditures.

A significant capacity-building development occurred in the second quarter of 1995, when the government issued domestic debt for the first time, in the form of "Treasury Bills," raising KBV 20.4 trillion (or 0.4 percent of GDP). Although the 1995 T-bills amounted to a mere 7.4 percent of Ukraine's net budget financing requirement, they partially offset losses in external budgetary assistance. Further, issuing domestic debt was required in order to restore loan installments (termed "tranches") from the IMF, which had been suspended earlier in the year due to Ukraine's noncompliance with terms of the Standby Loan Agreement. Under the Standby Agreement, a net debt issuance target of no less than KBV 17 trillion was to be met by December 31, 1995. The short-term nature of the initial offerings limited their use as a significant noninflationary financing vehicle, requiring significant emission of NBU credits that year (financing some 73 percent of the 1995 deficit), supplemented by external borrowings (20 percent of the deficit). Increasing the average maturity of new issues would become more critical over time, as Ukraine's new T-bills assumed a more prominent role in deficit financing in 1996 and beyond.

1996: Deficit Control and the Emerging Payments Crisis

The 1996 fiscal deficit was the first in Ukraine's early history to be financed largely without recourse to new money creation. The consolidated budget deficit target of 6.2 percent was more than met, coming in at 5.2 percent (including directed credits and extrabudgetary funds).[42] Further, passage of an austere 1996 budget on March 22 satisfied important conditions for resumption of tranches under the IMF Standby Loan Agreement. The previously suspended fourth tranche, worth around $350 million, was released in April, providing a welcome measure of fiscal cushion.[43]

Few further significant changes in Ukraine's tax structure were adopted in 1996. The government's tax policy proposals were rather modest in light of the need for revenue reform. The tax policy agenda included: permanently reducing VAT exemptions, unifying domestic and international excise rates, imposing new property taxes on enterprises and individuals, and making minor adjustments to the personal income tax schedule. Despite achieving a measure of fiscal stability, revenue targets were not met for the VAT (-4.7 percent), the enterprise income tax (-10 percent), or excise duties (the latter being attributable to a decline in domestic production of liquor). These declines were partially offset by increases in payroll tax collections, personal income tax receipts, and other taxes.

Expenditure pressures mounted early in 1996. The late passage of the 1996 Budget Law necessitated the continuation of spending at the 1995 level until the end of March.[44] Especially troublesome was a January 1 average increase of 12 percent in: wages and salaries for employees of state-subsidized institutions, military and law enforcement agencies; pensions (increased by 1.922 times); student stipends; assistance to families with newborns, many children, and single mothers; and compensation for the victims of Chornobyl. To meet its fiscal deficit targets, Kyiv was forced to exert aggressive control over expenditures by stemming the flow of budget and credit subsidies to inefficient and loss-making enterprises. Among the most drastic measures taken by the government was a Cabinet of Ministers decree that effectively cut the power supply to some 15,000 customers, mainly enterprises, for delinquent energy bills.[45]

In an ominous development, throughout 1996 the government's efforts to reduce both industrial credits and on-budget subsidies precipitated a serious crisis in unpaid wages, pensions, and interenterprise debts. At January 1, 1996, the total amount of mutual indebtedness of state enterprises and budgetary arrears to all sectors reached approximately KBV 5.5 quadrillion (the equivalent of UAH 55 trillion), exceeding in magnitude the total volume of 1995 GDP.[46] Virtually all of this amount (some 90–95 percent) pertained to domestic debtors; the remainder was due to payments delays in the external trade sector.[47] By December 31, 1996, total enterprise debt had grown to UAH 82 trillion, again exceeding annual GDP.[48] The interenterprise debt crisis had become so acute by May 1996 that the government replenished enterprises' working capital throughout the remainder of the year by exempting 10 percent of profits from taxation.[49] This contributed directly to the fall in enterprise tax receipts.

The partially offsetting increase in revenues from payroll and individual income taxes would have been greater still had it not been for the increase in wages arrears, which the IMF estimated at around five percent of GDP.[50] Further arrears of 1.3 percent of GDP were incurred as a result of underfunding contributions to the State Pension Fund. From June 1, 1996, to January 1, 1997, unpaid wages, pensions, and stipends climbed from $444 million to $1.7 billion (approximately UAH 3 billion). According to Deputy Prime Minister Vasyl Durdynets, by January 1997, unpaid wages had reached "disastrous proportions."[51] Consequently, President Kuchma issued a decree on May 12 ordering the timely payment of wages, pensions, and stipends by the government and state enterprises, stipulating that failure to pay salaries and pensions on time would be grounds for dismissal of ministers and enterprise directors.[52] Kuchma further ordered tough austerity measures to curtail foreign travel, office renovations, and other privileges for government officials until all back wages and pensions were paid.[53]

In May, parliament decided to allocate a portion of the fifth IMF tranche, worth around $953 million, to pay wages arrears.[54] The crisis was not so easily resolved, however. By July 1, Prime Minister Pavlo Lazarenko announced that Ukraine was using 80 percent of its internal and external revenues to clear the wage debt. By October, teachers and university professors were rallying in Kyiv to protest against unpaid wages.[55] The payments crisis continued into 1997.[56] The buildup of significant payments arrears was responsible for the government's improved budget management performance in 1996. Insufficient domestic debt financing capacity and the lack of developed financial markets to absorb government debt left the government with few alternatives to consider—the fiscal equivalent of the "devil's choice."

Domestic debt financing assumed more significant proportions in 1996 but was still insufficient to cover completely the fiscal financing requirement. Budgetary plans called for 35 percent of the anticipated KBV 427 trillion deficit to be financed through bond sales, with the remainder to be met through external borrowings (40 percent) and NBU credits (25 percent). In the first quarter, some 70 percent of gross revenues from new bond sales were spent redeeming maturing issues; in the second quarter, this situation improved somewhat but was still high at 52 percent. Increasing the average maturity on new issues was therefore a fiscal imperative throughout 1996. In February and March 1996, Ukraine introduced six-, nine- and twelve-month T-bills.[57] Throughout most of 1996, Ukrainian state bonds were available in maturities of three, six, nine, and twelve months, with effective yields ranging from 6–8 percent per month (a range of around 90–155 percent per year). Real returns before taxes in late 1996 were running at approximately 30 percent (annualized).[58]

Initial sales of nine- and twelve-month bonds were sluggish; however, sales of the six-month bills were more brisk, as investors came to view the six-month issue as an attractive alternative to three-month maturities. In the first six months of 1996, Ukraine collected only around one-third of the T-bill proceeds budgeted for that year, a disappointing result. Fear set in that a prolonged dip in state bond purchases would cause the financial system to collapse in "pyramid-like fashion."[59]

In the wake of the September currency reform, however, sales of state bonds improved dramatically. Successful introduction of the hryvnia appears to have had a positive effect on bond sales. In addition, a special Cabinet of Ministers resolution officially permitted nonresidents to participate in primary and secondary markets, thereby opening the door to much-needed foreign participation in the emerging domestic debt market.

1997: Tax Reform Fails

Preparation for the 1997 budget began in mid-1996, with the president spearheading efforts to radically reform the entire tax system. In fact, he made it a prerequisite for enactment of the budget.[60] Dubbed the Economic Growth '97 program, it would greatly simplify the tax system through a series of seven draft laws that, collectively, would spur growth by reducing overall taxes by 7.3 percent.[61] Crafted by youthful reformer Viktor Pynzenyk, the program's centerpiece was to be a cut in the average enterprise tax burden from 7.6 to 4.1 percent of GDP. A key objective of this proposal was to bring shadow sector business back into the official economy.[62]

Basic elements of the package included: reform and standardization of the VAT for all enterprises; introduction of a deduction for depreciation of fixed assets; reduction of Pension Fund and Chornobyl Fund contributions (with accompanying benefits reductions); reduction of the maximum personal income tax rate to 30 percent; cancellation of export duties; cancellation of tax on income from state-issued securities; and complete reform of the pension system. The accompanying budget also included deep cuts in social benefits, including elimination of all subsidies to residents for rents and utilities. Revenues were projected to rise substantially, to 42 percent of GDP, resulting in a targeted deficit of 4.6 percent of GDP—up from a cash deficit of 3.2 percent in 1996 (excluding local and regional government operations).

The fight over the tax package would delay enactment of the final budget for almost six months, to June 27. In the ensuing period, the original budget was replanned and resubmitted four times. During the first half of 1997, the 1996 spending levels were in effect.[63] The delay placed acute pressure on the government, with the IMF threatening to temporarily suspend or reduce considerably promised 1997 funding of more than $1.2 billion.[64] This would severely constrain Ukraine's ability to pay its energy debts to Russia and Turkmenistan. The tax package was only partially enacted, however, with minor changes to the VAT and a major amendment to the enterprise profits tax (levying the tax on "net profits"), including withdrawal of tax incentives for foreign investors. To the great disappointment of reformers, the remaining five bills were shelved indefinitely.

The state budget deficit rose to 6.6 percent of GDP, which resulted from a combination of unmet revenue projections, lax expenditure control, and unwillingness to cut spending in the face of the rapidly approaching 1998 parliamentary elections. Budgetary arrears, however, fell slightly (by some .4 percent of GDP) due to the diversion of foreign loan proceeds to pay a portion of back wages, pensions, and other outstanding social insurance obligations. Revenues from personal income and enterprise profits taxes fell, as did oil and gas transit fees. These were offset by sharp increases in taxes on goods and services. But unpaid taxes also increased sharply at this time, to 5.3 percent of GDP. (The problem of tax arrears, privileges, and offsets is discussed further in chapter 6.)

The 1997 deficit was covered primarily by the sale of T-bills (71.3 percent). The consolidated budget deficit amounted to 6.6 percent of GDP, 0.6 greater than the IMF target of 6.0 percent. Revenues fell short of planned levels by 11 percent, including 10 percent for VAT collections and 5 percent for personal income taxes. However, enterprise profits tax receipts were almost 50 percent above target, offsetting considerably other shortfalls. Expenditures were also under budget, by 7.8 percent, with the greatest reductions in capital investment (-27.9 percent), transfers to the Pension Fund (-52.1 percent), and foreign debt service (-19.5 percent). State domestic debt financing was on target at 57.9 percent of the deficit, up from the 1996 level but still insufficient to cover the total.

Failure of tax reform generally has been attributed to a lack of political will. While left-wing forces in parliament (socialists, communists, and agrarians, mainly) were mobilized against changes in the tax structure, there seems little doubt that lack of confidence in the government's ability to implement reforms did little to generate support for Pynzenyk's package among centrist and right-wing parliamentary factions. Especially important in this regard was the government's inability to effectively collect its taxes. A bright spot was the UAH 370 million reduction in budgetary arrears in 1997, compared to the UAH 2.3 billion increase during the previous year.

1998: Another Election Year Budget

Passage of the 1998 budget went much more smoothly than any of Ukraine's previous budgets. As 1998 was an election year, parliament and the cabinet cooperated closely, shelving tax and other budget bills where necessary.[65] In a virtual replay of the 1994 budget season, the budget was passed in record time, on December 30, 1997—for the first time prior to start of the fiscal year. The projected deficit was reduced to 3.3 percent of GDP, more in line with IMF targets. Two-thirds of the deficit was to be covered through foreign loans and the remainder through domestic borrowing. As in 1994, however, parliament gave the voters an election year surprise, largely in the form of generous tax concessions.

The relatively low planned deficit target therefore appears entirely unrealistic in light of the serious shortfall in revenues that could be anticipated from the many tax concessions granted in this election-year budget.[66] By April, the VAT had recorded four straight months of decline, running at only 70 percent of budgeted levels (and nearly 17 percent less than the same period in 1997). The first half-year VAT collections ran at 21 percent less than budget.[67] These shortfalls were again considerably offset by large, unplanned overages in enterprise income tax receipts, which through April already amounted to 72 percent of their annual plan. Fears of hefty penalties in the 1997 amendments apparently caused many enterprises to overpay the tax.[68] This led to serious reductions later in the year, in that the law permitted reduction of future tax payments by the amount of current overpayments.[69] Overall, half-year revenues fell 25 percent short of budget. Expenditures were reduced sufficiently to offset the fall in revenues.

Despite these developments, in the first half of the year, budgetary arrears rose by some UAH 700 million on wages, pensions, stipends, and social benefits. State budget revenues declined, owing to local governments' practice of permitting taxpayers to "net" tax liabilities against VAT refund claims. A sharp increase in fraudulent VAT refund claims, coupled with weak penalties and the lack of sufficient tax audit capabilities, precipitated an increase in netting transactions, from 13 percent of revenues collected during the first quarter of 1998 to 28 percent for the year.[70] Tax arrears also increased by over four times—to UAH 10.3 billion—as a result of the government's generous tax amnesty for agricultural concerns, as well as frequent individual tax revisions by the State Tax Administration (STA). President Kuchma issued a decree in March allowing for tax liens, seizure of property, and the eventual sale of such property to satisfy tax liabilities. However, the STA had only begun to exercise these powers at the end of the year, too late to impact 1998 fiscal performance.

Concerned about the realism of the enacted budget, and seeking to appear responsible to the voters, Kuchma announced on January 21 an economic austerity program designed to cut the projected 1998 budget deficit to 2.2 percent of GDP.[71] This effort failed, however, as the cumulative deficit through June ran at 3.7 percent (4.6 percent, including the Pension Fund). This was due to large increases in expenditure on construction (3.5 times budget), transportation (a 200 percent increase), and debt service (up 24 percent). Kuchma acted again in late summer to reduce the deficit. While parliament was preoccupied with selecting a new speaker after the elections, the president decreed draconian spending cuts to reduce the annual deficit to 2.5 percent of GDP.[72] A nominal cut of 19.4 percent was ordered, with most of the cuts coming in just two areas: reduced transfers to local governments (-50 percent), and Chornobyl relief (-43 percent).[73]

To compound matters, the Russian currency crisis (precipitated by the economic crisis in East Asia a year earlier) negatively affected T-bill sales, raising the likelihood that Ukraine would have to resort to new inflation to cover the deficit. For a time, activity in the T-bill market actually ceased altogether. Ukrainian currency bonds were downgraded by Moody's in September, from B2 to B3, with a negative forecast.[74] Also, a decline in gold and hard currency reserves to critical levels raised the risk of default on external debt, causing Standard & Poor's to rate Ukraine's fiscal position as "unreliable."[75] During late 1998, Ukraine successfully negotiated with three major groups of external creditors to voluntarily convert its short-term debt into longer-term hryvnia-denominated government bonds, at a 40 percent return to participants for one year, followed by a floating, benchmark-linked rate thereafter. The bonds would mature from 2002–04, according to a predetermined schedule. Next, Kuchma took the more drastic step of forcibly rescheduling Ukraine's internal debt. This effectively postponed the liquidity crisis until 1999. Domestic commercial banks agreed to exchange UAH 803 million of treasury bonds, amounting to one-third of their overall portfolio.[76] In order to meet the government's immediate cash needs, in November the president called for printing more money and stripping the NBU of its independence.[77] Fortunately, neither event occurred, but Ukraine's debt problems would reach acute proportions in 1999.

1999: Debt Burdens Decrease Flexibility

The 1999 budget was difficult to both enact and to execute. The budget law was passed on December 31, 1998, just hours before the start of the fiscal year.[78] An indication of how contentious the budgetary politics were is that it took 21 ballots to garner the bare legal minimum of 226 votes necessary for approval, out of only 235 deputies present (according to the roll call). Most members of leftist and left-center parties

(Communists, Socialists, Progressive Socialists, Peasant, and Hromada Parties) refused even to vote, in protest against what they perceived as inadequate funding for social programs, and no provision for satisfying outstanding wages and pension arrears.[79]

The adopted budget projected revenues of UAH 23.9 billion (around $6.83 billion), and expenditures of UAH 25.14 billion (approximately $7.2 billion). The resulting budget deficit of just 1 percent of GDP would be well within IMF-negotiated limits, but it did represent an increase over the balanced budget proposal in early December by parliament's Budget Committee and its chair, Yulia Tymoshenko. The Budget Committee made drastic changes to the government-submitted budget it had received—by law—on September 15. The changes included increasing social, health, and education expenditures by 33 percent (including a 300 percent increase in the minimum wage) and balancing the budget with highly optimistic revenue projections.[80]

1999 was a presidential election year, and the fight over the budget clearly marked the unofficial start of the campaign season. Tymoshenko's proposal was roundly criticized for engaging in "economic populism" and pandering to voters. But the government's September draft, it seems, was being criticized by everyone, from President Kuchma[81] and chief government auditor Valentyn Symonenko[82] to Parliament Speaker Oleksandr Tkachenko[83] and Tymoshenko's own Deputy Budget Committee head, Yevhen Zhovtyak.[84]

Zhovtyak represented the more professional deputies, who were livid that the government's draft budget did not take account of the effects of the Russian currency crisis or the consequent dramatic devaluation of the hryvnia that was then underway. In a feeble attempt at greater realism, parliament raised the deficit projection, but only to a mere 1 percent of GDP, on the basis of revenue and expenditure plans that were no more realistic than Tymoshenko's alternative. It seems incredible just how conservative parliament had become after 1998's poor showing, when the government collected only around one-half of the expected revenues. In retrospect, it appears that the original draft may have been closer to reality.

Other deficiencies in the 1999 Budget Law included: failure to address the overall fiscal burden, which continued to run at over 35 percent of GDP (including the revenues of off-budget funds); lack of funds for badly needed new capital investment (which actually decreased); an unexplained doubling of expenditures on construction; insufficient funding for foreign and domestic debt service; and very little effort to reduce the size of the government sector.[85]

The budget as enacted incorporated certain positive elements that should be noted, however. For one thing, the low deficit target reflected widespread agreement among elites that the fiscal deficit should be reduced. Second, serious efforts were made to revise existing taxes in beneficial ways: VAT liability was to be calculated on an accrual basis for most transactions; the zero-rate for VAT on coal and imported gas was cancelled; likewise, the VAT exemption on critical imports; payroll taxes were reduced from 48 percent of the wage bill to 38 percent; excise taxes were raised to 2.6 percent of GDP (from 1.6 percent in 1998); gasoline consumption taxes were increased; and the depreciation allowance for enterprises was fully restored (previously, it had been only 60 percent of the full allowance). Third, and perhaps most significantly, a simplified procedure was established for collecting taxes from small businesses.

Despite these positive aspects, a major risk was posed throughout 1999 by Ukraine's rapidly accumulating public debt obligations. Debt service had become the largest component of expenditures in 1998, growing further still in 1999, reaching 16.2 percent (excluding the Pension Fund, local government expenditures, and state grants to local governments). Both domestic and foreign liabilities dramatically increased after Ukraine began issuing T-bills in 1995. By the start of 1999, domestic debt had grown to UAH 13.45 billion (around $5.5 billion). The compound annual growth rate of domestic debt was 45.7 percent from 1995 to the start of 2000.

Taking account of Ukraine's burgeoning external debts, the picture was even bleaker: a combined total national debt of UAH 65.2 billion at January 1, 2000 (net of NBU liabilities to the IMF), or around $15 billion. Though growing at a slower rate than domestic debt, Ukraine's foreign debt was larger, so that the annual growth rate of 20.8 percent per year since 1995 actually placed a more serious squeeze on the state budget. To complete the picture, government guarantees extended to Ukrainian private sector enterprises for purposes of enabling foreign trade added another approximately $579 million to the total, bringing the entire stock of public debt to just under $16 billion through 1999.

In view of the increasing seriousness of Ukraine's burgeoning debt, debt policy planning seems to have gone terribly awry in 1999. The budget deficit was to have been plugged with UAH 610 million in domestic borrowing, and UAH 630 million in borrowing from abroad.[86] But the structure of deficit financing was dramatically different from that embodied in the budget. The government raised only 81 percent of the budgeted amount of foreign loans, which proved insufficient even to cover current expenditures for foreign debt repayment. This resulted in a negative balance of UAH 80.97 million in external financing. On the other hand, domestic borrowing greatly exceeded planned levels, with the Cabinet of Ministers raising the authorized borrowing to UAH 750 million in January, and again to UAH 4,288 million in September.[87]

The amount actually realized was UAH 1,724 million, some 80 percent higher than the amount originally approved (though barely 40 percent of the amount that was ultimately authorized). The amount of additional domestic borrowing vastly exceeded what was necessary to finance the budget deficit. In fact, internal borrowing occurred even in months where budget surpluses were recorded. The numbers therefore suggest that the government was using domestic borrowing to repay foreign debts throughout much of the year. This drove internal borrowing up so much that, by year's end, over 40 percent of debt service expenditures were dedicated to satisfying internal liabilities.

In order to limit its debt service expenditures, the government in February 1999 had mandated a conversion of T-bills, together with a loan from ING Barings that had originally been scheduled to mature several months later, on June 9. With foreign investors shying away from Ukrainian debt, the NBU was to remain almost the only purchaser of T-bills at auction for the remainder of the year. By July 1, 1999, the NBU T-bill portfolio would amount to UAH 15 billion (including interest), or approximately 88 percent of all bonds then in circulation. It does not seem to have occurred to anyone in official circles that this constituted the de facto NBU financing of government deficits—albeit "through the back door" (as it were)—in clear violation of the May 1999 Law on the National Bank of Ukraine.[88]

In addition to the 40 percent devoted to domestic debt, another 22.2 percent was devoted to interest paid on short-term ("fiduciary") loans from foreign commercial banks, and 12.1 percent went to servicing the external government loan of 1995 (Gazprom). Further, the government continued to pay the interest on the state-guaranteed debt of Ukrainian enterprises that were in default, amounting to 6.8 percent of the total. The crucial point is that none of this debt servicing was part of any overall public debt strategy; nearly all of it resulted from unplanned contingencies that had clearly placed the government in a reactive mode.

A case in point is the vast increase in the 1999 public debt stock due to devaluation of the hryvnia in the wake of the Russian currency crisis. As is discussed in Appendix 7.1, Ukraine really had no choice but to devalue in response to Russia's 50 percent devaluation of August 17, 1998. The fall from 3.4 to 5.2 UAH per U.S. dollar caused Ukraine's dollar-denominated debt to rise by some UAH 15.6 billion (around $3 billion). As to the sources of growth in Ukraine's 1999 public debt, around 70 percent of it resulted from the currency devaluation. These newly inflated debts would have to be repaid with real hryvnia, either from increased taxes or fresh borrowing. Neither could be considered a limitless source of funds, however.

What was of serious importance was that Ukraine was building a spiraling "debt pyramid." Refunding maturing debt issues with new debt is a common practice among the governments of the world. It works well as long as the government is able to make credible commitments to repay and the debt-to-GDP ratio remains within limits of affordability, say 30–40 percent. Generally, the government is the most reliable guarantor, backed by its full taxing power and a growing economy. But Ukraine's commitment to structural reform was increasingly doubtful in 1995–98, and it became clear that the long-awaited turnaround in output would not soon materialize. Ukrainian and foreign banks then signaled that they were prepared to credit the government only at very high (that is, risk-adjusted) interest rates.

The government permitted nonresidents to purchase T-bills, which helped to dampen the interest rate rise somewhat. But it also had the effect of increasing Ukraine's dependence on foreign capital flows. Debt pyramids that are not supported by ample amounts of economic growth are never sustainable in the long run. In the absence of more plentiful amounts of foreign credit, and with a public revenue system in crisis, fears arose that Ukraine would either default or resort—once again—to printing money.

2000: Ukraine's First Balanced Budget

The impending debt crisis did not break loose during 2000. Ukraine and its new prime minister, the youthful Viktor Yushchenko, benefited from an unexpected amount of economic growth, with GDP actually climbing 6.0 percent for the year. This was the first year-on-year growth recorded in the post-Soviet era. Ironically, the devaluation that had caused Ukraine's public debts to swell in 1999 also had the effect of improving the price competitiveness of Ukrainian goods, thereby increasing exports and also enabling sufficient amounts of import substitution (especially for consumer goods) so that GDP rose steadily, beginning in the first quarter. These factors propelled Ukraine's fully executed budget into surplus for the first time.

The fiscal year did not start out all that smoothly, however. Enactment of the 2000 budget was as contentious as in 1999, taking until February 17 for parliamentary approval. In order to head off opposition in advance, and to improve the quality of budget projections, a "joint working group" comprised of legislators and cabinet members was formed under a Cabinet of Ministers resolution of May 27, 1999.[89] The group was chaired jointly by Finance Minister Ihor Mitiukov and secretary of the parliamentary Budget Committee Valeriy Khoroshkovskyj.

The committee's status was advisory only; its main purpose was to improve communications on budgetary matters between the government and the various parliamentary factions. The working group does not appear to have fulfilled its main objective, however. The budget was presented on October 7, 1999, to parliament, which rejected it in the first reading, objecting that it contained a planned surplus of UAH 554.5 million (around $121.4 million, or 0.4 percent of GDP). Parliamentarians rejected the government's draft on the basis that social and economic conditions in Ukraine would not tolerate a balanced budget.[90] Further controversy surrounded the government's projected 2000 GDP growth of 2 percent, the optimistic assumptions about continuing accessibility to foreign credit markets, the contribution of privatization proceeds to revenues, and the level of debt service actually to be paid in 2000.[91]

With controversy as the backdrop, then, the final enacted budget was balanced, with targeted revenues and expenditures for the consolidated state budget (that is, including local governments' budgets) amounting to UAH 41,694.423 million.[92] In an important improvement in budgetary transparency, the budget was split—for the first time—between a general fund and a new "special fund," that would include all nonbudget funds of budget-financed organizations of the state budget in 2000. All extrabudgetary funds were required to be included in the budget's special fund, through which all previously off-budget revenues and expenditures would flow.[93]

Other aspects of the 2000 budget that represented improvements over prior practices are also worthy of mention. The 2000 Budget Law prohibited the restructuring or write-off of tax debts incurred after January 1, 2000, and prohibited postponement of tax payment deadlines. The State Tax Administration (recently renamed the "State Tax Service") was also authorized to seize as "tax collateral" property of individuals and enterprises owing back taxes. The law also permitted the Ministry of Finance—in exceptional cases—to redistribute appropriated amounts (that is, to "re-program" funds) among budgeted organizations within the overall total, with approval of the parliamentary Budget Committee. A further provision restricted the government's ability to increase spending for state administration and governing bodies at the expense of reductions in other appropriations, including salaries of state employees. The government was also prohibited from increasing capital spending by reducing spending on current items.

The most radical provision of the law specifically abolished subsidies to the population, except for individuals with severe disabilities, war veterans, families of soldiers killed in action, and those who suffered severe disabilities linked to the Chornobyl nuclear disaster. Thus, the budget law suspended all previous legislation that provided housing, communal services, electricity, gas, public transport, telephone fees, and other consumer subsidies. In return, the 2000 budget contained a number of "protected items," including wages and salaries of employees of public institutions, state-owned enterprises, purchases of medicine and basic health care supplies, food for state institutions, interest on the state debt, social security payments, and transfers to regional and local governments. The law further prohibited the payment of wages and salaries of public sector employees in-kind, rather than in cash.

Two particularly troublesome provisions of the law, however, appeared to open fresh opportunities for illicit payments, influence-peddling, and extortion on the part of officials of certain budget-funded entities. Specifically, the law provided for publicly funded institutions in education, health care, culture, science, and sports to receive voluntary (that is, charitable) donations and contributions from private organizations and individuals for the needs of the institutions.[94] Even more bothersome was the provision that sought to stimulate tax collections by permitting the State Tax Service to retain a portion of revenues collected (excepting fines and penalties) for its operations.[95] The budget also contained a separate line item for planned collections of UAH 153 million in fines and penalties. There were concerns that this provision was likely to invent overly active assessments of fines and penalties.

During 2000, there were a number of strikes, mainly focused on demands that the government pay wages arrears. Labor tensions arose early in the year, when teachers from 34 schools and 1 kindergarten in the city of Kherson struck but returned to work based on the government's promises to pay.[96] Indeed, a decision was taken in early May to give teachers, health care workers, and employees in the cultural and arts sphere a salary increase.[97] Salaries were paltry; health care employees received UAH 130 a month (less than $25), which is less than half the average wage in industry. Further, the salary had not been raised for four years. The proposed salary increase was explicitly built into planning for the 2001 state budget.[98]

As the government began to draft its 2001 budget, some 40,000 coal miners in 19 mines went on strike to protest against both low wages and the burgeoning arrears. Mines were affected in Donetsk, Luhansk, and Volynska oblasts. According to the State Committee on Statistics, in mid-April 2000, wages arrears to miners amounted to UAH 747 million (around $144 million).[99] The miners returned to work by the end of May without achieving a resolution to the problem of arrears. Total arrears to industry at that time were UAH 6.5 billion, with the largest amounts owed in eastern oblasts: Donetsk (UAH 988.6 million), Luhansk (UAH 593.6 million), and Kharkiv (UAH 450 million).[100] By June, the average arrears to workers throughout the country were UAH 739.[101] For many, this was more than 3 months back wages. It is reasonable to conclude that the government was once again relying upon build-up of payments arrears in order to reduce the budget deficit.

On May 11, 2000, amendments were formally made to the state budget, increasing both consolidated revenues and expenditures by UAH 880,000 thousand (an increase of 2.1 percent), reflecting anticipated increases in enterprise profit taxes, VAT receipts, personal income taxes, and collections from customs duties.[102] The budget amendment also reflected higher local government own-source revenue collections (other than from the personal income tax, which was allocated in its entirety to local governments), which were expected to rise 5.7 percent (net of transfers to/from the state budget). In fact, revenues remained so buoyant throughout 2000 that the Yushchenko government was able to substantially reduce wages arrears and to completely satisfy all outstanding pension arrears by October. Even despite the reduction in arrears, the 2000 budget ended in a surplus position, ending the year at UAH 1.164 billion, or 0.7 percent of GDP.

Building Fiscal Management Capacity

The foregoing discussion suggests that there is a strong relationship between economic policy making, policy implementation, and the capacity of a country's governmental fiscal institutions.[103] Already by early 1994, it was clear that reform of the fiscal management apparatus was critical to Ukraine's effective transition to the market; it was precisely the lack of fiscal management institution-building that plagued—and that continues to plague—the structural reform effort in Ukraine. What efforts were made to improve Ukraine's fiscal management capabilities came largely at the insistence of foreign donors and international lending institutions. But these measures have been weakly and inconsistently applied and have been subject to frequent reversal. They have not been made part of any comprehensive improvement program. Consequently, there remain several critical areas where building fiscal management capacity is of vital concern:

(1) Tax administration;
(2) Budget formulation process and procedure;
(3) Public expenditure and deficit control;
(4) Domestic debt issuance;
(5) Sovereign (external) debt management; and,
(6) Role of the National Bank of Ukraine.

Tax Administration

Building an effective capacity to administer taxes is of crucial importance. Too many vestiges of the Soviet past survived well into the 1990s. The institutional arrangements under the former central planning regime were designed to collect revenues of the socialist economy. The central bank performed the major role in tax collections and settled the government's budgetary accounts.[104] As Ukraine has sought to establish a tax system that is broadly similar to Western European varieties, new tax administration challenges have emerged. These include: new and larger numbers of taxpayers; expanded volumes of taxable transactions; reduced governmental information concerning taxpayers and their activities; and a more limited role for the central bank.[105]

The limited capacity of the State Tax Administration to administer the new taxes constitutes an obstacle to effective tax policy change in support of economic transition objectives. As economist Richard Bird observes, in general, "limited administrative capacity is a binding constraint on tax reform"; hence, "the administrative dimension must be placed at the center rather than the periphery of tax reform efforts."[106] World Bank economist Jayati Datta-Misra puts the matter more bluntly: "There is no point in reforming tax structure if tax administration is poor."[107] Obviously, tax administration problems are not independent of tax policy problems, starting with the overall structure of the tax system.

Movement toward a western-style tax system pressed Ukraine in 1991 to establish a State Tax Inspectorate (STI) as a semi-autonomous entity within the Ministry of Finance.[108] In 1996, the STI was renamed the State Tax Administration (STA) and accorded ministry-level status.[109] Customs administration remains a separate organization. Until January 1, 1994, the STI was organized partly by type of tax, by type of taxpayer, and by function. Its various divisions pertained to the VAT, personal income tax, and enterprise income tax. Under the Soviet regime, tax administration was geared toward state enterprises, so that a capacity to deal with the large numbers of new private firms had to be developed in the period following independence. Consequently, new divisions were created for state enterprises, joint ventures, and cooperative enterprises, respectively. There is also a division of internal audit.

The early STI organizational structure may have hindered efficient tax policy making and administration. There is a preference in the literature for tax departments to be organized on a functional basis, which was achieved in Ukraine only in 1994.[110] A continuing problem has been the intrusive nature of tax administration. Each citizen, collective, and enterprise is assigned a "personal tax inspector," whose role is to monitor all aspects of their taxable activities. This approach is costly, slow, and terribly intrusive. It also provides myriad opportunities for extortion by tax authorities.[111] However, a much-needed Taxpayer Services Division was developed in 1994–96 to assist, inform, and educate taxpayers.[112]

Effective tax administration cannot be separated from well-formulated tax policy, however. Tax yields (what the government collects) and tax incidence (who actually pays the tax) are as affected by how taxes are designed and administered as they are by vigorous enforcement of the law.[113] New taxes are also difficult to evaluate, insofar as it is difficult to predict separately their consequences as opposed to changes in the effectiveness of tax administration.[114] The perceived need to legislate new tax law changes also is increased by inefficient administration, in that the inability to administer the legislated taxes prompts parliament to seek new taxes. This only worsens the situation. Frequent tax law changes actually lead to reduced collections, as confusion and uncertainty reign. Taxpayer compliance plummets. In an oft-cited work, Stanley Surrey recommended addressing tax administration through proper drafting and codification of tax laws, adequate staffing and organization, and taxpayer registration.[115] A properly designed tax and clear and unambiguous legislation can greatly increase compliance and yields.[116] This highlights the need for effective tax policy, which is the subject of chapter 6.

Budget Formulation Process and Procedure

In budget formulation and execution, outcomes tend to be driven by both the budget's structure and the budgetary process. The international experience is that almost all countries that fail to cut current expenditure levels have weak budgetary systems.[117] From 1990–95, budgeting in Ukraine was regulated under a law adopted during the late Soviet period.[118] This law was amended in 1995,[119] and again in 1998, to be more consistent with modern international standards.[120]

A budget code was formally adopted by parliament on March 22, 2001, in a 391 to 8 vote (with 29 deputies either abstaining or not voting and 22 absent).[121] The new budget code lays out principles of the budget system, its structure and functioning, the basics of internal budgetary relations, and sanctions for violation of budget laws.[122] The principles of the budget system according to the Budget Code may be summarized as follows:

(1) Integrity of the Budget System—The budget system is based on a unified legislative framework, unified monetary system, unified regulation of budgetary relations, unified budget classification system, and unified procedures for the execution of budgets and budgetary accounting and reporting.

(2) Budgetary Balance—Budgeted revenues and expenditures shall be in agreement.

(3) Independence of State and Local Budgets—Legal and practical independence of budgets at all levels of government is provided by the assignment of specific revenues and expenditures, and the respective powers and authorities of the organs of government.

(4) Complete Inclusion—Budgets are to include all receipts and expenditures implemented on the basis of regulations and legal directives of bodies of state power at all levels of government.

(5) Rationality—Budget amounts are to be based on realistic macroeconomic and socioeconomic indicators and related calculations of revenues and expenditures in keeping with the established methods and rules.

(6) Effectiveness—In the formulation and execution of budgets, all participants are to seek economy and efficiency in achievement of goals, with the expenditure of budget revenues.

(7) Subsidiarity—Expenditure responsibilities must be divided between the state and local government budgets, as well as across budgets, so that social services may be provided at the level that is closest to the direct consumption of such services.

(8) Appropriate and Targeted Use of Funds—Budget funds may be used only for the purposes defined by legal appropriations.

(9) Equity and Impartiality—The budget system shall be based on the principles of equitable and impartial allocation of public wealth among citizens and territories.

(10) Publicity and Transparency—The state budget and local budgets shall be approved and decisions and reports on budget execution shall

be approved according to the established legislative processes at their respective levels of government.

(11) Accountability—Each participant shall be accountable for his/her actions or inaction.[123]

Many provisions of the Budget Code represent marked improvements over previous practice. In fact, it would not be too much to say that, if faithfully implemented, the final vestiges of Soviet-era budgeting have been removed. The overall intent of the Budget Code is to, at once: rationalize and formalize fiscal relations between all levels of government, increase fiscal flexibility, improve budgetary transparency, and provide a more predictable flow of budgetary resources, particularly to local governments. A most significant improvement is that, in the future, central, regional, and municipal government budgets will be developed simultaneously and independently.[124] The former "matrioshka doll" model of interlocking budgets has been abandoned.

The groundwork is laid for a new formula-based approach to intergovernmental fiscal relations. The code also introduces a system of national and local budget fulfillment via the Ukrainian Treasury in the Ministry of Finance. Cities with populations in excess of 800,000 are authorized to issue external debt, provided that debt service not exceed 10 percent of a city's current expenditures. Any and all off-budget funds are prohibited. With the passage of the new Budget Code, the 1995 Law on Budget System was repealed.[125]

The Budget Code formalizes the parliamentary budget process. The budget must now be subject to three readings, with specific votes—and, if necessary, revision—before enactment. (Previously, a vote on the third reading was taken only if necessary.) This greatly enhances budgetary openness and transparency. Specific dates are required for the cabinet's transmittal of the budget to parliament and for the first, second, and third readings. Under the new process, the draft budget may be returned to the cabinet for "correction" even before a vote on the first reading, should it be found to lack conformity with other applicable standards and guidelines. Should corrections be necessary, they are to be made jointly by members of the cabinet and the parliamentary Budget Committee, thereby enhancing inter-branch communications on fiscal matters. This process is a marked improvement over previous practices.

Under both the 1990 law and subsequent revisions, Ukraine's budget system continued to embody characteristics of the former administrative-command system.[126] Most of the following problems—but not all—were addressed by the 2001 Budget Code:

- Budgets were not comprehensive as to expenditures;
- Extrabudgetary funds proliferated into the hundreds;
- Budget formulation was not unified;
- Account classifications were vague;
- Earmarking of funds was common;
- Control was inadequate, spread among many agencies;
- Budgets tended to be fragmented;
- Implicit subsidies were common; and
- Transparency was lacking, generally.

Without belittling the many significant improvements incorporated in the Budget Code, it must be noted that budget preparation still is not the sole responsibility of the Department for Budget Preparation, or even of the Ministry of Finance. Other departments share in the work of preparing industry sector-specific budgets on the basis of budgetary norms developed by the Ministry of the Economy. Fiscal policy planning is not conducted based on a consistent macroeconomic framework. This is improving but is still not as rigorous as it ought to be. The Ministry of Finance, at best, performs an accounting and high-level reconciliation process; it performs virtually no microanalysis of program spending requests for conformance with government policy. Cost-benefit analysis of spending programs, even the most elementary cost analysis, is hardly ever performed.[127] Budget analysis thus continues to be a haphazard undertaking.

Ukraine's extrabudgetary funds proliferated during the 1990s, climbing to over 500; however, the significant ones are the State Pension Fund, Unemployment Fund, Social Insurance Fund, and Chornobyl Fund. In 1997, the vast majority of these funds were abolished, along with their associated fees and charges. Of the remaining five large off-budget funds in 1996, three were transferred on-budget (the Road Fund, Fund for the Protection of the Environment, and Social Protection Fund). The Pension Fund, which had been incorporated into the budget in 1994, was again moved off-budget in 1997, apparently in order to remove disputes over pension benefits from other budgetary issues (which is a dubious rationale).

In response to domestic political pressure, and on the advice of its international creditors (particularly the IMF), Ukraine steadily reduced the number of extrabudgetary funds throughout the late 1990s. By early 1997, in addition to the Pension Fund, among the larger funds only the Social Insurance, Industrial Development, and Pension Funds remained off-budget.[128] In 2000, all previously off-budget funds were moved on-budget, included in the newly created "special fund," the status of which was formalized in the Budget Code. This reform greatly simplifies matters and increases budgetary transparency.

By order of parliament, budget account classifications were developed in late 1996 to conform with the IMF's Government Financial Statistics (GFS) system.[129] This rationalizes the system of accounts and greatly enhances comparability with other countries. The new Budget Code contains provisions that empower the Ministry of Finance to specify the format of ministries' budget appropriation requests. There are also specific reporting requirements indicated for monthly, quarterly, and annual reporting (on routine expenditures, extrabudgetary funds, and public debt). Annual audits by the Ukrainian Accounting Chamber will also help to further the evolution of accounting standards and procedures. The reports of the Accounting Chamber are timely—occurring about four months after year's end—and are available for inspection by citizens. The IMF reports that the present accounting system operates on a "modified cash basis," which includes useful data on accrued cash arrears.[130] Further, reconciliation between budget appropriations and bank accounts appears timely and effective.[131] An effort was initiated in late 1999 to develop a government-wide balance sheet that would be inclusive of all financial assets and liabilities, on a "modified accrual basis" (which would be more in keeping with governmental accounting practice in western countries). An immediate improvement would be the publication of a statement of significant accounting policies, so that government budgetary reports and financial statements might be interpreted properly.

Public Expenditure/Deficit Control

At many points during the 1990s, government policymakers revealed a preference for direct control over troublesome economic variables rather than for the more indirect economic policy levers employed in Western countries. Despite repeated attempts since 1992 to exert "control by decree," the institutional basis of expenditure control was yet under development as late as 2000.[132]

In the areas of cash management and expenditure control, parliament appeared to favor establishment of a "budget bank." The 1995 Law on the Budget System, in Article 32, states that, "deposits in the budget will be made through branches of the State Budget Bank of Ukraine."[133] Full implementation would have the state transfer all budgetary accounts of state-budgeted agencies and enterprises directly to the new bank. The Budget Bank would be directly and solely accountable to parliament.

Reformers in the government, fearful that deposits at the bank could possibly be used for commercial lending, viewed it as an attempt to nationalize Ukraine's financial system. There is something to this concern, insofar as parliament would then control an entity through which more than half of GDP would flow. The operation of such an institution would have been a clear violation of the separation of powers; hence, the proposed bank may be viewed as part of the ongoing struggle between president and parliament for control over the executive function. Forces allied with the president have prevailed, however, and the role of the Ministry of Finance strengthened through the creation of a State Treasury of Ukraine in 1995.

President Kuchma decreed in 1995 the creation of the State Treasury of Ukraine within the Ministry of Finance. Its role was to establish control over expenditures, ensure repayment of public debt, and monitor spending by extrabudgetary funds.[134] The treasury was to gradually establish full control over budget funds in stages beginning on May 1, 1997. The objective was to eventually close ministerial and departmental bank accounts, thereby assuming the dominant role in the government's budgetary relations with state enterprises and other budget organizations.[135] By May 1998, the treasury was executing the budgetary business of nearly all government organs, except for three security agencies.[136]

The IMF reported in May 1999, however, that there were delays in full implementation of the treasury and that many spending agencies have kept certain accounts outside of the treasury system, amounting to some 2.5 percent of GDP in 1998.[137] Consequently, the Ministry of Finance could not yet adequately monitor and control expenditures at all levels of government. The government continued to depend upon the National Bank for cash management services into the late 1990s. In 1998, however, the treasury established a cash management unit to operate a cash concentration and disbursement function, providing the rudiments of a central budget system for the first time.

Until full implementation of the state treasury is completed, budgetary accounts of state-supported organizations and enterprises are maintained by the NBU and certain authorized banks, including Prominvestbank, Ukrsotsbank, and Bank Ukrayina (until its liquidation in early 2001). The number of commercial banks handling budgetary transactions has been reduced from 17 to 6 banks. Until full enactment of the Budget Code, the continuing involvement of the NBU, state enterprises, and autonomous spending decisions by sectoral ministries and subnational governments will make it extremely difficult to conduct a unified expenditure policy.[138] The NBU has played the dominant role in administering Ukraine's budget, settling the government's accounts, and financing budget deficits. The Budget Code mandates that the state treasury assume the lead role in budget execution, accounting, and control. But the deficit financing function of the NBU poses a potentially destabilizing intermingling of fiscal and monetary policies that, unless remedied permanently, continues to threaten the stability of the hryvnia.

Some state enterprises continue to perform various quasifiscal functions (such as housing employees and providing hospitalization, child care, and pensions). These activities are obviously difficult to monitor. Further, Kyiv has no effective means with which to enforce expenditure priorities at the local level. Local authorities have routinely drawn funds from local STA offices before a full accounting could be provided to the center. Budget relations with the Crimean Autonomous Republic are more formalized, however, being regulated according to a treaty concluded in 1995.[139] In late 1998, serious efforts were made to rationalize budgetary relations between Kyiv and local governments, whose fiscal independence is guaranteed under provisions of the Ukrainian constitution. The most promising development, however, was the move to a formula-based system of budgetary transfers to the regions, which was enacted with the state budget for 2001. (See chapter 6 for a fuller discussion of Ukraine's intergovernmental fiscal relations.)

Domestic Debt Issuance

As noted above, the government began in 1995 to employ domestic debt financing.[140] Rapid development of internal debt capacity after 1995 brought considerable benefits by permitting a decoupling of monetary policy from budget execution, which enabled the NBU in 1997–2001 to check considerably the fiscal excesses of the government. Issuance of significant amounts of securities will also, over time, permit the NBU to constrain liquidity in the financial system through use of western-style "open market operations."[141]

Steadily growing in volume during 1996–97, treasury bills became in 1997–98 the main instrument of deficit financing. The bulk of T-bills were purchased by foreigners throughout 1996–98. However, the Asian currency crisis struck Ukraine in mid-1998, and foreign investors withdrew from Ukrainian securities, resulting in a sharp reduction in T-bill sales. Nonetheless, some UAH 10.6 billion of short-term state bonds were outstanding at the end of 1999. The major obstacles to fuller participation by Ukrainian citizens in public debt issues have been the absence of fully-functioning securities exchanges, and brokerage houses and the lack of broad investor confidence.

Development of the secondary market is obviously crucial for state bonds to serve as a monetary policy instrument. Measures taken in 1996 to improve the liquidity of Ukrainian T-bills included: introducing a Lombard-type repurchase facility for commercial banks, secured by domestic government bonds; establishing a depository for government securities; increasing bond denominations and lengthening maturities; and launching a secondary market. Reverse "repos" (repurchase orders), and repo tenders were introduced in 1997, with the latter intended to replace credit auctions as the prime open market operations instrument of the NBU.[142]

Ukraine issued its first government securities on March 10, 1995.[143] Acting as the issuing agent for the Ministry of Finance, the NBU conducted auctions of state bonds (T-bills) according to a weekly timetable that was established in mid-August 1995 (with Tuesday as "auction day" at NBU). In 1995, bond sales generated some KBV 30.4 trillion (around $150 million). Approximately three-quarters of the bonds were for 91-day maturities; the average maturity in 1995 was 122 days. After payment of required debt service, the amount outstanding at year-end 1995 was KBV 26.3 trillion. This was used to finance approximately 7.4 percent of the fiscal deficit for that year.

To broaden investor appeal, in April 1996, the government approved issuance of noninterest-bearing (that is, "deep discount") bonds for 1996, with a face value of KBV 10 million (UAH 1,000, or around $500 at that time), and maturities from one month to one year.[144] Debt outstanding would rise to KBV 222 billion (or UAH 2.22 billion) by the end of 1996. That year, nearly 37 percent of the deficit was financed through sales of T-bills. In 1997–99, T-bills covered an average of over three-quarters of the accumulated deficits.

In May 1996 new small-denomination "retail" bills were introduced having a nominal value of KBV 10 million, permitting the public to buy bonds for the first time. In February 1997, the government approved introduction of savings bonds having a face value of UAH 50, with maturities of six months, one and two years, and an "inflation-proof" interest rate of the CPI plus one percent.[145] Expanding sales to commercial banks also was an important objective over the longer haul. But the small deposit base of just KBV 400 trillion in late 1996 constrained significantly banks' ability to buy bonds. Several foreign banks applied for licenses to purchase bonds directly from the NBU, including Credite

Suisse, Societe General, and Dresdner Bank.[146] A government regulation of January 1996 requiring that secondary trading of state bonds be made exclusively through the Ukrainian Interbank Currency Exchange (UICE) was reversed in March of that year, when over-the-counter (OTC) trading resumed.[147] Obviously, it is important for market development that simultaneous exchange and OTC trading be permitted to follow parallel paths.

By spring 1998, the government was issuing only 9-month and 12-month bonds, with the 1-year bonds by far the most popular. Also issued were so-called "bonds with fixed redemption date" (BFRD), which were issued for the difference between the date of issue and the fixed date of redemption that was set for each installment. Terms of redemption varied between short-term (114–140 days to maturity) and long-term (287–366 days to maturity).

Ukrainian state bonds in 1995–96 were not rated. Through year-end 1996, Ukraine had met all of its debt service obligations, without exception. Over time, however, rating of Ukraine's T-bills has become increasingly linked to its official external debt, especially its Eurobonds. In February 1997, Ukrainian Eurobonds received a rating of "BB+," somewhat better than Russia's "BB-." However, Ukraine's late 1997 $409 million Eurobond was priced at a whopping 12 percentage points above German government bonds, the highest spread ever paid by a sovereign borrower on that market.[148]

In order to provide the government with an appropriate assortment of debt instruments for policy purposes, longer maturities are imperative. Repeated attempts throughout 1996 to issue 18-month bonds failed due to lack of investor interest, until a stable hryvnia brought market acceptance in June 1997.[149] Issuance of 3-month bonds was discontinued in May 1997. That same month, the government approved issuance of 36-month bonds.[150] The key to Ukraine's plans to issue longer-term bonds (for 1-, 2-, 3-, 5-, and 10-years) is to develop a viable secondary market. An important development in this direction was the long-awaited equalization of tax treatment of gains on both the primary and secondary bond markets in August 1997, with amendments to the enterprise income tax law.

Significant volumes of government securities take years to build, as both investor confidence and per capita incomes rise. Luring foreign investors was therefore highly desirable and, in fact, accounted for some 50 percent of volumes traded on both the primary and secondary markets in 1996, rising to nearly 80 percent in early 1997.[151] Before 1998, foreign participation had grown so rapidly that the NBU was considering measures to restrict nonresidents' market activities due to fears over increasing vulnerability of Ukraine's foreign currency reserves. As of May 1997, the only such regulation required that banks register foreign ownership of government bonds with the NBU.[152]

A major constraint on expanding sales of Ukrainian state bonds was the 30 percent VAT on profits from bonds sold prior to their maturity. The VAT on financial transactions was lifted in August 1997, to the great relief of investors. Individuals may purchase bonds on a retail basis from Ukrainian banks, which retain custodial responsibility for the bonds. Custodial fees ranged from .5 to 1.5 percent in 1996. The banks may purchase bonds on a wholesale basis from the NBU. Each bank is responsible for maintaining a registry of individuals who own bonds and for making payments when the bonds mature. Since only some half-dozen banks were considered "safe," the financial strength of a bank was an additional important consideration for investors until the NBU opened a National Register for Government Securities in late 1996.

A marked decline in foreign investor interest in Ukrainian treasury securities began in the second half of 1997. The autumn 1997 "mini-crisis" actually started at the beginning of the year, when the government sought gradually to reduce the yield on its bonds. In August, interest rates were 22 percent, which was the lowest level since T-bills were first issued. Then the Asian economic crisis struck in mid-1997, diminishing investor confidence in all emerging markets. Foreign participants left the Ukrainian market in droves, with capital outflows extending into the winter months of 1998. Despite increases in T-bill yields to 45 percent by year-end 1997, investor interest was difficult to sustain in the face of concerns about the government's ability to maintain the exchange rate.[153]

The NBU attempted to prevent collapse of the hryvnia by expending some UAH 483 million in foreign exchange reserves. Monetary policy was tightened, with the bank discount rate raised twice, from 17 to 25 percent, then to 35 percent. The commercial bank reserve ratio also was increased from 11 to 15 percent. In the end, the NBU was forced to accept a partial devaluation, announcing a new currency corridor of 1.85 to 2.25 UAH to the U.S. dollar. By the end of 1997, foreigners held some 45 percent of outstanding T-bills and domestic banks 28 percent, with the remainder in the hands of the NBU. Holdings by Ukrainian citizens was negligible.

On August 17, 1998, the Central Bank of Russia announced a new currency corridor for the ruble; within 48 hours the ruble suffered a 50 percent devaluation against the U.S. dollar. In addition, the government announced that Russia had defaulted on its foreign debt obligations. A few days later, the crisis hit Ukraine. In the face of the Russian currency crisis, foreign investors in 1998 departed the T-bill market altogether. Further strains were placed on the state budget at this time by the reluctance of domestic banks to purchase large amounts of T-bills. The significant volumes of borrowing sought by the government further eroded investor confidence in Ukraine's ability to repay its debts. Ukrainian currency bonds were seriously downgraded in September 1998. Foreign purchases of T-bills dropped to approximately 6.7 percent. Consequently, the NBU was forced to take up the slack, purchasing up to 73 percent of T-bills in 1998.

In September 1998, the government started a voluntary exchange program for nonresident holders of treasury bills. Nonresidents who had instruments carrying the previously mentioned exchange rate guarantee, or who had contracts with the NBU, were eligible for a special deal. In exchange for their bonds, each would receive an up-front cash payment equal to 20 percent of the value of their bonds, plus a two-year U.S. dollar–denominated 20 percent Eurobond for the balance. Holders of unhedged bonds received the same Eurobond, but no cash payment. The internal debt held by banks was forcibly restructured.

From the beginning, the authorities began pyramiding its debts, "rolling over" outstanding securities into new issues as they matured.[154] T-bill debt climbed rapidly until 1999 but has decelerated since then. The NBU has become the chief purchaser of T-bills, with a nearly two-thirds share after mid-1998 (when foreigners held more than 50 percent). In July 1999, the NBU portfolio of T-bills was UAH 15 billion (including interest), or 88 percent of bonds in circulation. This was an increase of UAH 5.7 billion in the first six months of 1999 alone. The May 1999 "Law on the National Bank of Ukraine" prohibits the NBU from extending credit directly to the government.[155] However, the NBU has become the most active participant in T-bill auctions, in direct violation of the law. Once again, the NBU has become the government's chief creditor, albeit through the back door.

As the NBU has purchased T-bills, the money supply has expanded, and with it has come renewed inflation. Large NBU purchases of T-bills also hampered the bank's ability to react to the Russian currency crisis of 1998. This illustrates the dramatic need to bring down the budget deficit permanently. Another exceedingly important reason to do so is the government "crowding out" private firms from the domestic credit market. Perhaps most tragic of all, the opportunity to reform fiscal affairs afforded by the development of the T-bill market has been squandered. Debts must now be repaid, but Ukraine has precious little to show for the effort.

Sovereign (External) Debt Management

Short of developing effective domestic capital markets, external (foreign) deficit financing has been necessary to cover budget deficits. At the time of independence, Ukraine had no foreign debt outstanding; however, by the end of 1996, Ukraine already had accumulated significant amounts of debt. Ukraine's indebtedness grew from an estimated $396 million in late 1992 to over $8.2 billion by the start of 1997. This sum reached $12.4 billion at the start of 2000. Despite this dramatic growth, according to the standard indicators of debt burden, Ukraine's external debt remains low by international standards. The principal creditors at the start of 2000 were Russia, the IMF, World Bank, Germany, and the United States.

The institutional arrangements in this area have been deeply flawed and slow to improve. No single institution has had the decisive role in determining Ukraine's external debt policy.[156] The Ministry of Finance is responsible for debt repayment but has only a partial influence over borrowing policy. The Export-Import Bank of Ukraine and the Ministry for Foreign Economic Relations negotiate foreign loans, but coordination with the Ministry of Finance has not been routinized. To remedy this situation, the government in late 1995 created the "State Credit Investment Company" to serve as Ukraine's official agent for servicing its external debts.[157]

Decision making regarding foreign loan guarantees appears to be heavily influenced by sectoral lobbies (for example, agriculture), which work through the sectoral ministries of the Cabinet and the Ministry of the Economy. Beginning in 1994, greater attention was paid to debt analysis in the context of the macroeconomy and balance of payments. The result is that decisions on individual loans were increasingly being made in consideration of Ukraine's ability to pay. By 1996, Ukraine had adopted legal debt limits:

- 55.0 percent foreign debt-to-GDP ratio (In 2001, this was raised to 60 percent);
- 100.0 percent foreign debt-to-exports ratio; and,
- 30.0 percent debt service-to-exports ratio.[158]

At the end of 1999, Ukraine's debt-to-GDP ratio stood at around 57 percent; the debt-to-exports ratio (present value basis) was 77 percent; and debt service-to-exports ratio was 16.1 percent. These measures indicate that Ukraine's debt remains within the limits of affordability, despite the country's ongoing payments crisis. The situation even improved somewhat in 2000, as exports increased, mainly to countries other than the CIS.

In 1991–94, the overall debt situation was aggravated by Ukraine's ongoing disputes with Russia over both its share of the former Soviet Union's debt (16.37 percent of the Soviet total, or approximately $38 billion) and Ukraine's burgeoning Russian oil debt, estimated at over $3.6 billion as of October 1996. In December 1994, Ukraine agreed to the controversial "Zero Option" settlement with Russia over debt of the former USSR, under which Ukraine renounced its claims on Soviet foreign assets (that is, embassies and other properties) in exchange for Russia assuming full responsibility for Ukraine's share of the liabilities. However, at mid-1997, the Ukrainian parliament had yet to ratify this agreement. Regarding Ukraine's oil and gas debt to Russia, its principal repayments in 1996 amounted to nearly 80 percent of all such payments, so that Ukraine's indebtedness to Russia, while high, was dwindling late in this period.[159]

After delays of almost two years, Ukraine placed its first-ever Eurobond issue of $396 million, one-year, 12 percent bonds in August 1997. In October, Ukraine raised another $99 million via a one-year fiduciary loan put together by Chase Manhattan Bank at 10 percent. Additionally, Ukraine borrowed $200 million from the World Bank and $100 million from the European Union. But external borrowing was barely sufficient to cover foreign debt amortization, which amounted to approximately $680 million.[160] Overall, external financing covered only around 27.1 percent of the 1997 budget deficit.

Consistent with the 1997 pattern, 33.9 percent of Ukraine's 1998 budget deficit was covered by foreign borrowing and 66.1 percent through domestic financing. With the reduced interest in its T-bills, however, Ukraine became more active in foreign markets after 1997. Ukraine placed a three-year, 16 percent DM 750 million Eurobond issue in February 1998, and a two-year, 14.75 percent ECU 500 million Eurobond in March, followed by a second tranche of the February issue at DM 260 million for 14.99 percent in May. The underwriters were Deutsche Morgan Grenfell and J.P. Morgan.

But Ukraine's history of default on its international debt obligations has burdened the country with a debt rating of less than "speculative" grade.[161] Ukraine was in arrears throughout 1992–94 on its foreign agricultural loans and payments to Russia and Turkmenistan for natural gas imports. In 1995, Ukraine's debt to Russia's Gazprom was rescheduled and converted into debentures, which were trading in late

1996 at only around 10 percent of face value. Thus, despite its low debt levels, international markets have not overwhelmingly embraced Ukrainian debt issues.[162]

Through the late 1990s, Ukraine's external debts grew increasingly unaffordable, especially in view of the large and growing domestic debt. By the end of 1999, foreign debt exceeded 57 percent of GDP. In 1999 alone, net foreign debt climbed 9.6 percent in U.S. dollar terms, but fully 83.2 percent in terms of the devalued hryvnia. In his 1999 annual address to parliament, President Kuchma stated flatly that, "we have approached the threshold [at] which . . . a country loses the practical ability to get out of the debt pit and turns into a chronic debtor."[163] Ukraine would start to encounter serious liquidity problems by mid-year.

In June 1999, Ukraine defaulted on a $155 million ING Barings loan.[164] In January 2000, Ukraine missed its scheduled payment of $18 million in principal and interest due on its fiduciary loan with Chase Manhattan Bank, a loan that had already been rescheduled once, eighteen months earlier. Subsequently, Ukraine would seek to restructure nearly $2 billion of its debts, proposing to swap all of its private foreign debts for a single Eurobond with a 7 to 10 year maturity. The same month, Moody's Investors Service lowered Ukraine's long-term country ceiling for foreign currency bonds and notes from "B3" to "Caa1," with a negative outlook.[165] At the same time, Moody's indicated that a further downgrade was possible in the near future.

Among the government's liabilities to private creditors were: the 1995 external bonds issued in payment for Ukraine's gas debts to Russia's Gazprom (the so-called "*gazpromovka*" bonds), for the nominal sum of $1.4 billion; the DM 1.538 billion Euroloan maturing in February 2001 issued through Chase Manhattan Luxembourg S.A.; a Euroloan worth EUR 500 million maturing in March 2000 issued through Banker's Trust Luxembourg; and $258 million of Merrill Lynch zero-coupon bonds issued in September 1998 in the voluntary exchange of domestic bonds held by nonresidents through E.M. Sovereign Finance B.V., maturing in September 2000. Further, in August 1999, about half of the Merill Lynch bonds issued in October 1998 were exchanged for around $74 million of Eurobonds denominated in D-marks and due in October 2000.

Ukraine would have trouble paying the debts coming due in 2000 and 2001. At the end of 1999, Ukraine's foreign currency reserves totaled just $1.25 billion, against more than $2 billion in debt service due in 2000, another $1 billion due in February 2001, and another $2 billion by the end of 2001. Ukraine has thus encountered increasingly severe liquidity problems that have forced the country to seek debt relief. To their credit, government officials have not asked for debt forgiveness but for a rescheduling of payments. This approach appeared to strike a positive chord in credit markets, where the price of Ukrainian Eurobonds rose from 50 to 70 percent of face value.[166]

During 2000–2001, Prime Minister Yushchenko took advantage of the relief afforded by the partial rescheduling of Ukraine's foreign debt, the repudiation of much of the government's pre-1997 debts to the NBU, and the budget surplus to pay down Ukraine's external debts by nearly $2 billion. It was expected that this would bring only shortrun benefits, however. The poor functioning of Ukraine's fiscal system, particularly the decline in real terms of tax receipts, places severe pressure on the budget. Although the ratio of debt to GDP fell in 2000, debt service has consumed an increasing share of the state budget (excluding both net transfers to local governments and the special fund). In these terms, debt service in January–April 2001 claimed 24.7 percent of general budget income.[167] Expenditures on debt are therefore displacing funds for necessary spending on social and economic development programs. It is obvious that the "Ukrainian debt pyramid" requires immediate dismantling.

Status and Role of the National Bank

As previously mentioned, a legacy of the former Soviet economy was that the NBU initially played the pivotal role in fiscal management. The government's weak deficit financing capabilities in 1991–96 thrust the NBU into the dominant fiscal role, both in providing credit subsidies to state enterprises and financing directly budget deficits. The bank in 1992–94 almost completely accommodated the government's budget deficits through credit expansion. During this period, it was extremely difficult to disentangle fiscal and monetary policies, a requirement for effective stabilization.

Under such circumstances it is extremely difficult to measure the true size of the fiscal deficit.[168] As a prerequisite for effective fiscal and monetary reform, then, the bank has had to abandon many of its traditional fiscal management functions and assume a more independent, strictly monetary role. Until the development of the state treasury, other governmental institutions were utterly unprepared to absorb these functions from the bank, effectively preventing its transformation into a central bank in the mode of its Western counterparts. Effectively severing the budget from the NBU was an important step toward imposing a "hard budget constraint" on both the state and the enterprise sector.[169] This required that liquidity limits be imposed on both state enterprises and the government, a feat that was accomplished only in 1995–96. It is unclear how long this can be sustained, however, given Ukraine's undeveloped domestic debt market and reduced access to foreign capital.

The international experience has been that central bank independence is highly correlated with sustained monetary stability.[170] A positive step would be to guarantee permanently the independence of the National Bank. Its subordination to parliament in 1992–95 constituted a significant impediment to effective monetary policy. The relative independence of the NBU was improved with the new procedures for appointment of the NBU Governor under the Constitution of Ukraine, ratified in 1996. Previously, the bank had acted as the philanthropic agent of Parliament in pursuit of its populist agenda. In 1994, President Kuchma submitted legislation for an independent bank as part of his October economic reform agenda, although he has wavered in his commitment to the NBU's autonomy.

In May 1999, parliament enacted new legislation that significantly limits the NBU's independence.[171] The bank has been made jointly subordinate to parliament and president, with supervision over its operations exercised through a 14-member "supervisory council," half of whom are legislators.[172] The first set of members included four former heads of commercial banks.[173] Under the law, this group has the final word on NBU board decisions. The NBU chairman (or "governor") can be dismissed for failure to comply with the general direction of monetary and credit policy developed by the council. This is a decided step backward; previously, the NBU chair presided over the board, which had sole responsibility for its decisions. The previous arrangement virtually guaranteed that the NBU would not be coerced into inflationary financing of parliament's populist spending programs.

Conclusion

Ukraine's fiscal policy experience during its first decade has been one of conflicting objectives, contradictory policies, false starts, and slow learning. Mistakes were made that rendered subsequent corrections more difficult to achieve. This is especially evident respecting punitive tax policies, which have driven much commercial activity underground and encouraged rapid growth of an enormous shadow economy, the activities of which almost entirely escape taxation. The politics of reform have prevented parliament from embracing rigorous market-oriented budget reform, to the detriment of microeconomic restructuring of industry, which is the very essence of the transition to the market.

As long as there is more to be gained from lobbying parliament for cheap budget subsidies and preferential tax treatment than from engaging in production and real output increases, Ukrainian industry cannot be expected to improve substantially.

To be fair, Ukraine inherited from the former Soviet Union very little fiscal management infrastructure or professional staff, which severely hampered the country's ability to stabilize the public finances. However, lethargic management, half-hearted attempts to improve control over expenditures, and frequent turnover of key ministerial staff are not to be blamed on the former Soviet leadership or on the transition to market. Development of Ukraine's fiscal management institutions is a task that only Ukraine can address. Building fiscal management capacity has become an imperative.

Much progress has been made, particularly in developing capacity for domestic debt financing and in delineating the respective roles of the Ministry of Finance and NBU. These achievements were greatly facilitated by the monetary stabilization that accompanied the currency reform of September 1996. But Ukraine has borrowed heavily abroad in order to buy the time necessary to implement these improvements, and this is not a limitless source of funds. In fact, Ukraine from 1996–99 built a pyramid of debt that is unsustainable in the long run. International capital markets will remain open to Ukraine only to the extent that tangible reforms are forthcoming. Additionally, the critically important need for comprehensive tax reform was no closer to achievement in 2000 than it was in 1992. At the beginning of 2001, this remained the greatest single challenge facing Ukraine's public finances. That is the subject to which we turn in chapter 6.

Chapter 6

Tax Policy and Subnational Finances

Tax Policy Reform Challenges during the Transition

The primary function of any country's tax system is to generate revenue. The international experience with developing and transitional economies has been that sustained deficit reduction occurs primarily through long-term revenue enhancement rather than expenditure reform. Budgetary politics tend to make current expenditures "sticky-downwards": easier to raise than to reduce. Further, the political consensus needed to cut spending is generally elusive, and this is true in both the developing and western industrialized countries.[1] Finally, The World bank experience has been that fiscal adjustment tends not to be sustained in countries that reduce deficits through mainly short-term increases in revenues or spending cuts; a more sustained effort is required.[2] Thus, long-term revenue enhancement through tax system development and administrative capacity-building is an imperative for countries like Ukraine.

In general, sustained fiscal improvement may be expected where tax policies result in broadening the tax base and simplifying the tax system, rather than in raising tax rates. Raising tax rates is tempting to governments in budget deficit. But high effective tax rates are associated with low collection yields.[3] As Ukraine's experience in 1992–96 demonstrates, narrowly progressive tax structures and high marginal rates provide disincentives for compliance, reduce the perceived fairness of taxes, and lead to high levels of evasion. Under such circumstances, broadening the tax base in conjunction with lowering rates may both enhance the perceived equity and fairness of taxes and render evasion more difficult. Tax simplification via a reduction of exemptions and tax privileges brings benefits of greater ease of administration and increased compliance. Together, broadening and simplification can greatly facilitate making necessary improvements in tax administration.[4] These steps will generally lead to increased tax yields.

The Ukrainian tax system in mid-2001 was still in need of comprehensive reform. During much of its first decade, Ukraine's taxes exhibited many of the common features of a system in crisis:

- Falling tax revenue-to-GDP ratios (especially in 1994–96);
- Highly progressive, poorly functioning taxes, with high effective rates;
- Highly differentiated rates structures, narrow tax bases, and extensive exemptions and tax incentives;
- Small personal income tax receipts, relative to overall revenues; and
- Serious compliance problems.

Ukraine's tax reform challenges are conditioned by the many characteristics it shares with developing countries, including: segregated and inefficient markets, poor levels of factor mobility, a lop-sided dependence on foreign markets, and significant political and administrative constraints.[5] Despite these parallels, Ukraine's lingering state dominance of the economy has propelled it to collect a greater proportion of GDP in revenues than most developing countries. Whereas for developing countries the average share of GDP in revenues climbed over 25 percent in the 1980s, from 1992–96 Ukrainian consolidated state budget revenues averaged over 42 percent of GDP.[6] It has stabilized at around 36–38 percent since 1996.[7]

The Ukrainian "tax bite" appears broadly comparable to that in Western nations. OECD countries, for example, collect an average of 38–40 percent of GDP as revenues.[8] However, the array of taxes, tax rates and tax bases, and the way in which taxes have been introduced and administered in Ukraine are incompatible with the needs of a market-oriented economy.[9] The challenge for Ukrainian fiscal reform, then, is to reduce the tax drag on the economy without aggravating the fiscal deficit or placing the kind of pressures on monetary policy that resulted in Ukraine's tragic bout with hyperinflation in 1993–94.

Legal Basis and Structure

Ukrainian tax policy is embedded in the laws of Ukraine, presidential decrees, edicts of the Cabinet of Ministers, and regulations of the Ministry of Finance and State Tax Administration (STA, formerly the State Tax Inspectorate). In December 1996, some 400 tax laws were in force, regulating 35 types of taxes and fees, along with numerous exemptions and privileges granted to specific activities and taxpayers. Due to its increasing complexity, parliament laid out the basic principles of a comprehensive tax policy for Ukraine in December 1996, which provided the framework for extensive revision of the original "Law on the Taxation System."[10] Enacted February 18, 1997, this was the third major revision to the original June 25, 1991 law.[11] The basic principles governing Ukrainian tax policy follow below. These principles are broadly consistent with modern international standards.[12] However, the realization of these principles has proved to be elusive.

(1) Stimulation of Entrepreneurial Activity and Investment—Exemption will be granted only for purposes of stimulating production;
(2) Compulsoriness—Payment of taxes is a mandatory obligation of the taxpayer;
(3) Equivalence and Proportionality—All similar taxpayers are to be treated alike (to ensure horizontal equity); greater taxes are to be exacted from taxpayers with greater abilities to pay (vertical equity).
(4) Equality and Prevention of Tax Discrimination—An identical approach to the determination of tax liabilities of all economic subjects (including individuals, organizations, and nonresidents) will be assured.
(5) Social Justice—The neediest segments of society are to be supported by a tax-exempt minimum income level; the overall tax system is to be progressive in its rate structure.
(6) Stability—Taxes and fees, and their associated rates, as well as tax privileges, are not subject to change during the fiscal year.
(7) Economic Feasibility—Taxes and other compulsory payments are determined on the basis of a balanced budget approach.
(8) Payment Uniformity—Payment terms will be established so as to ensure the timely arrival of revenues in order to finance budget outlays.
(9) Jurisdiction—The establishment (and repeal) of taxes and fees and granting of taxpayer privileges will take place in accordance with legislation exclusively enacted by the Supreme Councils of Ukraine, the Crimean Autonomous Republic, and rural, settlement, and city councils.

(10) Unified Approach—A unified approach to the determination of the taxpayer, the object of taxation, tax period, tax rate(s), the means of payment, terms and procedures for payment, and grounds for the granting of tax privileges will be assured.
(11) Simplicity—Taxpayers will be able to easily understand the rules and norms of tax legislation.[13]

The basic structure of the tax system distinguishes between taxes on individuals and those levied on activities of legal entities (businesses and other organizations recognized by law). Both are subject to an imposing array of direct and indirect taxes. The tax structure is further bifurcated into state (that is, national) and local (including regional) taxes and fees. As discussed further below, the central government progressively narrowed the tax sources available to subnational governments in 1992–96, reserving control over the most abundant revenue sources for itself, leaving the much lower-yielding taxes to oblasts and municipalities, placing many of them in a perpetual revenue squeeze.

Summary of Major Taxes

For most of the 1990s, an average of between 50–70 percent of consolidated budget receipts were attributable to four taxes: value-added tax (VAT), excise duties, enterprise income tax, and personal income tax. The contributions of these four taxes fell steadily throughout this time period, however. In 1996–99, contributions of these four taxes stabilized at 48–50 percent of consolidated general revenues. Of the remaining 31 taxes and fees, not 1 accounts for more than 10 percent of total receipts (excepting Pension Fund revenues). Most are of far smaller consequence. Table 6.1 presents the tax mix as a percent of consolidated state budget receipts for 1992–99.

The Social Insurance Fund, State Pension Fund, Chornobyl Fund, and State Employment Fund are financed through a payroll tax levy that was fixed at 51 percent of total wages and salaries payable by an enterprise until 1999, when the 10 percent employer contribution for the Chornobyl Fund was eliminated.[14] (A portion of the VAT is now earmarked for relief of victims of the Chornobyl nuclear disaster.) Collectively, these funds accounted for approximately 13.7 percent of GDP in revenues in 1997, and 13.4 percent of GDP in expenditures.[15] As noted in chapter 5, since 2000, all formerly extrabudgetary funds have been incorporated in the "special fund," which accounted in 2000

Table 6.1
Tax Mix as Percent of Consolidated State Budget Revenues, 1992-99

	1992	1993	1994	1995	1996	1997	1998	1999
Value-Added Tax (VAT)	58.2	29.9	24.4	22.1	20.9	22.3	19.8	19.2
Enterprise Income Tax	16.5	25.2	26.8	23.6	18.1	15.7	15.1	14.0
Personal Income Tax	8.8	5.1	6.4	7.8	8.8	8.9	9.5	10.1
Excise Taxes	3.5	4.4	3.2	2.0	2.2	3.3	4.3	4.0
Total of Four Taxes	87.0	64.6	60.8	55.5	50.0	50.2	48.7	47.3
Memorandum: Percent of GDP								
Four Above Taxes	28.5	25.9	29.9	22.3	18.7	19.8	18.3	16.3
Total Tax Revenues	28.8	26.4	30.4	23.8	34.7	35.6	34.3	32.9
Total Revenues	32.8	40.0	49.2	40.2	37.4	39.5	36.7	34.5

Note: Columns may not sum precisely due to rounding.
Source: Author's computations based on data in Table 5.1 of this book.

for some 16.1 percent of state budget revenues (net of local governments) and 2.9 percent of GDP.

As can be seen in Table 6.1, since 1992, the VAT share of total receipts has fallen sharply, with increasing reliance placed on income taxation. However, the overall contribution of the four main taxes also fell, both as a percentage of revenues and of GDP. Graph 6.1 depicts the eroding value of total revenues and the four main taxes from 1992–2001. As can be seen, Ukraine's revenue system is quite burdensome—claiming some 30 percent of GDP in the late 1990s—yet has been steadily failing to produce sufficient revenues to cover expenditures (until quite late in the decade). Frequent tax law changes, extensive exemptions and ad hoc privileges granted to specific taxpayers, as well as outright evasion, have contributed to Ukraine's falling tax receipts. Further, as we will see, as late as 2001, a large proportion of some of these taxes still were not collected in cash.

VAT: Ukraine's Revenue Dynamo

The value-added tax (VAT) is generally regarded as Ukraine's revenue workhorse, having contributed 58 percent of budget revenues in its year of inception, 1992. From 1993–99, however, there was a steady decline in the proportion of consolidated state budget revenues contributed by the VAT, to less than 20 percent in 1999, and a concomitant increase in the prominence of the enterprise and individual income taxes. As a proportion of total budget revenues, total tax proceeds, and GDP, the VAT has been declining as a revenue source since 1992. This reflects a steady shift in tax policy toward more direct forms of taxation,

Graph 6.1
Eroding Value of Major Taxes in Ukraine, 1992-2001

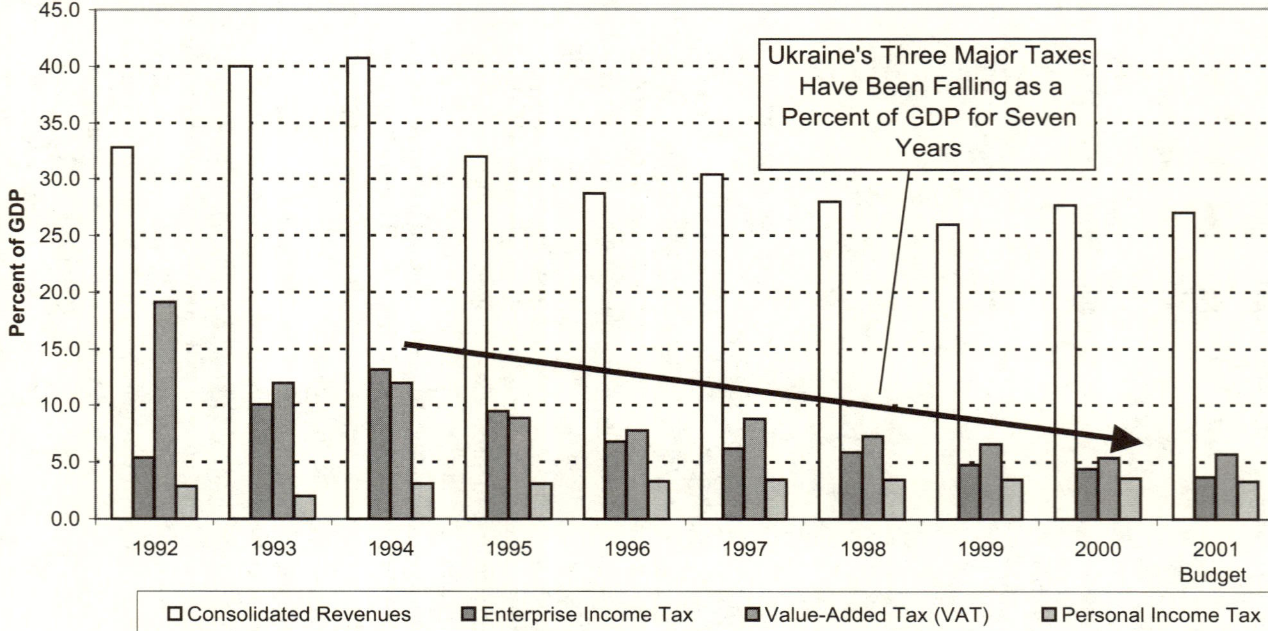

Source: Data are from Table 5.1 in this book. Total consolidated revenues excludes Pension Fund.

particularly income taxation, which from 1993–99 exceeded VAT collections by between 25 and 35 percent (however, income tax receipts were also falling).

As a rule, there has been considerable convergence in the structure of taxation in Organization for Economic Cooperation and Development (OECD) countries.[16] There has been a decided shift toward more indirect forms of taxation, with an emphasis on the VAT. (The United States is a notable exception.) There are certain advantages to a VAT over other forms of taxation. The VAT is levied on consumption rather than on income. It is less distortionary than income taxes, which tend to affect decisions concerning savings and investment.

A properly designed VAT does not distort domestic production and distribution or the choice of production technology (that is, labor- versus capital-intensive). It is neutral with respect to foreign trade, in that exports are free of tax and imports can be taxed on the same basis as domestic production. Opportunities for tax evasion are more limited than with income taxes, and the VAT is relatively simple and easy to understand. To work well, the tax base should be defined broadly, have uniform tax rates, and be neutral between taxpayers, with few exemptions.

The VAT was introduced early in Ukraine, far earlier than in other post-communist countries at similar stages of transition. Effective January 1, 1992, the VAT was levied without adequate administrative preparation.[17] A period of two years of advance preparation generally is necessary for VAT introduction.[18] In its haste to adopt the rudiments of a western-style tax system, Ukraine speedily replaced its Soviet-era turnover tax (in use in the former USSR since 1931) and the 5 percent sales tax that had been introduced in January 1991 as a supplement to the turnover tax.[19] However, the State Tax Inspectorate was wholly unprepared to monitor taxpayer compliance or to keep adequate records, resulting in major tax compliance problems in 1992–96.[20]

In Ukraine, the VAT was levied primarily as a revenue-raising vehicle for a state budget that was dangerously out of balance. Initially, there were few exemptions to the flat 28 percent rate, and virtually no privileges were available to specific sectors or industries. However, the list of exemptions grew dramatically, lessening the relative neutrality of Ukraine's VAT. The VAT exemptions and other tax concessions can erode the revenue base significantly. Indeed, VAT tax concessions in 1996 and 1997 were estimated by the Ministry of Finance to total some 59.8 percent of the total potential VAT throw-off.[21]

The situation worsened two years later. In the first half of 1998, VAT exemptions amounted to three times the amount collected. In 1996, there were no reduced rates for any class of goods or services.[22] However, substantial exemptions applied to coal and electric power, securities and hard currency transactions, insurance premiums, and certain services. Some exports also were exempted. Under the VAT law of April 3, 1997, and subsequent amendments, export operations, certain energy products (until January 1, 1999), copyrights, patents and licenses are zero-rated. Substantial exemptions exist for a vast array of other goods and services. The reduction in VAT rates in 1994–95 to a 20 percent single rate reduced somewhat the VAT's inherent regressivity, but also shifted the government's relative revenue dependency increasingly onto more direct forms of taxation. As a result of these combined factors, VAT collections in constant terms and as a percent of GDP have eroded steadily since 1992.

There has been some confusion over the precise nature of the VAT tax base in Ukraine, insofar as the tax itself appears to be paid on the volume of product and service sales turnover, as opposed to the "value-added" proper. Under a well-functioning VAT system, the value-added represents the difference in value in a product before and after its processing (where value-added at each intermediate stage of production sums to the total value-added of the finished product). As the Ukrainian VAT was computed in 1992–96, however, indices of national income (or "value-added") were employed in calculating the VAT, aggregated within industries and firms on the basis of material production, whether such products had been sold or not. This means that the amount of estimated manufactured product on which the VAT is levied will vary between capital-intensive and labor-intensive industries and firms. This situation arises due to the legally prescribed system of enterprise accounting, which excludes the computation of the true value-added at each stage of production. This is hardly a minor problem.

Collection of the VAT has also been fraught with difficulties. Before October 1, 1998, liability for the VAT arose when a product was shipped or when services were rendered, regardless of the timing of final payment. When a financial advance for goods yet to be manufactured was made, the VAT was liable to be paid, despite the fact that no value-added had yet been rendered. The VAT could therefore be collected not only on (1) goods at intermediate stages of production and (2) goods that had been sold to their final customers, but also on (3) goods that had not yet been delivered to the customer and (4) goods that had not yet begun to be manufactured.[23] The VAT was therefore subject to overpayment.

When the VAT is overpaid by enterprises, it represents a form of interest-free credit to the state budget. A February 21, 1996, decree of the Cabinet of Ministers admitted this possibility in the case of a single industry, shipbuilding, stipulating a temporary procedure for reimbursement for VAT overpayments. A new VAT law was enacted in 1997, but it was a much watered down version of the 1996 proposal of Viktor Pynzenyk that would have tightened up the law, and so did not deal with overpayments specifically.[24] In 1998, President Kuchma addressed the overpayment problem by decree, ordering that enterprise accounting for the VAT be moved from a cash basis to an accrual basis.[25]

Several VAT law changes were effective in October 1998, including elimination of some exemptions on transportation, imports, and household consumption of natural gas. Enterprises were also required to employ the accrual accounting method effective October 1, 1998. However, a presidential decree granted a five-year exemption to the agricultural sector from VAT, which has had a serious impact on VAT receipts. But generally, reform of the VAT has been slow in coming. In 2001, there was some possibility that parliament would set the VAT rate at a greatly reduced rate of 10 percent for 2002 and abolish the VAT altogether in 2003. This action would likely throw the state budget into an acute deficit position. There was no further word on this possibility at the time of this writing, however.[26]

Enterprise Income Taxation: An Uncertain Business

The tax on enterprise profits has been a source of great frustration to both Ukrainian entrepreneurs and foreign investors. Tax issues are consistently rated as among the main legal impediments to doing business in Ukraine.[27] Polls conducted in Ukraine by the Kyiv-based International Centre for Policy Studies during 1998–99 indicated an overwhelming agreement (in the 75–85 percent range) that "excessive taxation" was the chief factor limiting output growth in Ukraine.[28] In general, critics consider Ukraine's taxation of enterprises to be overly complex and burdensome, its rules and regulations ambiguous, the framework of taxation subject to frequent and unpredictable change, the implementation often made on a retroactive basis, and the tax officials prone to selective enforcement efforts. Obviously, enterprise taxation in Ukraine is not "investor-friendly."

Like the VAT, the enterprise income tax was established within three months of Ukraine's referendum on independence, on February 21, 1992. Also like the VAT, enterprise income taxation has been amended or overhauled frequently.[29] The basic tax rates and tax base tended to change annually:

- 1992: 35 percent of net profits;
- 1993: 18 percent of gross profits (including the wage bill);
- 1994: 22 percent of gross profits;
- 1995–99: 30 percent of net profits (wages and salaries are now deductible).

Differential tax treatment applied to various activities, including higher rates for lotteries, casinos, and video arcades; lower rates applied to dividend earnings. Many exemptions also applied, and withholding rates varied according to the source of income, making enterprise taxation a complicated affair.[30]

The most serious problem in enterprise tax policy, however, has been the changing definition of the tax base. Initially, the tax base excluded the wage bill. There were persistent concerns, however, that enterprises would seek to avoid taxes by increasing wages and salaries, especially to managers and directors (many of whom operated as de facto owners of their firms). As IMF economist Vito Tanzi writes, "In state-owned enterprises, when the government no longer fully controls them, the distinction between owners and employees becomes fuzzy and so does the distinction between wages and profits."[31] The government was unsure just how to deal with this issue; thus, the tax base was changed twice in 1992–93: It began by including wages, then excluded them, then once again included wages.[32] At the end of 1995, however, it appeared that the issue had been resolved in favor of the internationally accepted practice of exempting wages from income taxation, treating them as a deductible item.[33]

Taxable income included a firm's worldwide profits, calculated on a quarterly basis. But taxes are payable monthly, which is a significant administrative burden for businesses.[34] Income and expenses are accounted for on the accrual basis. The basic tax rate on profits was 30 percent in 1995–99, payable by both resident and nonresident entities. In addition, foreign-owned enterprises were exempt from income taxation provided that revenues were wholly from export or foreign sources, all settlements were made through Ukrainian banks, and managers and all administrative personnel were Ukrainian citizens. Foreign income taxes were creditable against Ukrainian taxes. Exchange rate gains and losses were included in the computation of taxable income. Straight-line depreciation had been prevalent, but accelerated depreciation (that is, pooled and declining-balance) methods are permissible under the enterprise income tax law effective July 1, 1997.[35] Certain activities remain exempt from taxation.[36] Financial disclosure requirements to tax authorities can only be described as onerous.[37]

While the flat 30 percent income tax rate does not seem particularly burdensome, it is the combination of business taxes—both direct and indirect—that impose a heavy burden on business development in Ukraine. It turns out that capital-intensive firms are more heavily burdened than labor-intensive ones. In the case of a capital-intensive firm, the purchase price of the product contains around 36 percent in taxes (including VAT, payroll taxes, and enterprise income tax) and 24 percent in earnings. Of the earnings, 73 percent is paid to the state. In the case of the more labor-intensive concern, there are higher VAT and payroll tax levies. In this firm, the price contains roughly 38 percent in taxes, resulting in 34 percent in earnings, of which 78 percent is paid to the state as taxes.

The discriminatory nature of the tax structure is apparent. What is also striking is the combined heavy burden of the taxes on both types of firms. Some analysts estimate that enterprises "worked for the state" some 18 days out of every 21 working days.[38] The heavy taxation of earnings has placed a serious drag on expansion of legitimate business and has no doubt contributed to the enormous growth of the shadow economy (especially since small business owners were also subject to high personal income taxes on their business earnings).

Local tax inspectors have had great latitude to assess tax liability, reportedly on an arbitrary basis. There is always an element of negotiation between tax authorities and businesses, even in western countries. However, owing to numerous ambiguities and (often) contradictory statutory provisions, the range for negotiated settlement of the tax bill in Ukraine largely makes the enterprise income tax what Kornai describes as a "soft tax."[39] This is highly problematical, as Bird points out, "The more room there is for negotiations between [tax] official and potential taxpayer, the more scope there is for bribery by the one, arbitrary exaction by the other, and collusion by both."[40] Efficiency and effectiveness of the tax system are both reduced. Contributions from the enterprise income tax have been eroding steadily since 1994.

Not only is revenue lost, but the elasticity of the tax system also is reduced, especially during periods of high inflation. The so-called "Tanzi Effect" suggests that higher levels of inflation and weak tax discipline strengthen the forces that erode budgetary revenues.[41] State enterprises and private businesses both delay remittance of taxes, with the latter more prone to outright evasion in the face of the state's administrative shortcomings. As a consequence, Ukraine's payments arrears have rippled throughout the economy.

The increased tax bite on enterprises also impacts adversely on future revenue collections, insofar as the payment delays contribute to increased interenterprise arrears, weaken enterprise liquidity, and threaten solvency. The squeeze in working capital feeds on itself, contributing to increased levels of interenterprise debts, which have accumulated to the point that future tax collections have been threatened. Firms are only able to pay taxes when their customers (which are often other firms) pay their bills.

The enterprise tax system is especially irksome to foreign investors.[42] The lack of predictability over the medium to long term has made it difficult to estimate tax liability and therefore earnings and investment returns. Some foreign investors litigated what they saw as tax officials' capricious enforcement of the law, making use of Ukraine's Courts of Arbitration to settle their disputes. However, the judgments of these courts, while binding on the government, do not establish legal precedence for future litigation; they apply only to the specific case at issue. The result was a spate of cases after 1995, most of them involving application of the import VAT to enterprises with foreign investment, in contradiction to the law. The tax authorities lost every case but continued "to force taxpayer after taxpayer to go through the cost . . . of senseless litigation."[43] Probably, this was in the hopes of encouraging out-of-court settlements. As the tax offices were permitted to keep a percentage of taxes they raised, they had incentives to pursue additional tax, even when its collection was unlikely and they might be litigated.

Officially, joint ventures with foreign partners registered before January 1, 1995, were granted tax privileges for five years.[44] In May 1993, a Cabinet of Ministers decree on foreign investment suspended the March 13, 1992, law "On Foreign Investment" (no. 2198–12-VR) as it applied to joint ventures, granting a five-year immunity from all new taxes and tax law changes. By 1996, however, this law was being routinely flouted by the government, which levied new taxes on enterprises (including joint ventures) without necessarily officially labeling such revenue measures as "taxes." Such maneuverings only increased foreigners' wariness of Ukraine as a country in which to do business. As if to confirm foreign investors' worst fears, on February 17, 2000, parliament enacted legislation withdrawing the tax privileges previously enjoyed by joint ventures (estimated to be worth some UAH 3 billion in 2000).[45]

Personal Income Tax: "Bracket Creep" Prevails

The personal income tax was adopted early in Ukraine, having an effective date of July 1, 1991. This tax has been subject to as much, if not more, variation as the enterprise profits tax. During 1992–96, dramatic shifts in tax rates, the number of brackets, and tax-exempt wage levels produced dramatic fluctuations in effective tax rates from year to year. Further, due to state-mandated wage adjustments in response to price inflation, effective tax rate levies in some years rose significantly each month. Table 6.2 summarizes the effective personal income tax rates on average state sector wages from 1992–2000. The year 1994 stands out sharply as a period of punitive personal income taxation, with a total of seven tax brackets and a maximum marginal rate of 90 percent.

Revised dramatically several times since its inception, Ukraine's personal income tax has always had an inherent progressivity, which varied considerably from 1992–96, especially at the upper income levels. There is no tax on minimum incomes in Ukraine, but the progressively higher marginal tax rates in 1992–96 had, in the words of one analyst, "a debilitating effect on employee motivation."[46] Since the personal income tax only accounted for around 8.8 percent of consolidated state budget revenues in 1996 (a five-year high), and exempt wage levels were low, the high progressive tax rate structure can only be viewed as an instrument to discourage entrepreneurial activity.

From 1992–96, Ukraine's personal income tax placed roughly similar burdens on individuals with wages and salaries in the range of one to ten multiples of the nontaxable minimum wage. This is, in fact, where most of Ukraine's wage earners fell, except for 1995, when the average wage consistently exceeded ten times the minimum wage all year. (Around 88 percent of all Ukrainian wage earners fall in the range of between one and ten multiples of the minimum wage.) Most Ukrainians were therefore not affected, but a great burden fell squarely on the emerging commercial class.

A serious problem during the period of rapid price increases (1993–95) was that the effective tax rate on average state sector wages tended to rise each month as wages were raised in response to price inflation. It is possible to discern the devastating effect that wage inflation had on Ukrainians' take-home pay by scanning the changes in effective income tax rates in Table 6.2. This "bracket creep" phenomenon is clearly discernible. In this case, 1995 stands out as the year when average wage earners were subject to the highest tax, due largely to the government's delay in adjusting upward the official minimum wage that year.

Table 6.2
Personal Income Tax Levy on Monthly Average Wages

Fiscal Year	Personal Income Tax Regime Effective Date	Official Minimum Wage [Note 1]	Nontaxable Minimum Wage [Note 2]	Average State Sector Wage [Note 3]		Effective Tax Rate (%) [Note 4]	
				January	December	January	December
1992	1-Jul-91	RUB 400	RUB 400	RUB 1,686	KBV 20,073	9.1	25.2
1993	15-Apr-93 [Note 5]	KBV 4,600	KBV 60,000	KBV 15,175	KBV 792,797	0	12.2
1994	1-Jan-94	KBV 60,000	KBV 120,000	KBV 763,396	KBV 3,312,000	8.4	18.8
1995	1-Oct-94 [Note 6]	KBV 120,000	KBV 240,000	KBV 3,291,000	KBV 12,250,000	18.5	39.0
1996	1-Jan-96	KBV 1,700,000	KBV 1,700,000	KBV 11,452,000 (or, UAH 114.5)	KBV 16,369,000 (or, UAH 163.7)	9.8	11.4
1997	1-Jan-97	[Note: Official	UAH 17	UAH 139.5	UAH 178.3	10.7	11.9
1998	"	Poverty Line	UAH 17	UAH 152.2	UAH 188.3	11.1	12.3
1999	"	= UAH 73.7	UAH 17	UAH 148.2	UAH 218.9	11.0	13.4
2000	"	per Month]	UAH 17	UAH 181.0	n.a.	11.4	n.a.

Notes: [1] The official minimum wage is employed as a benchmark by which to define the minimum salary as well as levels of various social benefits.

[2] The nontaxable minimum wage is equal to the official minimum salary (a multiple of the minimum wage) plus the bread supplement. The nontaxable "floor" was raised twice in 1992: in May to RUB 900, and in November, to KBV 2300. It was raised from KBV 60,000 to KBV 120,000 over the course of 1993, and to KBV 780,000 in 1994. In 1995, the nontaxable wage was again raised to 1,700,000 (or UAH 17), where it remained through 2001.

[3] The average state sector wage was subject to rapid inflation during 1992-95; hence, January and December levels are provided. The "state sector" is comprised of state enterprises, privatized enterprises in the official economy, and the government sector.

[4] The effective personal income tax rate on average state sector wages.

[5] Effective retroactive to January 1, 1993.

[6] Subsequently revised by presidential decree (no. 94-100) on February 3, 1995.

Sources: IMF, *IMF Country Studies: Ukraine* (1992, 1993); IMF, *Ukraine: Recent Economic Developments* (1995, 1996, 1997, 1999, 2001); Marcin Luczynski and Oleg Novoselsky, "Ukraine in Numbers Year-End 1996 Review," *The Ukrainian Legal and Economic Bulletin* (March 1997): table 3, p. 35. Effective tax rates are author's calculations.

Bracket creep remains a problem for Ukrainian individual taxpayers, even after some stability in the personal income tax was achieved in 1996–2000. Inflation, even after the stabilization of 1996, is a factor pushing Ukrainian taxpayers into ever-higher tax brackets. Economist Maurice Downey provides estimates as to the increase in effective tax rates due to inflation over the period 1995–99.[47] The accumulated inflation over the four years in his estimates was 119.5 percent. The difference, then, between actual effective rates and inflation-adjusted rates—which would have taxpayers paying the same tax, in real terms—for various monthly income levels was as indicated in Table 6.3. It is clear that the individual income tax scheme works to the advantage of the state over the individual taxpayer. This is the principal reason that individual income tax receipts have been more stable than other taxes, both in terms of constant hryvnia, and as a percent of GDP.

Excise Taxes: Underutilized Revenue Potential

Indirect consumption taxes, like the VAT and excise levies, are an underutilized source of governmental revenues. The estimates in Table 6.1 indicate that indirect taxes (VAT plus excises) dropped from 61.7 percent of total revenues in 1992 to 23.2 percent in 1999. It seems clear that the steady erosion in the value of overall taxes cannot be reversed without increasing the contribution from indirect taxes.

The VAT and excise taxes have the advantage of more effectively taxing the burgeoning shadow economy than other forms of taxation. (Even shadow operators have to spend their money on something, after all.) Excise tax collections peaked in 1998 due to increased consumption of taxable items (especially alcoholic beverages) during the two currency crises in 1997 and 1998. However, excises have not provided much additional revenue since 1997 and actually have declined as a percent of GDP.

The "Tax Gap" and Its Sources

There are many reasons for the steady erosion in value of Ukraine's revenue stream, including: tax privileges, mutual settlements, tax arrears, and evasion. It is difficult to measure precisely the revenues lost to the state from the combined effect of these factors. The following approach has been adapted from that employed by Serhiy Yurhelevych and Maurice Downey and has been updated and corrected.[48] Crude estimates of lost revenues can be made by comparing actual collections with the hypothetical potential for major taxes. Like Yurhelevych and

Table 6.3
Year 2000 Effective Personal Income Tax Rate (%)

Monthly Income in hryvnia	Actual	Inflation-Adjusted	Percentage Real Increase
100	9.1	6.3	43.7
200	12.8	8.5	50.7
300	15.2	10.7	42.6
500	17.1	13.7	25.3
1000	18.6	16.8	10.2
2000	25.7	18.4	39.4
3000	30.5	21.5	41.8
7000	35.9	31.0	15.8

Source: IMF, *Ukraine: Recent Economic Developments* (Washington, D.C.: International Monetary Fund, 2001).

Downey, we will estimate these figures for each of three major taxes: the enterprise income tax, VAT, and personal income tax. In each case, the applicable tax rate is applied against the hypothetical tax base.

The "tax gap" is simply the difference between the amounts actually collected and the hypothetical throw-off. As can be seen in Table 6.4, the amounts of lost revenue are considerable, reaching as much as 60 percent of the VAT and 36 percent of the personal income tax in 1999. The overall tax gap from these three taxes exceeded 10 percent of GDP from 1996–99 and topped 13.6 percent in the terminal year of the series. It is obvious that the Ukrainian tax system operated well below its potential for much of the late 1990s.

Tax Burden: High Despite a Large Tax Gap

Despite a large tax gap, the overall tax burden is excessive by international standards. According to the figures in Table 6.1, taxes ran at between 33–36 percent of GDP throughout the late 1990s, which is extremely high for a low per capita income country like Ukraine, where the international average is closer to 22 percent. The Ukrainian economy is therefore 50–60 percent more burdened with taxes then countries that are similarly situated.

To put it differently, the tax burden in Ukraine is more typical of countries having annual per capita incomes of $15,000 to $25,000. (Ukraine's per capita income is less than $750.) The excessive tax burden in Ukraine appears to derive from a mismatch between revenues and expenditures brought about by the unwarranted politicization of

Table 6.4
Estimated Revenue Potential, Tax Gap and Throw-Off Rates
(Millions of hryvnia, Unless Otherwise Indicated)

	1996	1997	1998	1999
Enterprise Income Tax (30% Rate)				
Total Income	19073	22414	20762	27090
Revenue "Potential"	5722	6724	6223	8127
Actual Collections	5456	5792	5694	6125
Tax Efficiency (Actual as % of Potential)	95.3	86.1	91.5	75.4
Tax Gap	226	932	529	2002
Tax Gap as % of GDP	0.33	0.10	0.52	1.57
Value-Added Tax (20% Rate)				
GDP	80510	93365	102593	127126
Revenue "Potential" [note 1]	13614	15592	17133	21230
Actual Collections	6299	8242	7460	8399
Tax Efficiency (Actual as % of Potential)	46.27	52.86	43.54	39.56
Tax Gap	7315	7350	9673	12831
Tax Gap as % of GDP	9.09	7.87	9.43	10.09
Personal Income Tax (Average Rate)				
Wages and Salaries [note 2]	38900	45400	49300	58700
Average Nominal Wage [note 3]	138	156	167	177
Average Tax Rate [note 4]	10.8	11.2	11.4	11.8
Revenue "Potential"	4201	5084	5620	6927
Actual Collections	2653	3296	3571	4436
Tax Efficiency (Actual as % of Potential)	63.75	64.83	63.54	64.04
Tax Gap	1548	1788	2019	2491
Tax Gap as % of GDP	1.92	1.92	2.00	1.96
Aggregate Tax Gap	9129	10070	12251	17324
Tax Gap as % of Revenues [note 5]	39.44	35.41	42.58	52.46
Tax Gap as % of GDP	11.34	10.79	11.94	13.63

Notes: [1] Tax applied at a net rate of 16.7 percent of GDP, taking account of legitimate allowances.

[2] Total wages and salaries are taken from the labor payments component of GDP published by the IMF. These figures are greater than the official wage bill in the state sector, but approximately equal to the totals for household consumption each year, net of savings and increases in cash balances. The author considers it to be a better number than that used by Yurhelevych and Downey.

[3] Average nominal wages from IMF, *Ukraine: Recent Economic Developments* (various years).

[4] Average personal income tax rate calculated from IMF data (See note 3). Yurhelevych and Downey used the marginal income tax rate of 15 percent, which is not correct to apply to total wages.

[5] Consolidated budget revenues less Pension Fund revenues.

Source: Adapted from Serhiy Yurhelevych and Maurice Downey, "Taxing Problems," *Ukrainian Economic Trends* (December 2000), pp. 42-49. Additional data from IMF, *Ukraine: Recent Economic Developments* (various years)

tax policy decision making. The unfulfilled potential of Ukraine's main taxes derives from several sources:

- Tax privileges;
- Mutual settlements (offsets);
- Tax payments arrears; and
- Tax evasion.

Tax Privileges

Since the mid-1990s, the number of tax breaks and special privileges has proliferated.[49] The value of these tax breaks is quite significant. According to STA data, in 1998 and 1999, the estimated budget losses due to tax privileges exceeded 32 percent of consolidated budget revenues and 11 percent of GDP. In the case of the VAT, exemptions have been very costly, amounting to three times the actual amount of collections in the first half of 1998.[50] The number and value of such privileges apparently increased greatly during the 1999 presidential election year, so much so that Prime Minister Yushchenko made the abolition of tax privileges one of the top priorities of his first hundred days in office.[51] Tax breaks in Ukraine number in the hundreds and can be found in many forms. However, the major ones are the following (figures are STA estimates):

- VAT exemptions on imports (UAH 272.9 million in 2000);
- VAT exemptions on medical supplies and drugs (UAH 678.4 million);
- Enterprise income tax exemptions (UAH 3,271 million);
- Land tax exemptions (UAH 1,341.1 million);
- Personal income tax exemptions (UAH 511.73 million); and
- Excise exemptions for Ukrainian manufactured goods (UAH 728.96 million).

In addition, there were tax breaks for accelerated depreciation on capital assets of selected industries (for example, aerospace), support of local manufactures through tariffs, and "special economic zones" where exemption from nearly all taxes is granted.

Emboldened by the looming $3 billion in external debt service payments that would come due in 2000, the Yushchenko government took on vested industrial interests by reducing the number of tax privileges, especially for the VAT. Specifically, the VAT would henceforth be calculated strictly according to the accrual basis, rather than on a cash basis; the zero-rate on coal and imported gas was cancelled; and the exemption on certain critical imports was eliminated. Insofar as tax privileges had mushroomed beyond what would be considered reasonable, these steps were all to the good. Care must be taken when interpreting the policy of reducing tax breaks, however, in that many governments have employed tax benefits to spur economic growth and development.

An example of a tax benefiting development in a specific sector is the agrarian "single tax," adopted in December 1998.[52] Some 12 taxes and duties were eliminated, with a single tax put in their place. Taxes on agricultural producers that were replaced included: the enterprise income tax, land tax, and contributions to the Social Security and Pension Funds. Through the operation of the new tax, every year the general tax burden on the agrarian sector is reduced by UAH 1.4 billion. In 2000, under the law, agrarian firms were paying just 70 percent of the fixed tax due, of which 68 percent went to the Pension Fund and 2 percent to the Social Security Fund. On top of the tax holiday already granted through the year 2004, and the VAT exemptions enacted on agricultural producers, this amounted to an extraordinary level of tax support for Ukrainian agriculture.

Great care must be taken in the design and implementation of tax breaks. The general rule is that the cost of tax privileges should be exceeded by their benefits to the overall society. Downey cites as a classic example of an unwarranted tax break the protection of the AutoZaz-Daewoo project.[53] The imposition of a protective tariff on imported automobiles increased the price of new and used cars in Ukraine, which effectively shifted the tax burden to Ukrainian taxpayers. He notes that, "while the project itself created around 20,000 new jobs, The World Bank estimated that the cost of protecting each job at several thousand US dollars per month."[54] Thus, in order to protect jobs paying an average of $46.50 per month, a large multiple of the estimated benefits was expended. It is clear that a rigorous cost-benefit analysis of tax breaks in Ukraine is in order.

Mutual Settlements

A serious difficulty for the government is that many taxes are not collected in cash at all but in the form of "mutual settlements," or offsets (so-called *vzaimozachet*). This essentially occurs where outstanding budgetary (that is, expenditure) arrears to enterprises are netted against their current tax obligations. It is a problem that affects all levels of government, as the figures in Table 6.5 indicate.[55]

Mutual settlements at all levels of government totaled UAH 5,557 million in 1999, or 16.8 percent of total on-budget revenues in that year. Offsets were also a problem for off-budget funds, where some UAH 4,593 million was cleared in energy-related mutual obligations

Table 6.5

	Proportion of Total Revenues			
	1997		1998	
	Cash	Offsets	Cash	Offsets
State Budget Revenues	74%	26%	88%	12%
Local Budget Revenues	66%	34%	68%	32%

Source: Fiscal Analysis Unit of Verkhovna Rada.

standing on the books at year-end 1998.[56] The largest amounts of offsets in terms of total revenues are for the enterprise income tax and the VAT, accounting for 25.1 percent and 47.4 percent of total offsets, respectively.

The problem of offsets as means to settle tax debts is obviously a serious problem in Ukraine. In early 1998, President Kuchma signed a decree to prohibit mutual settlements to the state budget, except for those that are specifically permitted by decisions deliberately taken by the Cabinet of Ministers.[57] But to no avail. Mutual settlements continued throughout 1998 and into 1999 with only modest reductions. The sums involved were quite significant. To put matters into perspective, had these amounts been collected in cash, Ukraine's foreign and domestic debt restructuring in 1998–2001, a result of the government's acute liquidity problems, may well have been avoided altogether.

Tax Arrears, Forgiveness, and "Moral Hazard"

The shrinking amount of tax collections in cash is exceeded by the growing level of tax arrears. Tax arrears include taxes and duties not paid within the established time period. Tax arrears grew steadily in the 1990s. By late 1996, almost 48,000 enterprises and organizations had incurred debts for unpaid taxes.[58] The volume of tax arrears outstanding grew from UAH 2.9 billion in 1996 to UAH 4.9 billion in 1997, reaching the enormous sum of 13.8 billion by year-end 1998 before falling a bit in 1999, to UAH 10.2 billion. But the arrears climbed again in 2000, reaching UAH 15.0 billion by August 1, which was equal to some 37 percent of consolidated budget revenues projected for that year.[59] The worst offenders are the VAT and the enterprise income tax (which are both considered by Ukrainian entrepreneurs and foreign investors as burdensome and a drag on economic growth).

There are several reasons for the build-up of tax arrears: short-term enterprise liquidity problems, increasing amounts of inter-enterprise arrears, accretion of budgetary payments arrears, and the general unprofitability of many enterprises. Barter transactions are also a notorious source of arrears accumulation, as are the use of notes payable as payment for goods (essentially unsecured, nontraceable IOUs), debt transfers to third parties (especially in eastern Ukraine and in the energy sector), payment of wages in-kind, and shadow market transactions—all of which may take the STA time to detect, measure, and assess the applicable tax.

The sums involved are quite large. Mutual indebtedness of enterprises exceeds the total value of GDP.[60] Enterprises are increasingly illiquid, with the share of cash working capital decreasing more than tenfold from 1990–97, from 15.6 to 1.5 percent.[61] Barter transactions accounted for over 40 percent of total industrial sales in 1998, and 32–35 percent in 1999. The IMF reports that there were over 25,700 loss-making enterprises in Ukraine in mid-1998, amounting to 53.8 percent of all firms, with losses totaling 13.4 percent of GDP.[62] Finally, shadow sector activities have been estimated at 50–60 percent of Ukraine's actual output.[63]

The VAT and enterprise income tax account for one-half of all tax arrears. Ironically, repeal of the zero VAT rate on coal and electricity as of January 1, 2000, and elimination of other exemptions on that date had the effect of increasing liability of enterprises to the state. Further, in order to reduce VAT liabilities to the budget, the Cabinet of Ministers in 2000–2001 permitted the use of mutual settlements for this purpose, thereby pitting one policy objective against another.[64] In the case of the enterprise income tax, the problem appears to be the accretion of mutual debts between enterprises (that is, accounts payable and receivable), especially in the energy sector. Based on a proportion of total arrears, more than half (58 percent) of tax arrears originate in the fuel and energy complex.

A serious problem of the government's own making has arisen from the policy of tax debt restructuring and even outright cancellation of tax debts, in order to provide relief to firms in critical sectors (that is, energy and agriculture). This practice has had the unfortunate effect of generating the widespread attitude that unpaid debts may be deferred, perhaps indefinitely. Enterprises thereby come to view unpaid tax debts as interest-free loans from the budget, if not outright "gifts." In 1997, some UAH 1.8 billion of tax debts were written off, and UAH 3.2 billion restructured for ten years.[65] But only a small amount of the restructured arrears was paid starting on January 1, 1998, so that arrears continued to mount. On May 23, 1997, parliament deferred for five years repayment of arrears of agricultural and food-processing enterprises.[66]

The policy of canceling or deferring tax debts has continued through 2001. On June 18, 1998, the president issued a decree canceling fines, penalties, and other sanctions payable to the state budget, Pension Fund, and Social Insurance Fund retroactive to January 1, 1998, and restructuring tax arrears as of the same date.[67] A Cabinet of Ministers resolution dated March 11, 1998, approved a list of enterprises in the military-industrial complex whose 1997 arrears were cancelled.[68] Further, while the 2001 state budget law maintains the principle of banning the restructuring or cancellation of tax debts, it provides for the cancellation of sanctions and debts for many firms and sectors accumulated before December 1, 2000.[69] Finally, two weeks after passage of the 2001 state budget law, parliament approved a law that wrote off tax debts accumulated by January 1, 2000, and postponed payment of year 2000 debts by 60 days.[70] Not only did these measures not improve enterprises' performances, but they engendered a serious "moral hazard" problem that made a mockery of the tax laws.

Tax Evasion

Under normal circumstances in modern western countries, detecting, preventing, and reducing tax evasion is a matter of administrative capacity. The tax authorities develop capabilities to inform taxpayers as to their liability, means and modes of payment, and compliance deadlines. They conduct both randomized and targeted audits designed to yield additional tax collections. Ideally, the cost of these taxpayer advisory, compliance, collection, and enforcement capabilities is far exceeded by the benefits in terms of tax yields.

Ukraine has thousands of STA employees involved in the assessment and collection of taxes. The STA is regulated according to the provisions of the amended law of Ukraine "On State Tax Administration in Ukraine."[71] There are serious issues in STA's relations with taxpayers, however[72]:

- Arbitrary interpretation and enforcement of tax laws;
- Restricted rights of taxpayers to appeal STA decisions;
- Widespread accusations of bribery and corruption;
- Capricious decisions regarding tax debt forgiveness and postponement;
- Harassment of certain taxpayers;
- Undue administrative burdens associated with record-keeping, frequent assessment and payment rules, and numerous tax inspections;

- More lenient treatment accorded to state owned enterprises; and
- Confiscation of property without right of appeal.

Prior to 1996, the STA (then known as the State Tax Inspectorate) was a constituent unit of the Ministry of Finance, headed by a deputy finance minister. Following an August 1996 presidential decree, the STA was elevated to ministerial status but had unclear reporting lines to the cabinet and president. Both tax policy and tax administration fell under the STA's purview. As a result of the numerous complaints against it, in December 1999 the Yushchenko government moved tax policy making to the Tax Policy Department of the Ministry of Finance and initiated steps to merge the STA with the Finance Ministry. Further positive steps would include separation of the tax assessment and collection functions and elimination of the practice of permitting STA offices to retain a portion of any additional tax that is collected.

Weaknesses in the basic administrative functions will obviously undermine the effectiveness of the tax system. Strengthening tax administration is critical to reform of the overall fiscal system. Ukraine's plight is far more serious, however, in that owing to the tax policy problems discussed in this chapter, there is a widespread belief that taxes can be deferred and that they may not have to be paid at all. Public attitudes in Ukraine work against effective tax administration. To put it differently, whereas most modern western systems of taxation are based on a social ethic of voluntary compliance, no such ethic prevails in Ukraine. Tax administration is very much a game of cat and mouse between the STA, customs service, and taxpayers in Ukraine.

There is broad consensus that tax evasion has become rampant in Ukraine, but it is too difficult to measure it accurately. There simply are too many opportunities to escape detection. Nonmonetary payments (for example, in-kind wages paid to employees, or notes payable given in payment for goods) result in much hidden income. Barter transactions are inherently difficult to evaluate in monetary terms, and shadow sector gains may only be taxed indirectly, via the VAT and excises. So many enterprises are loss-makers that even profitable firms are able to overstate their losses artificially. Audits can catch but a fraction of the taxes owed. The real challenge, then, is to compel citizens to voluntarily comply with the tax laws.

The authorities have made various attempts to combat evasion. In June 2000, President Kuchma ordered a crackdown on tax evasion and money laundering.[73] Taking note of large amounts of "conspicuous consumption" in Ukraine, the authorities were targeting taxpayers who were obviously living beyond their means. For instance, in a country with an average annual income of less than $750, over 5,000 people purchased limousines in 1999, worth more than $100,000 apiece.[74] Further, the STA reported that 40 new millionaires were registered the same year, but that they owed the state large amounts of back taxes. In November 2000, the Ukrainian Tax Police reported recovery of some UAH 3.3 billion (around $600 million) in unpaid taxes in the first ten months of the year.[75] During the same ten-month period, the tax police closed down approximately 3,200 fictitious companies that had been established for laundering money and detained some 2,500 chronic tax-dodgers.

More positive measures were also taken to increase compliance with the tax laws. An experiment in Zakarpatska (Transcarpathia) Oblast provided certificates of compliance to enterprises voluntarily contributing not less than UAH 3,000 per employee to local and state coffers.[76] Certificates conferred certain privileges; however, they were not automatic. They had to be applied for. Only around 70 percent of all applications were granted by the STA. The certificate secured the holder against some inspections by state bodies and gave priority for bank credits, tenders, and other privileges. Such measures are of limited usefulness, however. The international experience suggests strongly that resolution of the other tax policy and design issues discussed in this chapter will better serve to increase compliance.

Dilemmas of Tax Reform

There is a limit to the tax tolerance on the part of any public. Based on historical data, the renowned British economist of the 1930s, Colin Clark, estimated in 1945 that a tax-to-income ratio of 25 percent was the threshold beyond which a pro-inflation coalition developed in favor of a reduction in the government's real tax rate to the maximum tolerable limit of 25 percent.[77] The implication of Clark's work was that the source of a country's macroeconomic imbalance lies in the government's attempts to accomplish too much for the conditions of consent.[78] Although there is no way to establish a "correct" tax-to-income ratio on an a priori basis, economist Robert Skidelsky suggests that historical analysis would place the sustainable ratio for developed countries in the range of 30–35 percent. Ukraine's tax burden has been in excess of the 30 percent threshold for much of the 1990s, in some years exceeding 50 percent, including revenues of extrabudgetary funds. It comes as no real surprise, then, that the country has encountered such severe tax compliance problems and developed such an array of formal and informal means to escape taxation.

Taxes in Ukraine are set at simply too high a level, and tax authorities are much too intrusive in their activities. Despite many opportunities and repeated attempts to initiate change, tax reform has proved to be rather elusive. There can be no doubt that tax policy has placed a severe drag on output recovery in Ukraine. To be fair, the government has had to balance the need for budgetary revenues against its economic growth objectives. The main imperative has been stemming the fall in output, which authorities initially attempted to achieve through a policy of directed credits and consumer price controls. But Ukrainian tax policy has served only to circumvent in substantial measure the achievement of output recovery. The prevailing governmental attitude regarding the fiscal role of enterprises, which treated them largely as mere tax collection vehicles, prevented consideration of a more enlightened tax policy, to the great frustration of both foreign and domestic entrepreneurs and investors.

Increasing tax rates on existing tax bases clearly is counterproductive in transitioning economies like Ukraine's. In the experience of the World Bank, "where the prevailing tax structure is deficient, . . . increasing rates on existing bases, such as imports, will aggravate the distortions arising from taxation and complicate the pursuit of other goals."[79] In order to generate higher revenues without inducing distortions, it is more productive to have lower rates applied to a broader base.[80] Broadening the base permits reducing tax rates in the presence of revenue constraints and/or raising additional revenue without unduly aggravating existing economic distortions. It is also administratively more cost-effective to implement.

"During the transition, simplicity should be the guiding norm," according to IMF fiscal policy guru Vito Tanzi.[81] He goes on to say that "sophisticated systems and the pursuit of multiple [social] objectives for the tax system must be resisted." Also, taxes should be as broad-based and single-rated as possible. "Attempts . . . to promote industrial or social policies through the tax system would be misguided," as these efforts inevitably lead to proliferating tax (dis)incentives, preferences to particular taxpayers, privileges, and other concessions.[82] Unfortunately, the Ukrainian government has been unable to resist the temptation to implement a complex, western-style tax structure. The government has been too ambitious in its desire for overarching tax reform. The upshot is that by the mid-1990s, the tax system had become overly complex; tax legislation was vague and non-specific; regulations were rifled with exemptions, deductions and privileges; administrators were prone to selective enforcement; and the overall system was perceived as unfair. In the face of such complexity, Tanzi cautions against piecemeal reform solutions, given the compelling need to achieve and sustain budgetary balance.[83] Too much badly needed revenue may be lost in the short run.

The path to effective resolution of these difficulties is not entirely clear. The World Bank counsels that "even though the outlines of a desirable [tax] framework are reasonably clear, the design of transitional arrangements remains a critical problem. Poorly thought-out interim schemes may cause the reform to be aborted in the transition period or may necessitate large and costly zig-zags."[84] There was an abundance of such "zig-zags" in Ukrainian tax policy in 1992–96. The government has sought additional revenues through discretionary and ad hoc tax rate and base changes, as well as through seemingly spontaneous introduction of new taxes. Where revenue pressures persist, "*ad hoc* measures cumulate to result in a highly complex and internally inconsistent tax structure that is difficult to administer and costly in terms of efficiency, growth, and equity."[85]

There is thus a need for a systematic approach to tax reform in Ukraine. While a complete redesign of the tax system—such as that promoted by Viktor Pynzenyk in 1996–97—would likely have caused as many problems as it solved, Ukraine's piecemeal reforms would have benefited from the comprehensive vision that Pynzenyk could have provided in order to guide their implementation. If taken seriously, the basic principles of Ukrainian tax policy articulated in the law of February 18, 1997, provide such a framework. Comments on specific tax reform imperatives follow.

Concerning the VAT, broadening the base of the existing tax would require reducing the number of exclusions and eliminating concessions, permitting deduction of asset depreciation, and standardizing the VAT on the basis of invoice amounts. Such VAT reforms were proposed as part of the government's "Economic Growth '97" tax reform package in late 1996. Indeed, a new VAT law was enacted on April 3, 1997, incorporating many of these features, and further changes were introduced in October 1998.[86] However, despite these reforms, Ukraine's VAT basically remains a somewhat modified tax on asset turnover.

Broadening the enterprise income tax base usually involves extending the tax to more enterprises as well as reducing preferences and concessions. This can have far-reaching effects, insofar as many tax incentives are responses to pressure from sectoral lobbies and cannot be justified analytically. In Ukraine, determining taxable volumes of commercial activity, and even setting tax rates by negotiation, must be supplanted by a firm, stable, and binding regime, with fixed rates on qualified activity and clearly defined tax bases. Unfortunately, Ukraine sought to expand revenues by canceling long-standing tax incentives to foreign investors, a poor source of additional revenues. Thus, enterprise income taxation was revised on May 22, 1997, changing dramatically the calculation of profits and tax liability but also abolishing tax privileges for enterprises with foreign investment organized before January 1, 1995.[87] This change was damaging to Ukraine's image abroad, but as long as no further dramatic shifts occur, Ukraine will be able to repair its damaged relations with foreign investors.

Regarding personal income taxation, Ukraine's experience parallels that of developing countries, in that it has levied comparatively high rates on a narrow base, generating little revenue. Most wage earners in Ukraine earn relatively little, and much of it goes unreported in the shadow economy. Ukraine was therefore correct to reduce the rates and number of brackets in 1995. However, much personal income remains hard to tax, particularly incomes generated through shadow sector activity. In order to broaden the base at reasonable cost, presumptive taxation schemes can be introduced to assess tax liability, replacing voluminous documentation and lengthy audits and dispensing with Ukraine's army of "personal tax inspectors." Presumptive taxes applied using simple criteria might also be adopted as means to tax new and small entrepreneurial enterprises and other such activities that cannot as easily be taxed. Admittedly, however, such a reform is unlikely to find political expression in Ukraine, despite its potential.

Finally, it would seem prudent to expand use of excise taxes to help buoy revenues and to tax—albeit indirectly—shadow sector and criminal incomes. Excise taxes are an underutilized source of revenue in Ukraine. These could be extended to other classes of goods without introducing the types of wide-ranging distortions that income taxes would involve.

The Basic Structure of Subnational Finances

The consolidated budget structure of Ukraine incorporates the central government and all regional (oblast) and municipal (city, town, village, and rayon) budgets. As late as 1996, the assignment of expenditure responsibilities at various levels of government in Ukraine remained closely similar to the former Soviet framework. Ukraine remains a unitary state under the 1996 constitution, with the central government dominating the intergovernmental fiscal system. The intergovernmental fiscal principle of subsidiarity is generally followed. Analysts have observed that "the current assignment [of functions] respects to a large extent the basic principle of assigning expenditure responsibilities according to the benefit area for the public service."[88] As we shall see below, however, this has been a shifting variable. Central government ministries tend to specialize in activities of national economic significance, defense, law and order, foreign relations, major public works, and unemployment and pension outlays. Subnational governments focus mainly on the social and cultural spheres (that is, health, education, sports, and recreation).

However, during 1993–96, in response to fiscal retrenchment at the center, subnational governments increasingly assumed responsibility for "social protection of the population," which meant providing other social safety net programs in addition to the traditional mix of housing and communal services. Municipal governments also undertook many functions previously performed by enterprises. In preparation for privatization, many enterprises cleansed themselves of costs for activities that were unrelated to their core industrial functions.

In the 1990s, the devolution of functions from above and below acted as a "vise" upon the increasingly meager fiscal capacities of Ukraine's subnational governments. To compound matters, the allocation of budgetary resources to regional and municipal governments has fluctuated wildly throughout the decade, which has complicated fiscal planning at the subnational level and at times threatened the solvency of oblast and municipal governments.

The Public/Private Distinction

Expenditure assignment has two dimensions. First, there is the public/private division of activities: those that ought to be the prerogative of government, and those that are best left to the private sector. Second, there is the question of the proper allocation of functions among the various levels of government. Ukraine has had difficulty in addressing issues along both dimensions, pursuing very much an ad hoc process of shifting costs between sectors and levels of government. Concerning the public/private distinction, there is no uniform pattern across Ukraine. The roles of government and enterprises remain considerably blurred, as in Soviet times. As we shall see below, the Budget Code of Ukraine enacted in 2001 should greatly clarify matters. (However, as in all matters concerning the Ukrainian political economy, everything will depend on the details of its implementation.)

Under the former regime, much infrastructure spending (on roads, housing, and certain public works, such as electric power generating stations) was made by enterprises. Further, in the former USSR, the quality of housing, health care, employment training, and even access to cultural and recreational facilities depended more on one's place of employment than on one's place of residence. Vast disparities have been noted both between and within regions as a result of former Soviet expenditure policies.

Municipal enterprises provided generous subsidies to their workers for housing and communal services (that is, residential utilities), which varied considerably across enterprises. Large subsidies have gone for heat and hot water. However, these have diminished as rates have been progressively raised by the central government since 1994 in order to increase cost recovery levels. Cross-subsidization from enterprises to households continued during the period covered by this book, however, though the extent and level of subsidy is very uneven across Ukraine. Further, to the extent that many enterprises have continued to receive operating subsidies, this amounted to an implicit national subsidization of households from the state budget.[89] Enterprises' ability and interest in continuing to provide their traditional menu of social and cultural services diminished markedly after 1993, the result of falls in production and sales, decreasing operating subsidies from the budget, and the persistent payments crisis. For instance, many previously enterprise-provided services, such as kindergartens and daycare facilities, were either transferred to local governments or closed permanently.[90] The long-term trend was clearly one of shifting functions to the state sector, where the problem became one of assigning functions to the appropriate level of government.

Major Expenditure Assignments

In order to properly interpret the oblast-level functions, it should be observed that the main fiscal function of oblasts has been to redistribute and redirect to municipalities (that is, cities, towns, rural settlements and villages) national taxes shared with regional governments, and direct budgetary transfers from the center. The oblasts' direct service provision activities are actually much more limited. Oblasts have tended to fund services the impacts of which are primarily felt on a regional basis. For instance, oblasts are the primary providers of health, education, and housing and communal services. Oblast expenditures for social safety net programs did increase sharply (to 65 percent) in 1994, but this was mainly owing to increases in price subsidies rather than direct transfers to individuals and organizations. Subnational governments thus accounted for a large share of price subsidies, but the apportionment between oblast and municipal governments varied broadly.

Individual oblasts have great discretion to reassign expenditures among oblast, municipal, and rayon (district) governments. There is no national standard, which results in a highly checkered pattern of subnational expenditure assignments across Ukraine. In 1995–96, oblast and lower-level governments accounted for over one-third of all spending on public administration, which was expected to rise with the devolution of functions from the center. The share of subnational expenditures in other functional areas was relatively low.

As to their unique functions, despite improvements in the rate of privatization, oblasts and municipalities owned and managed hotels and tourist camps, ran restaurants, operated shops, and provided other services that in market-based economies are typically privately owned and operated. For instance, in 1994 the city of Kharkiv operated more than two-thirds of all retail and consumer shops in that city.[91] A similar situation existed in all large cities; however, small-scale privatization reduced the proportion of city-owned municipal shops, restaurants, and services after 1994.

Municipal governments primarily serve the local population, providing public transit, primary education, basic health and medical care, communal services, and sanitation. In addition, devolution of new functions from above has been quite extensive since 1993. Starting with the 1994 budget, oblast and municipal governments became responsible for certain expenditures previously the functional responsibility of the central government, including those for the social protection of the population (child allowance, bread allowance, and housing); social safety net (retirement homes, aid to families with blind and disabled children, and additional allowances for families with children); and further price subsidies for items as disparate as school lunches and housing construction. Housing and communal services were largely provided by municipal enterprises. These are quasipublic entities, possessing a measure of fiscal independence from the local governments to which they are subordinated. Previously, communal services were heavily subsidized (by as much as 88 percent of costs, equal to 20 percent of GDP).[92]

Problems with Expenditure Assignments

There were several shortcomings to Ukraine's assignment of expenditure responsibilities. First, a fragmentation of functions produced inefficiency and unevenness across regions, militating against effective administration. A classic example is in basic education, where oblast governments pay to build schools, rayons pay teachers' salaries, and city districts and settlements pay wages of support staff and maintenance personnel. Unified school budget management thus did not exist. Second, the central government shifted expenditure responsibilities to subnational governments on a fairly ad hoc basis, with little long-term planning. Municipal and regional finance officials were almost universal in their opinion that Kyiv was shifting those expenditures downward that would face the most politically unpopular funding cutbacks. Similarly, oblasts shifted functions to rayon or city governments in order to meet momentary fiscal and political objectives.

This resulted in a third problem, in which social safety net programs, a national responsibility in most market-based economies, since 1994 have been funded on a highly decentralized basis. Fourth, and as a consequence of the above, the system does not serve expenditure equalization objectives. Fifth, the continuing devolution of expenditure functions from both above and below (that is, the shift from enterprises to their respective oblasts or localities) worked against effective budgetary planning in the regions. Finally, the legislative basis for regional and local fiscal management has been ever changing, internally contradictory, and subject to selective implementation.

In general, expenditure needs and responsibilities at the municipal and oblast levels increasingly exceeded the available resources throughout much of the decade. One indication of the desperately acute nature of the subnational fiscal situation was that, despite shifting expenditure functions to lower-level governments, the subnational share of public expenditure shrank in real terms, owing to both the 1993–96 inflation and falling tax receipts generally. Due to the dwindling real value of budget resources transferred from higher level governments, cities and towns were under considerable pressure to maintain service levels. According to interviews conducted by the author in 1993–95, most city and oblast officials expected a continued decline in service levels for the foreseeable future. They were right. In the ensuing years, these expenditure pressures have been made more severe by a deteriorating intergovernmental revenue situation.

Revenue Assignment among Levels of Government

Due to a sharp deterioration in their fiscal circumstances, fiscal independence from Kyiv became a critical objective of regional and local governments in the 1990s. The need to develop "own-source" revenues was argued vociferously by President Kuchma's regional policy advisor, Volodymyr Hryniov, who viewed "serious and profound financial-budget reform in general, and taxation reform in particular," as "certain preconditions" for regional political and economic development.[93] In fact, Hryniov would "overturn the taxation pyramid to place its foundation not in the center, but in the regions." Hryniov's remarks largely reflected the prevailing regional view that Ukraine's intergovernmental fiscal system was "a mill working in vain." There were several noteworthy problems with the basic framework and operation of the system as it evolved after 1992:

- Unclear distinctions between national ("regulating") and subnational ("fixed") revenue sources;
- Continually shifting tax-sharing rates complicating regional and municipal fiscal planning;
- Fluctuating budgetary transfers to subordinate levels; and
- Deteriorating oblast revenue structures throughout 1992–2000.

Unclear Distinctions Between Own-Source and Shared Revenues

Budgetary relations between the central government and regional/local governments involves a somewhat complex system of tax sharing and revenue retention mechanisms, supplemented by transfers from higher-level governments. Intergovernmental fiscal relations in Ukraine retain many vestiges of the former Soviet budgetary system, especially the distinction between "fixed" revenues and state "regulating" revenues. Fixed, or own-source revenues, include taxes, charges, and fees that have been assigned by law to subnational governments. Regulating revenues are central government taxes that are shared with oblasts on a derivation basis, with varying rates of retention set according to the total tax anticipated to be collected in each oblast. Subnational governments also receive budgetary transfers from the central government. Local governments, in turn, may also receive transfers from the oblast administration. These transfers have varied considerably from year to year.

A serious problem for subnational governments was that the central government would periodically change the definition of "fixed" revenues, diminishing both their number and economic value to subnational governments. To cite two such instances, until the enactment of the 1994 Budget Law, the Personal Income Tax and Land Tax were defined as fixed revenues, with 100 percent being assigned to oblast and municipal governments.[94] Thereafter, they were shared with the center on a percentage basis. Effective with the 1995 budget, the Tax on Profits of Enterprises of Communal Subordination was also redefined as a state regulating revenue, which significantly diminished the already meager fiscal resources of subnational governments.[95]

Over the decade, exclusively subnational revenue sources became much more limited, including taxes on motor vehicles, payments for water consumed by industry, housing and communal services (utility) fees, revenues from privatization of communal property, and other nontax revenues (hotel occupancy, parking fees, apartment occupancy, pet licenses, advertising, lotteries, auctions, market stall rentals, etc.). Unfortunately, these taxes have very nominal yields with little growth potential.

The central government routinely violated legal norms to suit its fiscal convenience. For instance, the provisions of both the 1994 and 1995 Laws on State Budget, which changed the composition of oblast-fixed revenues, stand in contradiction to provisions of both the then-effective Law on Local Self-Government and the Law on the Budget System, which fully assigned these taxes to subnational governments and made the fiscal relationship between oblasts and their subordinate municipal jurisdictions solely a matter of oblast policy.[96] Far from serving as the basis for a rational distribution of resources, legal requirements did not prevent Kyiv from acting in its own fiscal interest at the expense of the regions.

In an effort to rationalize the system and to increase budgetary control over subnational expenditure, the 1996 Constitution of Ukraine (chapter 2, article 143) effectively reconfigured intergovernmental budget relations. In principle, a system of more formalized subventions replaced the complex web of tax sharing relations, with all state budget revenues transferred to the center for redistribution among the regions. The IMF reported in late 1997, however, that "the national government [still] has no effective control over local spending to ensure that budgetary spending requirements are being carried out," because "local authorities are able to secure funds from the [local tax] offices before they are passed on to the national administration."[97] This precludes withholding resources from local authorities that do not spend in accordance with budget priorities and fosters build-up of arrears. According to the Budget Code of Ukraine, in the future, the State Treasury would have responsibility for tax receipts and disbursements of all levels of government. The new scheme therefore depends upon the full implementation of the State Treasury system.

Shifting Tax-Sharing Rates

From 1990–2000, regulating revenues were shared between the central government and subnational governments according to tax retention rates, which entitled the regions to retain a proportion of the tax raised on their territory. (The 27 "regions" subject to retention rates included Ukraine's 24 oblasti, the Crimean Autonomous Republic, and the strategically important cities of Kyiv and Sevastopol.) Retention rates were set annually in the Law on State Budget. Oblasts, in their turn, assigned a proportion of their respective tax-sharing rates to their subordinate governments, which did the same for their districts and settlements.

Retention rates varied considerably by type of tax (for example, VAT, personal income tax, enterprise income tax, and excises) and between the regions for each type of tax.[98] Not all taxes were shared each and every year, however, to the great consternation of local governments' fiscal authorities. The rationale offered for the differential oblast retention rates was that it equalized differences in per capita expenditure across Ukraine's regions. However, it is not clear that lower-income oblasts benefited from higher retention rates, or that per capita expenditure levels were significant determinants of an oblast's level of fiscal contribution from the central government.

Budgetary planning was rendered all but impossible at the subnational level by the rather dramatic shifts in retention rates from year to year, especially for the VAT.[99] The VAT and enterprise income tax, which together accounted for between 40–60 percent of total oblast revenues during this period, were subject to the widest variation in retention rates. In fact, from 0–100 percent change per year was possible during 1992–2000. This obviously injected great uncertainty and stress upon the annual budget process at all levels of government and wreaked havoc upon the efforts of oblast and municipal budget officials to pursue a consistent fiscal policy.

Fluctuating Budgetary Transfers to Subordinate Levels

In addition to regulating revenues, the central government provides budgetary transfers, or "subventions," to the regions. In principle, such transfers are intended to promote revenue equalization objectives. The evidence suggests that subventions actually have been increasingly used for this purpose, becoming more selective (that is, targeted) over time. Indeed, since 1994, wealthier regions (especially Donetsk, Dnipropetrovsk, Zaporizhzhia, Kyiv City, and Poltava) either received no subvention or were subject to additional exactions from their budgets to the state budget.[100]

The level and pattern of subventions/exactions changed annually, however, reflecting the level of regulating revenues to be retained by the oblasts in each fiscal year. Effective with the 1994 budget, the central government introduced a system of uniform tax retention rates for all oblasts, supplemented by a more extensive (and generous) set of budgetary subventions, especially to oblasts with relatively narrow tax bases. This short-lived experiment was abandoned the following year, however, in favor of variable retention rates.[101] It has been argued that revenue equalization objectives may be more readily achieved with variable, rather than fixed rates.[102] However, the vast inherent differences between oblasts' natural endowments, industrial development, population, and income result in significant differences in oblast revenue capacities. These differences are of such magnitude that the potential beneficial effects of a derivation-based revenue system is limited, necessitating supplementary transfers from the center to the regions.

In general, as Jorge Martinez-Vazquez, Charles McClure, and Sally Wallace point out, the goal of revenue equalization is "undermined by the lack of objective rules or principles for determining sharing rates and subventions."[103] Absence of such rules had the effect of placing oblast budgets solely at the mercy of political decisions made in Kyiv. Further, as a consequence of the inflation of 1993–95, the falling real value of oblast revenues placed unprecedented fiscal pressures upon subnational governments, which has continued since then (albeit not as sharply).

Increasing Oblast Dependence on Kyiv

The revenue structure of oblasts has fluctuated widely, but the general pattern is clearly one of increasing regional budgetary dependence upon the central government. The degree of oblasts' dependency on state budget transfers and subsidies varied considerably; in the 2001 budget, Crimea was fully independent from Kyiv, while—at the other extreme—Ternopil was 70 percent reliant upon Kyiv for its revenues. This is also reflected in the fluctuating share of consolidated government (central plus subnational) revenues going to subnational governments. Fixed revenues were grossly insufficient to fill the gap left by falling regulating revenues, in that real per capita expenditures fell an average of 12.1 percent per year from 1997–2001. No oblast has been spared a deterioration in real expenditure capacity. The burden has fallen disproportionately on the more heavily industrialized oblasts of eastern Ukraine, particularly Dnipropetrovsk, Kharkiv, Zaporizhzhia, and Donetsk.[104]

This situation placed regional finances in a double bind: Even as the real value of oblasts' share of regulating revenues and budgetary transfers declined, their fiscal dependence on the center increased to more than half (measured as the proportion of oblast revenues constituted by regulating revenues plus budgetary transfers). Competition between Ukraine's regions for fiscal relief from the center became more intense, even as the real value of such relief fell. Further, the progressive redefinition of "fixed" revenues as state "regulating" revenues in 1994–95 meant that even the higher-income oblasts of eastern Ukraine, which were relatively fiscally independent in 1992, by 1995 approached or even exceeded the average for budgetary dependence upon Kyiv. As this would imply, poorer regions such as Ternopil and Rivne had become utterly dependent upon the center by the end of this period.

Other Regional Budgetary Pressures

Regional and municipal governments in the 1990s suffered from many of the same fiscal problems as the central government, some of them caused by the uncertain flow of resources from Kyiv. For instance, budgetary payments arrears as a percent of oblast budgets averaged 19.4 percent as of January 1, 1999, but were spread very unevenly across Ukraine. In the case of these expenditure arrears, there does not seem to be any clear inter-regional pattern from east to west. The magnitude of the payments arrears is therefore likely a function of a region's individual circumstances and its own fiscal relations with Kyiv.

Tax arrears also varied considerably across the regions. In fact, arrears as a proportion of total tax liability to the regions leapt rather dramatically in 1998, after three years of relatively modest increases. Tax offsets were also problematical for the regions, fluctuating between 22–33 percent of total tax revenues from 1996–99. These had been merely 5.2 percent of revenues in 1995. Finally, just as at the national level, the VAT and enterprise income tax have been the main problems. These problems will be resolved only with the advent of comprehensive national tax reform. Unfortunately for the regions, formulation of national tax policy is a matter well outside of their cognizance.

The Movement to "Formula-Based" Fiscal Relations

The 2001 Budget Code of Ukraine opened a new chapter in intergovernmental fiscal relations in Ukraine. The new code supercedes the 1996 Law on Budget System and offers a practical mechanism to implement the principle of fiscal decentralization. The Budget Code is the result of close collaboration among parliament, the cabinet, local government officials, and academic experts. It stipulates specifically, and for the first time, that intergovernmental budget relations shall be based on "budgetary sufficiency standards," which are in principle intended to equalize budget expenditures in different regions. Obviously, equalization of spending on necessary public services in Ukraine's regions is an urgent fiscal reform objective. The Budget Code also envisages a common approach to revenue allocation, one that provides greater predictability of revenue flows, which has been a key objective of local government officials.

The Budget Code has its origins in Articles 140 and 143 of the Ukrainian constitution, and in provisions of the 1997 Law on Local Self-Government. The constitution enjoins district, municipal, and oblast councils to carry out their service provision responsibilities through a mixture of own-source funds, transfers from the state budget, and assignment of general taxes to their budgets. It also provides that any delegated powers be fully funded by the state. Further, expenditure norms are to be developed according to a new approach, based on the relative oblast needs. Funding at the minimum level is to be guaranteed by the state.

The Budget Code enshrines the fiscal separation of oblast, rayon, and municipal budgets, which are to be independent and separately developed. The state budget and oblast budgets are no longer to be connected to the budgets of cities and rayons in any formal sense. Local government units are to have considerable discretion over the use of the budgetary resources at their disposal. However, budgetary discipline at all levels is to be strengthened by servicing budgets (that is, cash receipts and disbursements) through the State Treasury.

In addition to revenues specifically devoted to local budgets, the personal income tax proceeds are assigned solely to local budgets, to be allocated as follows: 100 percent in the case of the cities of Kyiv and Sevastopol; 75 percent to the budgets of cities of oblast or republican subordination (in the case of the Crimean Autonomous Republic); and 25 percent to the budgets of towns, villages, settlements, and smaller communities. Interbudgetary transfers may take the form of equalization grants to assist in carrying out delegated functions, subventions to compensate for revenue losses in fulfilling their own functions (and due to changes in national legislation), targeted subventions for state-mandated social protection programs and investment projects, direct transfers from the state budget for other purposes, and other grants. The most important of these are formula-based equalization grants. The amounts of grants and other transfers will be directly provided for in the state budget, greatly increasing transparency.

Equalization grants are intended to serve the dual purposes of providing sufficient resources for local budgets to fulfill their obligations and equalizing the revenue capacity of local budgets possessing different sized "revenue baskets." Revenue baskets are comprised of the total proceeds raised by a local jurisdiction from the personal income tax, land tax, stamp duties, licenses, trade patents, fees, and other revenues listed in the code. The revenue basket is to be 75 percent allocated to the budgets of cities and rayons, and 25 percent to fund activities of oblast budgets and the budget of the Crimean Autonomous Republic. Rayons are required to return at least 25 percent of the revenue basket collected in each town, village, or settlement to those jurisdictions.

The equalization grant amounts are to be calculated on a formula basis as the product of population and a percentage of the difference between a jurisdiction's per capita expenditure need and its per capita revenue capacity.[105] In general, the formulas that are specified for use are long, cumbersome, difficult to comprehend, and include certain extraneous items pertaining not to all regions but to particular ones.[106] Undoubtedly these formulas will be subject to revision and improvement.

Certain benefits are expected from the changes the Budget Code mandates in intergovernmental fiscal relations:

- Increased certainty of revenue streams, with an accompanying improvement in budgetary planning and execution;
- Enhanced transparency of state and regional budget decision-making;
- More per capita expenditure equity across regions;
- Greater accountability of local governments; and
- Improved incentives for local officials to economize on budget resources and mobilize local revenue capacities.

Conclusion

The revenue and intergovernmental policy challenges facing Ukraine in the 1990s were serious ones, and many of them could have been avoided. The issues described in this chapter are resolvable, however, with enlightened leadership and an appropriate degree of political leverage. The Ukrainian tax system continued to underperform throughout the late 1990s owing to an array of other (that is, nonfiscal) political and economic factors that limited considerably its potential to generate revenue. Among the list of factors are the declining liquidity of enterprises, proliferation of tax privileges, and rise of the shadow sector. The poorly performing revenue system was both a cause and an effect of these other problems. By the end of the decade, it was abundantly clear that tax reform could not be addressed in isolation.

Chapter 7

From Hyperinflation to Stabilization, 1991–96

Ukrainian Monetary Trends

This chapter concerns Ukraine's monetary policy from independence to the currency reform of 1996. Perhaps no other issue concerning the Ukrainian political economy has been more vexing than the country's two-year slide into hyperinflation in late 1993, followed by its long drive toward stabilization by 1996. From 1991–93, Ukraine had the worst inflation record of any former Soviet republic, with average monthly price increases of 33 percent from 1992 to mid-1994, when the long road to monetary stabilization began.[1]

Economist Phillip Cagan defined hyperinflation as general price increases in excess of 50 percent per month. According to this definition, Ukraine has had seven instances of hyperinflation, six of them constituting the entire second half of 1993.[2] The seventh, November 1994, occurred on the verge of Ukraine's drive to stabilization.[3] The early independence period was thus plagued by problems of monetary management, which exacerbated the problems associated with the output decline and issues concerning the necessary industrial restructuring. In a transition economy, this can be very serious, for as economic historian Robert Skidelsky observes, "High inflation redistributes free resources to the very sectors in need of restructuring, and hence delays the recovery of output."[4]

As economic theory would predict, Ukraine's price inflation was accompanied by a rapid expansion of the money supply. Changes in Ukrainian monetary aggregates between 1989–96 are presented in Table 7.1. Ukrainian definitions of money largely correspond to the usual conventions, so that interpretations of "narrow money" (M1), and "broad money" (M2) aggregates are fairly straightforward. The period of greatest expansion was 1992–94, followed by a prolonged and dramatic fall in the rates of monetary growth after the second quarter of 1994. Changes in the rates of money growth are the main concern. Thus, 1994 represents a watershed in the inflationary process, with monetary growth rates consistently falling from the second half of 1994 through year-end 1996. The data indicate that monetary stabilization was achieved, roughly, by mid-1996, permitting the introduction of Ukraine's permanent currency, the hryvnia, in September.

Examination of the fiscal deficit reveals that real revenues and expenditures were remarkably robust in the face of the output collapse, especially during the period of highest price inflation in 1992–93. (See chapter 5 for a more detailed discussion.) This would suggest that political factors played perhaps a more significant role in fiscal policy than economic factors. The consolidated budget results in Table 5.1 indicate that between 1992 and 1996, 45–60 percent of GDP was redistributed annually through the national budget. Further, when extrabudgetary funds and off-budget subsidies to state-owned enterprises and agricultural concerns are included, the percentage climbs to between 51–63 percent. During the same period budgetary revenues, though high, never exceeded 50 percent of GDP. The inevitable results were large and persistent deficits.

There are three ways to finance the fiscal deficit: borrow domestically, borrow externally, and/or inflate the currency (that is, print money). Thus,

$$D = \Delta B + \Delta F + \Delta M$$

where: D = fiscal deficit (including quasifiscal expenditures, extrabudgetary fund balances, and directed credits to state enterprises);
ΔB = change in state domestic debt;
ΔF = change in foreign debt; and,
ΔM = change in money creation.

Ukraine has employed a combination of all three financing devices to cover its fiscal deficits but overwhelmingly resorted to new money creation in 1992–94. From 1992–95, no more than 20 percent of the fiscal deficit was financed from borrowing, either domestically or from abroad. Rather, due to the immaturity of Ukraine's domestic securities market, and its limited capacity to borrow from abroad, monetization of the deficit was vigorously employed.

The persistent fiscal deficit, rapid price increases, and changes in the money supply from 1992–96 raise certain important questions concerning the government's management of the economy: What was the process by which the fiscal deficit resulted in hyperinflation by 1993? What changed in 1994–96 to bring inflation down? What was the magnitude of the "inflation tax" reaped by the government? And who paid it? Was the successful stabilization in 1996 the result of the political will of President Leonid D. Kuchma? Or was the liquidation of Ukraine's inflation the product of the self-limiting dynamics of the inflationary process?

This chapter addresses these and other questions through a review and analysis of the critical developments in Ukraine's monetary history during the young country's first five years. Early developments included efforts to maintain the "ruble zone" in 1991–93; Ukraine's issuing a temporary, transitional currency, the karbovanets, (or "kupon") to alleviate shortages of cash rubles; and the country's eventual exit from the ruble area. Especially important for understanding Ukraine's subsequent inflation, and the plunge into hyperinflation by late 1993, are the government's credit policies and its concomitant efforts to suppress inflation through administrative means. Also examined are the inflation response to credit emissions, the erosion of the "inflation tax base," and the dynamics of stabilization in 1995–96.

The picture that emerges from this examination of Ukraine's inflationary process is of a government groping for the means to maintain a steady flow of credit subsidies to enterprises without imposing the enormous redistributive costs that this inevitably entails. These measures were unable to overcome the irresistible inflationary forces that it had set in motion, forces that progressively narrowed the range of options available to the authorities by year-end 1995. Stabilization had, in effect, become the sole option open to Ukraine in 1996, to the happy relief of Ukraine's citizens, many of whom who had seen their life savings depleted by inflation in 1992. This chapter will conclude that the primary cause of Ukraine's hyperinflation was excessive financing of the fiscal deficit by money creation. It will also conclude that the period of rapid price increase ended only when the government abandoned in 1994–96 its practice of financing deficits through expansionary monetary policy. It further concludes that Ukraine's adoption of a more

Table 7.1
Ukraine--Changes in Monetary Aggregates, 1989-1996
(End of Quarter, Billions of KBV)

Period	Currency in Circulation	Demand Deposits	Time Deposits	Foreign Currency Deposits	M1 (Narrow Money)	% Chg.	M2 (Broad Money)	% Chg.	M3 (M2 plus FCD)	% Chg.
1989	17.2	61.8	34.4	n.a.	79	n.a.	13.4	n.a.	13.4	n.a.
1990	17.4	76.2	37.1	n.a.	93.6	18.5	130.7	15.3	130.7	15.3
1991-4Q	33.8	142.1	87.2	0.1	175.9	n.a.	263.1	n.a.	263.2	n.a.
1992-1Q	60.8	201.4	113.4	0.1	262.2	49.1	375.6	42.7	375.7	59.1
2Q	168.6	443.7	152.7	8.1	612.3	133.5	765	103.7	773.1	105
3Q	343.2	654	206.1	59.6	997.2	62.9	1203.3	50.1	1262.9	56.3
4Q	647.4	1538.8	316.1	183	2186.2	119.2	2502.3	107.9	2685.3	108
1993-1Q	896	2956	710	895	3852	76.2	4562	82.3	5457	118.1
2Q	1710	4790	1377	3325	6500	68.7	7957	74.4	11282	106.7
3Q	5246	17567	3257	4933	22813	250.9	26070	227.6	31003	174.8
4Q	12790	20814	4423	9177	33604	47.3	38027	45.9	47204	52.3

1994-1Q	23615	24391	7479	11282	48006	42.9	55485	45.9	66767	41.4
2Q	34066	43279	16737	14634	77345	61.1	94082	69.6	108716	62.8
3Q	52541	84443	24001	25318	136984	77.1	160985	71.1	186303	71.4
4Q	79104	107030	30272	99059	186134	35.9	216406	34.4	315465	69.3
1995-1Q	113444	112744	41957	125390	226188	21.5	268145	23.9	393535	24.7
2Q	178241	164666	42541	145985	342907	51.6	385448	43.7	531433	35
3Q	223527	196117	44757	174231	419644	22.4	464401	20.5	638632	20.2
4Q	262330	205859	58741	157703	468189	11.6	526930	13.5	684633	7.2
1996-1Q	280007	207411	68798	152402	487418	4.1	556216	5.6	708618	3.5
2Q	332400	203401	71854	144578	535801	9.9	607655	9.2	752233	6.2
3Q	333000	212900	76100	137200	545900	1.9	622000	2.4	759200	0.9
4Q	333020	229348	98780	131118	562368	3	661148	6.3	792266	4.4

Note: Ukrainian definitions of monetary aggregates largely correspond to the usual conventions:

M1 = Currency in Circulation + Demand Deposits

M2 = M1 + Time Deposits

M3 = M2 + Foreign Currency Deposits

Sources: Marcin Luczynski and Volodymyr Husak, "Ukraine in Numbers," *Ukrainian Legal and Economic Bulletin* (October 1996; December 1996; March 1997); Table 8.The data for 1989 and 1990 are from IMF, *Ukraine: Recent Economic Developments* (Washington, D.C.: International Monetary Fund, 1993), Table A21, p. 65

restrictive monetary policy was less the enlightened embrace of responsible policy than the result of a diminishing ability to employ inflationary financing of budget deficits.

The Ukrainian Coupon System, 1992–96

Political independence did not automatically lead to economic sovereignty for Ukraine. Disentangling its trade and monetary policies from those of Russia and the former USSR would prove to be a lengthy process. Difficulties emerged almost immediately in the monetary sphere. Throughout 1992 the Soviet ruble continued to circulate in Ukraine. Problems coordinating monetary policy with Russia manifested themselves in the form of acute goods shortages, propelling Ukraine in June 1991 to issue rationing scrip to its residents. These multi-use "coupons" circulated as a parallel currency to the old USSR ruble. The USSR's Gosbank (not yet renamed but in 1992 firmly under control of the Russian Federation's monetary policy) proved unable to supply sufficient quantities of banknotes to ruble zone states in order to meet their current needs, including wage payments. Even more acute shortages of banknotes were projected for 1992 and beyond. Especially troublesome to the authorities was the substantial diversion of Ukrainian goods to Russia, purchased with her more ample supply of rubles but with little prospect of Russian imports due to serious shortages of goods, both in that country and in other former Soviet republics.

The shortage of banknotes was resolved on January 8, 1992, through the introduction of a noncash counterpart to the ruble, the karbovanets. Under the new currency regime, the karbovanets (KBV) would be legal tender for use in all state stores; the still-circulating ruble would be confined to the payment of rents, communal services (that is, household utilities), public transport, certain other services, and purchase of goods in the "private economy." Karbovantsi, popularly known simply as kupons, were issued in the form of wages to workers in state enterprises, pension recipients and those on the government payroll. Both residents and nonresidents of Ukraine would be able to purchase kupons in exchange for hard currency at a face value of one ruble per coupon. Introduction of the kupon solved the currency availability problem.

The shortage of goods problem required more bitter medicine, however. The root cause of the goods shortage was the prevalence of price controls in Russia and other former Soviet republics. Chronic shortages and long lines at state stores were the inevitable result. Only freely floating prices would overcome these problems. Therefore, both Russia and Ukraine took appropriate steps in January 1992 to liberalize prices broadly.[5] But by signaling in late 1991 its intention to raise prices early in the next year, Ukraine unfortunately precipitated a rash of "panic buying," so much so that in December 1991, many state stores had no bread, milk, eggs, or other staple products for sale.[6] Monthly price inflation in January 1992 topped out at 435 percent; however, the late 1991 anticipatory purchases apparently overshot free market prices, as evidenced by a fall in prices in February (-6 percent) and March (-3 percent). But relative price stability in *kolkhoz* markets was to prevail only until July 1992.

The National Bank of Ukraine (NBU) originally intended to limit the issue of kupons to levels required to cover retail purchases and continue to use rubles for wholesale trade and interenterprise payments. However, the first issue paid workers around only 25 percent of their monthly wages in kupons; the balance was paid in rubles. A concern raised by the IMF at the time was that, because workers would spend a significantly greater proportion than 25 percent of their incomes in state stores, rubles would be diverted into the private market, driving up prices there and depressing even further an already weak state retail sector.[7] In order to purchase necessary goods in state stores, households sought to increase their holdings of kupons by turning to the black market, where street rates for karbovanets rose to levels well in excess of their face value.[8]

A related issue raised by the IMF was the possibility of trade distortions with other former Soviet republics, as excess goods were attracted to Ukrainian markets by the higher ruble prices that would prevail there. Ukraine's CIS trading partners would object to the situation on grounds that their reciprocal access to Ukrainian goods was artificially constrained by Ukraine's inability to convert rubles to kupons. The possibility that other republics would erect trade barriers to Ukrainian goods, to the detriment of all of the countries concerned, appeared imminent. To avoid this outcome, the IMF recommended much broader conversion possibilities for kupons, rubles, and hard currency. Ultimately, the IMF argued for full monetary autonomy for Ukraine, including introduction of the new national currency, the hryvnia.[9] Achieving monetary independence would take place in November 1992. But introduction of the hryvnia would take until September 1996.

The Ruble Zone, 1991–93: A Temporary Expedient

Collapse of the Soviet Union by year-end 1991 resulted in a massive disruption of trade between the former Soviet republics.[10] International lending institutions initially encouraged NIS states to cooperate in a single currency area due to uncertainty over the costs of breakup of the Soviet economic space, as well as fears that the new states would pursue even more expansionary monetary policies than Russia's.[11] Apparently, Russia was against the idea of a common currency area from the start, due to the vague means by which policy decisions were to be rendered. Russian economist Petr Aven observed that, "under IMF pressure, the Russian government kept the ruble zone alive," but that, "from the beginning of 1992, [Russia] never wanted to keep alive the fuzzy decision-making ruble zone."[12] Simply put, it was extraordinarily difficult to coordinate the monetary policies of the ten participating countries. Until its complete demise in July 1993, the ruble area consisted of ten FSU republics, including (in addition to Russia herself): the Baltic republics, Kyrgyzstan, Azerbaijan, Belarus, Georgia, Moldova, and Ukraine.

As early as 1991, economists Oleh Havrylyshyn and John Williamson warned that the ruble zone arrangement would provide member governments with "irresistible inflationary incentives," which would work to the disadvantage of the Central Bank of Russia (CBR).[13] As a consequence, Russian monetary policy initially was quite restrictive in nature, even going as far as to limit deliveries of cash rubles.[14] However, several republics responded by introducing parallel currencies, or coupons, with which to augment or replace the harder to obtain rubles. Under CBR Governor Viktor Gerashchenko,[15] Russia in the second half of 1992 reverted to a policy of promoting industrial production through a rapid expansion of credits.[16] It was apparent that the Russian monetary authorities now viewed unemployment as a more serious problem than inflation.

By July 1992 it was becoming clear that Ukraine was unable to control its inflationary appetite. In the first half of 1992, budget deficits were rather modest compared to what would follow. From July 1992 onward, deficits assumed more serious proportions, rising dramatically through the end of the year. With the "monetary borders" open, there was no effective limit to the level of inflationary finance available to Ukrainian authorities. Similar opportunities existed for other ruble zone states. Under the arrangements of the ruble zone, a participating republic could run deficits in its current trade account financed, to one extent or another, via the export of its own inflation to other republics. Provided that the others did not reciprocate, an individual republic could inflict serious monetary "pain" upon the others. What is clear, however, is that the entire ruble zone could not escape the inflationary consequences of its members' profligate ways. In an important sense, then, the collapse of the zone as it then existed was inevitable.

With such expansionary country policies, participating states suffered acute "cash shortages" in the first six months of 1992. In the third quarter of 1992, Russia partially alleviated the situation by printing larger denomination notes. In Russia, a growing proportion of currency in circulation consisted of 10,000-ruble banknotes printed only in 1992, while the CBR supplied other former Soviet republics with bills issued prior to 1992, having denominations of less than 10,000 rubles. The demand for rubles was thus only partially met, resulting in sharp increases in money demand in the second half of 1992.[17] In order to free up rubles to pay for Russian imports, several countries introduced their own national coupons, including Latvia, Lithuania, Belarus, Moldova, and Ukraine.

In the fourth quarter of 1992, the CBR under Governor Gerashchenko issued currency on a largely unrestricted basis to ruble zone states. In early 1993, these states were rapidly approaching their negotiated 1993 credit limits, whereupon the CBR would apply payment restraints to their unfunded transactions. As a consequence of fears that a severe disruption in interstate trade and payments would result, on June 30, 1993, the Supreme Soviet of Russia decreed that the CBR should quote exchange rates for noncash (that is, bookkeeping) rubles. Thus, a dual exchange rate system was born.

Further, in the so-called "demonetization" of 1993, on July 24, the CBR announced a package of measures that eliminated as legal tender in Russia all pre-1993 ruble notes having denominations of less than 10,000 rubles. Effective July 26, this had the effect of isolating the cash component of Russia's own money supply from that in other ruble zone states. The other states would be free to participate in a new monetary union (pending negotiations), but with strict limits on financing and state credits. Under the conversion rules to "new rubles," Russian citizens were permitted two weeks in which to convert up to 35,000 rubles into "new rubles," with the balance of "old rubles" deposited in savings accounts to be frozen for six months. Noncitizens were permitted to convert only 15,000 old rubles.

On July 26, Russian President Boris Yeltsin eased somewhat the terms of conversion by issuing a decree permitting up to 100,000 rubles to be converted by citizens through August 31. He also decreed the unlimited conversion of 1992 10,000-ruble notes, and that smaller denominations of "old rubles" would continue to circulate freely until the end of that month, in order to permit smaller-value transactions. As the end of August approached, CBR extended the period for converting smaller notes again, for 10-ruble notes and smaller, until December 31, 1993. Yeltsin's decree frustrated CBR's attempt to employ the conversion process to squeeze some of the inflationary pressures out of the Russian economy. It also had the politically popular effect of significantly curtailing CBR's opportunities to benefit from what otherwise amounted to a partial currency confiscation. Citizens of other ruble zone states would not fare nearly as well. However, Ukrainians with banking connections in Russia would have been able to take advantage of Yeltsin's more favorable conversion terms by sending their old rubles to Russia.

At the time of the July 1993 Russian currency reforms, many former Soviet states were unable to decide whether to exit the ruble zone. Technical problems, lack of a viable domestic currency alternative, and absence of the necessary domestic consensus to introduce strong stabilization policies were all reasons for their indecision. Additionally, some energy-dependent states were concerned that exiting the ruble area would reduce access to Russian-subsidized energy imports.[18] A "framework agreement" provided for an interim period in which signatory states would continue to use their own currencies, as well as "old rubles," while a timetable was worked out for a shift to "new rubles." Under such a monetary union, exchange rates would be maintained at stable levels by coordinating domestic monetary and fiscal policies. As a practical matter, this would mean that each member state would cede a degree of economic sovereignty to Russia. Divergent domestic policy interests, including the imperative of each state's consolidating its independence, effectively prohibited most participants from unifying their currency regimes, however appealing the notion of an economic union with Russia may have appeared at the time. For states leaving the ruble zone, each committed itself to repatriating their ruble holdings or crediting the amount as a liability owed to Russia. Ukraine's liabilities at year-end 1993 totaled some $2.5 billion.[19]

After the Russian demonetization, monetary policy coordination in the ruble zone proved as elusive as ever. In the absence of mechanisms to ensure coordinated fiscal and monetary policy, including the sharing of seigniorage by participating states, maintaining the zone would prove difficult. When Russia refused to accept non-Russian rubles for the settlement of debts by other republics, the ruble zone collapsed in ignominious death. In October 1992, Russia forbade the sale of oil to Ukraine in exchange for rubles. On November 12, Ukraine formally exited the ruble area to pursue its own inflationary policies.

Could the ruble zone have been reformed enough to preserve it? Economists Jeffrey Sachs and David Lipton suggested that an appropriate mechanism for coordination could have been worked out, whereby ruble zone central banks collectively negotiated the rate of monetary expansion, subject to rules for allocating the inflation tax among the member republics.[20] Such a mechanism would result in a republic bearing at least a proportionate share of its own monetary expansion, thereby reducing incentives to "cheat" on its neighbors. Further, any republic that was unwilling to remain in the zone on such terms would be free to leave, subject to buyback of its outstanding rubles with its own new currency. In principle, this scheme may have stood a good chance of succeeding. But no serious attempt to bring monetary policy under control within the ruble area was ever made.

Ukraine Leaves the Ruble Zone

Ukraine initially issued rationing coupons in June 1991, further expanding their use in January 1992. In November 1992, the Ukrainian kupon, circulating as a parallel currency to the ruble, was designated as a "transitional" national currency, pending introduction of the permanent currency, the hryvnia. On November 7, 1992, President Leonid Kravchuk issued a decree removing the ruble as legal tender for all monetary transactions, at 11:00 P.M. on November 12, 1992.[21] The official exchange rate of 1:1 would remain in force until November 16, when the NBU established a new rate of 1 ruble per 1.454 kupons. Thereafter, exchange of rubles and kupons was to be governed by the market, with different ruble-to-kupon rates for each CIS country established, due to differences in the purchasing power of rubles in each country (largely a consequence of CBR's currency regulations).

In order to implement the president's decree, the Cabinet of Ministers on November 8, 1992, adopted a resolution subjecting all economic subjects to its provisions.[22] At a press conference on November 13, Viktor M. Pynzenyk, deputy prime minister and minister of the economy, outlined additional measures, including reparations for payments to Russian enterprises that had been frozen by the CBR and the National Bank of Ukraine.[23] NBU governor Vadim Hetman estimated the total amount of such suspended payments outstanding in mid-November to be approximately 400 billion rubles, which were to be converted at a ratio of 1:1 and repaid at market rates. This amounted to a little less than $1 billion. Further, NBU would establish terms for removing the ruble from circulation and reestimating assets and liabilities of state enterprises, registered organizations, banks, and the public (including nonresidents).

The official rationale for Ukraine's exit from the ruble area was to "normalize trade with Russia and end the payments crisis that threatened to shut down Ukrainian industry."[24] Pursuant to Russian trade "normalization," NBU cleared only bills for payment for imports by state enterprises under guarantee of the Cabinet of Ministers, including oil and oil products, natural gas, and timber. Enterprises would have to pay for all other imports out of their own foreign currency earnings. Of primary concern was repatriation of payments previously made for Russian goods. In reaction to Ukraine's action, Russia suspended its freeze on Ukrainian enterprises' accounts on its territory and extended credits worth 75 billion rubles to Ukraine, primarily for fuel purchases.

Ukraine's withdrawal from the ruble zone was generally orderly and smooth.[25] Like other participants exiting the zone, Ukraine agreed to repatriate its rubles, but this was delayed inadvertently, due to an anticipated devaluation of the karbovanets against the ruble. Existing bank balances were converted from noncash rubles to noncash kupons at a ratio of 1:1. New transactions would be subject to the official rate of 1.454 kupons per ruble, with the apparent intention of reducing or eliminating the current account deficit with Russia. Thus, the monetary reform contained a significant element of devaluation.

Further, although Ukrainian banks would be free to set exchange rates between the kupon and the ruble, this was subject to a requirement that the bank rates not deviate from the official NBU rate by more than 3 percent. Almost immediately, the semifixed rate began to diverge sharply from the black market rate, falling to 1.6 kupon per ruble within a mere ten days' time. (This implicitly translates to a further devaluation of 10 percent.) Restricted access to rubles in coming months would lead to even more serious gaps between the official and black market rates. In response to such developments, confidence in the kupon deteriorated sharply. Initially introduced at par with the ruble, and selling for 425 per U.S. dollar, the karbovanets fell precipitously throughout 1993, reaching its low ebb in December at KBV 23 per ruble, and KBV 26,900 per dollar.

The partial monetary reform of November 1992 accomplished the purpose of enabling purchases of oil from Russia, but little else. In retrospect, it removed from Ukraine an important anchor of stability in the economic sphere, albeit an imperfect one. Full monetary independence—a goal supported by the IMF—actually made inflation more probable through the unrestricted emission of credits.[26] As to prospects for introduction of the hryvnia, Deputy Prime Minister Viktor Pynzenyk and new NBU governor Viktor Yushchenko[27] both stated, sensibly, that the inflation rate would have to be brought down to the level of a few percent per month before monetary reform could take place. Apparently unaware of the inflationary process that had been set in motion throughout 1992, in December Pynzenyk would boldly predict a monthly inflation rate of 3 percent by the end of 1993. In fact, by the end of 1993, Ukraine would experience six months of hyperinflation, with a one-month increase of 90.8 percent in December alone.[28] Concerning the demise of the ruble area, Havrylyshyn, Miller, and Perraudin observe that "it is striking that exit from the ruble zone did not remove the inflationary bias in government policy for most former Soviet Union republics."[29] Ukraine, in particular.

Credit Emissions and the Inflation Response

It will be demonstrated that the root cause of the inflation of 1992–95 was a policy of emitting currency in the form of budgetary and off-budget credit subsidies to state-owned enterprises and agricultural concerns. During this period, Ukrainian economic policy emphasized loose and cheap credit to enterprises, coupled with the interposition of administrative controls to reduce or suppress the inevitable inflationary pressures. Emission of cheap credits to industrial enterprises and agricultural concerns is frequently identified as the root cause of Ukraine's slip into hyperinflation in 1993.[30] In 1992, off-budget subsidies and directed credits to industrial and agricultural enterprises amounted to some 16 percent of GDP. In 1993 and 1994, the central government continued to mandate that the financial sector extend huge amounts of nearly interest-free credits to enterprises. Here we examine the extent to which such credits drove the general increase in prices and increases in the money supply.

First, we examine the effects of credit emission on the growth rate of the consumer price index (CPI). The quarterly exponential growth rate in the CPI index was regressed over that for broad money (M2), net banking system credits to state-owned enterprises, NBU and commercial bank credits to the government, and an index of energy price growth, which was derived from residential electricity price data from December 1991 to the end of 1996.[31] (Other models were tested that included growth in net domestic credit and net domestic assets, but these variables were found to have no statistically significant effects on the CPI or M2 growth.) The energy price growth index was included in these, and in subsequent models, on the basis that it is reasonable to expect that at least a portion of Ukraine's general price rise over 1991–96 may be attributed to the general tendency for prices in transition economies to rise to world market levels. In fact, such energy price adjustments were dramatic during this period.

Table 7.2 presents the results of three models, one of which includes all four independent variables; the other two selectively exclude credits to government and the energy price index in order to more clearly discern their effects. It turns out that the growth of enterprise credits is a significant and powerful determinant of the rate of change in the CPI. In fact, growth of broad money (M2) is completely overshadowed by growth in enterprise credits, signifying the greater significance of credit emissions in the inflation transmission process.[32] We may infer from these results that the main factor aggravating inflation in Ukraine has been the large quantities of cheap credits extended to the enterprise sector, including agriculture. These results are consistent with earlier tests by Olexander Babanin, who examined the more limited period from the first quarter of 1992 to the second quarter of 1993, finding that enterprise credits were the prime cause of the 1992–93 price surge.[33]

A refinement of this analysis examines the possibility of a lag in the effect of monetary growth on inflation rates in the presence of enterprise credits. Lags in the inflation response may be due to such factors as the adaptation of the public's inflationary expectation, payment lags, and informational frictions that prevent instantaneous responses to price information by firms and households. Such lags have been observed in the case of several former Soviet and eastern European republics. Economist Brigitte Granville determined in the case of Russia that the period of monetary transmission was approximately four

Table 7.2
Ukraine: Effects of Enterprise Credits and Money Growth on Inflation
Quarterly Data, 1992-1996
[Dependent Variable = CPI Growth Rate]

Independent Variables	Regression Coefficients		
	Version 1	Version 2	Full Model
M2 Growth Rate	-.465	-.461	-.472
	(-.973)	(-.776)	(-.858)
Enterprise Credits Growth Rate	.853	1.009	.837
	(2.413)*	(2.656)*	(2.294)*
Government Credits Growth Rate		.084	.0050
		(.518)	(.032)
Energy Price Index Growth Rate	.381		.379
	(1.975)		(1.819)
Constant	16.048	25.812	15.969
R-square	.536	.418	.536
F-statistic	5.385	3.346	3.751
(*F* Significance Level)	(.011)*	(.050)*	(.031)*
Durbin-Watson	1.826	1.686	1.826

Notes: [1] * Significant at .05 level. (*t*-ratios in parentheses.)
[2] Sample Period: 1Q:92 - 2Q:96.
[3] Growth rates are quarterly exponential growth rates.
[4] The variables Changes in Net Domestic Assets, Net Domestic Credits and Changes in Currency in Circulation were not found to have an effect.

months.[34] French economist Georgés de Ménil estimated that the relationship between monetary emission and inflation in Ukraine in 1992–93 followed approximately a three-month lag.[35] American econo mist Jack Strauss found that it took up to six months to complete price adjustments in response to Kyiv's monetary emissions, but with diminishing effects after 2 months had elapsed.[36]

In order to test for the existence of lagged effects in monetary transmission, a model was tested that employed quarterly exponential M2 growth lagged 0 months, 1 month, and 2 months, together with the growth rate of credits to enterprises and the energy price index growth rate. (Models were also tested with M2 quarterly exponential growth rates lagged 3, 4, and 5 months, but no statistically significant influence on inflation was present.) Results of the lagged M2 growth model were as follows:

$$
\begin{aligned}
GCPI = \underset{(-.160)}{-2.995} - \underset{(-.317)}{.367GM2} - \underset{(-.872)}{1.063GM2LAG1} + \underset{(2.205)}{1.560GM2LAG2} + \\
\underset{(2.352)}{.748GSOE} + \underset{(1.890)}{.334GENERGY}
\end{aligned}
$$

(t-statistics in parentheses)

$R^2 = .673$
F = 4.932 (.011 significance level)
Durbin-Watson = 1.564
Sample period: 4Q:1991 to 3Q:1996.
Durbin's h = (not defined)

Where: GCPI = growth rate of CPI index;
GM2 = M2 growth rate;
GM2LAG1 = M2 growth rate lagged one month;
GM2LAG2 = M2 growth rate lagged two months;
GSOE = growth rate of state enterprise credits; and
GENERGY = growth rate of energy price index.

In this case, the CPI rises with positive changes in both cheap credits to enterprises and a two-month "transmission belt" lag in monetary expansion. While the estimated regression coefficient for the two-month lagged M2 growth variable is substantially larger than that for enterprise credits, it is best to keep in mind that these two really amount to the same thing: for it is well known that the NBU during this period routinely covered (that is, monetized) deficiencies in commercial bank accounts resulting from the parliamentary-mandated extension of credits to enterprises. (Hence: the collinearity in this model was to be expected.)

Consistent with these findings, Strauss found that in Ukraine, the price response to increases in the money supply takes a total of six months to run its course, with the bulk of the resulting increase in the price level coming within the first three months.[37] He also found that the period of greatest price adjustment occurred in the second month following monetary emission. Using data from January 1992 through December 1994, Strauss's model explains over 95 percent of the long-run price level rise as a consequence of monetary changes, primarily arising from credit emissions. Further, the effects of inflation were temporary, insofar as new credit issues dissipate after six months, having no permanent effect on inflation. Both Strauss's results and the present analysis suggest strongly that there has been no "inflationary inertia" in the Ukrainian economy. It was the continuing injection of cheap, nearly zero-interest credits to industry that propelled increases in the CPI; the lagged effects have only given the appearance of momentum. Contrary to the arguments of some Ukrainian officials, there is no evidence that any such inflationary momentum exists in Ukraine.

If inflation truly had no inertia in Ukraine, then we would expect that the rise in the CPI would have no effect on monetary growth rates. Strauss employed a Granger Causality Test to determine the statistical likelihood that money growth caused inflation, and not vice versa.[38] He found that the growth of NBU credits was the primary determinant in the expansion of M2, and not the other way around. To verify Strauss's finding, both M2 and M3 growth rates were regressed over quarterly growth in the CPI Index, enterprise credits, net banking system credits to the government, and the energy price growth index.[39] The results in Table 7.3 indicate that CPI growth is not a statistically significant determinant of money supply growth. Rather, the growth rate in credits to enterprises is the main determinant of money supply growth. Inflation truly had no "echo" in Ukraine. A further test examines the rate of growth in broad money (M2) as a function of enterprise and government credits, and real GDP growth, lagged one quarter. The results are presented in Table 7.4. Again, the price rise is not a significant determinant of money growth; neither is the rate of change in real GDP (that is, its rapid decline). Falling output cannot account for the increase in prices. Rather, enterprise credits remain a robust and significant determinant of money growth.

Seigniorage and the Inflation Tax

In order to understand what compelled Ukraine to abandon its policy of inflationary financing of budget deficits, we must examine the extent to which the government benefited from inflation. John Maynard Keynes wrote in 1923 of the insidious ability of governments to raise revenues by inflating their currencies. In an oft-cited passage, Keynes wrote about a country's ability to "live for a long time . . . by printing paper money"; indeed, it can "live by this means when it can live by no other."[40] Ukraine, in the absence of a modern system of taxation, and lacking the administrative capacity to collect taxes in any case, possessed few options to finance its generous enterprise credits and still quite extensive social benefits other than to print money.[41]

The government's advantage in this regard derives from its exclusive right to issue new money. This maneuver involves nothing short of deceiving citizens as to the value of its money holdings, expropriating the difference between the currency's perceived worth and its real value. The purchasing power that the government obtains by issuing new money is termed *seigniorage*. The reduction in value of existing money due to the issuance of new money is the *inflation tax*. The sum of the inflation tax and seigniorage is equal to the real (that is, inflation-adjusted) change in monetary holdings, or *real balances*. The relationship between them is:

Table 7.3
Ukraine: Test for Effects of Inflation Growth on Money Growth
(Quarterly Data, 1992-1996)

Independent Variables	Dependent Variable Regression Coefficients: M2 Growth Rate	M3 Growth Rate
CPI Index Growth Rate	-.114	.023
	(-.858)	(.167)
Enterprise Credits Growth Rate	.499	.436
	(3.111)**	(2.578)**
Government Credits Growth Rate	.118	.098
	(1.699)	(1.343)
Energy Price Index Growth Rate	.047	-.016
	(.414)	(-.132)
Constant	13.278	15.035
R-square	.618	.568
F-statistic	5.266	4.269
(*F* Significance Level)	(.010)**	(.020)**
Durbin-Watson	1.370	1.081

Notes: [1] ** Significant at .01 level. (*t*-ratios in parentheses.)
[2] Sample Period: 1Q:92 - 2Q:96.
[3] Growth rates are quarterly exponential growth rates.
[4] The low Durbin-Watson statistics here suggest the presence of positive serial correlation; however, a Lagrangian multiplier test of residual serial correlation does not indicate the presence of serial correlation at the .05 level.

$$\Delta\text{Real Balances} = \text{Seigniorage} + \text{Inflation Tax}$$

The Ukrainian government benefited extensively from its inflationary policies, especially in the period from 1992–94. Appendix Table 7.1 provides computations of real balances, monetary velocity, seigniorage, and the inflation tax for the five-year period from 4Q:1991–4Q:1996. From late 1991 through mid-1994, the government derived a significant amount of revenue from its monopoly in supplying base money.[42] In fact, during this period, the government's command over economic resources reached magnificent proportions, in some periods exceeding 100 percent of quarterly GDP. This obviously means that the government not only confiscated vast amounts of the social product (that is, output) but effectively liquidated a portion of net wealth as well (that is, enterprise capital). The numbers are simply staggering.

Starting in the first quarter of 1995, both seigniorage and the inflation tax declined precipitously, however. There is broad agreement that the reduction of Ukraine's inflation in 1995–96 is largely attributable to the adoption of an IMF-sponsored program of fiscal reform that was initiated in the third quarter of 1994. The question is whether the government voluntarily adopted a policy of fiscal restraint to reduce

Table 7.4
Ukraine: Determinants of M2 Growth
(Quarterly Data, 1992-1996)

Independent Variables	Regression Coefficients: Lagged CPI Growth	Lagged CPI and Real GDP	Lagged Real GDP
Enterprise Credits Growth Rate	.708 (6.680)**	.680 (5.849)**	.702 (5.542)**
Government Credits Growth Rate	-.019 (-.315)	.0014 (.021)	.020 (.335)
Real GDP Growth Rate	.252 (1.641)		
Real GDP Growth Rate, Lagged One Quarter		-.061 (-.304)	-.139 (-1.705)
CPI Index Growth Rate			-.051 (-.530)
CPI Index Growth Rate, Lagged One Quarter	.129 (1.526)	-.082 (-.561)	
Energy Price Index Growth Rate	.067 (.989)	.058 (.771)	.082 (1.000)
Constant	5.018	5.468	8.395
R-square	.867	.836	.835
F-statistic	14.345	11.203	11.163
(*F* Significance Level)	(.000)**	(.001)**	(.001)**
Durbin-Watson	2.263	2.590	2.405
Durbin-h statistics	CPI: -.5789	CPI: -1.4709 GDP: -2.1502	GDP: -.9860

Notes: [1] ** Significant at .01 level. (*t*-ratios in parentheses.)
[2] Growth rates are quarterly exponential growth rates.
[3] Sample Period: 1Q:92 - 2Q:96.

inflation or if it faced a rapidly declining ability to engage in inflationary finance. The answer to this question turns on the apparent erosion of the "inflation tax base" in 1995–96. The inflation tax base basically represents the potential to raise revenues through inflation. We adopt here the conceptually straightforward definition of the inflation tax base as real money holdings as a percent of GDP. The decline in inflation tax yields after 1994 indicates that Ukraine's appetite for inflation exceeded at some point the maximum potential yield from the inflation tax. Visual inspection of Appendix Table 7.1 reveals that this stage probably was reached in the second quarter of 1993, reducing drastically the demand for money and shrinking the inflation tax base sufficiently enough to set the stage for hyperinflation to break out by the end of that year. Examination of the process by which this occurred provides a picture of the government's rapidly narrowing set of policy options from 1994–96.

It is a widely understood feature of the inflation tax that it will rise with inflation up to a certain point, beyond which it actually can decrease.[43] This occurs when inflation rises to the point that the demand for money falls. This point is reached, for instance, when people place large proportions of their wealth into hard currencies (that is, a "dollarization" of the economy occurs), or when cash incomes are rapidly converted into real goods, through hoarding critically needed goods for self-consumption or for trading at a later date (perhaps through barter, in order to avoid cash transactions altogether). To one extent or another, Ukraine provided evidence of such karbovanets-avoiding behavior throughout the early 1990s.

The flight from money—effectively a reduction in demand for money balances—reduces the inflation tax base, which necessitates increasingly large monetary emissions in order to reap an equivalent amount of inflation tax revenue. Falling real balances would then require larger infusions of cash and higher inflation levels for the government to finance the same level of fiscal deficits. This could precipitate an "upwards spiral," as the inflation tax rises even as the tax base falls, and the effect becomes its own cause, in the monetary equivalent of the dog who chased his own tail. Hyperinflation can be the result; should the public become convinced that the government is incapable of bringing inflation under control, then M. A. Roberts has argued that a complete collapse of the currency can take place instantly.[44] Even in circumstances that fall short of hyperinflation, however, at a certain point, the revenue-producing potential of the inflation tax base may be exceeded, and incremental amounts of new inflation will produce incrementally less inflation tax revenue.[45]

Beyond a certain point, as real balances fall, the tradeoff between marginal amounts of inflation and inflation tax revenue becomes increasingly unfavorable to the government. The precise point at which this occurs depends on the semi-elasticity of real balances to changes in inflation.[46] On the basis of a limited number of quarterly observations, Havrylyshyn, et al. took a "first cut" at the semi-elasticity, estimating it at around 3 months, implying a maximum sustainable inflation rate of 33 percent per month at a maximum seigniorage tax yield of 12 percent of GDP.[47] Cheikbossian estimated the maximum yield at 21 percent of GDP, on the basis of monthly data from February 1992–March 1994.[48] De Ménil employed data not previously available to the others to estimate the maximum sustainable rate of inflation at the enormous level of 100 percent per month, and the maximum seigniorage yield to be 37 percent.[49] Despite divergencies in these estimates, it appears that the threshold of sustainability probably was passed in Ukraine in the third quarter of 1993, lasting for a period of at least six months. This tracks closely with trends observable in the last two columns of Appendix Table 7.1.

Consistent with earlier findings, the present analysis reveals that the functional relationship between real balances and the inflation tax assumed a nonlinear form, involving a change of sign from positive to negative at some critical level of inflation.[50] Graph 7.1 depicts the nonlinear relationship between M2 inflation tax and real broad money balances. It is estimated that the inflation tax yield peaked in 1992–93, falling steadily throughout 1993 and into 1994. It remained relatively stable in the 1–7 percent range from mid-1995 to the end of 1996. From the graph, we can discern that the inflation tax exceeded its maximum yield after mid-1993, never again providing as fruitful a basis for the government's obvious preference for inflationary finance.

It is clear that the inflation tax in 1992–96 was a nonlinear function of the demand for real balances. Using these results, it can be estimated that the turning point in the inflation tax yield was reached at approximately 125 percent of GDP, which was surpassed in the second half of 1993. At the time, this corresponded to a quarterly inflation rate of between 100–110 percent. We may infer from these results that the government's policy options narrowed considerably after 1994, steadily reducing inflation as an option to finance the fiscal deficit.

Who Paid the Inflation Tax?

There is a presumption in the literature that, in transition economies, state ownership of industrial enterprises will thrust the burden of inflationary finance onto households. For instance, Havrylyshyn, et al., and de Ménil both argue that households in Ukraine paid *all* of the inflation tax, because, argues de Ménil, "the seigniorage collected from banks and nonfinancial enterprises is offset by a corresponding reduction in the real profits accruing to the state."[51] Havrylyshyn and his collaborators are more blunt, writing that, "the government sector broadly defined clearly cannot finance its overall deficit by taxing itself!"[52] There is nothing wrong with this view, on a priori grounds. However, there is nothing to prevent the state from denuding enterprises of their cash or partially liquidating enterprise fixed assets. In fact, during 1992–94, the government was criticized repeatedly for attempting to revalue enterprise assets, with the intention of transferring the difference between the new and old appraisals to the state

Graph 7.1

Relationship of M2 Inflation Tax to Real Broad Money Balances

(1Q:1992 – 4Q:1996, Inclusive)

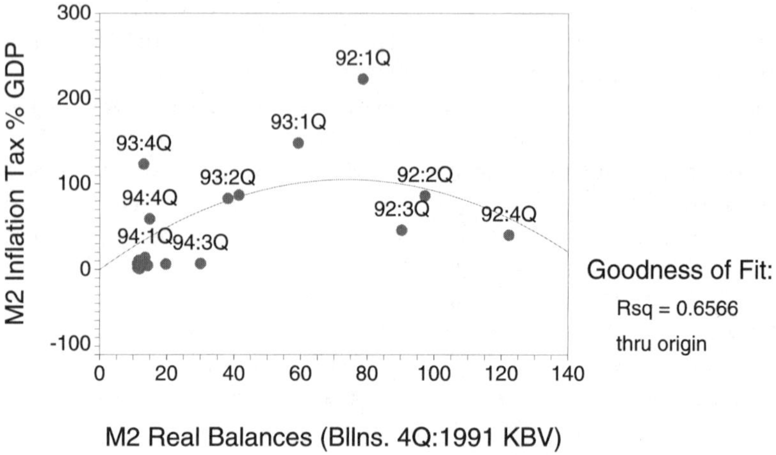

budget.[53] This indicates a willingness on the part of the government to "spend down" enterprises' net worth that is largely not reflected in the literature on the subject.

Segregating M2 into its household and enterprise components is instructive. (Here I have attributed currency in circulation to households, a not unreasonable assumption, given Ukraine's still quite rigid financial sector[54]). Although cash holdings accounted for an increasing share of household financial assets from 1992–94, throughout 1993 the household share of broad money (M2) grew from just 30 percent to only around 50 percent, the balance being held in the form of enterprise deposits in banks.[55] From Appendix Tables 7.2 and 7.3, it can be observed that, while households paid most of the inflation tax (as a percent of GDP) in some quarterly periods, in others enterprises accounted for the preponderance of the inflation tax paid. It seems doubtful that household assets were sufficient throughout this period to finance such magnitudes of inflation; the numbers are simply too large.

Analysis of the relationship of real monetary holdings to the inflation tax paid, respectively, by enterprises and households reveals two very different processes at work in the two sectors. The quadratic relationship that characterized the M2 inflation tax also pertains to the enterprise sector. Graph 7.2, however, reveals a downward-sloping curve for households (reading from right-to-left), with a very rapid decline after 1992. The functional form clearly is different, having a mildly curvilinear shape, but not the "Laffer Curve" shape that one observes in the case of broad money. Erosion of the inflation tax base therefore occurred earlier for households than it did for enterprises.

Such anomalous findings raise questions concerning the extent to which nominally state-owned enterprises are able to exert influence upon government economic policy, either directly or through their respective sectoral lobbies. The literature on enterprise governance and privatization in former Soviet republics maintains that, in the late perestroika and early post-Soviet periods, many enterprises have been run by their directors for the benefit of themselves, their workers, and their political patrons.[56] Directors can, and often do, behave more as de facto owners rather than merely as the state's custodians. Not all enterprises, or even industrial sectors, possessed (then or now) equal access to key government policymakers.[57] Further, many of the most privileged sectors simply did not manufacture for the domestic retail sector, so that their influence on general price changes must have been of an only indirect nature.

Sectoral differences can also be observed for seigniorage. Household seigniorage remained relatively flat during this five year period, gradually falling to nearly zero by early 1995. Enterprise seigniorage, on the other hand, tracks much more closely with total M2-calculated seigniorage, spiking in mid-1993 but falling precipitously later that year as inflation began to consistently exceed the maximum sustainable level. It appears that, with inflation in 1992 having thoroughly depleted the household inflation tax base, the ill effects of inflationary finance fell almost entirely onto the enterprise sector. Thus did the state's appetite for monetary expansion force it to begin "eating its own children." The government's opportunities to play this game after mid-1995 were severely curtailed, however, as enterprises accumulated ever-larger amounts of foreign currency, a development that also contributed significantly to the accelerating velocity of money in the enterprise sector in 1994–95. Such a pattern flies in the face of the conventional view that households pay the entire inflation tax.

Graph 7.2

Relationship of Household Inflation Tax to Household Real Balances

(1Q:1992 – 4Q:1996, Inclusive)

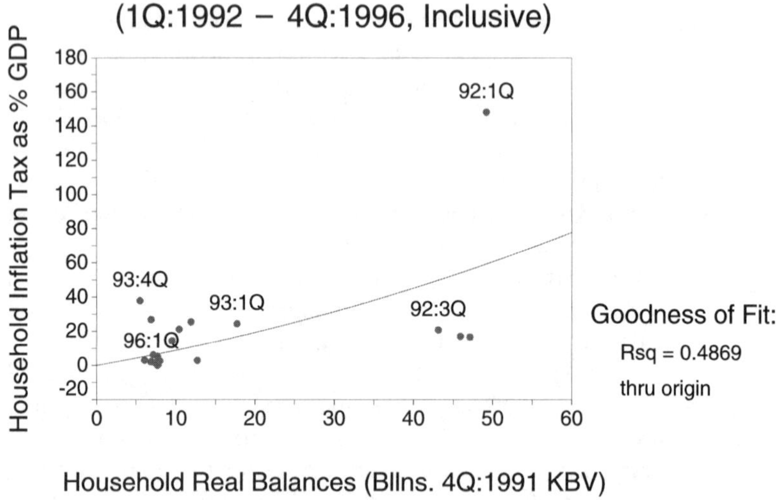

The 1996 Currency Reform

By far, the most important success of Ukraine in the economic sphere for the entire decade of the 1990s was the September 1996 currency reform. President Kuchma announced on Independence Day, August 24, 1996, the long-awaited introduction of Ukraine's permanent national currency, the hryvnia.[58] Coming on the fifth anniversary of Ukraine's independence, the announcement was greeted with much fanfare. Indeed, it seems that the timing could not have been better.[59]

While it is true that the June 1996 Constitution of Ukraine designated the hryvnia as the national currency, there were many practical reasons for replacing the karbovanets. Even simple transactions could require millions of karbovantsi, making huge wads of cash necessary and rendering record-keeping difficult, time consuming, and error prone.[60] In order to ensure a stable transition, and not to disadvantage anyone in the reform, currency conversion had to come at a time of relative monetary and price stability. The low levels of inflation throughout the summer months created a nearly ideal opportunity for currency conversion, with monthly inflation rates of a mere 0.1 percent in June and July. Independence Day celebrations were planned for August, and the time seemed ripe to introduce the hryvnia.

According to the decree signed by President Kuchma, the hryvnia would be introduced on September 2, 1996, at an initial conversion rate of 100,000 karbovantsi to 1 hryvna, effectively lopping off five digits from all shop prices. Ukrainians and foreigners were afforded two weeks, until September 16, to exchange their karbovantsi for hryvniy in unlimited quantities at some 20,000 exchange counters across Ukraine. Exchange of more than 100 million KBV (about $600) were to be placed into special bank accounts, in order to conserve quantities of banknotes. No restrictions on depositors' accounts were imposed, making the conversion truly nonconfiscatory. During the conversion period, both karbovantsi and hryvniy would circulate as legal tender.

Obviously, it was important to maintain public confidence in order for the monetary reform to succeed. Previous attempts to introduce the hryvnia were defeated by a lack of public trust. For instance, in July 1995, President Kuchma announced that the government would introduce the hryvnia in October of that year, precipitating a run on U.S. dollars, which increased inflation sharply in August. In hindsight, it is clear that the Ukrainian public, still reeling from the material and psychological effects of inflation in 1992–94, possessed little confidence in the government's ability to carry out a nonconfiscatory reform. Not until government credibility had been restored, in part, by returning to key positions such respected economic reformers as Deputy Premier Victor Pynzenyk and controlling inflation for several months' time, was introduction of the new currency possible.

Hryvniy were introduced in 1-, 2-, 5-, 10-, 20-, 50-, and 100-hryvniy banknotes. Also issued were coins, for the first time since 1991, in denominations of 1-, 2-, 5-, 10-, 25-, and 50-kopecks. It was well known that the banknotes issued in 1996 had been printed abroad over three years earlier, in 1992 and 1993 by the Canadian Banknote Company, and that sufficient quantities of the currency were present in NBU's vaults and at several other key locations around the country since early 1994.[61] Technically, the National Bank and government had been ready to introduce the new currency for quite some time. Ukraine has since opened a domestic engravery and mint to print and coin money.[62]

Introduction of the hryvnia, while generally smooth, was not without its challenges.[63] At the time of its introduction, Ukraine was still in the process of negotiating with the IMF an agreement for an IMF-backed "currency stabilization fund." Lack of ample quantities of stabilization reserves (Ukraine had approximately $2 billion in gold and hard currency reserves at the beginning of September) raised questions about the NBU's ability to defend the hryvnia from devaluation. At a press conference on August 25, however, NBU governor Yushchenko indicated that the bank's position was that "introduction of the new currency does not depend on the IMF," thereby signaling his confidence that the NBU could defend the hryvnia.[64]

Almost immediately, however, Ukrainians rushed to exchange their karbovantsi for hard currency. By August 27, the karbovanets had lost 30 percent of its value against the dollar at exchange kiosks. Some shops refused to accept payment in karbovantsi, prompting the government on August 26 to impose a 30-day freeze on retail prices and vow to prosecute vendors who were unwilling to accept karbovantsi as legal tender. In Kyiv, some fourteen currency exchange offices were closed, and four banks had their licenses revoked for currency speculation, sharply inflating the dollar exchange rate in the days leading up to the reform. For its part, the NBU intervened aggressively to maintain the karbovanets in the interbank market, putting to the test Yushchenko's declaration of August 25. By August 31, on the eve of introduction, it was clear that the government's measures to support the karbovanets would be successful, with the dollar exchange rate falling back to the interbank level.

NBU Governor Yushchenko estimated that the stock of cash karbovanets was KBV 337.3 trillion (approximately $1.8 billion) at the beginning of the reform, including KBV 23.6 trillion in bank vaults.[65] The preliminary data indicated that, during the period from September 2–16, approximately 95.5 percent of cash in circulation on September 1 had been converted. During the same two-week period, the NBU issued UAH 3,995 million in fresh notes. Yushchenko reported that the proportions of hryvniy put into circulation through various means are as shown on page 209. Cash collected by banks from the retail trade sector amounted to UAH 826 million (20.7 percent of that which had been issued), bringing the total amount of hryvniy in circulation on September 16 to UAH 3,168 million.

Conversion went so smoothly after September 2 that the government was able to cancel the retail price freeze after just two weeks.[66] Further, in an effort to afford all corners of the country ample opportunity to convert, the period of conversion was extended until mid-October.[67] Prices increased by 5.7 percent in August; however, this increase was not due to the flight from karbovantsi in the panic-selling of August

Means of Emission	mlln. UAH	Percent
• Direct Exchange	2,023	50.6
• Wage Payments	750	18.8
• Pensions, Social Benefits	474	11.9
• Special Deposit Accounts	165	4.1
• Assorted Other Means	583	14.6
TOTALS	3,995	100.0

24–27, but resulted from previously scheduled administrative increases in rents and communal services (that is, utility) charges. More valid indicators of success were the modest increases in consumer prices of just 2 percent in both September and October, which were in line with Ukraine's agreement with the IMF. Indeed, IMF Managing Director Michel Camdessus praised Ukraine for adhering to tight monetary and fiscal policy during the currency reform.[68]

Another indicator of the government's success is the relative stability of the hryvnia-to-dollar exchange rate in the period following the reform. The NBU initially set its exchange rate at UAH 1.76 per dollar, 1.18 to the D-mark, and 3,000 Russian rubles per hryvna. At the Ukrainian Interbank Currency Exchange, the hryvnia started trading at 1.76 to the dollar. It held this value through October, climbing to 1.82 per dollar by November 1, and 1.88 at December 1. This amounted to a cumulative devaluation of approximately 6.5 percent over three months, a modest fall in light of recent history. A further indicator of success was the increase in savings deposits at Ukrainian banks during the reform. Household time deposits climbed by 3 percent in the first two weeks of September alone. Enterprise time deposits rose by 6 percent. Deposits of one year's duration rose by 30 percent during the same period.[69] The liquidity of Ukrainian banks, and the financial sector generally, therefore improved as a direct result of the reform.

In retrospect, it was the public's restored confidence in the government that enabled the successful currency conversion. A public opinion poll of 400 people conducted in Kyiv on September 7 by the Democratic Initiatives Foundation indicated that Kyivans overwhelmingly welcomed the new currency.[70] When asked whether the introduction of the hryvnia would change the situation in Ukraine, 58 percent responded "yes," 29 percent said "no," and 13 percent responded that "it is difficult to say." This contrasts with a September 1995 poll, in which 23 percent were optimistic about a new currency and 42 percent pessimistic. In the 1996 poll, 69 percent responded as feeling that the conversion to the hryvnia was conducted "in an open and honest manner"; a mere

13 percent disagreed. At the same time, 68 percent predicted that the hryvnia would either hold its value or lose only a small amount of value against the dollar within the next year. Only 4 percent predicted a dramatic drop in value. Thus, it seems, Ukrainians were more favorably disposed to currency reform at the time of its occurrence, a factor of immense benefit to the government during the conversion. We consider next the process of monetary stabilization in Ukraine and the important question of whether or not stabilization was inevitable.

The Drive to Monetary Stabilization

Why did Ukraine stabilize the currency when it did? What factors propelled Kyiv to curb its inflationary habits? What were the actual dynamics of the process? And what lessons can be drawn from Ukraine's experience? Given that the long drive to stabilization began in the second half of 1994, it is tempting to credit the political changes that swept through Ukraine that year, particularly the election in July of former prime minister Leonid Kuchma as president of Ukraine. However, it was decidedly to the advantage of state enterprises and their patrons in the *nomenklatura* to inflate the karbovanets. It is difficult to imagine this group willingly relinquishing access to the "monetary pump."

Additionally, stabilization itself is a politically and procedurally difficult objective to achieve. It often takes more than one attempt to succeed.[71] A "credible commitment" on the part of the government to reducing inflation is necessary in order to convince citizens of the reality of the coming stabilization. It is usually necessary to signal such commitment with very painful cuts in the fiscal deficit, such as occurred in 1995–96. What prompted the government to take this unpleasant road?

There appears to be little doubt that excessive fiscal deficits pose a significant threat of runaway inflation and even collapse of currencies.[72] The issue is not without controversy, however. Economists Thomas Sargent and Neil Wallace explored the "unpleasant arithmetic" of monetarism, arguing that, in an environment of increasing inflation, even short-term financing of government deficits via bonds would be insufficient to contain the inflationary impulse.[73] Their model implies that, although tight monetary policy may be able to fight inflation temporarily, it will eventually lead to higher inflation.[74] Such a situation logically results only where monetary policy fully accommodates fiscal laxity. Unfortunately, until 1996, Ukraine did not have an independent monetary authority capable of imposing fiscal discipline on the government. During 1991–96, the NBU remained subordinate to parliament and/or the government and a captive to "soft budget" policies.[75] That being the case, in the absence of an independent monetary authority, how did Ukraine achieve stabilization?

German economist Willem Buiter contradicts Sargent and Wallace, arguing that runaway inflation under conditions of large and growing budget deficits cannot lead to ever-higher inflation.[76] He argues that unsustainably high deficits actually may cause inflation to decline and can even lead to deflation,[77] but not hyperinflation. The difference between Buiter and other theorists consists of the assumptions they make about the public's behavior in response to changing prices. The issue is an important one, for if he is right, Buiter's analysis circumvents the standard "heterodox" IMF recommendation to stamp out inflation through a stringent process of fiscal reform.

The controversy basically turns on whether a "rational expectations" or an "adaptive expectations" process is at work in the public's evaluation of future inflation. Under rational expectations, the public would fairly accurately anticipate the government's moves to inflate the currency, incorporating such assessments in its money demand function, thereby (at least partially) counteracting and frustrating the government's actions. Under adaptive expectations, the public largely reacts to the government's actions based on new price information as it becomes available. The government obviously has greater advantages under adaptive expectations, insofar as the public's expectations tend to remain below actual inflation.

Havrylyshyn, et al., overcome Buiter's criticism of Sargent and Wallace by decoupling actual from expected inflation, making seigniorage a stochastic variable subject to a degree of uncertainty.[78] Under these conditions, the public will have difficulty getting a true fix on the government's long-run money supply function. Jurgen von Hagen argues that "if this is done in the right way, high and even increasing inflation rates can persist for quite a while in a rational expectations equilibrium although the deficit is unsustainably large."[79] If that is the case, then it would be possible to observe rather long periods of accelerating inflation before stabilization were to occur. Indeed, we might even expect to see inflation reach its apex immediately preceding stabilization. The potential for inflationary financing of deficits can erode quite suddenly, regardless of how expectations are formed, where the growth in the real money stock butts up against the economy's resource constraint. Ultimately, then, all cases of accelerating inflation are unsustainable and must reach an end, as it did in Ukraine.

It seems that one can sidestep this controversy somewhat by focusing on the essentially adaptive nature of expectancy formation in transition economies. This has implications for interpretation of the Ukrainian path to stabilization. Michael Bruno and Stanley Fischer argue that the assumption that economic agents form their inflationary expectations adaptively makes sense under conditions in which reliable data on government budget deficits is not available, and/or when the government's policy and data pronouncements possess little credibility.[80] Both conditions were abundantly present in Ukraine during 1991–96; government-provided economic information was widely distrusted. The only reliable source of information about inflation available to the public was the changing price level itself.

To compound matters, the Ukrainian public experienced shocks resulting from partial price liberalizations, which caused monetary velocity to temporarily overshoot the equilibrium level.[81] Such price shocks had the effect of confusing the public by obscuring the real source of the price rise. Another source of confusion were government authorities themselves, who were prone to attribute rising prices, variously, to consumer price liberalization, monopoly pricing by state firms, rising costs of Russian energy imports, and/or currency speculation.[82] Even the fall in output was blamed.

If inflationary expectations are formed adaptively, then the real money stock held by households will be determined by the public's expectation of future inflation.[83] But with a lag. Both households and enterprises will reduce their money holdings in response to anticipated inflation. Dollarization can and did occur in Ukraine. Such broad conversion into hard currencies actually can accelerate inflation, as people jettison their money at ever-faster rates. MIT economist Rudiger Dornbusch argues that lags in forming expectations will tend to shorten as inflation accelerates.[84] Despite the best efforts of the public to seek new information about changing prices, in periods of accelerating inflation, expected inflation remains below actual, current inflation. This means that the demand for real balances can fluctuate, or even increase, and with it the inflation tax base. The government will therefore have tremendous latitude to benefit from inflation, at least for awhile.

It is doubtful that the public can be deceived for very long, however. Dornbusch writes that economic actors and institutions will adapt to accelerating inflation by rearranging their financial affairs and shortening their commitments, so that, "with sufficient adaptation, the inflation tax can be almost totally evaded, and hence the budget deficit cannot be financed."[85] This situation occurred in Ukraine after 1994, when the demand for real balances fell, resulting in erosion of the inflation tax base. When this happens, stabilization becomes the only alternative to wholesale abandonment of the currency.

To summarize: Under conditions of hyperinflation, the government must print money at ever-increasing rates. Because the public's expectations are formed adaptively in response to new price information, expectations will lag behind actual inflation, never quite catching up. Under these conditions, the inflation tax base may shrink dramatically and with it the opportunity to finance budget deficits with inflation. Theoretically, the government can continue to finance its deficit as long as the rate at which it prints money outpaces the rate of public adaptation. However, a threshold exists beyond which a weary public becomes convinced that deficits cannot be controlled and that inflation will "never end." At that stage, currency collapse can occur almost instantly.

While a complete collapse did not occur in Ukraine, that does not invalidate the logic of adaptive formation of inflationary expectations, which has the effect of progressively narrowing the government's policy options. The theory holds that, at some critical point, the government will have no choice but to stabilize the money supply. Kyiv built up significant payments arrears in 1995–96 in order to meet its minimum social expenditure obligations.[86] Time was running out. The Ukrainian stabilization and currency reform of 1996 was thus no great product of the government's will to reform the monetary system. The government had simply exhausted its options.

Conclusion: Why Did Stabilization Occur?

The root cause of Ukraine's tragic experience with inflation in 1992–94 was not price liberalization, the collapse in output, monopoly pricing practices, or rising energy costs. Rather, it was the government's policy of extending cheap, practically zero-interest budgetary and off-budget credits to enterprises. The benefit to the state from inflation reached its pinnacle in mid-1993, when the inflation tax base began to erode. The Ukrainian public changed its aggregate financial behavior in ways that frustrated and circumvented government policies, including shifting to hard currency.

The inflation tax and seigniorage peaked at different times for households and enterprises. An important finding is that enterprises paid a major share of the inflation tax, especially during 1993, household monetary holdings having been depleted thoroughly by year-end

1992. Stabilization became increasingly likely in 1995–96 as the government exhausted its options to continue financing fiscal deficits through inflation. Rather than the product of the government's will to reform the public finances, the liquidation of Ukraine's inflation in 1996 was the result the self-limiting dynamics of the inflationary process. In the absence of ample internal and external sources of debt financing, and with the inflation option exhausted, the government had no choice after 1994 but to pursue budgetary balance.

Appendix 7.1

Monetary Policy after the 1996 Currency Reform

Overview

This appendix concerns Ukraine's monetary policy following introduction of the hryvnia in the third quarter of 1996. Prior to the currency reform of September 1996, the inflationary dynamic was driven by a "transmission belt" process that began with state budget deficits and ended with rather large currency emissions. The main problem in 1992–96 was the lack of coordination between fiscal and monetary policy. The currency reform of September 1996 changed completely the monetary dynamic in Ukraine. Budget deficits persisted, however. In the years following introduction of the hryvnia, the effort to decrease the budget deficit was undermined by the rapid accumulation of internal and external government debts and the build-up of budgetary arrears. Budget deficits therefore continued into 1999, but at least the inflationary link had been broken.

The share of government spending in GDP remained high throughout the late 1990s, however, which reflected a budget dominated by extensive redistributive programs, social expenditures, and implicit subsidies to enterprises and households. Despite this, price stability was largely achieved, as can be seen from the trends tracked in Table 7.1.1. The truly interesting problem (which simply "leaps" out from the table) is just how the inflationary dynamic changed in the late 1990s, from what it had been prior to the currency reform.

Essentially, after 1996, the rate of growth of the money supply does not appear to bear any systematic relation to the rate of inflation. In fact, given the money growth rates in Table 7.1.1, we would have expected to witness a greater degree of price and exchange rate volatility than was actually present in the period before the Russian currency crisis of 1998. It is only in the period starting in the third quarter of 1998, and extending into 1999, that the hryvnia suffered devaluation and inflation again threatened to accelerate. Ukraine managed to come through the crisis without a financial panic, however, which is a testimony to its monetary management efforts, particularly the skill of the central bank governor, Viktor Yushchenko.

Policy from Late 1996 to the Russian Crisis of 1998

Positive Developments in 1997–98

In the period following introduction of the hryvnia, the NBU pursued a relatively tight monetary policy. In 1996 and 1997, rates of expansion of both domestic credit and broad money were somewhat limited. Broad money (M2 in Table 7.1.1) expanded by 38 percent in 1997 and just 13 percent in 1998. This reflects the extremely low level of monetization of the Ukrainian economy, but it did contribute to keeping the rate of price inflation to just 10.1 percent in 1997 and 19.9 percent in 1998.

Development of the government securities market in 1996–98 constrained direct NBU credit expansion. The relatively high yields on T-bills attracted foreign investor interest in Ukrainian government securities. This put upward pressure on the hryvnia, prompting the NBU to purchase significant amounts of foreign exchange in order to prevent a rapid appreciation. By and large, the currency was relatively stable until late 1998. Public confidence in the currency was engendered by the nonconfiscatory nature of the reform, which was reflected in a gradual decrease in the dollarization ratio (foreign currency deposits as a percent of total deposits plus currency in circulation), which fell from .23 in the fourth quarter of 1995 to .19 in 1996 and .134 in 1997. Consequently, inflationary expectations also fell, as evidenced by a rise in the ratio of M2 to GDP, from 7.68 percent in the fourth quarter of

Table 7.1.1

Ukraine--Money Supply, Real Balances, Seigniorage, and the Inflation Tax, 4Q:1996 - 1Q:2001

(Includes Household and Enterprise Sectors)

	(Millions of hryvnia)			Growth Rates [note 1]										
Period	M1 (Narrow Money)	M2 (Broad Money)	M3 (M2 + FCD)	M1	M2	CPI Index (4Q:96=100)	Quarterly Inflation [note 2]	M2 Real Balances	Velocity (Annual) [note 3]	Seigniorage [note 4]	Inflation Tax	Quarterly Real GDP [note 5]	Seigniorage as % of GDP	Inflation Tax as % of GDP
[note 6] 1996-4Q	6315	7306	9024	...	...	100.00	3.6	7306	...	...	...	...	...	..
1997-1Q	6967	8040	9514	9.8	9.6	103.53	3.5	7766	2.33	723.9	263.9	18089	4.0	1.5
2Q	7971	9279	10971	13.5	14.3	105.30	1.7	8812	8.83	1187.1	141.1	19454	6.1	0.7
3Q	8978	10464	12222	11.9	12.0	106.67	1.3	9810	9.97	1119.3	121.3	24445	4.6	0.5
4Q	9050	10775	12447	0.8	2.9	110.12	3.2	9785	10.42	241.7	266.7	25496	0.9	1.0
1998-1Q	9230	10973	12836	2.0	1.8	111.99	1.7	9798	7.61	234.0	221.0	18636	1.3	1.2
2Q	9226	11269	13256	0.0	2.7	113.45	1.3	9933	8.29	260.4	125.4	20597	1.3	0.6
3Q	9066	10873	14142	-1.7	-3.6	116.94	0.3	9298	10.64	-586.2	48.8	24720	-2.4	0.2
4Q	10331	12175	15432	13.1	11.3	132.13	12.2	9214	9.68	1054.7	1138.7	22286	4.7	5.1
1999-1Q	10130	11976	15631	-2.0	-1.6	135.81	3.5	8754	8.34	-144.4	315.6	18259	-0.8	1.7
2Q	12192	14242	18259	18.5	17.3	143.45	4.7	9928	8.20	1611.9	437.9	20353	7.9	2.2
3Q	13255	15360	20019	8.4	7.6	145.45	1.4	10560	9.80	1501.0	869.0	25873	5.8	3.4
4Q	14094	16367	21714	6.1	6.4	157.52	8.0	10390	8.63	680.0	850.0	22421	3.0	3.8
2000-1Q	14605	17331	23275	3.6	5.7	173.61	9.7	9983	7.51	579.9	986.9	18748	3.1	5.3
2Q	17024	19955	26359	15.3	14.1	186.94	7.4	10675	7.87	1456.3	764.3	21006	6.9	3.6
3Q	17953	21138	28076	5.3	5.8	191.61	2.5	11032	9.56	627.5	270.5	26357	2.4	1.0
4Q	20732	24178	31387	14.4	13.4	198.59	3.6	12175	8.75	1562.5	419.5	26622	5.9	1.6
2001-1Q	21159	25075	32382	2.0	3.6	203.99	2.7	12292	6.84	468.0	351.0	21013	2.2	1.7

Notes :

[1] Growth rates are exponential within quarters, such that g = ln(%growth) .

[2] Quarterly exponential growth rate within quarters. (See Note 1.)

[3] Velocity = (Annualized Nominal GDP)/M2.

[4] Seigniorage = (Change in Real Balances) x [M2 Growth Rate/(M2 Growth Rate - CPI Growth Rate)].

Inflation Tax = Seigniorage - Change in Real Balances.

[5] 4Q:1996 = 100. Expressed in millions of hryvnia. Data in this column are deflated by quarterly GDP figures.

[6] The 1996-4Q monetary aggregates were restated by the NBU after 1997, so that this line differs somewhat from the same line in Appendix Table 7.1.1. This does not affect the results of analysis in either chapter 7 or this appendix, however.

Sources :

M1: National Bank of Ukraine. Available online at http://www.bank.gov.ua.

M2 and M3: Ukrainian-European Policy and Legal Advice Centre, *Ukrainian Economic Trends* (March 2001), table 7.3, p. 46.

Real balances, velocity, seigniorage and inflation tax are the author's calculations.

1996 to 10 percent in 1997 to over 11 percent in 1998 (at times reaching 13 percent; See Table 8.1 in chapter 8.)

The increase in M2 real balances (a direct indicator of the demand for money) is provided in Table 7.1.1. This was very stable in 1997–98, as it was driven primarily by the increasing volume of transactions. Currency in circulation grew at rates faster than recorded price inflation, which indicates the growing prominence of activity in the shadow economy. Hence, the increase in money demand was smaller than what would have been predicted on the basis of the stable exchange rate and declining price inflation. Most likely, credit expansion took place through the "back door," through the rise of "surrogate monies" to be discussed in chapter 8. Consequently, there appears to have been a weak link between monetary growth rates and price inflation in 1996 to mid-1998.

Contraction of Demand for T-bills in Late 1997

Foreign investors soured on new purchases of Ukrainian T-bills in the second half of 1997, mainly on the basis of a fresh assessment of the risk in light of the rapid expansion of Ukrainian state internal and external debts. Short-term capital flowed outward, a trend that was only aggravated by the Asian economic crisis. A great deal of pressure was placed on the NBU to support the hryvnia by expending foreign exchange reserves. Unfortunately, the NBU did not change the level of reserve money. In order to prevent a complete collapse of the T-bill market, the NBU refinancing rate was raised from 16 percent in October 1997 to 35 percent in November. Bank reserve requirements were raised from 11 to 15 percent, and the maximum proportion of reserves that could be held in the form of T-bills was increased from 20 to 30 percent (while the highest permissible cash share was decreased from 30 to 20 percent).[1]

These moves proved to be insufficient to prevent the wholesale outflow of foreign capital, which rapidly exited developing markets worldwide. The contraction of market demand for T-bills was quite sharp. In late November 1997, the Finance Ministry failed to sell 9- and 18-month T-bills, while only some UAH 115,500 in 6-month bills and UAH 7.08 million in 12-months bills were sold.[2]

The decline in foreign investment to finance the consolidated state budget was replaced with large NBU purchases of T-bills in the primary market. In December 1997, the NBU held just 17 percent of the outstanding T-bill debt. By the end of 1998, the NBU held 66 percent, and by December 1999, the proportion had grown to 88 percent. The NBU also extended credit directly to the government, which grew in early 1998, owing to lax fiscal discipline in the period preceding the March 1998 parliamentary elections. NBU credit to the government grew by some 32 percent in the first half of 1998, making the bank once again the chief creditor of the state. The dollarization ratio also grew, rising from .134 at the end of 1997 to .211 by year-end 1998.

Impacts on the Foreign Exchange Position

As a direct result of the reversal in foreign capital flows and the ongoing Asian economic crisis, starting in the first quarter of 1998, in its efforts to defend the hryvnia, the NBU steadily depleted its foreign exchange reserves. Softening demand for T-bills also caused problems for the government in refinancing its internal and external debts. By mid-1998, international financial markets turned sharply against Ukraine.[3] Depletion of the NBU's foreign exchange reserves caused a downswing in foreign asset balances. Due to the masterful efforts of the NBU, however, the potentially precipitous fall assumed more of a controlled downswing, which was largely reversed by the second quarter of 1999.

The Russian Currency Crisis of August 1998

On August 17, 1998, the Central Bank of Russia (CBR) announced a 90-day moratorium on its foreign loan payments and at the same time unlinked the ruble from the U.S. dollar. Due to the lively trade between the two countries, Russia's fateful decision was to have serious deleterious consequences for Ukraine. In hindsight, neither country really could have avoided a sharp devaluation. The CBR's attempts to defend its ruble-to-dollar (RUR/USD) trading band had severely depleted Russia's foreign exchange reserves. Consequently, by mid-August, Russian authorities gave up supporting the RUR/USD exchange rate, defaulted on its T-bills, and introduced a foreign debt moratorium.[4]

The Russian crisis triggered a rapid depreciation of the hryvnia. The NBU responded with an official devaluation of the UAH/RUR exchange rate in order to maintain the balance of trade with Russia. On September 5, the NBU changed its announced currency trading corridor against the U.S. dollar from 1.8 to 2.25 to 2.5 to 3.5 UAH/USD. The

NBU's foreign exchange reserves fell from $2.3 billion in January to around $860–890 million in late September 1998, barely sufficient to meet the international debt payments coming due at year-end. The government closed the interbank market for foreign exchange and imposed new exchange controls.[5] By order of the NBU, market exchange rates were to be within +/-10 percentage points of the official rate announced by the bank. (This was further narrowed to +/-5 percentage points on September 7.) Mandatory conversion was required starting September 4 for 50 percent of the foreign exchange receipts of Ukrainian exporters. (This was raised to 75 percent on September 7 but lowered again to 50 percent on September 14.) Imports were discouraged through restrictions prohibiting prepayment and new certification procedures.

The government formally enacted an anticrisis program on September 10, 1998.[6] As happened in Russia, at the start of October, Ukraine restructured over 99 percent of the T-bills held by nonresidents and a large proportion of the T-bill portfolio of commercial banks. The T-bills were converted to Eurobonds maturing in 2000, and the holders of medium-term and hedged T-bills received 20 percent cash compensation for the inconvenience. The conversion was officially characterized as "voluntary" due to government fears that a mandatory conversion would be taken as a signal of default on Ukraine's domestic debts.

The extent of the hryvnia's devaluation can readily be seen in Graph 7.1.1. The government's policy moves appear to have prevented the kind of widespread panic witnessed in Russia during this time. Nonetheless, households and enterprises responded in a rational manner to protect themselves, withdrawing bank deposits and converting hryvniy to dollars. In August-October 1998, 18 percent of household bank deposits were withdrawn (including 10 percent of demand deposits and 22 percent of time deposits). Net purchases of hard currency also rose sharply in the fourth quarter of 1998 as a direct consequence of the exchange rate fall.

Relative stability in the exchange rate was restored in early to mid-1999, as indicated in Graph 7.1.1. Foreign exchange reserves stood at just $686 million at December 31, 1998, however. These were hardly sufficient to redeem debts coming due in the first part of 1999. Hence, the Russian currency crisis of 1998, which propelled the deep devaluation in the hryvnia that year, precipitated the Ukrainian debt crisis detailed in chapter 5. Now Ukraine's dollar-denominated debts would have to be redeemed with devalued hryvniy. This meant that foreign

Graph 7.1.1
Trend in the Hryvnia to U.S. Dollar Exchange Rate, 1995-2001

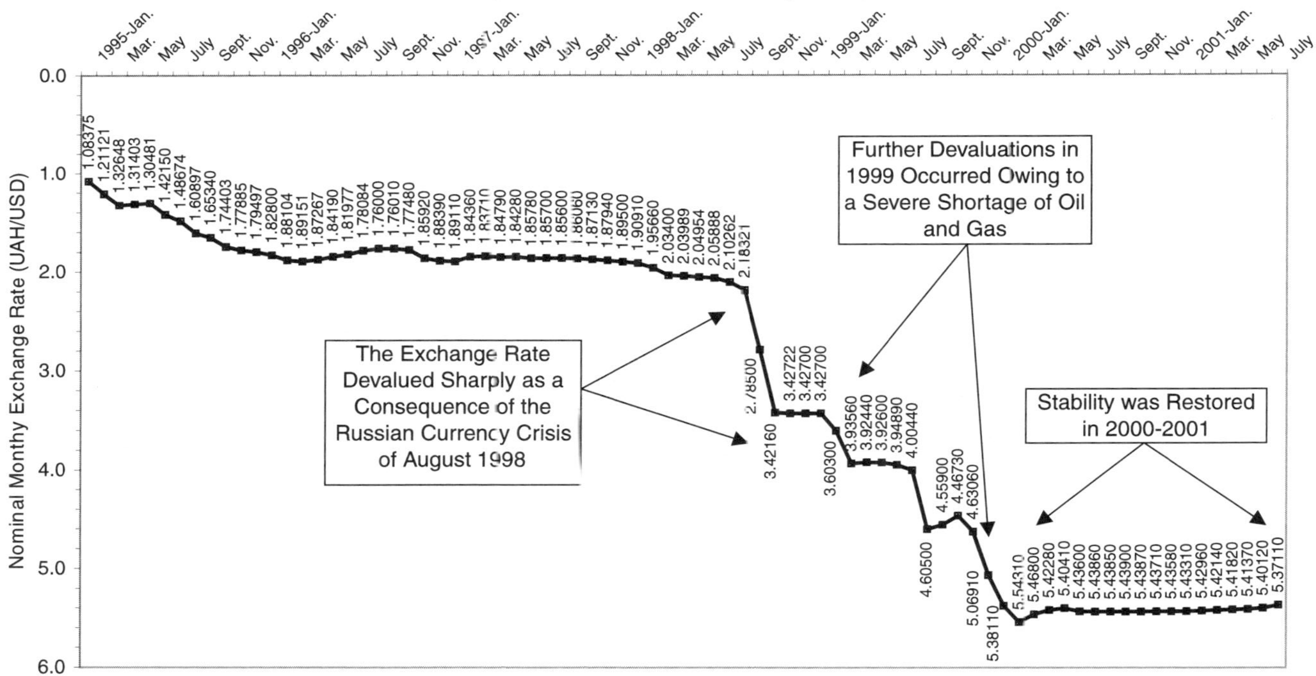

Source: National Bank of Ukraine and *Ukrainian Economic Trends* (various issues).

debts as a percent of GDP climbed sharply, due in large part to the devaluation. This would impose an enormous cost on Ukrainian taxpayers for some years to come.

Developments in 1999–2000

After having achieved relative stability in late 1998, the year 1999 began with a planned devaluation. The NBU intended to reopen the interbank foreign currency market, so it began on February 8 a gradual (UAH 0.02 per day) devaluation to bring the official exchange rate in line with the street (that is, black market) rate, which had stabilized at between UAH 3.85–3.92 per USD. It was also clear at this time that defending the hryvnia within the existing 2.50–3.50 UAH/USD corridor was unrealistic in face of the gradual devaluation. Consequently, Deputy Prime Minister Serhiy Tyhypko announced on February 9 a new corridor of UAH 3.40–4.60 UAH/USD.[7]

Unfortunately, the public interpreted the broad width of the newly announced trading band as a signal of the government's uncertainty about future devaluations. Commercial banks therefore started purchasing large amounts of U.S. dollars as the hryvnia worked its way up to the street rate. But this only increased pressure on the NBU to act, by raising required commercial bank reserves to 17 percent from 15 percent on February 22. Moody's reacted to this news on the same day, reducing its rating of Ukrainian government domestic debt obligations to "Ca" (highly speculative).

The NBU expanded the money supply fully 17 percent in May, apparently lulled by the low level of monetization into believing that the economy could sustain monetary expansion with few inflationary effects. On May 24, the NBU imposed a maximum UAH 3,000 cash payment for transactions, in order to limit the flow of currency outside of banks, which had always been a concern for NBU and government officials. Official hard currency reserves were boosted on May 27, when the IMF granted Extended Fund Facility (EFF) tranches for April and May worth $130 million, plus another $50 million to compensate for losses sustained as a result of the Russian currency crisis.[8] Ukrainian officials were delighted at the prospect that the hryvnia would remain stable for some time.

In July 1999, however, Ukraine entered a severe domestic oil crisis. Much of Ukraine's energy trade with Russia tended to be mostly U.S.

dollar denominated and was conducted largely on a barter basis. In the energy sector in the first quarter, less than 10 percent of transactions involved cash.[9] Since so much of the energy trade with Russia was being conducted via barter, government officials at first believed that the further deterioration of the ruble rate in 1999 would leave the hryvnia unaffected. However, the terms of trade can serve just as effectively as cash transactions to transmit inflation from one country to another.

The depreciation of the hryvnia began July 20–22 with the start of the gasoline crisis.[10] Gasoline all but disappeared from retail outlets. The crisis ended with a 20 percent devaluation less than a week later, July 28–29, sliding down to 4.605 UAH/USD. Expectations of further devaluation provoked frenzied, speculative demand for foreign currency, which put much downward pressure on the hryvnia. On August 10, the NBU acquiesced somewhat, lowering its official exchange rate to 4.6784 UAH/USD, above the UAH 4.60/USD upper bound of the currency corridor that had been set the previous February. However, Deputy Premier Tyhypko on August 12 reiterated the government's commitment to maintaining the February 9 trading band until the end of the year and predicted that the rate would soon stabilize in the 4.4–4.5 UAH/USD range.[11] In fact, the UAH/USD rate was to strengthen somewhat, rising to 4.44 on the foreign exchange market by mid-September.[12]

Inflationary expectations continued to plague NBU officials' efforts to shore up the hryvnia throughout the remainder of 1999. In December, the NBU ceased efforts to reduce the hryvnia's slide.[13] As can be seen in Graph 7.1.1, the downward slide did not end until the beginning of 2000, but the hryvnia was to fall to a record low of 5.5431 UAH/USD before stabilizing. The appointment of NBU Governor Viktor Yushchenko as Prime Minister in late 1999, together with renewed flows of IMF financing, certainly helped to stabilize the currency. Further, for the first time in its ten-year history, the Ukrainian economy began to grow in real terms. The devalued hryvnia enhanced competitiveness of Ukrainian consumer goods in the domestic and international market. Strengthening world commodities prices also encouraged exports of Ukrainian raw materials and basic unfinished goods. The state budget threw off surpluses for the first time, and hryvnia-denominated debts became more affordable (even as U.S. dollar-denominated ones were burgeoning). The result was a relatively stable currency that actually appreciated steadily against the dollar throughout 2000 and into 2001.

New Monetary Policy Instruments

By the end of the decade, the NBU had at its disposal the full panoply of traditional instruments of monetary management. However, the extent to which these instruments were skillfully employed varied considerably. These instruments were:

- Bank reserve requirements;
- Open market operations;
- Interest rate policy; and
- Bank certificates of deposit.

Bank Reserve Requirements

Bank reserves have a direct effect on the volume of money supply; the higher the required reserves, the lesser the effects are of the money multiplier that operates via the banking system. Starting January 1995, regulations required that the NBU-set reserve requirements apply to all deposits, including those in foreign currency. Whereas prior to April 1997, there were dual reserve requirements for domestic (11 percent reserves) and foreign currency deposits (15 percent), the requirements were unified at 11 percent in that month. In a move to encourage commercial bank purchases of government T-bills, starting in November 1997 banks were permitted to use T-bills to partially or fully meet their reserve requirements.[14] As can be seen in Table 8.1 in chapter 8, the required reserve ratio reached as high as 17 percent in 1999 but ended the decade at a level of 16 percent.

In response to the Russian currency crisis, in September 1998 the NBU disallowed the use of T-bills to meet their required reserve levels. Further, daily monitoring of bank reserves was instituted at that time but was pared back to every ten days in November. Of critical concern was the many and frequent changes in the required reserve ratio in 1998–2000. Changing reserve requirements is not an effective instrument of short-term liquidity management. Such changing requirements may also only punish the very best banks, which have made longer-term asset commitments based on a sound matching of liability maturities to asset maturities.

Open Market Operations

Sales and purchases of government securities on the open market are the most effective tools for ensuring short-term financial stability. Issuance of government treasury securities in April 1995 enabled open market operations, which became more feasible with the increasing sales of

T-bills throughout 1996–97. However, in the wake of the Asian economic crisis of 1997, and the resulting Russian currency crisis a year later, the market for Ukrainian government securities all but evaporated. After the "voluntary" conversion of T-bills in October 1998, commercial banks lost much of their interest in them. In early 2000, the NBU held some 88 percent of outstanding T-bills and was unable to effectively operate an "open market window."

Interest Rate Policy

Prior to September 1996, commercial bank lending rates were linked statutorily to the NBU commercial bank refinancing rate. Despite breaking the direct linkage that previously existed, the refinancing rate of the NBU remained the key reference rate in the economy. It was largely true throughout the 1990s that the average interest rate charged on refinancing commercial banks was lower than the statutory rate. This was an implicit break for the banks that also reduced the effectiveness of the NBU's use of interest rates to manage short-term liquidity in the banking system.

Commercial bank lending rates largely moved in conjunction with movements in the NBU refinancing rate, but after September 1996, the two were only loosely correlated. Effective yields to maturity on Ukrainian T-bills also tracked closely with the refinance rate. The average spreads between lending and deposit rates widened in the late 1990s, to over 2.0 percentage points in 2000. Both commercial bank lending rates and the refinancing rate have been positive in real terms (with few exceptions) since the beginning of 1996.

The high costs of refinancing, together with the inherent riskiness of lending to Ukrainian enterprises (many of them loss-making), made many banks more cautious than before. High levels of unprofitable excess reserves and relatively large holdings of T-bills (at least, until 1998) are indications of the poor credit of many Ukrainian borrowers. Unfortunately, NBU interest rate policies did little to enable banks to extend badly needed credit to high-potential growth enterprises in the nascent private sector. Perpetually starved for capital, these firms turned to the more informal sources of financing discussed in chapter 8.

Bank Certificates of Deposit (CDs)

Certificates of deposit (CDs) were introduced by the NBU in January 1998, with the first CD auction conducted on February 5. In Ukraine, CDs are documents evincing a bank's deposits at the NBU and having a specific interest rate and maturity, which can range from 1 to 180 days. CDs may be traded on the secondary market by anyone, but the auctions are closed to all but participating banks.[15] The NBU has the option to call back CDs before maturity, at the prevailing interest rate.

CDs have the potential to become an important instrument for the orderly expansion of credit in the economy. However, the procedure for their issuance in the late 1990s placed a great deal of discretion in the hands of the NBU, rather than in the banks themselves. Banks were required to apply to the NBU and to propose terms and conditions, but the NBU retained the final word on which "bids" it would accept. Hence, the process contained both market-based and administratively determined attributes. As of early 2001, this policy instrument was yet at an early stage of development.

The Ukrainian Currency Market

In 1998, the Ukrainian currency market consisted of the Ukrainian Interbank Currency Exchange (UICE), Interbank Currency Market (IBCM), International Currency Market (ICM), and the cash market (CM). The volume of trade in foreign currencies increased in U.S. dollar terms from $9.2 billion in 1995, and reached a peak of $37.7 billion before falling to $15.1 billion in 2000. The main currencies traded have been the U.S. dollar, Deutsche mark, and Russian ruble. On January 11, 1999, the Euro was traded at the UICE for the first time. It has not attracted as much interest from traders as the other currencies, however, since arbitrage opportunities were limited due to the absence of a cash Euro.

Policy Effectiveness

Effectiveness of Ukrainian monetary policy in 1997–2000 can be a subject of intense debate. The NBU by 2001 possessed the classic range of monetary policy tools and used them masterfully in several instances. Nominal interest rates, particularly, were controlled, and the rate of monetary emission subjected to discipline. The government also substantially reduced its tax "take" from inflation compared to the prereform days. A source of continuing concern is the rather low level of monetization of the economy, which reflects the small size and ineffectiveness of Ukraine's commercial banking industry.

A closer look at the monetization levels indicates that, while low for broad-based measures like M2 and M3, on an M1 basis, the money supply as a percent of GDP—ranging from 8.6 to 10.0 percent from

1997–99—is in line with most other transition countries and some developed ones. Currency in circulation accounts for an inordinately large proportion of the money supply. The real culprit thus appears to be the inability of banks to attract depositors, which is largely the result of government policy failures relating to the banking system. As detailed in Appendix 8.1, Ukraine's banks are relatively small, financially weak, and shy of assuming the risks inherent in lending to many Ukrainian enterprises. It would be entirely valid to conclude that the poor state of Ukrainian banks is a direct reflection of the state of their clients.

The widespread use of barter and arrears as means of financing (to be discussed in chapter 8) implies that they are both cheaper and more accessible to many enterprises than bank credits. Barter is an effective means of reducing the risks of doing business by collateralizing transactions. Arrears are a manifestation of "moral hazard" resulting from the absence of a hard budget constraint on enterprises. Both are means to overcome a lack of liquidity and weak enforcement of contracts. They are also a means of tax evasion. For present purposes, we may conclude that they serve as an alternative source of working capital. A related indication of failure of the financial system is the broad use of foreign currency, both as a store of value and as a means of exchange.

We may conclude, therefore, that the NBU has largely controlled inflation but that it has done so by permitting development of unregulated alternatives for credit expansion that operate outside of the NBU's monetary policy framework. It has no effective tools to manage these surrogate monies, which ultimately represent latent inflationary pressures building up outside of—and parallel to—the monetary system.

Looking to the Future

The line on inflation has been largely held since the currency reform of 1996. Monetary emissions have been subject to much-needed discipline. But as the decade came to a close there were warning signs that renewed inflation—derived from lax monetary policy—was still a possibility. Much of the pent-up inflationary pressure was present in the form of surrogate money, such as the extremely high and growing level of interenterprise debts.

The huge mutual indebtedness may be viewed as a potentially volatile source of instability in the monetary system, despite the rather low rates of inflation in the official statistics. If public expectations grow that these debts will be monetized at some point, inflationary expectations will mount, confidence in the currency will plummet, and inflation will be the inevitable result. It should be added that lack of confidence in the hryvnia would be entirely justified, given the stunning failure to implement structural reforms in both the industrial sector and the banking system, the lack of collateralization of enterprise assets as security for their debts, and the recurring government bailouts for "deadbeat" debtors.

As mentioned, the low ratio of broad money (M2) to GDP was seriously touted by government officials as a strong indication that an expansionary monetary policy would pump up production without an attendant increase in the price level. But fresh currency emissions are unlikely to elicit the desired supply-side response. In fact, they would have completely the opposite effect: an increase in the velocity of circulation, a collapse in confidence, an increase in the dollarization ratio, a deterioration in the rate of exchange, and rapidly increasing prices. Further, whatever policy course is selected, government and NBU officials will find that monetary policy is difficult to conduct successfully absent a well-developed, vibrant banking industry.

Appendix Table 7.1
Ukraine--Real Balances, Seigniorage, and the Inflation Tax, 1991-96
(Includes Household and Enterprise Sectors)

Period	M1 (Narrow Money)	M2 (Broad Money)	M3 (M2 + FCD)	Growth Rates [note 1] M1	Growth Rates [note 1] M2	CPI Index (4Q:91=100)	Quarterly Inflation [note 2]	M2 Real Balances	Velocity (Annual) [note 3]	Seigniorage [note 4]	Inflation Tax	Quarterly Real GDP [note 5]	Seigniorage as % of GDP	Inflation Tax as % of GDP
1989	79	13.4	13.4											
1990	93.6	130.7	130.7											
1991-4Q	175.9	263.1	263.2	n.a.	n.a.	100	n.a.	263.1						
1992-1Q	262.2	375.6	375.7	39.9	35.5	478	156	73.6	5.46	54.6	239.1	107.3	50.9	222.8
2Q	612.3	765	773.1	84.8	71.1	787	50	97.2	4.99	62.7	44.1	122.5	51.2	86.1
3Q	997.2	1203.3	1262.9	48.8	45.3	1332	53	90.3	4.35	40.6	47.5	103.2	39.3	46
4Q	2186.2	2502.3	2685.3	78.5	73.2	2048	43	122.2	7.7	77.3	45.5	113.1	68.3	40.1
1993-1Q	3852	4562	5457	56.6	60.1	7708	133	59.2	9.57	51.9	114.9	77.6	45.1	148.1
2Q	6500	7957	11282	52.3	55.6	20372	100	38.1	6.01	26.4	47.3	57.3	46.1	82.9
3Q	22813	26070	31003	125.6	118.7	63020	111	41.4	5.29	50.9	47.6	54.8	92.9	86.9
4Q	33604	38027	47204	38.7	37.8	290195	153	13.1	9.42	9.3	37.9	30.8	30.2	123.1
1994-1Q	48006	55485	66767	35.7	37.8	411698	35	13.5	10.59	5.4	5	35.7	15.1	14
2Q	77345	94082	108716	47.7	52.8	476548	15	19.7	8.06	8.7	2.5	39.8	21.9	6.3
3Q	136984	160985	186303	57.2	53.7	535648	12	30	5.87	13.3	3	44.1	30.2	6.8
4Q	186134	216406	315465	30.7	26.6	1453691	100	14.9	9.39	5.5	20.6	34.9	15.8	59
1995-1Q	226188	268145	393535	19.5	21.4	2317981	159	11.6	12.58	0.5	3.8	36.3	1.4	10.5
2Q	342907	385448	531433	41.6	36.3	2688366	15	14.3	11.57	4.6	1.9	41.5	11.1	4.6
3Q	419644	464401	638632	20.2	18.6	3378329	23	13.8	12.58	2.1	2.6	43.2	4.9	6
4Q	468189	526930	684633	11.1	12.6	4094330	19	12.9	12.63	1.8	2.7	40.6	4.4	6.7
1996-1Q	487418	556216	708618	4	5.4	4954330	19	11.2	12.1	0.7	2.4	33.9	2.1	7.1
2Q	535801	607655	752233	9.5	8.8	5114524	3	11.9	11.92	1.1	0.4	35.4	3.1	1.1
3Q	545900	622000	759200	1.9	2.3	5519687	8	11.3	13.3	0.2	0.8	37.5	0.5	2.1
4Q	562368	661148	792266	2.9	6.1	5720740	4	11.6	15.06	0.9	0.6	43.5	2.1	1.4

Notes:
[1] Growth rates are exponential within quarters, such that g = ln(%growth)
[2] Quarterly exponential growth rate within quarters. (See Note 1.)
[3] Velocity = (Annualized Nominal GDP)/M2.
[4] Seigniorage = (Change in Real Balances) x [M2 Growth Rate/(M2 Growth Rate - CPI Growth Rate)].
Inflation Tax = Seigniorage - Change in Real Balances.
[5] 4Q:1991 = 100.

Sources: Marcin Luczynski and Volodymyr Husak, "Ukraine in Numbers," *Ukrainian Legal and Economic Bulletin* (October 1996, December 1996, March 1997), Table 8.The data for 1989 and 1990 are from IMF, *Ukraine: Recent Economic Developments* (Washington, D.C.: IMF, 1993), Table A21, p. 65. Real balances, velocity, seigniorage, and inflation tax are author's calculations.

Appendix Table 7.2

Ukraine--Household Real Balances, Seigniorage, and the Inflation Tax, 1991-96

Period	(Billions of Current KBV) Held By Households: Currency in Circulation	Demand Deposits	Time Deposits	Household Financial Assets	Growth Rate [note 1]	Household Share of Broad Money	CPI Index (4Q:91=100)	Quarterly Inflation [note 2]	Household Real Balances	Velocity (Annual) [note 3]	Seigniorage [note 4]	Inflation Tax	Quarterly Real GDP [note 5]	Seigniorage as % of GDP	Inflation Tax as % of GDP
1989	17.2							n.a.							
1990	17.4							n.a.							
1991-4Q	33.8	73.8	74.7	182.3	n.a.	69.3	100	n.a.	182.3						
1992-1Q	60.8	90.2	84.1	235.1	25.4	62.6	478	156	49.2	8.73	25.8	158.9	107.3	24	148.1
2Q	168.6	105.1	88	361.7	43.1	47.5	787	50	45.9	10.66	17.5	20.8	122.5	14.3	17
3Q	343.2	155.1	75.3	573.6	46.1	47.7	1332	53	43.1	9.58	18.7	21.5	103.2	18.1	20.8
4Q	647.4	233.9	82.8	964.1	51.9	38.5	2048	43	47.1	9.61	22.7	18.8	113.1	20	16.6
1993-1Q	896	335	133	1364	34.8	29.9	7708	133	17.7	17.55	10.4	18.9	77.6	13.4	24.4
2Q	1710	568	217	2495	60.4	31.4	20872	100	11.9	19.17	8.8	14.6	57.3	15.4	25.5
3Q	5246	982	335	6563	96.7	25.2	63020	111	10.4	21.03	10.1	11.6	54.8	18.4	21.2
4Q	12790	2403	764	15957	88.8	41.9	290195	153	5.5	22.45	6.8	11.7	30.8	22.1	37.9
1994-1Q	23615	3007	3037	29659	61.9	53.5	411698	35	7.2	19.82	3.9	2.2	35.7	10.9	6.2
2Q	34066	4832	6428	45326	42.4	48.2	476548	15	9.5	16.73	3.6	1.3	39.8	9	14.4
3Q	52541	6725	8816	68082	40.7	42.3	535648	12	12.7	13.87	4.5	1.3	44.1	10.2	2.9
4Q	79104	9900	10920	99924	38.4	46.2	1453691	100	6.9	20.33	3.6	9.4	34.9	10.3	26.9
1995-1Q	113444	12397	16135	141976	35.1	52.9	2317981	159	6.1	23.76	0.3	1.1	36.3	0.8	3
2Q	178241	17612	17987	213840	40.9	55.5	2688366	15	8	20.85	3	1.1	41.5	7.2	2.7
3Q	223527	19965	17807	261299	20	56.3	3378329	23	7.7	22.37	2	2.3	43.2	4.6	5.3
4Q	262330	26932	26016	315274	18.8	59.8	4094330	19	7.7	21.11	0	0	40.6	0	0
1996-1Q	280007	28935	32012	340954	7.8	61.3	4954330	19	6.9	19.74	0.6	0.7	33.9	1.8	2.1
2Q	332400	31634	37304	401338	16.3	66	5114524	3	7.8	18.05	1.1	0.2	35.4	3.1	0.6
3Q	333000	35600	41700	410300	2.2	65.9	5519687	8	7.4	20.16	0.2	0.6	37.5	0.5	1.6
4Q	333020	41475	59837	434332	5.7	65.7	5720740	4	7.6	22.92	0.7	0.5	43.5	1.6	1.1

Notes:
[1] Growth rates are exponential within quarters, such that g = ln(%growth).
[2] Quarterly exponential growth rate within quarters. (See Note 1.)
[3] Household Velocity = (Annualized Nominal GDP)/Household Assets.
[4] Seigniorage = (Change in Household Real Balances)/[Household Assets Growth Rate/(Household Assets Growth Rate - CPI Growth Rate)].
Inflation Tax = Seigniorage - Change in Real Balances.
[5] 4Q:1991 = 100.

Sources: Marcin Luczynski and Volodymyr Husak, "Ukraine in Numbers," *Ukrainian Legal and Economic Bulletin* (October 1996, December 1996, March 1997), Table 8. The data for 1989 and 1990 are from IMF, *Ukraine: Recent Economic Developments* (Washington, D.C.: IMF, 1993), Table A21, p. 65. Real balances, velocity, seigniorage, and inflation tax are author's calculations.

Appendix Table 7.3
Ukraine - Enterprise Real Balances, Seigniorage, and the Inflation Tax, 1991-96

Period	(Billions of Current KBV) Enterprise Holdings Demand Deposits	Time Deposits	Enterprise Financial Assets	Growth Rate [note 1]	Enterprise Share of Broad Money	CPI Index (4Q:91=100)	Quarterly Inflation [note 2]	Enterprise Real Balances	Velocity (Annual) [note 3]	Seigniorage [note 4]	Inflation Tax	Quarterly Real GDP [note 5]	Seigniorage as % of GDP	Inflation Tax as % of GDP
1991-4Q	68.3	12.6	80.9	n.a.	30.7	100	n.a.	80.9						
1992-1Q	111.2	29.4	140.6	55.3	37.4	478	156	29.4	14.59	28.3	79.8	107.3	26.4	74.4
2Q	338.6	69.7	408.3	106.6	53.5	787	50	51.9	9.44	42.4	19.9	122.5	34.6	16.2
3Q	498.9	130.8	629.7	43.3	52.5	1332	53	47.3	8.73	20.5	25.1	103.2	19.9	24.3
4Q	1304.9	234	1538.9	89.4	61.5	2048	43	75.1	6.02	53.6	25.8	113.1	47.4	22.8
1993-1Q	262.1	577	3198	73.1	70.1	7708	133	41.5	7.48	41	74.6	77.6	52.8	96.1
2Q	4223	1240	5463	53.5	68.7	20872	100	26.2	8.75	17.6	32.9	57.3	30.7	57.4
3Q	16585	2922	19507	127.3	75.8	63020	111	30.9	7.08	36.7	32	54.8	66.9	58.4
4Q	18410	3659	22069	12.3	58.1	290195	153	7.6	16.24	2	25.3	30.8	6.5	82.1
1994-1Q	21384	4442	25826	117	46.5	411698	35	6.3	22.76	1.9	3.2	35.7	5.3	8.9
2Q	38447	10309	48756	63.5	51.8	476548	15	10.2	15.55	5.1	1.2	39.8	12.8	3
3Q	77718	15185	92903	64.5	57.7	535648	12	17.3	10.16	8.7	1.6	44.1	19.7	3.6
4Q	97130	19352	116482	21.5	53.8	1453691	100	8	17.44	2.5	11.8	34.9	7.2	33.8
1995-1Q	100347	25822	126169	8	47.1	2317981	159	5.4	26.74	0.1	2.7	36.3	0.3	7.4
2Q	147504	24554	172058	31	44.6	2688366	15	6.4	25.92	1.9	0.9	41.5	4.6	2.2
3Q	176151	26951	203102	16.6	43.7	3378329	23	6	28.77	1	1.4	43.2	2.3	3.2
4Q	178927	32725	211652	4.1	40.2	4094330	19	5.2	31.45	0.2	1	40.6	0.5	2.5
1996-1Q	178476	36786	215262	1.7	38.7	4954330	19	4.3	31.27	0.1	1	33.9	0.3	2.9
2Q	171767	34550	206317	-4.2	34	5114524	3	4	35.12	1.1	0.8	35.4	3.1	2.3
3Q	177300	34400	211700	2.6	34.1	5519687	8	3.8	39.07	0.1	0.3	37.5	0.3	0.8
4Q	187873	38943	226816	6.9	34.3	5720740	4	4	43.89	0.5	0.3	43.5	1.1	0.7

Notes:
[1] Growth rates are exponential within quarters, such that g=ln(%growth)
[2] Quarterly exponential growth rate within quarters. (See note 1.)
[3] Enterprise Velocity = (Annualized Nominal GDP)/Enterprise Assets.
[4] Enterprise Seigniorage = (Change in Enterprise Real Balances)/[Enterprise Assets Growth Rate/(Enterprise Assets Growth Rate - CPI Growth Rate)].
Inflation Tax = Seigniorage - Change in Real Balances.
[5] 4Q:1991 = 100.

Sources: Marcin Luczynski and Volodymyr Husak, "Ukraine in Numbers," *Ukrainian Legal and Economic Bulletin* (October 1996, December 1996, March 1997), Table 8. Real balances, velocity, seigniorage, and inflation tax are author's calculations.

Chapter 8

Financial Repression in the Ukrainian Economy

Financial Repression as a Policy Choice

Throughout the 1990s, Ukraine's macroeconomic policies posed certain dangers for the country. For instance, large and persistent budget deficits can lead to financial or balance of payments crises.[1] Persistent deficits may be interpreted by the populace as signals of future tax increases, greater inflation, a coming devaluation, or evidence of capital flight. The public can come to view fiscal deficits as unsustainable, touching off an inflationary spiral. The range of possible behavioral responses in the economy to incomplete, distortionary and/or discriminatory economic policies induced the government to undertake certain policy measures that would suppress the worst effects of its policy mistakes, at least for awhile.

Thus, in the attempt to avoid the immediate effects of such crises, the government employed a variety of instruments to suppress the effects of inflationary deficit financing on financial markets. Known collectively as tools of "financial repression," these consist of a broad set of policies, legal restrictions, rules and regulations, and controls and influences—both formal and informal—that inhibit the efficient operation of, mainly, financial and capital markets. (Although other markets may be also repressed, as well. For example, wage and price controls may be imposed.) In general, financial repression consists of policy measures that reduce economic efficiency generally, by erecting government-sponsored or sanctioned barriers to the timely and free assertion of opportunity-cost prices. This has been, perhaps, the most enduring legacy of Ukraine's first ten years of economic independence. And at the end of the 1990s, it showed little sign of abating anytime soon.

Instruments of Financial Repression

By their nature, instruments of financial repression distort interest rates, foreign exchange rates, patterns of investment, and the economic incentives of both borrowers and lenders. Financially repressed economies typically exhibit excessive demand for credit (because real interest rates are too low, or negative) and an undersupply of loanable funds (because there are serious disincentives to save). Exchange rates tend to be overvalued in terms of foreign currency, and protections of and subsidies to industry are too extensive.[2] Ukraine exhibited all of these symptoms of financial repression in the 1990s.

The effects of these measures can prompt governments to further actions, each introducing still further distortions. In order to deal with the economic pathologies introduced by the government's own credit and financial policies, they inevitably find that they must intervene further, to ration credit and impose controls, generally on prices, wages, interest rates, foreign exchange rates, and other transactions. Repressive measures may therefore tend to "snowball," as a chain of measures is set in motion in the effort to overcome distortions introduced by earlier repressive measures, and so on.

The basic policy instruments of financial repression are all too familiar in Ukraine, including:

- administered wage and prices;
- interest rate ceilings and controls;
- excessive bank reserves;
- foreign exchange regulations;
- rules specifying the composition of commercial bank balance sheets;
- the forcing of banks to purchase government securities;
- heavy or differential taxation of the financial sector; and
- specialized state-owned (or private) banks possessing lavish government-conferred privileges.

Governments may be tempted to employ such measures, since financial restrictions can mask from the public the inflationary effects of deficit financing (at least for awhile). In fact, to one extent or another, in the 1990s, Ukraine employed each of these measures (often in combination) as means to suppress the effects of excessive amounts of state consumption, the resultant inflation, and its own credit policies. In the long run, economic growth would suffer, however, because repression reduces the capacity of the financial system to respond to the needs of firms and households in the real economy.

Why Repression? The Government's Rationale

The traditional justification for financial repression is that it is presumed to increase the rate of economic growth.[3] This turns on the dubious assumption that money and real assets are perfectly substitutable. The basic idea is that increasing returns in real asset markets relative to money market instruments will induce a shift in investor behavior, out of money and into capital investment.[4] An important implication is that setting interest rate ceilings will reduce the rate of return on financial assets and induce a shift to investments in "productive" assets (that is, property, plant, and equipment), thereby increasing the rate of economic growth.

Economists Ronald MacKinnon and Edward Shaw both challenged the economic growth argument, however, arguing instead that high-yielding instruments may be "crowded out" of the market by distortions introduced by financial repression, creating a false preference for capital-intensive investment and discouraging savings.[5] The low real interest rates characteristic of a financially repressed economy will act to shrink bank deposits, resulting in shortages of loanable funds, which is especially hurtful to the efficient enterprises that can put them to productive use. The more attractive it is to hold real money balances, the greater the incentives are to invest. The clear implication is that economic growth rates will improve as interest rates are freed up so that they might rise to their equilibrium, market-clearing levels. On this view, productive investment occurs in direct response to a concomitant growth in the supply of loanable funds (that is, the real money stock). This is one reason that so many studies find inflation and economic growth to be inversely related.[6]

MacKinnon and Shaw have been criticized on the basis that raising interest rates rapidly in the absence of some amount of governmental regulation may not have the desired effect on savings and investment or induce a positive output response.[7] Such critics have generally argued for "optimal" levels of financial repression (that is, some, but not extensive governmental controls) on grounds of "market failure," the notion that markets cannot be left to govern themselves efficiently in the absence of some minimal set of government-enforced rules and regulations. In this case, it would be important to balance the positive and negative effects of intervention in financial markets, for the evidence suggests strongly that low real interest rates, high bank reserve requirements, and relatively low levels of financial "depth" in an economy (that is, a low level of monetization) are negatively correlated with real investment increases and GDP growth.[8]

There is some consensus that financially repressive measures are adopted in order for governments to exact resources from the financial sector with which to finance their own consumption and to cover fiscal deficits. The consensus position focuses on the revenue effects of financial repression.[9] The contention is that governments facing serious budget deficit problems have incentives to repress the financial sector. Repressive measures often are employed where tax systems are weak or porous, or there are significant levels of tax evasion.[10] Forcing artificial restrictions on financial institutions also serves to buoy the inflation tax base, thereby maintaining a steady flow of seigniorage to the government. Permitting financial systems to develop efficiently, on the other hand, would reduce the inflation tax base, along with the seigniorage opportunity.

There can be no doubt that financial repression can and does assist governments to cover fiscal deficits (that is, to live beyond their means). However, recent research questions the budget deficit financing rationale on the basis that institutional and historical-cultural differences between countries places the problem of policy choice into a variety of sociopolitical milieus, which has resulted in sharply different approaches to financial system regulation and development, even among countries facing substantially similar budget problems.[11] What can be said about Ukraine's specific circumstances?

Indicators of Financial Repression

During 1991–2000, Ukraine exhibited many of the classic symptoms of the financially repressed economy. Until the mid-1990s, banks were mandated to make available low interest rate loans to priority enterprises and sectors on a "directed credit" basis. In return, the banks were able to rediscount priority loans at the NBU on concessionary terms. This policy was apparently an effort to stem the fall in output in key industrial sectors. As can be observed from Table 8.1, real interest rates were negative throughout much of 1993–96, and though they recurred less frequently in 1996 and after, they nonetheless provided a clear incentive for over-borrowing. Another measure of repression is the level of real discount rates used by NBU for its refinancing operations, since it formally served as a base for other rates until September 1996. It was therefore a more accurate reflection of policy than deposit or lending rates. Table 8.1 also presents real NBU refinancing rates, calculated as the nominal refinancing rate less the annualized rate of price inflation. In many periods, this rate, too, was negative. Such interest rate linkages and ceilings distort economic activity by discouraging savings, reducing incentives to deposit money with banks, and stimulating demand for credit on the part of the worst borrowers.

High reserve requirements often are employed in conjunction with directed credit schemes in order to reduce availability of funds for low-priority, nonprivileged enterprises and sectors. Excess bank reserves thus have the implicit effect of reducing banks' own funds available for discretionary, nonpriority lending.[12] Bank profitability also is constrained, as mandatory reserves normally are not interest-bearing. Funds subject to mandatory reserve requirements in Ukraine are paid in cash and kept in the individuals banks' correspondent account at the NBU with no interest payments.[13] Where excess reserves are mandated, the central bank's assets may constitute a relatively large proportion of total assets in the financial sector. As can be observed in Table 8.1, the proportion of domestic credit held by the NBU in Ukraine exceeded 50 percent in many quarters throughout 1996–2000, a clear indication of rather severe shortages of loanable funds.

High reserve ratios also serve to increase the "tax base" on which the inflation tax is levied. For a given level of inflation, other things being equal, a higher reserve requirement results in higher inflation tax revenues. Governments that rely upon the inflation tax to finance budget deficits are likely to maintain high reserve requirements in order to buoy revenues rather than to reduce inflation.[14] However, it is also true that overall inflation can be reduced in the short run by raising sharply bank reserve requirements. To the extent that the inflation tax can be passed on to depositors, the real volume of deposits will shrink. A credit squeeze can occur, as the inflation tax reduces the real supply of loanable funds. Under these conditions, banks will have difficulty meeting normal credit demands from new and existing clients. Real output can fall, should banks be unable to meet the needs of worthy borrowers. In this way, economies can experience periods of both accelerating inflation and decelerating GDP growth, a condition that afflicted Ukraine throughout the early years of the decade.

There are obvious difficulties in measuring the degree of repression that may be present. Financial repression may rely upon implicit instruments, which are inherently difficult to detect and measure. Financially repressed economies may also exhibit characteristics that are not due to repression per se. The lack of maturity in the financial sectors of transition economies is an impediment to evaluating the

Table 8.1
Indicators of Financial Repression in Ukraine, 1992-2000

Quarter	Annualized Quarterly Exponential Rates of Inflation	Average National Bank Refinance Rates (APR %)		Average Commercial Banks' Deposit Interest Rates (APR %)		Actual Commercial Bank Reserve Ratio (%)	Required Commercial Bank Reserve Ratio (%)	Estimated Excess Bank Reserves	"Financial Depth" (M2 as % of Annualized GDP)	Percent Domestic Credit Held by NBU	Estimated Annual "Tax" Revenues on Domestic Credit from Repression (% Annualized GDP)
		Nominal	Real	Nominal	Real						
1992-1Q	624	n.a.	n.a.	12.5	-611.5	n.a.	10 to 15	n.a.	18.30	8.7	133.2
2Q	200	n.a.	n.a.	20.8	-179.2	n.a.	10 to 15	n.a.	19.97	52.9	56.5
3Q	115	n.a.	n.a.	34.4	-80.6	n.a.	10 to 15	n.a.	21.89	61.5	30.9
4Q	172	80	-92	57.3	-114.7	56	10 to 15	43	27.01	55.0	54.0
1993-1Q	532	80	-452	79.2	-452.8	70	10 to 15	57	19.20	41.7	162.7
2Q	400	80	-320	133.2	-266.8	96	25	71	16.65	33.7	85.7
3Q	444	240	-204	212.4	-231.6	57	25	32	18.89	43.4	64.7
4Q	612	240	-372	210	-402	52	25	27	10.66	41.7	60.7
1994-1Q	140	240	100	279.6	139.6	53	25	28	9.84	50.9	20.9
2Q	60	240	180	274.8	214.8	49	15	34	11.44	50.4	38.1
3Q	48	161.8	114	148.8	100.8	58	15	43	17.00	53.3	23.6
4Q	400	248.4	-100	130.8	-269.2	49	15	34	10.67	36.4	49.0
1995-1Q	644	239.5	-397	128.4	-515.6	21	15	6	7.94	37.5	72.4
2Q	180	109.7	-70.3	63.6	-116.4	20	15	5	8.64	36.7	16.0
3Q	92	66.7	-25.0	30	-62	17	15	2	7.98	43.1	8.7
4Q	76	97.6	21.0	43.2	-32.8	17	15	2	8.04	47.6	4.7

1996-1Q	76	102.4	26.0	49.2	-26.8	18	15	3	8.44	50.3	4.3
2Q	12	65.5	53.0	33.6	21.6	14	15	-1	8.60	49.2	3.5
3Q	32	40.1	8.0	26.4	-5.6	15	15	0	7.72	49.4	0.7
4Q	16	39.9	24.0	26.4	10.4	13	15	-2	7.68	52.9	1.1
1997-1Q	41.6	32.9	-8.7	22.8	-18.8	17	9	8	11.02	50.6	3.0
2Q	6.8	23.4	16.6	19.2	12.4	17	11	6	11.49	48.9	1.9
3Q	5.2	16.9	11.7	15.6	10.4	13	11	2	10.16	47.9	1.4
4Q	12.7	24.9	12.2	16.8	4.1	15	11	4	9.58	50.7	0.5
1998-1Q	6.7	40	33.3	19.2	12.5	12	15	-3	13.27	51.1	2.3
2Q	5.2	45	39.8	20.4	15.2	12	15	-3	12.27	54.1	2.9
3Q	12.1	80	67.9	24	11.9	15	16.5	-1.5	9.53	60.3	2.2
4Q	48.8	79.4	30.6	26.4	-22.4	18	16.5	1.5	10.51	61.3	4.3
1999-1Q	13.9	60	46.1	24	5.1	22	15	7	12.12	63.9	1.1
2Q	18.9	50.2	31.3	20.4	1.5	25	15	10	13.28	64.6	0.1
3Q	5.5	45	39.5	30	24.5	22	17	5	10.37	63.3	4.5
4Q	31.9	45	13.1	20.4	-11.5	22	17	5	11.70	64.4	2.4
2000-1Q	38.9	38	-0.9	16.8	-22.1	25	16	9	13.31	n.a	6.3
2Q	29.6	29.3	-0.3	12	-17.6	22	16	6	12.70	n.a	4.7
3Q	9.9	27.9	18	13.2	3.3	21	16	5	10.46	n.a	0.6
4Q	14.3	27	12.7	12	-2.3	26	16	10	11.43	n.a	0.4

Source: Ukrainian-European Policy and Legal Advice Centre, *Ukrainian Economic Trends* (various issues); International Monetary Fund, *Ukraine: Recent Economic Developments* (various issues); and author's calculations.

actual amount of deviation from market-clearing interest rates. Since there were only rudimentary financial markets in Ukraine in the 1990s, we can only estimate the "tax" that the government derived from financial repression. One approach is to calculate the difference between the world interest rate (taken as the long-run real rate in OECD countries, 0.9 percent) and the average domestic real rate, multiplied times the volume of domestic credit. This is an admittedly crude measure, but an effective one. The last column in Table 8.1 provides this measure for Ukraine. Throughout 1992–95, such "tax revenues" were quite high relative to GDP but fell to more moderate levels beginning in 1995.

Another measure of repression is "financial depth," defined as the ratio of money supply (M2) to GDP. This is employed as a rough proxy for more sophisticated measures of the level of financial intermediation, which cannot easily be calculated in the case of a transition economy like Ukraine's. Financial depth is consistently found to be lower in financially repressed economies than in market economies.[15] As can be seen in Table 8.1, M2 as a percentage of annualized nominal GDP fell dramatically in Ukraine from 1992–96. This indicates the extent of disintermediation in the wake of Ukraine's hyperinflationary episode. Others have also observed Ukraine's difficulties in attracting funds to the banking sector.[16]

Directed credit policies also require financial repression in order to work, since informal channels would develop spontaneously to reallocate administratively channeled capital subsidies to higher-yielding private uses. Governments therefore typically intervene to segment financial markets, by restricting the flow of funds between subsidized and nonsubsidized firms and sectors.[17] Rules for credit rationing therefore almost always accompany elaborate directed crediting policies. There are five major types of directed crediting policy instruments, all of which involve rationing to one extent or another: (1) subsidized interest rates; (2) differential rediscount rates; (3) direct budgetary subsidies; (4) credit floors and ceilings on banks' lending operations; and (5) use of specialized financial institutions. To one extent or other, Ukraine employed all five of these in the 1990s.

Research suggests strongly that preferential crediting of specific firms and industries is the primary objective and motivation of governments that engage in financial repression.[18] Stemming output falls and preventing mass unemployment are more acute concerns for governments than are budget deficits. On this view, selective credit schemes are not merely a secondary consequence of a government's policy of interest rate controls. Rather, directed crediting itself constitutes the policy choice. This implies that, in the case of Ukraine, financial repression has been employed mainly as the means to absorb losses of state enterprises, and only secondarily as a means to finance fiscal deficits. It is, therefore, a component of the government's expenditure policy.[19]

Evidence of Excessive Consumption by the State

The Yushchenko Hypothesis

Former prime minister Viktor Yushchenko lays the blame for Ukraine's economic woes on excessive consumption by the state sector relative to the private, household sector.[20] Since 1994, the diversion of extensive amounts of resources to satisfy the government's requirements has constrained growth of the private sector, promoted centralization of output, and driven legitimate private competitors into the shadow sector. Yushchenko regards this process as "the main reason behind all out macro- and micro-economic difficulties," and, more importantly, "the chief threat to the establishment of democracy and . . . national security of Ukraine."[21] There is some merit to this argument. Table 8.2 presents a revised and updated version of Yushchenko's analysis, which was originally published in 1998. Let us retrace his logic.

In the face of a rapid decline in real GDP, the growth in state sector consumption greatly exceeded that of the household sector throughout the 1990s. This can be seen in the data in Table 8.2, which indicates that real final consumption of the state sector exceeded that of the household sector by an average of 30 percent from 1990–99. Yushchenko classifies consumption by the state sector as "nonproductive." This is not quite fair, but his larger point is well taken. That is, the centralization of the economy has survived the demise of the command economy, and it has done so aided by a state that employed repressive means to accomplish its ends at the expense of the private sector.

Many of Ukraine's economic pathologies are direct outgrowths of this state of affairs, including: undermonetization of the economy; stunted development of the banking sector; enterprise liquidity problems; growth of the shadow sector; poor government tax receipts; and low investment levels. There is also a bias—apparent in the data—toward protecting state-owned and former state enterprises, which are considered "too big to fail." At first this policy was pursued by issuing large volumes of preferential credits, especially in 1992–94. The result was hyperinflation, which only aggravated the trend toward

Table 8.2

Indicators of Economic Centralization in Ukraine, 1990-2000

(Millions of hryvnia, Unless Otherwise Noted)

Indicator or Other Item	1990	1991	1992	1993	1994	1995	1996	1997	1998	1999	Est. 2000
Real GDP Index (1990=100)	100.0	93.4	94.0	76.1	47.0	42.6	42.2	44.4	43.1	42.2	45.5
GDP Deflator (1990=100)	1.00	1.92	33	1,117	13,761	71,533	114,162	125,846	142,474	180,492	230,272
State Sector Consumption:											
Final Consumption by State Sector (UAH mlln.)	0.27	0.52	6	236.99	2,330.69	11,595.45	17,738	20,368	23,600	24,100	27,600
Growth in State Consumption (Multiples of 1990)	1.00	1.93	32.74	877.74	8,632	42,946	65,696	75,437	87,407	89,259	102,222
Real Final Consumption in State Sector	0.27	0.271	0.268	0.21	0.169	0.162	0.155	0.162	0.166	0.134	0.120
Growth in Real State Consumption (Multiples of 1990)	100.0	100.3	99.2	78.6	62.7	60.0	57.5	59.9	61.3	49.5	44.4
Household Sector Consumption:											
Final Consumption by Household Sector (UAH mlln.)	0.92	1.56	21.12	653.5	5,331.39	27,093.74	43,469	50,600	58,400	73,000	88,000
Growth in Household Consumption (Multiples of 1990)	1.00	1.696	22.957	710.326	5,794.989	29,449.717	47,248.913	55,000.000	63,478.260	79,347.826	95,652.174
Real Final Consumption in Household Sector	0.92	0.813	0.64	0.585	0.387	0.379	0.381	0.402	0.41	0.404	0.382
Growth in Real Household Consumption (Multiples of 1990)	100.0	88.4	69.6	63.6	42.1	41.2	41.4	43.7	44.6	44.0	41.5
Economic Centralization Index (Ratio of Real Final Consumption of the State Sector Over Real Final Consumption of Households)	**100.0**	**113.5**	**142.5**	**123.6**	**148.9**	**145.6**	**138.9**	**137.1**	**137.4**	**112.5**	**107.0**

Sources: Adapted from Viktor Yushchenko and Viktor Lysytsky, "Excessive State Consumption: The Main Instability Factor for Ukraine," *Ukrainian Economic Trends* (June 1998); revised and updated by the author.

GDP Deflator: UEPLAC, *Ukrainian Economic Trends* (March 2001): table 1.1, p. 6.

Consumption Data: 1990-93: IMF, *Recent Economic Developments* (Washington, D.C.: IMF, March 1996), table 5, p. 33.

1994-95: IMF, *Recent Economic Developments* (Washington, D.C.: IMF, October 1997), table 2, p. 55.

1996-97: IMF, *Recent Economic Developments* (Washington, D.C.: IMF, May 1999), table 13, p. 76.

1998-2000: IMF, *Recent Economic Developments* (Washington, D.C.: IMF, January 2001), table 3, p. 6.

demonetization. With the liquidation of the hyperinflation and currency reform in September 1996, this game was at an end. However, as we shall see later in this chapter, a new dynamic was set in motion in 1997–99: hidden inflation through the vehicle of "money surrogates." This approach has permitted the government to retain "soft" budget constraints on enterprises while at the same time claim credit for tight monetary policy.

The Repression of Household Liquidity, 1988–96

We can provide further confirmation of the Yushchenko hypothesis through an examination of the government's efforts to boost production during the period immediately preceding the currency reform of 1966. The following analysis indicates strongly that the government reduced significantly household liquidity, transferring much of it to the enterprise sector. The theoretical justification for examining sectoral liquidity is provided by the socialist theory of money, a theory to which many Ukrainian officials apparently subscribed in 1992–96.[22]

Expressed succinctly by economist Gavin Peebles, the theory of socialist money is that, unlike the kind of fiat money used in other economic systems, households in the socialist economy have recourse to the state for the discharge of debts owed to them, which are represented by the paper money issued by the state.[23] Indeed, "the whole logic underlying this monetary system is that the currency has value as long as the state can supply all the goods people want in the correct assortment, at stable prices."[24]

Consequently, some economists have measured the money supplies in socialist countries in terms of the relationship of the money stock to the annual flow of retail goods supplied through state stores.[25] Indigenous economists have also employed this measure.[26] Economist Richard Portes, on the other hand, disagrees with this approach on theoretical grounds.[27] In any event, there is nothing conceptually incorrect with the view that financial assets held by households in socialist economies are debts of the government and the government-owned banking system. Further, concerning its applicability in Ukraine, it is hard to imagine that policymakers in this recently socialist country would be so quick to abandon their previous conceptions about the role of money in the economic system. Quite to the contrary.[28]

Movements in the ratio of household monetary holdings to retail sales (and the same for enterprises), therefore, may provide important clues as to the general drift of government economic policy. Two measures of household liquidity are pertinent, which we will label

"DSD liquidity" and "HM liquidity." DSD liquidity measures household liquidity as a function of demand and savings deposits (hence, the designation DSD). HM liquidity will be discussed presently. Peebles estimates that, in Soviet times, there was rapid growth in DSD liquidity, from around .15 of retail sales in 1960 to over .80 by 1989.[29] Consistent with Peebles's estimation of the long-term trend, the present study finds that Ukrainian household DSD liquidity was in the .95 to 1.00 range in 1989–90, on the eve of the Soviet collapse.

The year 1991 appears as a watershed period, with household DSD liquidity falling rapidly thereafter. Table 8.3 provides the quarterly data, based on a rolling four-quarters' worth of retail sales, in the interest of comparability. As can be seen, household liquidity fell by half in just one year, 1992, reaching its previous 1985 level. It fell by half again by mid-1994, which approximates Peebles's estimate of the 1975 level in the USSR. Not surprisingly, the proportion of household monetary assets held in the form of cash rose during this period, from 18.5 percent at the time of independence to 80 percent in late 1993, where it hovered since then, in a narrow band of 82 percent, plus or minus 3 percent.

DSD liquidity provides only a partial view of household monetary assets, however, since it excludes cash holdings. HM liquidity provides a much broader picture, incorporating cash as well as demand and savings deposits as a ratio of annual retail sales. According to Peebles, HM liquidity reached 1.054 in the Soviet Union by 1988, having risen from .182 on an all-union basis in 1960. Peebles's figures are roughly consistent with the present estimate of 1.16 to 1.23 for 1989–90 in Ukraine. Here, too, we witness Ukrainian HM liquidity falling precipitously after 1991, more than halving by the end of 1993.

Before proceeding to a discussion of what the decline in household liquidity means with reference to the government's policy, we must examine the trends in enterprise liquidity. Three measures were developed, which include: enterprise demand deposits (D), demand deposits plus savings deposits (S+D), and demand and savings deposits plus foreign currency deposits (S+D+F). For the lattermost measure, foreign currency deposits have been ascribed entirely to the enterprise sector on the basis that enterprises were in a much more favorable position than households to earn large quantities of foreign exchange from export trade. This is not an unreasonable assumption.[30] In any case, the intent was to examine whether the accumulation of foreign currency would serve to cushion adverse changes in enterprise liquidity during this period. It turns out that it was of only transitory benefit. Indeed, as Table 8.3 shows, enterprise liquidity, which initially rose during 1992,

Table 8.3

Ukraine - Quarterly Sectoral Liquidity Indicators, 1991-1996

Period	Annual Nominal Retail Sales (Rolling 4 Quarters)	Liquidity Expressed as a Proportion of Annual Retail Sales									
		Entire Economy [note 1]			Enterprise Sector [note 2]				Household Sector [note 3]		
		M1	M2	M3	D	S	S + D	S + D + F	DSD	HM	% Cash
1991-4Q	132	1.333	1.993	1.993	0.517	0.095	0.613	0.614	1.125	1.381	18.5
1992-1Q	198	1.324	1.897	1.897	0.562	0.148	0.71	0.711	0.88	1.187	25.9
2Q	343	1.785	2.23	2.25	0.987	0.203	1.19	1.214	0.563	1.055	46.6
3Q	689	1.447	1.746	1.333	0.724	0.19	0.914	1.001	0.334	0.833	59.6
4Q	1456	1.502	1.719	1.344	0.896	0.161	1.057	1.183	0.217	0.662	67.2
1993-1Q	3006	1.281	1.518	1.815	0.872	0.192	1.064	1.362	0.156	0.454	65.7
2Q	5848	1.111	1.361	1.929	0.722	0.212	0.934	1.503	0.134	0.427	68.5
3Q	14147	1.613	1.843	2.191	1.172	0.207	1.379	1.728	0.093	0.464	79.9
4Q	43824	0.767	0.863	1.077	0.42	0.084	0.504	0.713	0.072	0.364	80.2
1994-1Q	86425	0.555	0.642	0.773	0.247	0.052	0.299	0.429	0.069	0.343	79.6
2Q	140910	0.549	0.668	0.772	0.273	0.073	0.346	0.45	0.08	0.322	75.2
3Q	206929	0.662	0.778	0.901	0.376	0.123	0.449	0.571	0.075	0.329	77.2
4Q	283038	0.658	0.765	1.115	0.343	0.027	0.177	0.762	0.073	0.353	79.2
1995-1Q	434100	0.521	0.618	0.907	0.231	0.06	0.291	0.579	0.066	0.327	79.9
2Q	625600	0.548	0.616	0.849	0.236	0.039	0.275	0.508	0.057	0.342	83.4
3Q	885100	0.474	0.525	0.722	0.199	0.03	0.229	0.426	0.043	0.295	85.5
4Q	1196400	0.391	0.441	0.572	0.149	0.027	0.177	0.309	0.044	0.264	83.2
1996-1Q	1366200	0.357	0.407	0.519	0.128	0.027	0.158	0.269	0.041	0.249	82.1
2Q	1498300	0.358	0.406	0.502	0.115	0.023	0.141	0.234	0.046	0.268	82.8
3Q	1583900	0.345	0.393	0.479	0.112	0.022	0.134	0.22	0.049	0.259	81.2
4Q	1569600	0.358	0.421	0.505	0.12	0.025	0.145	0.228	0.065	0.277	76.7

Notes: [1] M1 = Cash in Circulation + Demand Deposits; M2 = M1 + Savings Deposits; M3 = M2 + Foreign Currency Deposits.

[2] D = Demand Deposits; S = Savings Deposits; F = Foreign Currency Deposits.

[3] DSD = Demand Deposits + Savings Deposits; %Cash = Cash as a Percent of Total Monetary Holdings.

Sources: Retail sales are from OECD, "Short-Term Economic Indicators--Transition Economies," various issues. Money supply data are from Marcin Luczynski and Oleg Novoselsky, "Ukraine in Numbers Year End 1996 Review," *Ukrainian Legal and Economic Bulletin* (March 1997); table 8, p. 40. Liquidity Indicators are the author's calculations.

the period in which household liquidity collapsed, also fell rapidly after the hyperinflationary period of late 1993, reaching approximately household levels by late 1995. Enterprises were therefore late to suffer the ill effects of inflation, as their liquidity remained at robust levels until the second half of 1993. Hyperinflation, it seems, spared no one.

Putting this all together, the general drift in Ukrainian financial policy can be discerned. Throughout 1992–93, the government sought to restore the previous balance between incomes and output levels, by consciously transferring liquidity from households to the enterprise sector. This served the perceived policy imperative of wringing inflation out of the retail trade sector while at the same time stemming the fall in output. In fact, the output collapse was viewed by many in the Ukrainian economic establishment as itself *the problem*, rather than the inevitable consequence of the inefficient organization of industry under the former Soviet regime.

The policy tools to pursue this objective remained available to the authorities throughout this period, owing to the still rather rigid walls of separation between the official household and enterprise sectors, which were reinforced by Ukraine's credit policies and heavy regulation of the retail sector. That Ukraine should squeeze household liquidity so is not surprising in light of the traditional Soviet method of suppressing inflation through manipulation of retail prices. Since in a socialist economy retail sales are the main channel for recalling excess currency, the Ukrainian government entered into a delicate tightrope act, attempting to strike the appropriate balance between wages and retail goods availability. This task was made all the more difficult by the new inflationary dynamic that had been set in motion in 1992–93, the causes of which the authorities apparently chose to remain largely ignorant.

Directed Credits to Industry

The directed credit policies (the effects of which have been described both above and in Chapter 7) increase the financial system's fragility while reducing its flexibility. There is no evidence that they improve the efficiency of resource allocation; quite to the contrary.[31] By their nature, directed credits place relatively severe restrictions on bank loan portfolios. Banks are directed to channel to certain enterprises or sectors a specified amount of total lending (or total assets). Such direction tends to segment financial markets, segregating enterprises according to their risk and economic potential and providing poor risks with incentives to borrow more. This can give rise to a serious "moral hazard" problem in the banking industry.[32] Interest rate ceilings on deposits also tend to encourage and promote development of bank cartels. Direct government intervention in the form of lavish privileges (for example, exclusive franchises or priority access to refinancing at the central bank) for favored banks and restrictions on others also can have this effect.

Governments can also own banks outright. Public sector ownership of lending institutions impairs financial flexibility due to the government bureaucratic management, lack of innovation, and the undue influence of political factors in lending decisions. As Maxwell Fry points out:

> A major problem with virtually all specialized financial institutions . . . springs from the fact that they are established to lend to borrowers that [other] financial institutions . . . have avoided. Hence, specialized financial institutions are set up deliberately to lend to high-risk borrowers.[33]

Government banks generally hold substantial proportions of nonperforming loans.[34] While generally understated, the true volume of default losses appears to be enormous.[35] Further, loan loss provisions are inadequate in most cases, so that these institutions can themselves become problems for their governments, as they load up the asset side of their balance sheets with substandard and nonperforming loans. In Ukraine, the banking sector started out on shaky ground. Even before many state banks were converted to joint stock companies, they inherited bad loans to state enterprises. Under such circumstances, foreclosure would threaten the solvency of the banks themselves.[36] These are problems that most governments are anxious to avoid.

The contours and performance of Ukraine's banking system are described in detail in Appendix 8.1. There is evidence of high levels of segmentation and concentration in Ukraine's banking industry. The top ten largest banks dominated Ukraine's financial system in the 1990s, despite the high levels of fragmentation that have been increasing over time. Further, the most prominent banks enjoy many privileges owing to their ties with the government and the NBU. The three largest banks in Ukraine were formerly state-owned, specialized banks. Confidence in the Ukrainian banking system has been consistently low, and this is reflected in the extremely low ratio of demand deposits and money supply to GDP, both measures of the "financial depth" of the economy. From this data, we can conclude that the Ukrainian economy has been, and remains, terribly undermonetized.

Commercial banks were too small in the 1990s to supply the credit needs of the industrial sector. Consequently, the NBU filled this role and has continued to do so even after the currency reform of 1996. In fact, the total amount of domestic credit held by the National Bank reached almost 65 percent in 1999, up from 50 percent in the third quarter of 1996. The NBU performs economic functions that go beyond (and in some cases, fall short of) the traditional functions of central banking and encroach on commercial bank operations. This is, and should be, clearly outside of the scope of any central bank's activities.

An examination of the growth in official net NBU credit to the general government helps a great deal to fill in the story. The NBU remains the chief supplier of credit to the general government. Official net NBU credit to general government increased eight-fold from 1995–2000 in nominal hryvniy. As a proportion of GDP, NBU credit to government has almost tripled, from a little over 5 percent in 1995–97 to an average of 12–15 percent in 1999–2000. These credits are not in themselves inflationary. However, the government has also turned to the NBU to absorb the vast majority of its T-bill issues, due to problems in refunding Ukrainian T-bills in the open market. As a consequence, by 1999, the NBU had again assumed the institutional role of chief lender to the government. This only increased the fragility of the financial system. It also made it difficult to avoid inflationary financing of budget deficits in the event of an external shock, such as a global economic downturn, or a national emergency. Just as critical for the state of the Ukrainian financial system in the short-run, there was ample evidence that the government was seriously "crowding out" private borrowing.

"Crowding Out" Firms from the Credit Market

An increasing share of banks' assets was held in government securities in the 1990s. Insofar as many banks were undercapitalized, and therefore tended to shy away from risk-taking, Ukrainian T-bills appeared as a more desirable alternative to lending in the real sector. The government was absorbing an increasing share of domestic lending in the late 1990s (until 1999, when the trend abated somewhat). As a consequence, less credit was available for the rest of the economy, a phenomenon known as "crowding out." It is extremely difficult to know how much of the flow of bank resources into the T-bill market would have otherwise been channeled to the private sector. The massive amounts of capital flight serve as one indicator of Ukrainian investors' low level of confidence in the domestic credit markets. What we can conclude, however, is that the vigorous use of T-bills for budget deficit financing has displaced private investment funds, raised interest rates, and reduced access to private financing, generally.

Private lending is risky for Ukrainian banks. Credit analysis is hampered by enterprises' Byzantine accounting practices, the difficulty in securing loans via collateral, and the effort involved in monitoring the financial fortunes of bank clients. Investment in T-bills was a less risky, more profitable alternative. The crowding out of private enterprises also had the consequence of rendering Ukrainian banks less competitive than they otherwise might have been, in that such passive investments provide little incentive to improve commercial lending expertise.

Insofar as the government has been unable to fill the budget deficit gap with foreign lending, and considering that domestic purchases of T-bills had fallen off dramatically by the end of the decade, the NBU has been forced into the role of "lender of last resort." By the start of 2000, the NBU held some 88 percent of the outstanding T-bill debt, up from 66 percent in 1998. Hence, although the NBU is constitutionally and legally prohibited from directly financing state budget deficits, it has the primary role in financing government operations. The budget surplus of 2000 obviated the need for placement of new T-bill debt, but the NBU continued to hold the overwhelming majority of outstanding government securities. This has thrust the NBU into the key role in both private and public finance, and made the bank a direct player in domestic credit markets, as opposed to its more appropriate role as a functionally disinterested regulator.

The Expanding Use of Surrogate Money, 1997–2000

After the currency reform of 1996, the domestic monetary situation was much improved. The hryvnia remained relatively stable against the U.S. dollar and other hard currencies, and the T-bill market was absorbing ever-larger amounts of government debt. For a few years, the government was able to finance the state budget deficit in a noninflationary manner. However, the enterprise sector remained perpetually starved for cash, the banking industry being too small and underdeveloped to supply even its working capital requirements. Consequently, enterprises turned to an array of more-or-less informal means of financing operations, which can collectively be referred to as "surrogate money," the presence of which constitutes a form of latent (but suppressed) inflation.

At the end of the 1990s, a majority of Ukrainian enterprises remained liquidity-constrained. To fill the need for cash, they increasingly resorted to nonmonetary means to settle their transactions. Many of these enterprises were loss-makers and therefore unable to generate working capital out of their normal operations. Reliance upon the government to supply their needs via direct subsidies—as in the early independence days—was no longer possible; budget "sequestration," the practice of postponing or canceling budgeted appropriations in order to balance the state budget, did a good job of matching expenditures to revenues but magnified the cash squeeze on enterprises. This prompted many firms to build up significant wages, tax, and other payments arrears. These are essentially a form of surrogate money, as it were: a way to finance operations "by other means."

Money substitutes may include mutual overdue debts, the netting out of tax liabilities, use of quasimoney (that is, bank notes, treasury bills, and IOUs), and barter. According to Poser, a critical means to evaluate the process of transition is to track the proportion of transactions that are settled on a monetary basis.[37] By the end of the 1990s, surrogate money was in broader use than cash in settling transactions in Ukraine. In 1997, over UAH 30.3 billion of industrial sales was paid in cash, or just 45.3 percent of total sales of industrial output.[38] In 1998, the figures were UAH 31.6 billion and 41.9 percent, respectively. Indications are that, in agriculture, the volume of transactions settled in terms other than cash was even higher. In an undermonetized economy, like Ukraine's, barter transactions, payments arrears of various kinds, and money surrogates act as substitutes for cash. They help to adjust the volume of output to market demand as surely as short-term borrowing (that is, use of commercial paper) would in a fully developed market economy.

One way to look at the Ukrainian situation is to understand that the government itself has provided the productive sector with credit, albeit through the back door, by facilitating creation of monetary surrogates. This serves the foreign economic policies of the state. The authorities have been clever in pursuing a very tight, anti-inflationary policy but have managed at the same time to maintain "soft budget constraints" on enterprises using nonmonetary means of financing. Use of money substitutes serves to adhere to the letter of credit agreements with the IMF and other international lenders but largely violates the spirit of such restrictions. The emergence of alternative means of payment in the economy since 1995 also suggests that the inflationary processes in

Ukraine assumed characteristics that are vastly different from those that pertained in the period 1991–96.

Basic Money Substitutes

Wages are the main item that enterprises pay in cash. The relative volume of wages arrears, plus wages paid in-kind, is smaller than other components of the stock of enterprise arrears. Tax arrears pose no special problem for enterprises, as mutual settlements (that is, offsets) and noncash payments have grown. The use of nonmarketable bills of exchange (essentially private IOUs) has also increased. Based on negotiated prices, these permit firms to "manage" profits on individual transactions. Further, they can be assigned to third parties in multiparty transactions, thereby serving as a (limited) instrument of credit expansion outside the banking system and remaining largely hidden from the NBU's view. Essentially, bills of exchange are "private money."

Payments Arrears

There were considerable volumes of overdue debts among Ukrainian enterprises at the end of the 1990s. Firms have received de facto loans by habitually paying their bills late (if at all). Such debts have exceeded 100 percent of GDP since the first quarter of 1998, climbing as high as 170 percent of GDP in 1999. The chronic nature of these debts suggests that actual prices of transactions probably are well below those reported by the enterprises involved. The fact that this state of affairs has persisted is a strong indication of its usefulness to enterprises in expanding credit and evading taxes. It also indicates that enterprises have alternative means of financing their working capital requirements.

British economist Mario Gara raises the possibility that the build-up of payments arrears is an alternative means of achieving output equilibrium operating alongside the classical and Keynesian varieties.[39] Government direct and indirect price controls and imperfectly competitive markets permit sellers to fix excessively high prices relative to demand. Arrears can operate as means to permit the value of demand to equate to the value of supply, "since buyers pay just for a share of what they actually purchase."[40] Should all transactions have been settled in cash, there is no doubt that recorded inflation would have been higher. Sellers, of course, know this, and mark up their prices accordingly, which raises the prices of barter (and partial barter) transactions over those settled in cash.

Another consequence of interenterprise arrears is that estimates of the actual GDP level were increasingly overstated over the 1990s. To convey some sense of the magnitude of error, the increase in payables between enterprises in 1999 and 2000 was +UAH 58.75 billion, and +UAH 26.07 billion, respectively, These amounted to 45.2 percent and 15.1 percent of GDP, respectively, during these two years. Of this amount, perhaps one-half represents real value-added, so that some 7.5–22.5 percent of official nominal GDP appears to be affected by this phenomenon. This estimate is even before consideration of the growth of the shadow sector (where the magnitude of error in the official GDP statistics becomes enormous).

Some causes of high repayment arrears include: unproductive investments, defective loan policies, misapplication of funds, ineffective loan supervision, lackluster loan and debt recovery efforts, and lack of industrial discipline and responsibility. Enterprises throughout the 1990s were unable to avail themselves of the means employed by the government to relieve the payments crisis on the budget: the "write-off." Significant amounts of enterprises' arrears to the state were written off or restructured in the late 1990s (5.8 percent of GDP in 1999 and 3.7 percent in 1998).[41] Enterprises appeared to be unwilling to sustain both the losses that would accompany such write-offs and the write-down in current assets that that would involve. (The government also was unwilling to permit it.)

An interesting problem in the late 1990s was that enterprise payables consistently exceeded receivables since 1993, and the spread grew steadily after 1994. The rise in net payables is an indication that the circular pattern of arrears was broken in some way. Thus, there has been a net inflow of credit to the enterprise sector, via the budget (through subsidies) and mechanisms of informal financing. Budget subsidies are an insidious problem in that credit is implicitly to be reallocated from economically viable enterprises that need financing to inefficient, loss-making, liquidity-constrained firms that can't survive without it. In effect, the state acts as a financial intermediary, extending interest-free credit to unworthy borrowers and transferring the interest costs and default risk to the state budget (where everyone pays for it).

Interenterprise debts have all but completely displaced bank lending as the preferred source of enterprise financing. Commercial bank credits to enterprises have fallen dramatically during the 1990s, from a high of over 130 percent in early 1993 to less than 10 percent by mid-1995. They have hovered at around 5 percent since early 1997. The implication is clear: Weaknesses in the banking sector have driven enterprises to seek informal financing, from special pleadings to the state on the one hand (voluntary), and from other enterprises on the other (more or less involuntary). In either case, serious distortions were introduced into the financial system that would hamper the necessary development of the lending capacity of banks. In other words, it is not necessarily the case that there is little demand for credit, but that it was satisfied through means other than banks.

Barter Transactions

The extent of barter transactions in industry has been extensive. The magnitudes vary by sector, however, exceeding 40 percent in total in 1997 and 1998 before falling to around 33 percent in 1999, and less than half of their 1998 level by early 2000. (This was the result of diligent efforts by the Yushchenko government.) Enterprises have certain incentives to engage in barter. Barter trade can be employed as an additional source of credit.[42] Accepting in exchange for goods other goods that are not of immediate use to the seller induces a voluntary increase in inventory investment. There are storage and other carrying costs involved, not to mention the loss in liquidity. The amount and cost of such credit is measured as a function of the lag between the initial transaction and the time that the holder either sells the goods, exchanges them, or uses them in its own operations.

It is not clear whether barter transactions involve different prices than cash transactions. In the case of Russia, economists Commander and Mumssen argue that the process of barterization is driven mainly by the demand for credit.[43] They found that barter deals result in prices that are much higher than cash prices but that the relative prices of goods involved in such exchanges are unaffected. Probably, some of these transactions are forced, in that one or both parties would not otherwise have purchased the goods. Barter involves somewhat higher risks than monetary transactions, and transaction costs are higher in that the quality and tradability of the goods to be bartered must be assessed and the right terms of trade determined.[44]

Barter and arrears appear to be interrelated. Arrears can be viewed as an interenterprise settlement mechanism, a sort of involuntary credit extended from the payee to the payer. In this vein, barter overcomes the inherent danger that arrears—viewed as another form of credit—will not be paid. Barter de facto ensures the completion of contracts, hence, "multiplication of the number of such deals does not lead to a potentially explosive accumulation of debts but only means expansion of the area of trade."[45] A deleterious consequence, however, is that an increasing share of enterprise capital is tied up in immobilized form in inventories of finished and unfinished products. Barter trade does nothing to increase firms' liquidity. Rather than being a means to overcome the nonpayments crisis, then, barter trade represents a further deepening of the crisis.

Conclusion

There is ample evidence that the Ukrainian government used the instruments of financial repression throughout the 1990s—sometimes vigorously, but at other times less so—as means to finance its own consumption. It did so in a way that also avoided imposing a "hard budget constraint" on enterprises. The use of administered interest rates, bank reserves, regulations on foreign exchange, forced purchase of government debt by commercial banks, and the government's specialized banks supported the government's own appetite for spending at the expense of development of the private sector. Indeed, the scale of repressive activity leads to the inevitable conclusion that this constituted, in fact, the government's main financial policy throughout the decade of the 1990s.

In order to reduce (or temporarily circumvent) the inflationary pressures generated by its profligate spending, the state has tolerated—and even facilitated—growing use of "money surrogates" as an alternative form of credit. Such substitute monies include the build up of overdue debts, tax arrears, netting out mutual debts, use of nonmarketable bills of exchange, and barter transactions. At the end of the decade, growth of these more or less informal means of credit expansion had changed the inflationary dynamic in Ukraine, placed the NBU in the position of chief lender to both government and the private sector, ensured the continuing fragility of the banking industry, and rendered the economy more vulnerable than ever to macroeconomic shocks. As long as these instruments are employed, it will be difficult for Ukraine to harmonize its economic system with that of Western economies.

Appendix 8.1

Contours and Performance of the Ukrainian Banking System

Profile of the Banking Sector

Prior to 1989, the Ukrainian banking industry consisted of the republican branches of the main Soviet banks. Between 1989–91, significant measures were taken to establish a "two-tiered" banking system. The purpose of these early structural reforms was to separate formally commercial banking activities from the Central Bank of Russia. In the spring of 1991, the republican branch of Gosbank in Kyiv was reorganized into the National Bank of Ukraine (NBU). In addition, a small number of commercial banks and credit cooperatives were held over from the Soviet period.[1]

Subsequently, four specialized Soviet-era banks were spun-off from the corresponding all-Union banks in 1990: Bank Ukrayina (the agricultural bank, formed on the basis of the former Agroprombank), Prominvestbank (the industrial bank, formed on the basis of the former Prombudbank), Ukrsotsbank (the social sector bank, formed on the basis of the former Zhtlosotsbank), and Oshchadniy Bank (the savings bank). A fifth bank, the Ukrainian Export-Import Bank (Ukreximbank) was established in 1992 as a matter of pure necessity, as the former Soviet Vneshekonombank ceased processing Ukrainian foreign trade payments. Ukreximbank has no formal connection with the former Soviet-era bank.

Banking activity is governed by provisions of the Law of Ukraine, "On Banks and Banking Activity," which was enacted in 1991, providing for a variety of ownership structures and banking activities, and their regulation.[2] Commercial banks can be formed as joint-stock companies or as limited liability companies having the status of legal persons. The range of possible banking activities includes: receiving enterprise, household, and institutional deposits; crediting interest on deposits; holding cash balances, securities, and reserves; providing settlement services; engaging in foreign exchange transactions; and setting up fiduciary trusts.

On December 31, 2000, there were 195 organizations registered as banks in Ukraine. Approximately two-thirds of all banks registered in Ukraine since 1992 were single-branch banks that operated exclusively within the oblast in which they were originally registered. A number of banks were not operational, due to their poor financial condition or failure to meet statutory requirements. Table 8.1.1 details the evolution of bank ownership from 1991–2000. Due to a fairly lackadaisical licensing scheme in place from 1991–95, the number of banking institutions grew to 230 by year-end 1995 but has since fallen away to 195. Licensing requirements were tightened during 1996, when the NBU placed some 45 banks into categories of: restricted licensure, rehabilitation, closure, or liquidation (depending upon their financial condition). At any point in time, the actual number of banks operating *as banks* is somewhat less than those registered.

According to the data in Table 8.1.1, of the 195 registered banks in Ukraine at the end of the decade, two held the status of "state banks" (the savings bank and export-import bank); 169 commercial banks operated as joint-stock companies (including 120 open-ended and 49 closed joint-stock companies); 26 commercial banks were established as limited-liability companies (down from 67 in 1994); and 31 had foreign capital participation (up from 12 in 1995), including 7 with 100 percent foreign interest. Some 149 banks held a general license to conduct foreign currency transactions.

In 2000, only 155 banks actually operated in Ukraine, with a total authorized capital of UAH 3.557 billion (an average of UAH 23.0 million per bank). The major banks operating in Ukraine were Prominvestbank, Privat Bank, Ukrsotsbank, Oshchadniy Bank, Ukreximbank, Bank Ukrayina (which was liquidated in 2001), and Aval. These seven were classified by the NBU as "system banks." A large number of small to medium-sized private commercial banks actually were subsidiaries of large industrial conglomerates (that is, they were constituent units of financial-industrial groups, or FIGs); for

Table 8.1.1
Number and Ownership of Banks in Ukraine, 1991-2000

	1991	1992	1993	1994	1995	1996	1997	1998	1999	2000
Total Number of Banks	76	133	211	228	230	229	227	214	203	195
State-owned Banks	...	...	...	2	2	2	2	2	2	2
Joint-Stock Companies:										
Open-Ended	...	...	...	96	119	125	133	125	124	120
Closed-Ended	...	...	...	63	50	52	51	53	49	49
Limited Liability Companies	...	...	...	67	59	50	41	34	28	26
Banks with Foreign Capital Investment	...	...	...	12	12	14	22	28	30	31
Banks 100 Percent Foreign-Owned	...	...	...	1	1	2	6	9	8	7
Banks Licensed to Conduct Foreign Currency Operations	...	...	...	115	134	146	157	161	153	149
Other Banking and Financial Institutions Licensed by the National bank of Ukraine	...	...	...	...	4	2	2	2	1	1
Banks Liquidated	...	3	6	11	1	11	10	16	11	0

Source : National Bank of Ukraine. Available online at: http://www.bank.gcv.ua.

instance, in the oil and gas sector a number of such banks operated. Others were closely linked to the government through contracts to service budgetary receipts and payments, though this relationship has ended with the establishment of the State Treasury of Ukraine.

Several banks were established with foreign capital, growing in number from 12 to 31 over five years. At first, only one foreign bank was present: Credit Lyonnais.[3] This bank was joined later by Societe Generale, the Netherlands-based Rabobank, and Citibank Ukraine. (Both Societe Generale and Rabobank subsequently closed their doors in Ukraine, in October 2000 and February 2001, respectively.) Two banks were established with 50 percent foreign capital. The first was the First Ukrainian International bank, which was established in Donetsk with capital from AIOC Corporation (30.0 percent), and the second was Meous Pierson Bank (20.0 percent). Antares Bank was established in Kyiv by two U.S. firms with a combined capital contribution of $273 million. The Vidergeburt Bank in Dnipropetrovsk was started with 49.5 percent foreign capital, and Odessa's Contact Bank with 35.0 percent foreign participation. The Ukrainian Credit Bank was established by three British companies with a combined capital contribution of $154.6 million (46.0 percent). Finally, two banks have 35.0 percent foreign capital: Yugtokobank of Dnipropetrovsk, and Polikombank; the others are smaller and less prominent. The total share of bank assets held by foreign-owned banks is less than 15 percent.

Industry Concentration

State-owned banks accounted for over 45 percent of the sector's total capital, around 48 percent of total assets, 47 percent of total lending, and 51 percent of deposits. This puts these institutions clearly in the dominant position in the Ukrainian financial system, which remained highly concentrated throughout the 1990s. At the time of their formation on the basis of the former all-union banks, the four formerly state-owned banks (plus Ukreximbank) possessed disproportionately greater capital, numbers of branch offices, and a vaster client base than their fledgling commercial bank competitors. They are all closely tied to the government. Even the three large banks holding the status of joint stock companies in 2001 continued to enjoy support from the government and the NBU. As late as 1995, the largest banks controlled 86 percent of the banking market, with exclusive rights conferred by the state.[4]

The Oshchadniy Bank inherited from its Soviet predecessor the largest network of clients in Ukraine and held a monopoly position in the household savings market. The other state bank, Ukreximbank, has exclusive rights to finance foreign trade. These state banks, together with the three former state banks, have managed to retain their monopoly position within their respective specialized sectors. Bank Ukraina, Prominvestbank, and Ukrsotsbank were corporatized in 1992, with the shares transferred to the Ministry of Finance. Shares were subsequently distributed widely—mainly to employees—over 1993–94. Ownership was so diffused, however, that decision making continued to be dominated by senior management, many of whom were hold-overs from the former regime. Due to their close ties to the government, these banks were pressured into directed lending to state-owned enterprises and other large concerns, which compromised the integrity of their loan portfolios. The banking sector remains highly concentrated. Around 175 of the 195 banks in Ukraine account for less than 25 percent of the sector's total assets. The industry is "top-heavy," with the ten largest banks overwhelmingly dominating Ukraine's financial system.

Capitalization of Banks

The large number of registered banks in Ukraine derived from the inadequate minimum capital requirements that pertained in the period immediately following independence, as well as limited NBU authority for supervising banks in the early 1990s (discussed below). At the end of 1992, minimum capital requirements were a mere KBV 500 million for all banks (or around $500 thousand at 1992 exchange rates). This was increased in January 1994 to KBV 2 billion (but actually was reduced in real terms to $80,000) for banks operating only in domestic currency, and KBV 4 billion for banks with licenses to engage in foreign exchange transactions. By mid-1994 the minimum was raised again—this time for all banks—to KBV 5 billion ($125,000). These amounts were hardly significant enough to exclude the large number of "fly-by-night" institutions that were established prior to 1996.

Starting in February 1996, however, the NBU exercised its newly acquired authority to license banks by systematically reviewing all previously granted licenses, now with a minimum statutory capital requirement of ECU 500 thousand. (Banks established on or after January 1, 1996, however, faced a minimum capital requirement of ECU 3 million.) The minimum was subsequently raised to ECU 750 thousand as of July 1, 1997, and ECU 1 million starting on January 1, 1998; but it was ECU 5 million for minority foreign-owned banks, and

ECU 10 million for majority foreign-owned banks. Hence, the virtually costless entry into the banking business was brought to a halt, and at the same time marginal banks were rehabilitated, closed, or liquidated.

An exceedingly important problem of the banking system in the 1990s was that commercial banks were undercapitalized. This increased the risk of insolvency and posed a threat to depositors. Even though the amount of statutory capital in the system more than doubled in 1996 to UAH 1.033 billion, nearly 20 banks still failed to meet the minimum requirement of ECU 500 thousand by January 1, 1997.[5] After the mid-1990s, however, there was a strengthening of capital, especially among medium- and small-sized banks. In 1994, 96 percent of banks had less than $1 million in statutory capital. By 1997, the number had shrunk to 29 percent. But 90 percent of banks still had less than $5 million in statutory capital by mid-1998, an indication of just how poorly developed Ukraine's banking sector was. At August 1, 2000, the volume of capital in the banking system was UAH 6.275 billion (around $1.15 billion), or only approximately 4.5 percent of GDP.

Banking Performance

Banking sector performance in a normally functioning economy is largely a reflection of performance in the real assets sector. As such, the post-independence contraction in output and the growth of the shadow sector, together with the rise of informal financing arrangements, have negatively affected bank profitability, mainly by limiting the extent to which banks are able to expand their lending activities. In 1999, interest earnings comprised 60 percent of income and were shrinking in percentage terms. Banks have therefore had to look elsewhere for profits. The period of high inflation in the early 1990s provided ample opportunities for banks to earn handsome returns, but not in traditional intermediation activities.

Banks earned substantial profits from currency exchange operations during the period of high inflation. They were often able to take advantage of the distortions introduced by rapidly changing prices to engage in highly profitable but speculative foreign exchange transactions. Bank profitability declined steadily after the hyperinflation of 1993–94 came to an end. By the time of the currency reform of 1996, this game was over. In 1999, return on assets (ROA) system-wide was 3.8 percent, and return on equity (ROE) 4.6 percent. But the returns were skewed positively toward medium-sized banks.

Both the high inflation and its reduction hurt banks. During the period of inflation, real interest rates were highly negative, which favored borrowers over lenders. There was therefore an extraordinary propensity to borrow (whether one needed the money or not), which was reversed by monetary stabilization after 1996. Consequently, the volumes of real credit in the economy declined significantly, having a negative effect on banks' asset portfolios. The sharp decline in interest rates reduced the spread between lending and deposit rates. From 1995 to 1997, interest rate spreads fell from more than 50 percent to 30 percent. The narrowing spread became particularly acute starting in early 1996. The declining interest margins were offset largely by increased lending, as evidenced by the increase in the loan-to-deposit ratio from .95 in 1995 to 1.14 in 1997. The statutory linkage between commercial bank lending rates and the NBU refinance rate was eliminated in September 1996. Since that time, interest rates have been the product of market forces rather than administrative fiat.

In 1995–2000, commercial loan rates exceeded the NBU refinance rate. Insofar as inflation rates fell more rapidly than the lending and refinance rates, these were positive in real terms, until late 1999, when inflation accelerated somewhat. Banks were constrained from taking advantage of the positive real rates, however, in that the still-high level of public expenditure "crowded out" private investments. Commercial credit, therefore, remained tight throughout the late 1990s. The structure of bank assets and liabilities reflects both the constrained demand for credit in the economy generally as well as the constrained ability of banks to meet the existing demand for credit. Loans accounted for just 43 percent of assets in mid-2000. This is very low. Approximately 90 percent of liabilities in the banking system in 2000 were short term (less than one year in duration). The state of affairs in the banking sector constituted a serious drag on expansion and development of the private sector economy, thereby frustrating an important reform policy objective.

The banks were not able to attract new depositors, so that the lending base could not expand sufficiently to meet the demand for credit. At the same time, the number of nonperforming loans increased. In mid-2000, the proportion of prolonged, doubtful, and overdue loans accounted for over 25 percent of loans outstanding. The pressure from the government to credit loss-making state enterprises has been discussed elsewhere in this volume. The losses of the large "system banks" in 1999 totaled approximately $15.8 million. These banks also held around 65 percent of all bad loans in that year.

Another factor affecting performance is that many large state enterprises also have acquired majority interests in banks servicing their sectors. Such enterprise-owned banks are compelled to meet the financing demands of their parent concerns. Further, such interrelationships provided, in many cases, the only access to loans in a banking system where credit analysis and risk-based lending decision making were largely nonexistent. Consequently, many substandard borrowers and investment projects received financing, while more creditworthy private concerns were unable to gain access to badly needed capital. Deterioration of banks' loan portfolios was the inevitable result.

As previously noted, state banks account for around half of all banking sector operations. However, at January 1, 1998, their share of industry profits was a meager 28 percent. This suggests that—despite their small size and capitalization—the new commercial banks were less affected by government pressure to credit loss-making enterprises. In fact, the smallest banks were the most successful. Banks with capital between UAH 6–20 million held under 20 percent of both deposits and loans but accounted for over 30 percent of industry profits. The data also indicate that they were the best-capitalized banks.[6]

Owing to the high degree of concentration in the industry, and due to their secondary status, newly established commercial banks were driven to seek clients among the more risky segments of the credit market. The financial frailty of many enterprises led to a relatively large proportion of nonperforming assets (that is, bad loans), which were estimated to be as high as 30 percent of outstanding loans.[7] Banks therefore sought other sources of income, mainly by investing in treasury bills and engaging in foreign exchange operations.

Legal Status and Functions of the NBU

The NBU was created with passage of the Law of Ukraine "On Banks and Banking Activity," but its status and major functions are largely governed by the Constitution of Ukraine and the more recently enacted law "On the National Bank of Ukraine."[8] According to Article 99 of the Constitution, the prime function of the NBU is to ensure stability of the national currency. The law on the national bank designates the NBU as the central bank of Ukraine, the functions of which include: conducting monetary policy, coordinating operation of the banking system, and managing the rate of exchange against foreign currencies.[9] The NBU is empowered to determine the number, denominations, and security of bank notes that it places in circulation. It serves as the custodian of the gold and currency reserves of Ukraine and represents the country to other countries' central banks and to international financial institutions (such as the IMF and World Bank).

The Council of the National Bank of Ukraine is the highest policy-making body of the bank. Created under the 1999 national bank law, it consists of 14 members—7 appointed by the President of Ukraine and 7 appointed by parliament. The Council of the NBU develops annually the general principles of monetary policy and approves the membership of the NBU board, whose names are submitted for approval by the NBU governor. The governor is appointed by the president, subject to approval of parliament, and serves for a renewable term of five years. Under this arrangement, the NBU is accountable jointly to the president and parliament, within the limits of their constitutional powers.

Until the establishment of the State Treasury of Ukraine, the NBU provided cash management services for the state budget of Ukraine through contracts with authorized banks. According to the 1999 national bank law, the NBU is specifically prohibited from directly financing state budget deficits. However, the bank has indirectly financed deficits through its increasingly large purchases of Ukrainian T-bills. This is in violation of the spirit, if not the letter, of the law, but the authorities apparently have no difficulty with this practice.

The NBU supervises commercial bank compliance with banking laws and prudential regulations, according to standards established by the NBU, sometimes in consultation with the commercial banks themselves. The NBU also serves as the "bankers' bank" by lending to commercial banks in order to meet their short-term cash and reserve requirements. Refinancing of commercial banks is conducted via auction. The NBU also credits directly projects intended to strengthen investment in the national economy. For this purpose, loans are extended to commercial banks under collateral and via repo-type securities against the banks' holdings of state treasury securities.

Bank Regulation

Prior to February 1996, banks in Ukraine were not formally licensed by the NBU but were established at the oblast level under laws permitting companies to engage in banking activity. During this period, around two-thirds of all banks operated only in the oblast where they were established. Many of them were single-branch operations. The NBU did not formally register banks as such but did grant licenses for cash and foreign exchange operations. The NBU at this time had limited ability to intervene to protect depositors from weak banks; it could not seize bank assets or initiate liquidation of failed banks.

Under NBU governor Viktor Yushchenko, the central bank nonetheless intervened aggressively in some banks, starting with 20 problem banks in 1995, by imposing management changes and revoking licenses for violations of the law or regulations. This affected mainly smaller banks. At that time, the NBU estimated that 95 percent of banks on the brink of ruin had charter capital of less than KBV 10 billion (around $77,000).[10] The NBU also has, from time to time, restricted the rights of a number of large private banks to conduct foreign exchange operations (due mainly to excessive amounts of speculation and illegal money transfers abroad). Between 1992–2000, 69 banks were liquidated for violations of banking laws or for financial insolvency. The most prominent of bank failures was the July 2001 liquidation of the former state agricultural bank, Bank Ukrayina.

To protect depositors, the NBU established certain requirements respecting bank solvency (for example, minimum capital ratios, solvency ratios, and equity ratios), risk (for example, maximum exposure to a single borrower), and liquidity ratios.[11] When all else fails, the NBU possesses power to intervene in bank management. The bank resolution department of the NBU was established in September 1996. Its specific role is to identify problem banks and work out and enforce agreements for their restructuring. Further, the NBU staff formulated stricter regulations for prudential reporting (under a revised "Regulation 10") and classification of loans by commercial banks, effective in mid-1997. Other departments were also established at the NBU to supervise banks.[12] There were persistent concerns throughout the 1990s, however, that political interference in regulation enforcement by the NBU contributed to the steady deterioration of many banks.

Prior to 1997, the prevailing accounting practices tended to obscure the true financial position of many banks. Consequently, in 1996, the NBU issued new regulations mandating that all commercial banks issue financial statements in accordance with International Accounting Standards (IAS).[13] The new financial statements must include a Balance Sheet, Profit and Loss Statement, Statement of Cash Flows, and a Statement of Share Capital. The NBU also drafted a new chart of accounts for banks, in order to facilitate IAS implementation. To assist banks to make the transition to IAS, the NBU also established a controllers unit and statistics unit. Conversion to IAS has greatly improved analysis of banks' solvency and performance, increased transparency of the entire banking sector, and enabled comparisons with foreign banking institutions.

Confidence in Ukrainian Banks

The Ukrainian public has had a low level of confidence in banks, which placed a serious limit on the ability of the banks to attract deposits. Deposits have not grown substantially in real terms, with domestic currency deposits hovering at around 5 percent of GDP throughout the late 1990s. The period of high inflation wiped out the savings of many Ukrainian households, especially in 1992–93. (See chapter 7.) Since that time, periodic bank closings (for example, Slavyanskiy Bank, Hradobank, and Dendy Bank) have shaken confidence of depositors and investors alike. But one of the most serious institutional impediments to expansion of banks' lending base has been the infamous "Kartoteka II" system retained from the former regime.

Under Kartoteka II (literally, "card file no. 2"), commercial banks are thrust into the role of de facto agents of the state tax authorities. This mechanism permitted tax inspectors to satisfy enterprises' tax indebtedness by seizing their bank accounts. Enterprises also were not permitted to open more than one account. Further, NBU regulations require that banks provide information about depositors' bank balances and transactions to tax inspectors and law enforcement agencies.[14] Enterprises have no right of appeal in the event that their bank accounts are raided or funds siphoned off to the state budget. Consequently, enterprises have been reluctant to expand their use of commercial banks.

In an effort to increase public confidence in the banking system, President Kuchma in 1998 issued a decree to establish an insurance fund for the compensation of depositors if he/she is unable to gain access to their deposits.[15] Household and enterprise deposits as a percent of GDP remain small, however, at less than 5 percent of GDP, having fallen from over 40 percent in 1992. As long as measures like the Kartoteka II system persist, it is unlikely that the public will warm to commercial bank accounts.

Stability in the Banking System

In Soviet times, the banking sector was highly undeveloped, with no genuine role for proper banks in the administrative-command economy. Development of financial intermediation in Ukraine was stunted by the post-independence economic contraction, combined with the inflationary episode of 1992–95 (which effectively wiped out many households' savings), and actions taken by the government that forced the financial sector to meet its requirements ahead of the private sector's. Consequently, as economist Urban Gorski has observed, the total assets of the Ukrainian banking system are equal in size to that of a medium-sized bank in Western Europe, around $11.5 billion.

The relatively small size of the banking sector—well less than 20 percent of GDP—is at least partially due to the erosion of bank assets and liabilities that took place during the inflation years. Unfortunately, in both nominal and real terms, bank assets and liabilities have not recovered during the late 1990s. Unfortunately, actions taken by the government have only thwarted the recovery of the banking sector. Problems with refunding T-bills in the open market—especially after yields began to drop—prompted the government to force them on unwilling commercial banks. Direct losses also were imposed on the banks in August 1998 through involuntary restructurings of T-bill debt.

The currency reform and monetary stabilization of 1996 provided a badly needed window for the banking system to achieve stability, restructure, and begin serving as a true intermediary between savers and borrowers. This opportunity was missed, however. The government continued to take advantage of the banking sector in order to meet its own financing needs. Thus, by the middle of 1998, T-bills accounted for some 12 percent of all banking assets and for some 30–40 percent of liquid assets (depending on the bank). Small banks, especially, have remained relatively illiquid after the forced T-bill restructurings, insofar as T-bills accounted for 30 percent of small bank assets. Further, since T-bills are the only acceptable form of collateral for interbank lending in Ukraine, it has been hard for the banks to deal without them. Many banks that were otherwise financially sound were not able to meet prudential regulations and were forced to appeal to the NBU to supply liquidity.

During the Russian currency crisis of 1998, banks took long foreign exchange positions (in violation of NBU regulations) in anticipation of the domestic currency devaluation. This did not involve as much undue risk as it normally does, however, due to the banks' avoiding so-called "off-balance sheet" transactions in the currency futures market. Their poor financial standing did not permit them to leverage their positions through international borrowings. Consequently, while Russian banks suffered from the ruble devaluation, Ukrainian banks were not nearly as exposed. Ironically, Ukrainian banks' weaknesses saved them from the fate of their Russian counterparts.

The high degree of concentration in the Ukrainian banking sector is a significant possible source of instability. Poor performance (or outright failure) of a handful of banks could significantly damage the industry, with serious reverberations throughout the economy. The limited liquidity of the overall banking system has been partially overcome by a highly efficient payments system. But attracting deposits has continued to be a serious challenge at the start of the new decade. The limited amount of interbank lending activity reduced the impact of several medium-sized bank closures and the liquidation of the Ukrayina Bank. But the heavy burden of bad loans and low levels of equity investment also made the banks sensitive to relatively small perturbations in the macroeconomy. It is a credit to the NBU that stability in the system has been maintained, despite the fragility of the banks themselves.

Appendix 8.2

Repeated Efforts to Repress Inflation, 1993–96

The Ukrainian government authorities' attempts to suppress inflation in the first half of the decade stand as a classic case study of financial repression. As was demonstrated in chapter 7, the root cause of the Ukrainian inflation in 1992–95 was a policy of emitting currency in the form of credit subsidies to enterprises. During that period, Ukrainian economic policy emphasized loose and cheap credit to state enterprises, coupled with the interposition of administrative controls to reduce the inevitable inflationary pressures or to suppress inflation outright. It was this combination of policy instruments that briefly gained for Ukraine a reputation as the "most economically illiterate nation on earth."[1] The actual situation was much more complex, and the choices facing the authorities much less straightforward than whether or not to stabilize the currency. The political economy of government decision making militated against the aggressive pursuit of monetary reform. It was only after the inflation tax base eroded precipitously that Ukrainian policymakers resolved to stabilize the currency. By that time, the monetary situation presented no option other than to stabilize.

Throughout 1991–96, state-owned enterprises and powerful sectoral interests lobbied aggressively for the continuation of government policies, which lavished large amounts of "soft credits" on industry and agriculture. This appeared to the government as an imperative in light of the collapse in output. However, somewhat ironically, the availability of cheap credits effectively postponed the necessary steps toward monetary stabilization and structural reform. In 1992, off-budget subsidies and directed credits to industrial and agricultural enterprises amounted to some 16 percent of GDP. In 1993 and 1994, the central government continued to mandate that the financial sector extend huge amounts of nearly interest-free credits to enterprises. To a great extent, liberal credit emissions were facilitated by the subordination of the NBU to parliament, which employed the bank to frustrate the government's economic reform efforts. For instance, a KBV 1.23 trillion emission in March 1993 prompted a brief but inconclusive struggle between the Cabinet and parliament over control of the NBU. The government was enraged that the release of fresh credits had caused the value of the karbovanets to fall by half against the dollar, hitting a record low (at that time) of KBV 3,000 per dollar, falling from KBV 2,000 within a week's time. Damaging as it was, the emission also wiped out existing interenterprise debts, making it nearly impossible for the government to discern the economically weak enterprises from the others. Indeed, clearing the mutual debts of enterprises was precisely parliament's intent.[2]

The Stage is Set: Fall 1993

On September 22, 1993, President Kravchuk named as acting prime minister the recently appointed First Deputy Premier, Yukhym Zviahilskiy.[3] A conservative member of the "Red Directors" group of peoples' deputies, the 60-year-old Zviahilskiy was also serving at that time as the mayor of Donetsk and director of the Zasiadko Coal Mine. He was one of a number of former communist lawmakers who were opposed to radical reforms. Kravchuk had obviously used his appointment as the means to appease energy interests in the Donbas region, especially among coal miners. With the elections looming in mid-1994, Kravchuk's policies increasingly favored his electoral constituency, mainly the rural districts where he had always been popular and those in eastern Ukraine. In the fall, he ordered Zviahilskiy to lavish huge amounts of credits on the agricultural sector in order to finance the harvest, and on state enterprises that were seemingly perpetually strapped for cash due the growing payments arrears problem.[4]

The government authorities had great difficulty weaning enterprises off their cheap credit diet. On October 1, 1993, Ukraine again issued a mass of credits, totaling KBV 16 trillion (approximately $500 million), and an additional KBV 3.6 trillion later in the fourth quarter (in what

Acting Prime Minister Yukhym Zviahilskiy termed a "non-monetary emission."[5]) Zviahilskiy believed that such credits were necessary to reduce inflation, by financing an increase in industrial output. The karbovanets thereafter went into a virtual "free fall" in October, on some days losing as much as 10 percent of its value. To their credit, officials at the NBU consistently counseled the government strongly against using credits on such a scale.[6] However, the institutional placement of the NBU made it virtually impossible to pursue an independent course as regards monetary policy. (Under these arrangements, the NBU was arguably as much a victim as it was a perpetrator.)

Apparently unable or unwilling to perceive the connection between credit emissions and the deterioration in the value of the karbovanets, President Leonid Kravchuk responded with a spate of new administrative controls. On November 2, 1993, he issued a decree instructing the NBU and Cabinet of Ministers to revise Ukraine's credit policy within ten days' time and to devise new policies for export promotion, presumably to generate more hard currency earnings.[7] The decree also temporarily suspended operations at the Ukrainian Interbank Currency Exchange (UICE) and instructed the NBU and Cabinet of Ministers to establish procedures for regulating the official exchange rate. Further steps were also to be taken to curb the flight of capital out of Ukraine. The government turned to administrative means to fight inflation, apparently in order to protect and preserve its own intrusive role in the economic sphere. Kravchuk's policy of economic reform "from above" in the search of the third, "Ukrainian way" to the market really had left him with no choice but to intervene further.

The basic problem was that the government was intent in 1993 on retaining its dominant role in the foreign trade sector, for which it badly needed foreign exchange. Further, due to its burgeoning oil debts to Russia and Azerbaijan, Ukraine had incentives to overvalue its exchange rate with the ruble. This was the primary motivation for fixing the karbovanets-ruble rate, wreaking havoc with the development of an efficient foreign exchange market. In February 1993, Ukraine had established the UICE as the official auction house for trade in foreign currency.[8] At the same time, the Cabinet of Ministers put into force a requirement that 50 percent of all foreign currency earnings be sold at the UICE within 90 days, in what amounted to an effective 50 percent surrender requirement, effective March 1, 1993.[9]

Loose credit emissions and worsening inflation caused the karbovanets to plummet against the dollar through the spring and summer, however, falling from KBV 3,000 to 5,760 per dollar by August 1. The NBU reacted on August 12, by setting the official exchange rate at a fixed KBV 5,970 per dollar. This measure forced Ukrainian businesses and residents to sell half of their foreign currency earnings to the state at an administratively set rate.

As the karbovanets continued to fall in the commercial market, the surrender requirement placed an increasingly large burden on Ukrainian exporters. Former deputy prime minister Viktor M. Pynzenyk estimated that the artificially induced divergences between the official and market exchange rates resulted in a "levy of an additional exchange tax on exports equal to two-thirds of export earnings."[10] This was a deplorable predicament for a country so badly starved for foreign investment and export trade. Another provision in Kravchuk's decree required that 10 percent of the required 50 percent sale of foreign currency income be placed into a "karbovanets stabilization fund." Far from stemming the fall of the karbovanets, however, the commercial rate continued to deteriorate, reaching KBV 31,000 per dollar by November 1, down sharply from the official rate of KBV 5,970. Such rapid deterioration prompted Kravchuk to take more drastic action.

Kravchuk Intervenes, Making Matters Worse

On November 25–26, 1993, the government took three measures designed to implement the policies mandated under Kravchuk's November 2 decree. First, all previously existing exemptions from the mandatory 50 percent surrender requirement were canceled as of January 1, 1994.[11] In addition, the period for selling hard currency at the UICE was cut from 90 to 30 days. This measure affected an estimated 80 percent of all Ukrainian enterprises, having the deleterious effect of greatly broadening the base for the government's implicit tax on export earnings.[12] Second, licenses granted to Ukrainian residents permitting them to open and maintain hard currency accounts abroad were revoked as of January 1, 1994.[13] This measure apparently sought to stem the capital outflow by preventing Ukrainian citizens from keeping money balances in legal offshore bank accounts—which only treated the symptom, rather than the disease. Finally, the official exchange rate was dropped to KBV 7,090 per dollar as of November 30, 1993. In the future, the official rate would be set by the NBU in consultation with the Cabinet of Ministers.[14] No longer frozen, the government in the future would periodically revise the official rate, presumably in accordance with its needs. The rate was dropped further, to KBV 12,610 on January 1, 1994, but, incredibly, this was still less than half of the auction or black market rates.

A new law on currency exchange policy enacted on November 25 uncoupled the UICE auction from Ukraine's official rate, effectively revoking previous legislation that moved in the direction of a fully commercial exchange rate.[15] Further complicating matters, a joint resolution of the Cabinet of Ministers and the NBU established no fewer than four exchange rates as of January 1, 1994[16]:

(1) The official rate would apply to all mandatory 50 percent surrenders;
(2) An auction or bank rate set at *twice* the official rate would apply to other commercial transactions between companies;
(3) A noncash bank rate would apply to currency exchange but was not to exceed the official rate by more than 2.5 percent; and
(4) A cash rate for currency exchange would apply at kiosks but was not to exceed the "auction rate" by more than 2.5 percent.

This cumbersome system reflected neither a wholly arbitrary nor a fully market-based valuation basis. Ukraine's exchange rate system would turn completely on the government's official rate, which would only indirectly reflect conditions in foreign exchange markets, if at all. The government thus reserved to itself a great deal of discretion to administer the rate of exchange between the karbovanets and hard currency.

The new exchange rate regime failed to dampen inflationary pressures, however, since it did nothing to stem the flow of credits. The consequence was that prices rose by an enormous 93 percent in December 1993, which was also the sixth straight month of price rises in excess of 50 percent. It was now abundantly clear that hyperinflation had broken out in Ukraine at mid-year.[17] This prompted Kravchuk to respond with further measures to address the inflation in a more explicit way. In early December, the government introduced a series of measures in the form of an "Anti-Hyperinflation Program."[18] The first stage of the plan was to "establish strict control over all forms of ownership." In direct contradiction to other recent measures to reassert control over prices and production, however, the government initiated a program to dramatically liberalize prices, removing controls over all but 20 percent of prices by the end of 1994. That represented a fall in the state's implicit subsidy to consumers from around 20 percent of GDP to less than 9 percent.

The first week of December proved to be a rough one for the Ukrainian consumer. Prices on consumer goods were increased by an average of 100 percent on Saturday, December 4, 1993. The following Monday, ration cards were issued for butter. On Tuesday, December 7, the price of eggs was raised to KBV 50,000 for ten eggs. (That was about $2.00!) The work day was changed in order to conserve energy, ending at 4:00 P.M. The work week for state enterprises, too, was staggered, with the week extending Thursday through Monday in Kyiv's Pechersky Rayon (including schools). Daytime television broadcasts were eliminated, universities were closed until the end of February, and heat was rationed in some cities.

In conjunction with the planned price liberalization, the government also proposed to adjust wages so as to cushion the effects of the price rises on consumers. Further, the Economics Ministry pressed for a gradual ratcheting up of prices and incomes, until the prices for basic goods—especially raw materials and energy products—rose to world market levels. While intended to protect consumers, this policy could not help but fuel inflation.[19] (Such policies are almost always self-defeating.) What was even more extraordinary was that, in the face of an anticipated—but highly doubtful—fall in inflation levels, in the words of one official, the government was now "free to exercise [its] own price policy."[20] This kind of talk was widely interpreted as a prelude to the reimposition of controls, once the immediate crisis had subsided. But the crisis did not subside so quickly.

The only measure that addressed the proliferation of cheap credits during this period came very late in the year, in the form of a government telegram from the Cabinet of Ministers and NBU, curtailing all enterprise loans and credits from December 2 until the end of the year, revoking all credits previously authorized, and demanding immediate repayment. Enterprises failing to return credits would have their hard currency accounts raided by the NBU.[21] Rather than a step toward fiscal sanity, however, the move was apparently in order to pave the way for the NBU to issue some KBV 23 trillion of new credits in December and January.[22] The bulk of fresh credits was slated for agriculture (KBV 9 trlln.), industry (KBV 8 trlln.), and pension indexing (KBV 5 trlln.). Further, parliament issued an order on November 26, allocating an additional KBV 1.5 trillion in credits to the agricultural sector. Deputy Prime Minister for Agriculture Volodymyr Demianov initially requested KBV 4 trillion, pleading that the government had no funds with which to complete the purchase of agricultural products ordered in 1993. This was sure to bring further inflationary pressures.

NBU governor Yushchenko protested the new emission on the basis that the NBU had already allocated more than KBV 12 trillion in agricultural credits and that the additional emission would frustrate ongoing measures to contain inflation.[23] By December 27, under pressure from farmers who threatened to sell their grain on the private market, Agriculture Minister Yuriy Karasyk promised to pay the full KBV 4 trillion debt by shifting the state's agricultural debt to enterprises that were indebted to the state for agricultural products.[24] However, the government had to face the fact that many of Ukraine's industrial and agricultural enterprises were insolvent and were in fact functioning only on the basis of government credits. This measure was thus too little, too late. By December, Ukraine had already been in the grips of hyperinflation for over five months.[25]

The UICE reopened on December 23, holding its first "tender auction" in nearly two months. It now functioned, however, in a very much changed role. According to instructions of the NBU, the UICE no longer actually conducted an "auction" per se but rather administered the receipt of karbovantsi from sellers and the transfer of hard currency to purchasers. As such, it became during this period merely the "back office" settlements operation for a new NBU-conducted auction. In order to place funds into the karbovanets stabilization fund, the NBU converted 10 percentage points of the required surrender of foreign currency earnings into karbovantsi at a rate set by the NBU, based on the need for foreign currency. In principle, this rate would be adjusted weekly in order to reflect market conditions. In practice, however, the rate was fixed at KBV 25,000 after January 1, 1994. The remaining 40 percent was sold at a fixed rate of KBV 12,610. In effect, a two-tiered system was in place for hard currency sellers. At the same time, the black market rate rose to KBV 30,000 per dollar. Sales of foreign currency through official channels, therefore, worked increasingly to the disadvantage of the seller.

For those businesses wishing to purchase foreign exchange, access to hard currency was to be strictly limited, subject to approval by two special committees on a case-by-case basis. Purchases could be made only through member banks of the UICE. The bank was required to submit detailed client documentation and payment receipts in advance to the so-called "Auction Committee," chaired by Deputy Prime Minister Valentyn Landyk, which would render an "expert opinion" prior to the auction. No definitive criteria were disclosed as to the basis for the committee's opinions. The Auction Committee's recommendation was next passed to a "Committee on Determining the Priority of Using Foreign Currency Income in Ukraine," also chaired by Landyk, which would make the final decision as to whether the applicant would be permitted to purchase foreign exchange.[26] Many legitimate businesses were turned away from the auction by this bureaucratic machinery.[27] Domestic capital was therefore subject to a degree of rationing, which tended to depress interest rates, reduce economic efficiency, and introduce new levels of financial repression into an already unduly constrained financial system. These measures would remain in place until after the 1994 elections, when newly elected President Leonid Kuchma would abandon the currency exchange regime established by his predecessor.

Experimentation with Credit Controls: Winter 1993

During this critical period, the government sought creative ways to maintain necessary levels of enterprise support while containing inflationary pressures. Unfortunately, such methods placed a heavy reliance upon administrative means. On December 17, 1993, Deputy Premier Landyk announced that the government would lift the ban on bank credits to enterprises in early 1994. UICE chairman Vadim Hetman explained that the new credits would be covered by hard currency sales from the NBU's reserves, and therefore not be inflationary. In principle, this would work as long as volumes of hard currency trades were brisk enough to provide for all of the government's needs. Confident that inflation could be contained through its new administrative mechanism, the government planned the fresh emission of KBV 23 trillion.[28] Trading volumes would never be on a scale sufficient to avoid an inflationary emission, however, as incentives for export through official channels had been significantly diminished.

In February, under pressure from industrial groups, including the Ukrainian Unions of Industrialists and Entrepreneurs (UUIE), headed by former prime minister Leonid D. Kuchma, the government announced the injection of another KBV 12 trillion to enterprises, in order to clear interenterprise debts.[29] In an attempt to limit the inflationary damage, Acting Premier Zviahilskiy indicated that the amount of credits granted would not exceed the value of the receiving plant's output.[30] The UUIE also spearheaded a drive to establish a KBV 6 trillion "financial credit fund" at the NBU, involving three prominent commercial banks, the use of which was limited to only those state enterprises that were indebted to other state plants.[31] Private firms and state enterprises with hard currency funds would not be eligible for credit from the fund. Further, all ministries were ordered to channel credits through the NBU fund account, in order to prevent the increase of cash in circulation. Essentially, it was to be a noncash (that is, bookkeeping) clearing mechanism for the cancellation of mutual debts.

The payments crisis only intensified through February, however. Despite KBV 11 trillion issued in January, and KBV 12 trillion in February, mutual debts rose to some KBV 76 trillion, up from KBV 46 trillion in January (approximately *twice* the monthly GDP, or 14 percent of February GDP on an annualized basis).[32] In late February, NBU Governor Yushchenko announced the issue of another KBV 5 trillion to indebted enterprises, to be paid off with products. Limited only to clearing interenterprise debts, Yushchenko claimed that this was "not a credit emission," because it was "backed up by specific goods, and, therefore, will not increase inflation."[33] Yushchenko failed to mention that this logic pertains only insofar as consumers for the products so purchased could ultimately be found. Since many of the manufacturers were producing subsidized industrial products, it appeared doubtful that a monetary emission could be avoided.

Recognizing that government control of hard currency transactions had failed, the NBU issued a telegram on February 3, 1993, announcing the gradual renewal of hard currency trading on the UICE.[34] Since the UICE suspended operations in November 1993, UICE chairman Hetman revealed that Ukrainian banks had been illegally using the currency market, as well as channeling funds to the Moscow auction through correspondent accounts with Russian banks.[35] In fact, volumes of U.S. dollars from Ukraine traded in Russia had the effect of doubling the amount of dollars traded on the Moscow exchange.[36] The effects of such slippage north to Russia were devastating to the government's program.

Whereas in June and July 1993, the UICE's monthly volume of dollars traded was around $145 million, in February 1994 a mere $35 million was exchanged at the Hard Currency Priority Committee's auctions. Further, according to the IMF, Ukrainian enterprises had some $1.3 billion worth of hard currency earnings in foreign banks.[37] Figures compiled by Ukraine's Western trading partners indicated that import-export turnover was some four times the amount reported by Ukrainian customs. NBU governor Yushchenko blamed the government's policy of exchanging currency at an official fixed rate, arguing instead for a 100 percent mandatory hard currency earnings conversion at a fully market-set rate. But changes in the official system for exchanging hard currency were to await Ukraine's new president.

Kuchma Relaxes Controls: Summer 1994

President Kuchma's victory in July 1994 brought a wave of change to the government's management of the economy. As a prelude to his October 1994 Program of Radical Economic Reforms, the president moved quickly to liberalize foreign exchange markets. On August 22, 1994, Kuchma issued a decree decentralizing the UICE, restoring its autonomy to set market rates of exchange.[38] This measure reversed President Kravchuk's November 1993 emasculation of the UICE and effectively unified the heretofore dual rates of exchange, canceling the NBU action of August 1993, which had set a fixed exchange rate at the discretion of the bank. Further, in the interim, enterprises were required to sell only 30 percent of foreign currency earnings at the fixed rate of KBV 25,000.[39]

On October 24, the NBU issued instructions requiring that a unified rate be determined at the UICE, thereby formally relinquishing its role in the matter.[40] The unified rate was to go into effect on October 28. The UICE would not be completely liberalized, however. In order to help stabilize the karbovanets on the UICE, the exchange installed guidelines that would immediately suspend trading if the karbovanets were to depreciate by more than 10 percent over the previous week's close. It was anticipated that this measure would reduce the potential for currency speculation. Additional measures would increase restricted access to karbovantsi further by rejecting applications for hard currency to purchase consumer goods, food products, and goods of former Soviet republics.[41]

The NBU also announced a new round of credit controls, issuing a resolution prohibiting commercial banks from extending new credits to enterprises from October 26 through the end of 1994, unless previous credits were first repaid.[42] Violations of the new rule would result in the NBU confiscating all of a bank's profits exceeding their October 25 level. Banks were also to register and report to the NBU all new credit agreements with enterprises. Further, all NBU loans to commercial banks were to take place within the parliamentary-approved credit limit of KBV 154 trillion and were to be allocated through auction. The NBU also canceled a previous restriction that limited the interest rate at which commercial banks could lend money to no more than 250 percent per year. These steps were advanced as "interim measures," pending the anticipated introduction in 1995 of the permanent national currency, the hryvnia.

The government also reported moderate success in recovering enterprise monetary assets from abroad. Newly appointed Prime Minister Yevhen Marchuk indicated that, by October, some $512 million had been returned from "illegal" accounts abroad, in accordance with President Kravchuk's decree of a year earlier.[43] Another $1 billion was estimated to remain in foreign accounts, however.[44] Sifting the activities of state enterprises for assets "hidden" abroad was an extensive, painstaking undertaking. By August 1994 nearly 120,000 enterprises had reported on their foreign business activities, with audits of 526 companies resulting in 25 criminal indictments. Tens of millions of dollars would be recovered through these investigations, but not the billions the government had hoped for. In a collateral effort to encourage Ukrainians to repatriate their hard currency, President Kuchma issued a decree that enabled citizens to open anonymous hard currency accounts in Ukrainian banks. However, in a move that would immediately undermine the potential attractiveness of the new "numbered accounts," the very next day the NBU issued instructions forbidding the owners of such accounts from withdrawing more than $10,000 per month. It is no surprise, then, that fears of further restrictions prevented Ukrainians from opening even a single anonymous hard currency account for the next 12 months.[45]

The October 27, 1994, auction of the UICE set the dollar exchange rate at KBV 78,600 per dollar. Trading volumes were sluggish, however, at $12.4 million, versus the $35 million weekly average of July 1993. At the November 3 auction, the rate moved down only slightly, to KBV 78,900 per dollar. As a confidence-building measure, the NBU on November 2 repealed the joint resolution of November 24, 1993, which set the cash rate according to trading at the UICE. Banks would now be free to establish rates independently for all currency trades, with a profit margin of no greater than 5 percent. Far from building confidence in the karbovanets, however, the commercial bank rate on November 11 fell to a record KBV 129,000 per dollar. The government then realized that its worries were far from over.

Some advisors to the president argued that only major currency reform involving a degree of currency confiscation would liquidate Ukraine's inflation. Kuchma was increasingly under pressure to introduce the hryvnia. In anticipation of issuance of the permanent currency in 1995, on November 16, 1994, at Kuchma's behest, the NBU issued a telegram banning foreign currency from circulation on the territory of

Ukraine as of February 18, 1995, three months hence. As the time of the ban approached, however, certain notable reformers raised concerns about the timing of a hard currency ban, fearing that a severe devaluation of the karbovanets would ensue.[46] Consequently, the NBU rescinded its decision on February 18, 1995, less than three hours before it was scheduled to take effect.

Kuchma Backtracks: Fall 1995

Another attempt to ban hard currency was made on August 1, 1995, in anticipation of an October introduction of the hryvnia; this time the ban was successful. Since early in 1995, the karbovanets had remained fairly stable against the dollar, trading at approximately KBV 150,000. No doubt, the stable karbovanets contributed positively to the "dedollarization" of official transactions. The karbovanets continued to fall in the wake of the hard currency ban, however. Over the first two weeks of August 1995, the kupon fell by KBV 16,000 against the dollar, losing roughly 10.5 percent of its value and reaching a new record low of KBV 167,700. It also fell against the Russian ruble, from RUB 34.6-to-1 on August 1, to RUB 36.4 by August 14. Aggressive intervention by the NBU reversed the fall temporarily, requiring the bank to buy $34 million worth of karbovantsi from August 6–18, an amount equal to all NBU purchases of karbovantsi in the preceding three months. The result was that the coupon rose a little, to KBV 165,200 per dollar and 34.0 per ruble.

Predictably, government officials, economists, and policy advisors were split over the reasons for the unanticipated fall in the karbovanets. President Kuchma's economic advisor, Anatoliy Galchinsky, blamed the fall on the banning of payments in hard currency, which was effective August 1. Deputy Premier Viktor Pynzenyk, however, asserted that a more plausible explanation was the unplanned credit emissions in the third quarter of 1995. Indeed, in an interview with the Ukrainian Press Agency, NBU Governor Yushchenko acknowledged that "the amount of unplanned monetary emission in the third quarter . . . was considerable," and that he had resisted, but in the end, "could not find concrete reasons to avoid [emissions]."[47]

The Pynzenyk-Yushchenko thesis is almost certainly correct. The available figures indicate that more than KBV 140 trillion (approximately $900 million at July 1995 exchange rates) in credits were released in the third quarter of 1995. The stage for this fresh emission actually had been set over the course of 1995, culminating in Kuchma's May 22 order to the NBU and Ministry of Finance to "consider the possibilities to provide individual support to enterprises," starting on June 1.[48] Such additional "support" had not been provided for in the 1995 state budget. On June 12, the president issued a decree ordering the government and NBU to provide an initial KBV 70 trillion for the purchase of some 3,300 Russian-built grain harvesters. Early in August, Deputy Premier for the Agricultural Sector Petro Sabluk announced that a further KBV 70 trillion was necessary to complete the purchase of grain from farmers, who had learned their lessons in 1992–94 and now refused to sell grain to the state on credit terms.

These credit infusions to the economy came during an apparent "softening" in 1995 of Kuchma's heretofore stalwart commitment to economic reforms. The president's wavering was discernible early in the year. In February, during a visit to L'viv, Kuchma for the first time used the term "correction" of reforms, raising concerns that his commitment to the October 1994 program of radical reforms might be waning. He elaborated further during his April 4, 1995, Economic Report to Parliament, explicitly employing the term to indicate a shift in emphasis from achieving stabilization by meeting aggressive inflation targets to spurring growth in industrial output.[49] In his April speech, he criticized so-called "blind monetarism," calling for an "intensification of social policy," with the emphasis on creating a "socially-oriented market economy."

On a June 22 trip to Uzhorod, in western Ukraine, on the occasion of the fiftieth anniversary of unification of Transcarpathia with Ukraine, Kuchma again asserted that it was necessary to "correct" the course of economic reform. He stated further that it would be necessary to discard the government's target of a 1–2 percent monthly inflation rate by the end of 1995. Kuchma's statements brought an immediate reaction from key reformers in the government, including Pynzenyk, who criticized the president. Finally, on August 24, in the president's address to a gala gathering in celebration of Ukraine's fourth anniversary of independence, Kuchma declared that, "the time that has elapsed since I first announced the correction idea has convinced me that it is something we need, so I will demand appropriate steps from the government."[50] Kuchma's remarks were carried by the national media, reaching a wide audience.

Kuchma's notion of "correction" implied a strengthening of the state in order to "enhance the control over all components of the economic process."[51] Kuchma's proposals to correct reforms were summarized and defended in a July 18, 1995, newspaper article by presidential economics advisor Galchinsky. Galchinsky explained that the cornerstone of Kuchma's idea was to establish financial-industrial groups (FIGs) that would "integrate into themselves banking institutions and enterprises with various forms of ownership."[52] Essentially, this would create a seamless network of financial relations, permitting credit creation from banks directly to enterprises controlled under the same institutional umbrella. With no market mechanism for the competitive allocation of capital and credit, fears were rampant that the inflationary floodgates would be opened wide. Predictably, many large enterprises supported the concept of financial-industrial groups.

Tight Budgets and Unpaid Bills: 1996

In 1995 it was clear that the government had been unable to resolve the thorny problem of stemming the free and easy extension of credits to inefficient, loss-making enterprises. Hopes for turning the corner on credits were raised, however, by Prime Minister Marchuk, who vowed to reduce budget expenditures and credit subsidies in 1996.[53] In fact, throughout 1996, the government's efforts to reduce both industrial credits and on-budget subsidies would precipitate a serious crisis in unpaid wages, pensions, and interenterprise debts. In May 1996, according to the NBU, the amount of nonpayments in the basic sectors of the economy were in excess of KBV 320 trillion.[54]

The danger appeared great that a chain reaction of bankruptcies would be set in motion, engulfing Ukraine during the summer months. The situation had been worsening for several months' time. The previous September, Kuchma had attempted to impose discipline on enterprises, with a decree requiring the conversion of mutual debts into 100-million-KBV-denominated promissory notes, payable on February 28, 1995.[55] The NBU was ordered to clear these debts by October 10, with repayment to be a direct obligation of the enterprises. Some 2,000 enterprises were affected, 90 percent of them state-owned. When the deadline for repayment of the notes passed without their redemption, however, Kuchma was forced to intervene a second time, with a March 1995 decree to "normalize payments between enterprises."[56] But mining and metallurgical unions and workers, among the hardest hit industrial groups, blamed the nonpayment of wages on the decree, which they claimed had forced enterprises to choose between paying their creditors and paying their workers.[57]

Kuchma acted once again in May, issuing a decree aimed at the bureaucracy, curtailing frivolous spending in government, and threatening dismissal of ministers and enterprise directors who failed to pay salaries on time.[58] On May 21, Marchuk announced that the government would use foreign currency reserves for three overdue payments of wages, pensions, and student stipends. At the same time, parliament began exploring the possibilities of using IMF credits to partially cover back wages. In fact, an estimated $953 million (KBV 177 trillion) in back wages, pensions, and stipends was partially paid with the $900 million IMF tranche in late May 1996.

The total arrears continued to grow, however, even as the government sought to satisfy at least the oldest debts. Unpaid wages, pensions, and stipends, while subject to some fluctuation over this period, climbed to some $444 million by June 1, 1996, rising further to $1.7 billion (UAH 3 billion) by November 1. By January 1, 1997, the total stood in excess of $2.3 billion (UAH 4.2 billion). First Deputy Prime Minister Vasyl Durdynets reported in January 1997 that unpaid wages had reached "disastrous proportions" in many of the most industrialized regions, including: Cherkassy, (having a low of UAH 21.8 per capita), Dnipropetrovsk, Donetsk, Kharkiv, Zhytomyr, Zaporizhzhia, Kyiv, Chernivtsy, and Volynska Oblast (having a high of UAH 59.7 per capita).[59] In some cases, wages were in arrears for up to 12 months. In the cities of Kharkiv and Zhytomyr, protest demonstrations were held in January 1997 to recover 4–5 months' worth of back wages. A new round of controls was expected to be imposed on the regions, reported Durdynets, due to "unlawful increases in oblast budgets," while at the same time their tax payments to the central government continued to fall. In the absence of a major increase in productivity, the first deputy premier noted, "the problem will continue for a long time."[60]

What seems clear is that the government employed arrearages in a systematic way to meet inflation targets agreed upon with its international creditors, particularly the IMF. In a somewhat perverse turn of events, however, the government also used some of its hard-earned IMF credits to cover back wages, thereby transforming a short-term domestic liability into a long-term external debt. This may have been politically expedient, but it also deprived Ukraine of badly needed funds with which to make strategic investments to improve industrial productivity. This raises the possibility that the perilous ascent of arrears in 1995–96 and afterwards was not entirely of the government's choosing but rather the result of a narrowing of the available policy options that the government found expedient to employ in place of direct credits and subsidies.

Chapter 1

1. Zbigniew Brzezinski, "The Premature Partnership?" *Foreign Affairs* 73, no. 2 (March/April 1994): 80.
2. Due to its strategic position in east-central Europe, foreign policy analyst Sherman Garnett calls Ukraine "the keystone in the arch" of European security. See Sherman Garnett, *Keystone in the Arch: Ukraine in the Emerging Security Environment of Central and Eastern Europe* (Washington, D.C.: Carnegie Endowment for International Peace, 1997). European analysts have expressed similar sentiments. For one, see Tor Bukkvoll, *Ukraine and European Security* (London: The Royal Institute of International Affairs, 1997). Regarding the positive effects that Ukrainian independence can have on progress in Russian democratic reforms, Paul D'Anieri writes that, "As long as [an independent] Ukraine exists, it will be an important check on Russian power in the region." Additionally, some have pointed out that Russia cannot, at once, be both an empire and a democracy. For this reason, many Russian reformers and democrats have opposed efforts to reintegrate Ukraine with Russia. For the full argument, see Paul J. D'Anieri, *Economic Interdependence in Ukrainian-Russian Relations* (Albany: State University of New York Press, 1999), pp. 11–14.
3. For comprehensive histories, see either Orest Subtelny, *Ukraine: A History* (Toronto: University of Toronto Press, 1988); or Robert Paul Magocsi, *A History of Ukraine* (Seattle: University of Washington Press, 1996).
4. See I. S. Koropeckyj, *Development in the Shadow: Studies in Ukrainian Economics* (Edmonton, Alberta: Canadian Institute of Ukrainian Studies Press, 1990). U.S. economist Volodymyr Bandera estimates that, "for well over half a century, at least 10 percent of Ukraine's national output has been given up [to Russia] annually." See V. Bandera, "National Income Transfers and Macroeconomic Accountability from the Standpoint of Ukraine," in I. S. Koropeckyj, ed., *The Ukrainian Economy: Achievements, Problems, Challenges* (Cambridge, MA: Harvard University Press, 1992), p. 386.
5. For a comprehensive review of the evolution of Ukraine's self-consciousness during this period, see Bohdan Krawchenko, *Social Change and National Consciousness in Twentieth Century Ukraine* (Edmonton, Alberta: Canadian Institute of Ukrainian Studies, 1984).
6. See Robert Conquest, *Harvest of Sorrow* (Cambridge, MA: Oxford University Press, 1986).
7. For an account of the people and events during this historic period, see Bohdan Nahaylo, *The Ukrainian Resurgence* (Toronto: University of Toronto Press, 1999).
8. See Adrian Karatnycky, "The Ukraine Factor," *Foreign Affairs* 71, no. 3 (summer 1992): 90–107.
9. See Nahaylo, *The Ukrainian Resurgence.*
10. See the World Bank, *World Development Report 1996: From Plan to Market* (Washington, D.C. and New York: World Bank and Oxford University Press, 1996), pp. 9–21. See especially Figure 1.2, p. 14.

11. See Adrian Karatnycky, Alexander Motyl, and Boris Sher, eds., *Nations in Transit 2000—Civil Society, Democracy and Markets in East Central Europe and the Newly Independent States* (New Brunswick, NJ and London: Transaction Publishers, 2000).
12. Among other countries, Ukraine ranked lower than Chile, Malaysia, Thailand, Jamaica, Uruguay, Panama, Columbia, and the Dominican Republic. See the World Economic Forum, *Global Competitiveness Report* (Washington, D.C.: The World Economic Forum, 2001).
13. "Ukraine Business Panorama for 9–17 April 2001," Moscow Interfax, 18 April 2001. FBIS-SOV-2001–0418. Original in English.
14. See Jayati Datta-Mitra, *Fiscal Management in Adjustment Lending* (Washington, D.C.: The World Bank, 1997), pp. 25–27.
15. The positive growth rates of 6.0–8.0 percent recorded in 2000–2001 are an exception. In any case, due to the continuing lack of structural reform (especially corporate governance reform, lagging agricultural restructuring, and lack of more fully developed capital markets), this author does not believe that Ukraine's recent growth will be sustained.
16. Shafiqul Islam, "Russia's Rough Road to Capitalism," *Foreign Affairs* 72, no. 2 (spring 1993): 56–66.
17. See, for instance, Taras Kuzio, Robert S. Kravchuk, and Paul D'Anieri, *State and Institution Building in Ukraine* (New York and London: St. Martin's Press and Macmillan, 1999).
18. See János Kornai, *The Socialist System* (Princeton University Press, 1992), pp. 361, 387–92.
19. See "Kuchma Aide Denies Ukraine Likely to Default on Debt," Moscow Interfax, 2 September 1999. FBIS-SOV-1999–0903. Original in English. See also "Moody's Lowers Ukraine's Foreign Currency Country Ceiling," *Ukraine Business Panorama for January 4–10, 2000,* Moscow Interfax, 9 January 2000. FBIS-SOV-2000–0109. Original in English.
20. See Daniel Kaufmann, "Desperately Seeking Economic Recovery: Why Is Ukraine's Economy—and Russia's—Not Growing," *The World Bank Transition Newsletter,* April 1997, pp. 5–8. Available online at http://www.worldbank.org.
21. According to former Polish Finance Minister Leszek Balcerowicz, the designer of Poland's "shock therapy" program, "A pure shock-type, or radical transition to a private market economy may be defined as a transition whereby all constituent processes are implemented with the maximum possible speed." The rationale is that radical reform is painful, tests the peoples' patience, and therefore has a limited amount of political capital to expend. See Leszek Balcerowicz, *Socialism, Capitalism, Transformation* (Budapest: Central European University Press, 1995), p. 179.
22. Freeing prices serves several purposes: It destroys the "shortage economy" and with it incentives to hoard goods and currency; it deprives the population of the "excess savings" that constitute the "monetary overhang," which reformers initially feared would fuel serious inflation; and it clears out industries of excess liquidity that would tend to prop up inefficient enterprises.
23. See James R. Millar, "The Failure of Shock Therapy," *Problems of Post-Communism* (fall 1994): 21–25.
24. See Ben Slay, "Rapid Versus Gradual Economic Transition," *RFE/RL Research Report* 3, no. 31 (August 12, 1994): 31–42; and Amanda Rose, "Sachs Was Right: Economic Assessments Under Rapid and Gradual Reform in Central and Eastern

Europe" (paper presented at the Annual Meeting of the American Political Science Association, San Francisco, CA, August 29, 1996).

25. See David Lipton and Jeffrey Sachs, "Creating a Market Economy in Eastern Europe: The Case of Poland," *Brookings Papers on Economic Activity 1* (Washington, D.C.: The Brookings Institution, 1990); and David Lipton and Jeffrey Sachs, "Privatization in Eastern Europe: The Case of Poland," *Brookings Papers on Economic Activity 2* (Washington, D.C.: The Brookings Institution, 1990); and Peter Murell, "What Is Shock Therapy? What Did It Do in Poland and Russia?" *Post-Soviet Affairs* 9, no. 2 (April-June 1993): 111–140.
26. See János Kornai, *The Road to a Free Economy* (New York: Norton, 1990).
27. Robert Skidelsky, *The Road From Serfdom* (New York: Allen Lane/Penguin Press, 1995), p. 142.
28. Murell, "What is Shock Therapy?"
29. See Ronald McKinnon, *The Order of Economic Liberalization* (Baltimore: Johns Hopkins University Press, 1991).
30. Kornai, *The Road to a Free Economy.*
31. See Tim Carrington, "Efforts to Ease Social Pain of Transition to Market Economy Often Can Backfire," *The Wall Street Journal,* May 2, 1994.
32. See Anders Åslund, "Lessons of the First Four Years of Systemic Change in Eastern Europe," *Journal of Comparative Economics* 19, no. 1 (August 1994): 22–53.
33. See Jozef M. van Brabant, "Governance, Evolution, and the Transformation of Eastern Europe," chapter 7 in Kazimierz Z. Poznanski, ed., *The Evolutionary Transition to Capitalism* (Boulder, CO: Westview Press, 1995): 157–182.
34. D'Anieri, *Economic Interdependence.*
35. See Michael Ellman, "Transformation, Depression, and Economics: Some Lessons," *Journal of Comparative Economics* 19, no. 1 (August 1994): 1–21.
36. van Brabant, "Governance, Evolution."
37. Millar, "The Failure of Shock Therapy."
38. For a detailed review and analysis of Ukraine's recent institution building experience, see Kuzio, Kravchuk, and D'Anieri, *State and Institution Building.*
39. See John Williamson, ed., *The Political Economy of Policy Reform* (Washington, D.C.: The Institute for International Economics, 1993).
40. See Paul Kubicek, "Post-Soviet Ukraine: In Search of a Constituency for Reform," *Journal of Communist Studies and Transition Politics* 13, no, 3 (September 1997): 103–126.
41. Gary Ferguson, "Public Opinion in Ukraine, 1998," Report of SOCIS-Gallup, Kyiv for the International Foundation for Electoral Systems, Washington, D.C., n.d. Report in the author's possession.
42. Ibid., p. 112.
43. See Alexander J. Motyl, "Structural Constraints and Starting Points: The Logic of Systemic Change in Ukraine and Russia," *Comparative Politics* 29, no. 4 (July 1997): 433–47.
44. Marshall I. Goldman, *What Went Wrong with Perestroika* (New York: Norton, 1992).
45. See Robert W. Campbell, *The Socialist Economies in Transition* (Bloomington, IN: Indiana University Press, 1991).
46. Jan Winiecki and Andrzej Kondratowicz, eds., *The Macroeconomics of Transition* (London and New York: Routledge, 1993).

Chapter 2

1. Among the post-socialist countries, only Albania and Turkmenistan have suffered worse declines.
2. "Ukraine Posts 9 Percent GDP Growth in 2001," Moscow Interfax News Service, 14 January 2002. FBIS-SOV-2002–0115. Original in English.
3. See Jan Winiecki, "The Inevitability of a Fall in Output in the Early Stage of a Transition to the Market: Theoretical Underpinnings," *Soviet Studies* 43, no. 4 (1991): 669–676.
4. See Gisela Meyer Escoe, "The Demise of Soviet Industry: A Regional Perspective," *Journal of Comparative Economics* 21 (1995): 336–352. On the general economic history of the entire Soviet period, see Martin Malia, *The Soviet Tragedy: A History of Socialism in Russia, 1917–1991* (New York: The Free Press, 1994).
5. On the legacy of the Soviet organization of industry, see Clifford Gaddy, *The Price of the Past: Russia's Struggle with the Legacy of a Militarized Economy* (Washington, D.C.: The Brookings Institution Press, 1996).
6. See the World Bank, *World Development Report, 1997: The State in a Changing World* (New York: Oxford University Press, 1997).
7. See János Kornai, "Transformational Recession: The Main Causes," *Journal of Comparative Economics* 19 (1994): 39–63.
8. See Michael Ellman, "General Aspects of Transition," in Michael Ellman, Yegor Gaidar, and G. W. Kolodko, eds., *Economic Transition in Eastern Europe* (Cambridge, MA: Basil Blackwell, 1993).
9. See Robert W. Campbell, *The Socialist Economies in Transition* (Bloomington, IN: Indiana University Press, 1991).
10. See Kornai, "Transformational Recession," p. 44.
11. In purely economic terms, bankruptcy entails reallocation of productive assets to the most efficient uses. It is widely agreed that this will serve to increase long-run efficiency. In the short run, however, bankruptcy and plant closings will also have demand-reducing effects, insofar as redundant labor is shed and demand for input materials is curtailed. This cannot help but contribute to the general output fall.
12. Kornai sees this as "possibly the main cause behind the recession" in formerly socialist countries. See "Transformational Recession," p. 44.
13. David Dyker, "Capital Formation, Capital Stock, and Capital Productivity," in I. S. Koropecskyj, ed., *The Ukrainian Economy: Achievements, Prospects, Challenges* (Cambridge, MA: Harvard Ukrainian Research Institute, 1992), p. 148.
14. Ibid., p. 149.
15. See Abram Bergson, *Productivity and the Social System—The USSR and the West* (Cambridge: Harvard University Press, 1978).
16. From a speech by Prime Minister Valeriy Pustovoitenko, reprinted in Kyiv *Uryadoviy Kur'er,* 4 March 1999. FBIS-SOV-1999–0316. Original in Ukrainian.
17. Dyker, "Capital Formation, Capital Stock, and Capital Productivity," p. 163.
18. See Razumkov, et al., Report of the Ukrainian Center for Economic and Political Studies, "The Shadow Economy and Organized Crime in Ukraine," Kiev *Zerkalo Nedeli* 10 February 1996, p. 6. FBIS-SOV-96–094-S. Original in Russian.
19. Based on estimates of changes in electric power consumption in Ukraine, the real output decline has been far less than the official statistics indicate. The difference is accounted for by movement into the shadow sector, where such activity escapes

registration, regulation, taxation, and corruption. For estimates for formerly socialist countries in transition, see Istvan Dobozi and Gerhard Pohl, "Real Output Decline in Transition Economies—Forget GDP, Try Power Consumption Data," *Transition* 6, no. 1–2 (January-February 1995): 17–18.

20. Razumkov, et. al., "The Shadow Economy and Organized Crime."
21. See Alexander Paskhaver, "The Adaptation of the Ukrainian Economy to the Crash of the Government Management System," *Ukrainian Legal and Economic Bulletin* 2, no. 3 (March 1994): 37–41.
22. Kyiv UNIAN, 18:30 GMT, 30 January 1995. FBIS-SOV-95–020. Original in Ukrainian.
23. See Alexander Paskhaver, "Ukraine's Shadow Economy During the Period of Transition," *The Ukrainian Economic Monitor* III, no. 6 (June 1996): 6–11.
24. See the chapter entitled "Economic Crisis and Reform" in Paul D'Anieri, Robert Kravchuk, and Taras Kuzio, *Politics and Society in Ukraine* (Boulder, CO: Westview Press, 1999), p. 173.
25. Kiev *Uryadoviy Ku'rer,* 16 January 1999, pp. 7–8. FBIS-SOV-1999–0318. Original in Ukrainian.
26. Cited in Razumkov, et. al., "The Shadow Economy and Organized Crime."
27. See Taras Kuzio, "Crime Still Ukraine's Greatest Enemy," *Jane's Intelligence Review* (January 1997): 10–13.
28. Cited in Razumkov, et al., "The Shadow Economy and Organized Crime."
29. See Daniel Kaufmann and Aleksander Kaliberda, "Integrating the Unofficial Economy into the Dynamics of Post-Socialist Economies," chapter 4 in Bartlomiej Kaminski, ed., *Economic Transition in Russia and the New States of Eurasia* (Armonk, NY: M. E. Sharpe, 1996), pp. 81–120.
30. See Robert S. Kravchuk, "Budget Deficits, Hyperinflation and Stabilization in Ukraine, 1991–96," *Public Budgeting and Finance* 18, no. 4 (winter 1998): 45–70.
31. Ukrainian definitions of money largely correspond to the international conventions, so that interpretations of "narrow money" (M1) and "broad money" (M2) are reasonably straightforward.
32. See Robert S. Kravchuk, "The Challenge of Fiscal Reform in Ukraine, 1991–97" (paper presented at the international conference Institutional Reform in Ukraine: Implications for Emerging Markets, Yale University, New Haven, CT, April 24–25, 1998).
33. See International Monetary Fund, "Ukraine—Recent Economic Developments," IMF Staff Country Report No. 97/109 (Washington, D.C.: International Monetary Fund, October 1997), p. 45.
34. See Economist Intelligence Unit, *Ukraine Country Forecast—3rd Quarter 1998* (London: The Economist, 1998).
35. International Monetary Fund, "Ukraine: Recent Economic Developments," IMF Staff Country Report No. 99/42 (Washington, D.C.: International Monetary Fund, May 1999), p. 26.
36. See Ukrainian-European Policy and Legal Advice Centre, "On Privatization in Ukraine," *Ukrainian Legal and Economic Bulletin* (July 1997): 19–26.
37. *Author's Note*: These statistics are subject to some interpretation. The government's reported privatization statistics tend to over-inflate the results in several ways. First, the reported number of privatized enterprises includes those that have initiated the process but are not yet in private hands. Second, many formally privatized entities have had significant blocks of shares retained by the state due to the incomplete sale or purchase of all shares. Third, privatization "spin-offs" are

counted among the privatized firms, whereas they began the process as a single entity. To overcome some of these statistical reporting issues, starting in the first quarter of 1996, the State Property Fund began to register enterprises as "private" only if all shares were sold. Finally, it should be pointed out that the figures for small-scale privatization do not include new, *de novo* private enterprises.

38. In the wake of President Kuchma's July 1994 electoral victory, parliament voted overwhelmingly to suspend privatization by resolution, enacting a moratorium on concluding new lease-purchase agreements of medium- and large-scale firms. The resolution did not prevent enterprises and leasing associations from continuing the process themselves. It merely prevented sales from being consummated. An unanticipated consequence was that, when the moratorium was lifted in 1995, there was a burst in privatization activity owing to the more careful preparation of the firms waiting in the pipeline. See Resolution of the Supreme Council of Ukraine, "On Perfection of the Privatization Mechanism in Ukraine and Intensifying Control of its Conduct," July 29, 1994.
39. In December 1994, parliament approved a "negative list" of around 6,000 medium- and large-scale enterprises exempt from privatization, of which some 5,414 were in the energy, transportation, and communications sectors. Others were schools, kindergartens, and other organizations subordinated to the Ministry of Education. There has been considerable movement in the number and composition of the list since then. For instance, on February 23, 1995, the Cabinet expanded the list of such entities to 5,600. A parliamentary resolution on March 3, 1995, however, increased this number to 6,102. At the same time, parliament approved another list of some 90 enterprises in defense, oil, and food industries that would also be exempt. On November 22, 1996, the first list was expanded again, to 7,111. In early 1997, the list was reduced to 5,125. It was reduced considerably later that year, to 2,850, by removing educational institutions; health, cultural, and sports facilities; and catering firms. At the same time, 219 facilities in machine building, engineering, energy, and food processing industries were added.
40. The process was well under way the year before. Some 4,800 of eligible enterprises had sold more than 70 percent of shares at the end of 1998.
41. IMF, "Ukraine: Recent Economic Developments," p. 28.
42. Ibid.
43. See Ukrainian-European Policy and Legal Advice Centre, "On Privatization in Ukraine"; and International Monetary Fund, "Ukraine—Recent Economic Developments," IMF Staff Country Report No. 97/109 (October 1997), especially p. 23.
44. See Lidia Lyakh, "Enterprises in the Post Privatization Period," *The Ukrainian Economic Monitor* III, no. 3 (March 1996): 19–20; and Yves G. Van Frausum, et al., "Privatization and Industrial Restructuring in Ukraine," *The Ukrainian Legal and Economic Bulletin,* IV, no. 4 (April 1996): 15–27.
45. "Ukrainian Business Panorama, 17–24 January 2000," Moscow Interfax, 24 January 2000. FBIS-SOV-2000–0124. Original in English.
46. Ukrainian-European Policy and Legal Advice Centre—TACIS, "The Effects of Direct and Indirect Subsidies on the Ukrainian Economy," *Ukrainian Economic Trends,* quarterly issue, June 1999.
47. They write that "privatization is often about power and the distribution of property to those already close to power—the *nomenklatura.*" Paul Hare, Mohammed Ishaq, and Saul Estrin, "Ukraine: Legacies of Central Planning and the Transition to

a Market Economy," in Taras Kuzio, ed., *Contemporary Ukraine: Dynamics of Post-Soviet Transformation* (Armonk, NY: M. E. Sharpe, 1998), pp. 181–200. This citation appears on p. 194.

48. Cited in Paul J. D'Anieri, *Economic Interdependence in Ukrainian-Russian Relations* (Albany, NY: State University of New York Press, 1999), p. 102.
49. The proportion of Ukraine's industrial production accounted for by monopolists has grown steadily, from 67 to 78 percent from 1990 to 1993, finally reaching 90 percent at the end of 1997. See "Big Monopolies Breaking into Many Smaller Ones," *IntelNews* (January 21, 1994): 4; and Anatoliy Revin, "Capital Markets: Who Is the Fairest of Them All?" *Kiyevskiye Vedomosti,* 12 February 1998, p. 9. FBIS-SOV-98–054. Original in Russian.
50. See Dr. Halyna Kozoriz, "Antimonopoly Legislation in Ukraine," *The Ukrainian Legal and Economic Bulletin* 5, no. 5 (May 1997): 9–11.
51. Approval of the Antimonopoly Committee is required if the total value of assets of the combined entity exceeds $2 million. Resolution of the Cabinet of Ministers of Ukraine, "On Adoption of the Mechanism of Preventing the Commodities Markets Monopolization," no. 765–94, November 11, 1994.
52. Law of Ukraine, "On Protection from Unfair Competition," no. 327–96-VR, January 11, 1997.
53. Law of Ukraine, "On Changes to the Law of Ukraine, 'On Protection from Unfair Competition,'" no. 154–98-VR, March 3, 1998.
54. See Gleb Vyshlinskiy, "The President Declared War on Officials," *Kiyevskiye Vedomosti,* 29 December 1997, p. 6. FBIS-SOV-98–013. Original in Russian.
55. See Igor Aksyonov, "How to Improve the Regulatory Conditions for Small Business," *The Ukrainian Legal and Economic Bulletin* 5, no. 4 (April 1997): 9–11.
56. Kevin Manninen and David Snelbecker, "Obstacles to Doing Western Business in Ukraine," *The Ukrainian Legal and Economic Bulletin* 1, no.4 (April 1993): 20–30.
57. Myron Rabij, "Top Twenty Legal Impediments to Doing Business in Ukraine," *The Ukrainian Legal and Economic Bulletin* 4, no. 8–9 (August-September 1996): 19–20.
58. Igor Aksyomov, "How to Improve the Regulatory Conditions for Small Business," *The Ukrainian Legal and Economic Bulletin* 5, no. 4 (April 1997): 9–11.
59. See Roman Woronowycz, "Kuchma Administration Announces Program to Cut Regulations for Business," *The Ukrainian Weekly,* 8 February 1998, p. 1.
60. This includes the State Tax Administration (STA) and the Customs, State Treasury, and Audit Department. See IMF, "Ukraine: Recent Economic Developments" (1999), p. 26.
61. For observations at two points in time, see Manninen and Snelbecker, "Obstacles to Doing Western Business in Ukraine"; and Rabij, "Top Twenty Legal Impediments to Doing Business in Ukraine."
62. Ukrainian-European Policy and Legal Advice Centre—TACIS, *Ukrainian Economic Trends,* quarterly issue, September 1999, Table 3.1.
63. The World Bank, *Ukraine Restoring Growth with Equity: A Participatory Country Economic Memorandum* (Washington, D.C.: The World Bank, 1999).
64. Ibid.
65. See Margarita Shalenko, "Labor Market in Ukraine: The Problem of Latent Unemployment," *Kiev Times,* 17–24 September, 1993, p. 5.
66. See Elena Kuzmenko and Alexander Usenko, eds., *Ukraine Human Development Report 1996,* International Labor Organization (New York: United Nations, 1996), chapter 4, "Employment and Wages."

67. By their nature, official statistics cannot capture or adequately describe the shadow sector. We may infer, from what is known about it, that it is large and therefore crucial to the livelihood of many Ukrainians, making a vital "safety valve" for social tensions.
68. A countervailing factor is that unemployment benefits are so low (approximately 40 HRV per month, or around $18) that many workers do not bother to register with the State Employment Service.
69. Kyiv, *Vechirniy Kyiv* (Internet edition), 15 April 1999. FBIS-SOV-1999–0430. Original in Ukrainian.
70. Ibid.
71. See Economist Intelligence Unit, *Ukraine Country Forecast—3rd Quarter 1998.* (London: The Economist, 1998).
72. The amount of wages subject to indexation is statutorily defined as an amount up to three times the official poverty line. (The poverty line was established at 73.7 HRV per month at July 1, 1998, which compares favorably to the average wage level that month of 55 HRV.) A 100 percent inflation adjustment is made for incomes up to one poverty wage; 80 percent for wages between one and two poverty wages; and 70 percent for wages between two and three poverty wages. The legal basis for indexation of incomes in Ukraine is principally contained in a law and subsequent decree of the Cabinet of Ministers: Law of Ukraine, "On Indexation of Monetary Incomes of the Population," July 3, 1991, revised April 25, 1997, published in *Vidomosti Verkhovnoi Rady Ukrayiny,* no. 2, 1998; and the Decree of the Cabinet of Ministers of Ukraine, "On Adoption of the Order of Indexation of Monetary Incomes of Citizens," no. 663, May 7, 1998, published in *Uryadoviy Ku'rer* 21 May 1998. The latter decree establishes the base period of the cumulative CPI index as January 1998.
73. Ihor Zhyliaev, "Surrogate Money in the Ukrainian Economy: The Scale and the Dynamics," Ukrainian-European Policy and Legal Advice Centre—TACIS, *Ukrainian Economic Trends,* quarterly issue, March 1999, pp. 50–56.
74. The World Bank, *Ukraine Restoring Growth with Equity,* Appendix Table 1.4, "Labor Productivity Indexes by Industry," p. 134.
75. Alex Granberg, "The Economic Interdependence of the Former Soviet Republics," in John Williamson, ed., *Economic Consequences of Soviet Disunion* (Washington, D.C.: Institute for International Economics, 1993), p. 70.
76. The budgetary and monetary spheres suffered considerably, especially since, in the absence of substantial forward progress on privatization and industrial restructuring, many enterprises counted on ample state budget subsidies and cheap bank credits in order to survive. Further, Ukraine inherited from the Soviet Union an overly generous social welfare system that the country could not afford but that its leaders were reluctant to abandon in the face of dramatic falls in the standard of living.
77. Cited in D'Anieri, *Economic Interdependence,* p. 112.
78. See *The Ukrainian Economic Monitor,* no. 3 (32) (March 1998): 3, table 7.
79. Ukrainian-European Policy and Legal Advice Centre—TACIS, *Ukrainian Economic Trends,* monthly update—February 2001, Table 8, p. 28.
80. Moscow Interfax, 11 January 1999. FBIS-SOV-99–011. Original in English.
81. *The Ukrainian Economic Monitor* (various issues).
82. See Economist Intelligence Unit, *Ukraine Country Forecast—Third Quarter 1998.* Until 1996, Russia implicitly subsidized Ukrainian energy imports, as measured by the spread between the import price and world market prices, to the sum of 30.5

percent of imports, or 1.3 percent of Ukrainian GDP, annually from 1992 to 1995. See Gregory V. Krasnov and Josef C. Brada, "Implicit Subsidies in Russian-Ukrainian Energy Trade," *Europe-Asia Studies* 49, no. 5 (1997): 825–843.

83. The World Bank, *Ukraine Restoring Growth with Equity,* Appendix Table 3.10, "Barter Trade in Foreign Goods," p. 153.
84. Ibid., Appendix Table 3.4, "Commodity Structure of Foreign Trade," p. 147.
85. Over 200 varieties of mineral resources have been discovered in Ukraine, in nearly 20,000 deposits. Ukraine produces up to 5 percent of worldwide raw materials and mineral products, valued at some $15 billion in 1997. See V. Chepizhko, "Land Caretakers are 80 Years Old," *Uryadoviy K'urer,* 7 February 1998, p. 8.
86. From a speech by President Leonid D. Kuchma before the Foreign Investment Consultative Council. Kyiv *Uryadoviy Ku'rer,* 25 May 1999, p. 3. FBIS-SOV-1999–0616. Original in Ukrainian.
87. See Tetiana Vakhnenko, "Balance of Payments as the Mirror of Domestic Economic Processes and Foreign Economic Relations of Ukraine," in Ukrainian-European Policy and Legal Advice Centre—TACIS, *Ukrainian Economic Trends,* monthly update—February 2001, p. 4–13.
88. See Oleksandr Bilotserkivets, "Ukraine's Foreign Trade: Structure and Developments," *The Ukrainian Economic Monitor,* no. 6–7 (June-July 1998): 23–28. See Also IMF, "Ukraine: Recent Economic Developments" (1999, 2000).
89. D'Anieri, *Economic Interdependence,* p. 53.
90. See Taras Kuzio, "Ukraine's Arms Exports Continue to Expand," *Jane's Intelligence Review* 9, no. 3 (March 1997): 108–111.
91. The CIS Customs Union includes Russia, Belarus, Kazakhstan, and Kyrgizhstan.
92. "Foreign Direct Investment: New Trends in Transition Countries," *Transition* (summer 1999): 7–8.
93. See German Consultative Group, "Foreign Direct Investment in Ukraine: From a Disappointing Trickle to a Salutory Flow?" *The Ukrainian Economic Monitor,* no. 3 (March 1998): 20–26.
94. See "Foreign Investments Inflow Rising, but Slowly," *Kiev Post,* 21 November 1997, p. 12.
95. Indeed, all CIS states ranked ahead of Ukraine in terms of cumulative per capita FDI, except Armenia, Belarus, Georgia, Tajikistan, and Uzbekistan. From this perspective, Ukraine's performance in attracting FDI may be regarded as a remarkably dismal achievement.
96. German Consultative Group, "Foreign Direct Investment in Ukraine: From a Disappointing Trickle to a Statutory Flow?"
97. See Yves G. Van Frausman, "Foreign Investment in Ukraine: The Investor's View," *The Ukrainian Legal and Economic Bulletin* (January-February 1996): 9–28.
98. "Foreign Investments Rising, But Slowly," *Kiev Post.*
99. See Ukrainian Press Agency, *UPressA,* 27 November 1995, p. 3. See also Interfax-Ukraine, "Excess of $20 Billion Transferred Abroad Over Four Years," 22 November 1996. FBIS-TDD-97–001-L. Original in English.
100. See "Prime Minister Declares Return of Ukrainian Money Successful," *IntelNews,* 13 April 1994.
101. Alex Sudakov, "Ukraine—International Trade Issues," unpublished manuscript in the authors' possession, dated May 1996.
102. Except for, perhaps, a *pro rata* share of the debt of the former Soviet Union. Such debts have long since been assumed entirely by Russia.

103. Ukrainian-European Policy and Legal Advice Centre—TACIS, *Ukrainian Economic Trends* (various issues).
104. Kiev, *Intelnews,* 13 April 2001. FBIS-SOV-2001–0413. Original in English.
105. "Ukraine: Premier Notes Growth in Ukraine's Foreign Debts," Moscow Interfax, 23 January 1999. FBIS-SOV-99–023. Original in English.
106. *Ukraine Business Panorama, 17–24 January 2000,* Moscow Interfax, 24 January 2000. FBIS-SOV-2000–0124. Original in English.
107. Ibid.
108. *Ukraine Business Panorama, 10–17 January 2000,* Moscow Interfax, 18 January 2000. FBIS-SOV-2000–0118. Original in English.
109. Specifically, the government offers to exchange Eurobonds worth EUR 500 million (around $505.3 million) due March 2000; $74 million maturing in October 2000; and bonds worth DM 1.5 billion (about $775.1 million) falling due in February 2001. The proposed rescheduling also involves $250 million in zero-coupon bonds due in September and bonds issued by the Finance Ministry in 1995 worth $300 million, maturing in 2000 and 2001. *Ukraine Business Panorama, 17–24 January 2000.*
110. D'Anieri, *Economic Interdependence.*
111. Ibid., p. 40.
112. Vesa Korhonen, "Swings over Russian Economic Transition," *Russian Economy: The Month in Review* (December 2000). Cited in the World Bank, *Transition* (November-December 2000/January 2001): 41.
113. "Government Approves Concept of Adapting to EU Laws," Kiev, *IntelNews,* 19 August 1999. FBIS-SOV-1999–0820. Original in English.
114. Yevhen Prokopenko, "Acceptance to WTO Hard," Kiev, *Uryadoviy Ku'rer,* 3 September 1998, p. 17. FBIS-SOV-98–275. Original in Ukrainian.

Chapter 3

1. Anders Åslund, "The Trouble with Economic Reforms in Ukraine," in Teofil Kis and Irena Makaryk, eds., *Towards a New Ukraine II: Meeting the Next Century* (Ottawa, Canada: Chair of Ukrainian Studies, University of Ottawa, 1999), pp. 103–120.
2. Bohdan Krawchenko, *Social Change and National Consciousness in Twentieth-Century Ukraine* (London: Macmillan, 1985).
3. Alexander J. Motyl, *Will the Non-Russians Rebel? State, Ethnicity and Stability in the USSR* (Ithaca, NY: Cornell University Press, 1987).
4. Taras Kuzio and Andrew Wilson, *Ukraine: Perestroika to Independence* (Edmonton, Alberta: Canadian Institute of Ukrainian Studies, 1994).
5. Andrew Wilson, *Ukrainian Nationalism in the 1990s: A Minority Faith* (Cambridge, England: Cambridge University Press, 1997), p. 93.
6. Volodymyr Zvigilyanich, "Analysis: Stability and Reform Pose Challenges to New President," *The Ukrainian Weekly,* 16 October 1994, p. 2.
7. Dr. Bohdan Havrylyshyn is the founder of the International Management Institute in Kyiv, Ukraine's first western-style business school M.B.A. program. His remarks are from a speech he delivered on the occasion of the publication of the second edition of his book *Road Maps to the Future,* in the Ukrainian language (Kyiv:

Osnoviy Publishers, 1993), at the Institute of Economics, Ukrainian Academy of Sciences, Kyiv, October 5, 1993. From the author's personal notes from the occasion.

8. See Paul D'Anieri, Robert Kravchuk, and Taras Kuzio, *Politics and Society in Ukraine* (Boulder, CO: Westview Press, 1999), p. 188.
9. Astonishingly, the author himself was present at meetings with high-level officials—including former Minister of Finance Hryhoriy Piatachenko—who stated flatly that printing money for distribution to enterprises was an "inflation fighter."
10. For more detailed discussions, see Robert W. Campbell, *Soviet Economic Power* (Boston: Houghton Mifflin, 1960); Alec Nove, *The Soviet Economy: An Introduction,* 2d rev. ed. (New York: Praeger, 1969); Michael Ellman, *Socialist Planning,* 2d ed. (Cambridge University Press, 1989); or János Kornai, *The Socialist System* (Princeton, NJ: Princeton University Press, 1992).
11. Pathologies of the Soviet economic system, and their root causes, are explored in Robert W. Campbell, *The Failure of Soviet Economic Planning* (Bloomington, IN: Indiana University Press, 1992).
12. For more on the reforms of 1965, see Gertrude Schroeder, "Soviet Economic 'Reforms': A Study in Contradictions," *Soviet Studies* 20, no. 1 (July 1968): 1–21; and David A. Dyker, *The Future of the Soviet Economic Planning System* (Armonk, NY: M.E. Sharpe, Inc., 1985), especially chapter 3.
13. For more on the Gorbachev-era reforms, see Gertrude E. Schroeder, "Anatomy of Gorbachev's Economic Reform," *Soviet Economy,* no. 3 (July-September 1987): 219–241; Marshall Goldman, *Gorbachev's Challenge: Economic Reform in the Age of High Technology* (New York: W. W. Norton, 1987); Padma Desai, *Perestroika in Perspective* (Princeton, NJ: Princeton University Press, 1989); and Anders Åslund, *Gorbachev's Struggle for Economic Reform,* updated and expanded ed. (Ithaca, NY: Cornell University Press, 1991). Excellent works by Russian scholars in English also are available, including some by Gorbachev's former advisors, such as Abel Aganbegyan, *The Economic Challenge of Perestroika* (Bloomington, IN: Indiana University Press, 1988); and Tatyana Zaslavskaya, *The Second Socialist Revolution* (Bloomington, IN: Indiana University Press, 1990).
14. For a detailed discussion of the effects of this law, see Desai, *Perestroika in Perspective.*
15. *Ekonomicheskaya Gazeta,* no. 12 (March 1989): 10–11. Cited in Leslie Dienes, "Energy, Minerals, and Economic Policy," in I. S. Koropeckyj, ed., *The Ukrainian Economy: Achievements, Problems, Challenges* (Cambridge, MA: Harvard Ukrainian Research Institute and Harvard University Press, 1992), pp. 123–147. The citation appears on p. 138.
16. Robert Skidelsky, *The Road from Serfdom* (New York: Penguin, 1996), p. 115.
17. Gross social product (GSP) and net material product (NMP) are Soviet-era measures of national income and output. Gross national product (GNP) and gross domestic product (GDP) are measures more commonly used in the West. It is not easy to translate from the Soviet measures (GSP, NMP) to the western measures (GNP, GDP). Soviet national income accounting focused mainly on output of the most important goods and not necessarily on all goods, and certainly not on all services that would be considered valuable in western capitalist economies. What we can say, simply, is that GDP differs from GNP insofar as the latter includes the foreign trade sector. Unlike GNP, NMP excludes depreciation of capital assets as well as output of the nonproductive sector (i.e., utilities, public services, transportation, and personal services). The ratio of GNP to NMP in the USSR as a whole was

approximately 140.7 percent in 1989. NMP as a ratio of GSP was approximately 40 percent in 1989.

18. For a more detailed discussion of the Ukrainian economy leading up to the Soviet collapse, see Ivan Lukinov, "Radical Reconstruction of the Ukrainian Economy: Reasons, Reforms, Outlook," in Koropeckyj, *The Ukrainian Economy*, pp. 21–44.
19. Ibid.
20. Raphael Shen, *Ukraine's Economic Reform: Obstacles, Errors, Lessons* (Westport, CT: Praeger, 1996), p. 39.
21. Erik Whitlock, "Ukrainian-Russian Trade: The Economics of Dependency," *RFE/RL Research Report*, 2, no. 43 (29 October 1993): 38–42.
22. Ibid.
23. For a more thoroughgoing discussion, see Paul D'Anieri, *Economic Interdependence in Ukrainian-Russian Relations* (Albany, NY: State University of New York Press, 1999), p. 119.
24. See Lucjan T. Orlowski, "Indirect Transfers in Trade among Former Soviet Union Republics: Sources, Patterns and Policy Responses in the Post-Soviet Period," *Europe-Asia Studies* 45, no. 6 (winter 1993): 1001–1024.
25. Whitlock estimates that Russian subsidization of Ukraine nearly doubled to 6.6 percent of GDP by 1992. See Whitlock, "Ukrainian-Russian Trade." To put this figure in perspective, 3–4 percent annual GDP growth for a large industrialized economy would be considered by economists to be quite impressive.
26. Gijsbertus van Selm and Emiel Dolle, "Soviet Inter-republican Capital Transfers and the Republics' Level of Development, 1966–1991," *Most*, no. 1 (1993): 133–149.
27. These are industries characterized by low capital-to-output ratios, rapid inventory turnover, and high operating margins.
28. Juergen Corbet and Andreas Gummich, *The Soviet Union at the Crossroads: Facts and Figures on the Soviet Republics* (Frankfurt, FRG: Duetsche Bank AG, Economics Department, 1990).
29. "Better Late Than Never, Maybe," *The Economist*, 22 July 1995, pp. 21–24.
30. Kuzio and Wilson, *Ukraine: Perestroika to Independence*, p. 14. In voting completed in March 1990, some 442 deputies from 450 districts were elected. Of these, 373 were Communist Party members, 102 were from the intelligentsia, 60 were employed in the state *apparat*, 67 were from industry, 44 from agriculture, 14 from the armed forces, 19 from trade unions and allied organizations, 27 from the working class, and 16 unknown. Ibid., pp. 125–26. For a detailed analysis of the Ukrainian elections of 1990, see Peter J. Potichnyj, "Elections in the Ukraine, 1990," in Zvi Gitelman, ed., *The Politics of Nationality and the Erosion of the USSR* (New York: St. Martin's Press, 1992), pp. 176–214.
31. Kuzio and Wilson, *Ukraine: Perestroika to Independence*, pp. 159–170.
32. See Volodymyr Paniotto, "The Ukrainian Movement for Perestroika: *Rukh*: A Sociological Survey," *Soviet Studies* 42, no. 1 (1991): 177–181.
33. Kuzio and Wilson, *Ukraine: Perestroika to Independence.*
34. D'Anieri, *Economic Interdependence*, p. 176.
35. At this time, Kravchuk was serving as Speaker *(holova)* of the Supreme Soviet of the Ukrainian Soviet Socialist Republic. Previously, he had served as second secretary of the CPU and chief of its ideological department, where—ironically—one of his concerns was purging Ukrainian society of reform and separatist movements, like Rukh.

36. See *Literaturna Ukrayina,* 21 September 1989.
37. Wilson, *Ukrainian Nationalism in the 1990s,* p. 169. He also includes a list of the relevant Ukrainian language literature of the time.
38. For an excellent analysis of Kravchuk's behavior at this time, see Kuzio and Wilson, *Ukraine: Perestroika to Independence*; and Bohdan Nahaylo, *The Ukrainian Resurgence* (Toronto, Canada, and Buffalo, NY: University of Toronto Press, 1999).
39. Kuzio and Wilson, *Ukraine: Perestroika to Independence,* p. 50.
40. *Holos Ukrayiny,* 31 October 1991.
41. Radio Kiev, 10 October 1991. FBIS-SOV-91–198, 11 October 1991, p. 64. Cited in D'Anieri, *Economic Interdependence,* p. 106.
42. TASS International Service, 26 November 1991. FBIS-SOV-91–229, 27 November 1991, p. 59. Cited in D'Anieri, *Economic Interdependence,* p. 107.
43. Kuzio and Wilson, *Ukraine: Perestroika to Independence,* p. 190.
44. Some members of the former Soviet *nomenklatura* did not even have to change offices. In fact, the presidential administration building in Kyiv now occupies the former offices of the Central Committee of the Communist Party of Ukraine. Warm thanks to Taras Kuzio for reminding me of this interesting fact.
45. Most of the following events are chronicled in detail in Taras Kuzio, *Ukraine: The Unfinished Revolution,* European Security Study No. 16 (London: The Institute for European Defence and Strategic Studies, 1992), chapter 4, pp. 21–25.
46. The Pylypchuk-Fokin program was approved by parliament on October 1, 1990.
47. For details on these and other early reform proposals, see Alexei Sekarev, "Ukraine's Policy Structure," *RFE/RL Research Report* 1, no. 32 (August 14, 1992): 60–63.
48. Leonid M. Kravchuk, *Yeh Taka Derzhava—Ukrayina* (Kyiv: Globus, 1992), p. 12.
49. Ibid., p. 44.
50. See D'Anieri, *Economic Interdependence,* p. 109–112.
51. Both the new currency and the early 1992 price liberalization are attributable to Lanoviy, who became known in the West as the "Ukrainian Gaidar." Lanoviy served as Deputy Prime Minister for Economic Reform and Minister of the Economy until his dismissal on July 11, 1992. See Thomas Gregory, "The Trembling Hand of Economic Reform," *East European Reporter* (September/October 1992): 32–34.
52. This attitude would not change easily. Former Deputy Prime Minister Viktor M. Pynzenyk, writing in 2000, states that "the government's fear of losing state control over the economy is a common concern among Ukrainian politicians." See Pynzenyk's chapter, "How to Find a path for Ukrainian Reforms," in Anders Åslund and Georges de Ménil, eds., *Economic Reform in Ukraine: The Unfinished Agenda* (Armonk, NY and London: M. E. Sharpe, 2000), pp. 78–93. The quote appears on p. 80.
53. See *Holos Ukrayiny,* 20 March 1992.
54. Sekarov, "Ukraine's Policy Structure."
55. Lanoviy's leadership of the "New Ukraine" faction, which was harshly critical of Kravchuk, was the pretext for his dismissal. In fact, most observers would later agree that Lanoviy was removed owing to what Kravchuk's cronies in the *nomenklatura* perceived as his overly aggressive pursuit of reforms.
56. *Holos Ukrayiny,* 8 July 1992.
57. See Council of Advisors to the Parliament of Ukraine, "Political Developments," October 14, 1992 (prepared by Laura Szkrbalo). See also, Resolution of the

Supreme Council of Ukraine, "On 'No Confidence' in the Cabinet of Ministers of Ukraine," October 1, 1992.

58. "Dream On," *The Economist,* 17 October 1992, pp. 56–57.
59. "Kuchma Granted Sweeping Powers for Six Months to Set Economy Right," *The Ukrainian Weekly,* 22 November 1992, p. 1. On his economic recovery program, see "Kuchma Outlines Recovery Plan," *The Ukrainian Weekly,* 31 January 1993, p. 2.
60. On the broad array of decrees adopted during this period, see Konstantin Vronsky, "Decrees Adopted by the Ukrainian Government in December 1992," *Kiev Legal and Economic Bulletin* 1, no. 2 (February 1993): 13–14. Regarding the Kuchma team, the prime minister brought into his cabinet several young reformers to help him formulate and execute his program, including: Ihor Yukhnovsky, First Deputy Prime Minister; Viktor Pynzenyk, Deputy Prime Minister for Economic Reform and Minister of the Economy; and Roman Shpek, Minister of De-Statization of Property and Demonopolization of Industry.
61. Compiled from various sources, including: *The Economist,* 17 October 1992, pp. 58–59; *The Economist,* 26 December 1992, p. 62; *Holos Ukrayiny,* 19 November 1992, p. 2, 3; *The Ukrainian Weekly,* 17 January 1993, p. 1; and *The Ukrainian Weekly,* 15 November 1993, p. 3.
62. Borys Klymenko, "Parliament Ok's Kuchma Government's Plan for National Economic Policy," *The Ukrainian Weekly,* 7 February 1993, p. 1.
63. "Man of Iron," *The Economist,* 26 December 1992—8 January 1993, pp. 62–63.
64. Moscow Interfax, 6 March 1993. FBIS-SOV-93–044, 9 March 1993, p. 36. Original in English.
65. Taras Kuzio, *Ukraine: Back From the Brink,* European Security Study No. 23 (London: Institute for Defence and Strategic Studies, 1995), p. 24.
66. "Tough Enough," *The Economist,* 13 March 1993, pp. 38–39.
67. Marta Kolomayets, "Kuchma Supports Introduction of Emergency State in Ukraine," *The Ukrainian Weekly,* 11 July 1993, p. 1.
68. Vladimir Kievsky, "Has the Sly Fox Outwitted Himself?" *Kiev Times* 8 June 1993, p. 1.
69. "Kuchma Seeks Extension of Special Powers," *The Ukrainian Weekly,* 16 May 1993, p. 2.
70. Marta Kolomayets, "Who will Control Ukraine's Cabinet? Kravchuk, Kuchma Struggle, PM Offers His Resignation," *The Ukrainian Weekly,* 23 May 1993, p. 1; and Serhiy Dmytrychenko, "Ukraine's Executive Power Crisis: Analysis of Recent Developments," *The Ukrainian Weekly,* 6 June 1993, p. 3.
71. Decree of the President of Ukraine, "On Urgent Measures for the Stabilization of the Economic and Political Situation in Ukraine," No. 215–93, 16 June 1993. Translated and reprinted in *The Ukrainian Weekly,* 20 June 1993, p. 3.
72. Marta Kolomayets, "News Analysis: Who Will Be Responsible for Economic Reform?" *The Ukrainian Weekly,* 30 May 1993, p. 2.
73. Marta Kolomayets, "Kuchma Unveils New Measures to Speed Market-Oriented Reform," *The Ukrainian Weekly,* 27 June 1993, p. 1.
74. The parliamentary elections were scheduled for the end of March 1994 and the presidential elections for July of that year.
75. In fact, it is widely understood that Zviahilskiy played a key role in instigating the strike. See "Zviahilskiy Operating Style Portrayed," Kiev *Nezavisimost,* 13 May 1994, p. 3. FBIS-USR-94–056, 26 May 1994, pp. 71–73. Original in Russian.

76. Marta Kolomayets, "Kuchma Quits," *The Ukrainian Weekly,* 12 September 1993, p. 1.
77. Council of Advisors to the Parliament of Ukraine, "Update on Ukraine," No. 9, September 29, 1993 (prepared by Myron Wasylyk).
78. See Serhiy Dmytrychenko, "From Troubled Seas to the Storm Ahead: A Parliament Waiting to Die Proves It Still Has Life," *IntelNews,* 26 December 1993, pp. 3–4.
79. See Roman Solchanyk, "Ukraine: A Year of Crisis," *RFE/RL Research Report* 3, no. 1 (January 7, 1994).
80. The first to depart was Ihor Yukhnovsky, who resigned as First Deputy Prime Minister in March, citing "bureaucratic red tape" and the lack of parliamentary cooperation. In April, Viktor Pynzenyk relinquished his post as minister of the economy but stayed on as deputy prime minister; he would resign altogether from the government in August, blaming conservatives who were blocking reforms. Viktor M. Pynzenyk, "Why I Resigned," *Kiev Times,* 17–24 September 1993, p. 3. See also Laura Szkrybalo, "Political Update on Ukraine," *Ukrainian Legal and Economic Bulletin* 1, no. 18 (August 1993): 11–15.
81. See *Financial Times,* 29 September 1993, p. 2.
82. Council of Advisors to the Parliament of Ukraine, "Political Update on Ukraine," No. 10, October 21, 1993.
83. Nahaylo, *The Ukrainian Resurgence,* pp. 465–66.
84. Ibid., p. 467.
85. See Marta Kolomayets, "President Decrees Signal Return to Command Economy," *The Ukrainian Weekly,* November 7, 1993, p. 1.
86. Decree of the President of Ukraine, "On the State Contract and State Order for 1994," No. 484–93, October 28, 1993. See also Resolution of the Cabinet of Ministers of Ukraine, "On the Procedure of Formulation and Placement of State Contract and State Order in 1994," November 12, 1993.
87. See "In Brief," *IntelNews,* 20 November 1993, p. 1.
88. Andrew Wilson, "Ukraine: Two Presidents and Their Powers," in Ray Taras, ed., *Postcommunist Presidents* (Cambridge, England: Cambridge University Press, 1997), pp. 67–105. The citation is on p. 81.
89. For Kravchuk's views, see Leonid Kravchuk, *Yeh Taka Derzhava—Ukrayina* (Kiev: Globus, 1992).
90. Åslund, "The Trouble with Economic Reforms in Ukraine," p. 103.
91. Ibid.
92. Wilson, *Ukrainian Nationalism in the 1990s,* p. 78.
93. For more on this aspect of Kravchuk's leadership, see ibid., p. 112.
94. D'Anieri, *Economic Interdependence,* p. 178.
95. Ibid., p. 179.
96. See Robert S. Kravchuk and Victor Chudowsky, "The Political Geography of Ukraine's 1994 Presidential and Parliamentary Elections," (paper presented at the 1996 annual meeting of the New England Slavic Association, April 19–20, College of the Holy Cross, Worcester, MA). [Note: This paper is available from the author upon request.]
97. Taras Kuzio, *Ukraine Under Kuchma* (London and New York: Macmillan and St. Martin's Press, 1997), p. 4.
98. D'Anieri, *Economic Interdependence,* p. 190.
99. Ibid.

Chapter 4

1. Paul D'Anieri, *Economic Interdependence in Ukrainian-Russian Relations* (Albany, NY: State University of New York Press, 1999), p. 176.
2. "Kuchma Tells Government to Draft Economic Reform," Moscow Interfax News Service, 28 July 1994. FBIS-SOV-94–146. Original in English. See also Adrian Karatnycky, "From Ukraine, a Surprise," *The Wall Street Journal,* 18 November 1994, p. 32.
3. Address of the President of Ukraine to the Supreme Council of Ukraine of 11 October 1994. See *"Shlyakhom Radicalnykh Ekonomichniykh Reform,"* *Holos Ukrayiny,* 13 October 1994, p. 9. Unofficial English translation of the Council of Advisors to the Parliament of Ukraine. (Copy in the author's possession.) For a summary of Kuchma's proposals, see Marta Kolomayets, "Kuchma Outlines Radical Program of Reforms," *The Ukrainian Weekly,* 16 October 1994, p. 1.
4. See Marta Kolomayets, "Parliament Approves Kuchma Reform Program," *The Ukrainian Weekly,* 23 October 1994, p. 1.
5. Address of Michel Camdessus, Managing Director of the International Monetary Fund, at the G-7 Conference on "Partnership for Economic Transformation in Ukraine," October 27, 1994, Winnipeg, Manitoba, Canada. Transcript in the authors' possession. See also Christopher Guly, "Ukraine Wins Pledge of $1.2 Billion in Assistance from G-7," *The Ukrainian Weekly,* 6 November 1994, p. 1.
6. *"Shlyakhom Radicalnykh Ekonomichniykh Reform,"* *Holos Ukrayiny,* 13 October 1994, p. 9. Also, the Unofficial English translation of the Council of Advisors to the Parliament of Ukraine. (Copy in the author's possession.) For a summary of Kuchma's proposals, see Marta Kolomayets, "Kuchma Outlines Radical Program of Reforms," *The Ukrainian Weekly,* 16 October 1994, p. 1. See also Oleh Borsuk, "Kuchma's Economic Proposals—A Point-by-Point Abstract," *IntelNews,* 14 October 1994.
7. Oleh Borsuk, "Kuchma's Economic Proposals."
8. Oleh Borsuk, "Karbovanets Rallies Against Gloomy Prospects," *IntelNews,* 21 October 1994.
9. "Deputies Vote in Favor of Price Liberalization," Moscow Interfax News Service, 9 November 1994. FBIS-SOV-94–218. Original in English.
10. Resolution of the Supreme Council of Ukraine, "On Streamlining the Mechanism of Privatization in Ukraine, and Strengthening Control Over Its Implementation," July 22, 1994. The ban did not apply to small or medium-sized businesses, or to housing privatization. However, the parliamentary resolution prohibited all sale-purchase agreements and those leasing agreements that would result in buy-outs. Further, it did not suspend all privatization activities but temporarily prevented sale-purchase agreements from being consummated. See Jannine MacNeil, "Parliament Halts Privatization," *IntelNews,* 31 July 1994, p. 5; and Marta Kolomayets, "Parliament Suspends Privatization," *The Ukrainian Weekly,* 7 August 1994, p. 2.
11. The ban was lifted on December 11, 1994. The list of objects not to be privatized consisted mainly of large enterprises in the transportation, communications, and energy sectors, as well as bread production and defense industries. See Marta Kolomayets, "Parliament Moves on Privatization," *The Ukrainian Weekly,* 11 December 1994, p. 3.
12. Roman Woronowycz, "Ousted Soviet-Era Prime Minister Brought Back to Head Government," *The Ukrainian Weekly,* 19 June 1994, p. 1.

13. Taras Kuzio, *Ukraine Under Kuchma* (London: Macmillan, 1997), pp. 142–144.
14. Marta Kolomayets, "Masol Resigns as Prime Minister," *The Ukrainian Weekly*, 5 March 1995, p. 1.
15. Ibid. See also Taras Kuzio, "After the Shock, the Therapy," *Transition*, 28 July 1995, pp. 38–40; as well as "Bank Chief Welcomes Marchuk's Appointment," FBIS-SOV-95–042, 2 March 1995. Original in Ukrainian.
16. Chrystyna Lapychak, "Kuchma's First Move: A New Cabinet," *Transition*, 28 July 1995, p. 8.
17. For Kuchma's economic address to parliament, see *Holos Ukrainy*, 6 April 1995, pp. 3–4. For a summary of the March 1995 report on which Kuchma's address is based, see "The Ukrainian Economy in 1994: Annual Report of the President of Ukraine to the Supreme Council," *The Ukrainian Economic Monitor*, no. 1 (3) (1995): 22–24.
18. See the discussion on "Correction of Economic Reform," in Taras Kuzio, *Ukraine Under Kuchma*, pp. 144–49.
19. "Kuchma Issues Edict on Entrepreneurial Activity," Kiev, Radio Ukraine World Service, 1700 GMT, 30 January 1995. FBIS-SOV-95–020. Original in Ukrainian.
20. "Kiev Said Ready for Economic Integration with Russia," interview with presidential aide Oleksandr Razunko. Moscow InterFax News Service, 1654 GMT, 1 March 1995. FBIS-SOV-95–041. Original in English.
21. Law of Ukraine, "On Industrial-Financial Groups in Ukraine," November 21, 1995. *Golos Ukrainy*, 21 May 1996, p. 8. Reprinted in English in FBIS-SOV 121 S. Original in Russian. See also, "Political Update on Ukraine," *Ukrainian Legal and Economic Bulletin*, III, no. 12 (December 1995): 46.
22. A Russian-Ukrainian interstate agreement on basic principles for the establishment of FIGs was signed in July 1995.
23. See Michael Blackman, "An Analysis of Industrial Financial Groups in Ukraine," *Ukrainian Legal and Economic Bulletin* III, no. 11 (November 1995): 11.
24. The "Law on Power," as it was called, had been introduced on December 2, 1994, and adopted in its first reading on December 28. The second reading did not take place until April 1995, however, due to delaying tactics on the part of parliamentary left factions.
25. Chrystyna Lapychak, "Showdown Yields Political Reform," *Transition* I, no. 13 (July 28, 1995): 3–7. See also "Political Reform," in Kuzio, *Ukraine Under Kuchma*, pp. 99–109.
26. One of the most significant aspects of the accord is the positioning of the presidential administration at the center of formulation and execution of economic policy, and a concomitant decrease in the Cabinet's role in the reform process. See "Some Aspects of the Constitutional Agreement between the Supreme Council and the President," *The Ukrainian Economic Monitor*, no. 2(4) (1995): 20.
27. Kuzio, *Ukraine Under Kuchma*, p. 109.
28. Kuchma's Inaugural Address, July 19, 1994. Radio Kiev World Service, July 20, 1994. FBIS-SOV-94–134, p. 35. Original in Ukrainian.
29. Kuzio, *Ukraine Under Kuchma*, p. 41.
30. *Financial Times*, 19 February 1993.
31. Kuzio, *Ukraine Under Kuchma*, p. 41.
32. On the treaty, see D'Anieri, *Economic Interdependence*, p. 116.
33. Marta Kolomayets, "Kuchma Stresses Irreversibility of Economic Reform's Course," *The Ukrainian Weekly*, 26 November 1995, p. 1. See also Kuzio, *Ukraine Under Kuchma*, pp. 147–49.

34. Kuzio, *Ukraine Under Kuchma,* pp. 148.
35. Marta Kolomayets, "Marchuk Named Prime Minister," *The Ukrainian Weekly,* 18 June 1995, p. 1.
36. "Marchuk Presents Economic Program," transcript of an address to parliament of October 11, 1995, Kiev, Radio Ukraine World Service, 19:15 GMT, October 11, 1995. FBIS-SOV-95-198. (Original in Ukrainian.)
37. Marta Kolomayets, "Parliament Approves Government Program," *The Ukrainian Weekly,* 15 October 1995, p. 1.
38. Danylo Yanevsky, "New Government Program Strikes a Discordant Note," *Transition,* 15 December 1995, pp. 56–58.
39. Kuzio, *Ukraine Under Kuchma,* p. 148. See also "Marchuk Presents Economic Program," FBIS-SOV-95-198; For a more detailed summary of Marchuk's program, see "The Program of Activities of the Cabinet of Ministers of Ukraine Is Adopted," *The Ukrainian Economic Monitor,* no. 4(6) (November 1995): 14–18.
40. Kolomayets, "Parliament Approves," p. 1.
41. Ibid.
42. Ibid.
43. "Government to Reduce Credits to Industry," *IntelNews,* 27 November 1995.
44. Marta Kolomayets, "Kuchma Reaffirms Determination to Stay the Course on Reforms," *The Ukrainian Weekly,* 7 April 1996, p. 1.
45. Hreohoriy Larin, "Nonpayment Crisis Climaxes in a Chain of Bankruptcies," Ukrainian Press Agency, UpressA, 7 August 1995.
46. Extended in April 1995, the value of the Standby Loan with the IMF was approximately $1.5 billion.
47. Hrant Bagratian and Emine Gürgen, *Payments Arrears in the Gas and Electric Power Sectors of the Russian Federation and Ukraine,* IMF Working Paper WP/97/162 (Washington, D.C.: International Monetary Fund, 1997).
48. Marchuk was formally discharged due to his violation of the law barring government ministers from concurrently serving as members of parliament. This was a pretext, however, as some 60 other members of the administration also served in parliament. See "Marchuk Fired Due to Shortcomings in Performance of Cabinet," Moscow Interfax, 17:06 GMT, 27 May 1996. FBIS-SOV-96-103. Original in English. See also Marta Kolomayets, "Kuchma Sacks Prime Minister, Replacing Him with Political Ally," *The Ukrainian Weekly,* 2 June 1996, p. 1.
49. "Marchuk Dismissal Seen Based on Rivalry with Kuchma," Moscow, *Pravda,* 30 May 1996, p. 1. FBIS-SOV-96-106. Original in Russian. See also Chrystyna Lapychak, "Power Struggle in Ukraine Reaches Climax with Prime Minister's Dismissal," *OMRI Analytical Brief,* no. 133, May 28, 1996.
50. Marta Kolomayets, "Parliament Approves Lazarenko as PM, President Names Six 'Power' Ministers," *The Ukrainian Weekly,* 14 July 1996, p. 1.
51. Marta Kolomayets, "Kuchma Reaffirms Determination to Stay the Course on Reforms."
52. "New PM Lazarenko Profiled; Statement," Kiev, *Uryadoviy Kur'er,* 30 May 1996, p. 1. FBIS-SOV-96-140-S. Original in Ukrainian.
53. See Anders Åslund, *How Russia Became a Market Economy* (Washington, D.C.: The Brookings Institution, 1995).
54. Ibid.
55. Ben Slay, "Ukraine's Economic Program—More Muddling Through?" *OMRI Analytical Brief,* no. 395, October 17, 1996.

56. On Kuchma's support for the Pynzenyk program, see "Government Issues Appeal to Parliament on Economy," Kiev UT-1 Television Network, 1900 GMT, February 4, 1997. FBIS-SOV-97–024. Original in Ukrainian.
57. Roman Woronowycz, "Pynzenyk Leads Public Relations Campaign to Push Reforms," *The Ukrainian Weekly,* 15 December 1996, p. 1.
58. "IMF Warns about Consequences of Delayed Budget Approval," Moscow Interfax, 17:04 GMT, 28 January 1997. FBIS-SOV-97–019. Original in English. After July 1, 1997, another $3 billion in economic reform loans would be withdrawn. See Roman Woronowycz, "Parliament Passes 1997 Budget after Seven Months of Wrangling," *The Ukrainian Weekly,* 6 July 1997, p. 1.
59. This was the third time Pynzenyk had lost a senior government post since 1993. He had resigned as minister of the economy and deputy prime minister in August 1993 and left his post in a cabinet shake-up in 1995.
60. Roman Woronowycz, "Kuchma Removes Lazarenko as Prime Minister," *The Ukrainian Weekly,* 22 June 1997, p. 1.
61. Ibid. See also Taras Kuzio, "Ukraine Changes Its Prime Minister—Again," Oxford Analytica, *East Europe Policy Brief,* July 4, 1997.
62. At the time of this writing (summer 2001), Lazarenko is being detained by the U.S. Immigration and Naturalization Service, accused of money laundering and traveling under a false passport. (Lazarenko has also confused matters a bit by seeking political asylum in the United States. This is probably a stalling maneuver, however.) He awaits extradition to Switzerland on similar charges, pending resolution of the U.S. charges against him. See Charles Clover, "Swiss Investigate the Profits from Unaccountable Ukrainian Gas Trading," *Financial Times,* 9 December 1998; and, Vitaliy Sych, "Lazarenko Faces Trial in Geneva," *Kyiv Post,* 8 December 1998.
63. Olena Yashchenko, "Pustovoitenko Wins Premiership," *Eastern Economist* 4, no. 26 (182) (July 21, 1997): 1. See also Institute of Statehood and Democracy, "Kuchma Goes for Safety in Nominating Prime Minister," *The Rukh Insider* 3, no. 7 (July 15, 1997). This may be found online at http:www.freenet.Kiev.ua/ISD/RUKHINSD/970715.htm.
64. Olena Yashchenko, "Profiles in Politics: Valeriy Pustovoitenko—The Compromise Candidate," *Eastern Economist* 4, no. 26 (182) (July 21, 1997): 11.
65. Anders Åslund, "The Trouble with Economic Reforms in Ukraine," in Teofil Kis and Irena Makaryk, eds., *Towards a New Ukraine II: Meeting the Next Century* (Ottawa, Canada: Chair of Ukrainian Studies, University of Ottawa, 1999), pp. 114–15.
66. Institute of Statehood and Democracy, "Tkachenko's Rise to the Post of Speaker and Its Aftermath," *The Rukh Insider* 4, no. 7 (July 13, 1998). This may be located online at the following URL: http:www.freenet.Kiev.ua/ISD/RUKHINSD/980713.htm.
67. Viktor A. Yushchenko, "Monetary Policy in the Transition to a Market Economy," in Anders Åslund and George de Ménil, eds., *Economic Reform in Ukraine: The Unfinished Agenda* (Armonk, NY and London: M. E. Sharpe, 2000), pp. 94–110.
68. "Ukrainian President Opens Parliament 12 May," Radio Kiev World Service, 0815 GMT, 12 May 1998. FBIS-SOV-98–132. Original in Ukrainian.
69. Economist Intelligence Unit, *Ukraine Country Forecast—Third Quarter 1998.* (London: The Economist, 1998).
70. Ibid.

71. Roman Woronowycz, "National Bank of Ukraine Chairman Under Fire From Verkhovna Rada," *The Ukrainian Weekly,* 25 October 1998, p. 1.
72. The decree was issued pursuant to Article 33 of the "Law on Budget System," which permits the president to order proportional cuts in the event of revenue deficiencies. The decree does not explicitly identify a target deficit level. See Decree of the President of Ukraine, "On Cutting Expenditures for the State Budget of Ukraine for 1998," no. 860–98, August 8, 1998.
73. The majority of cuts were made in just two areas: Chornobyl relief (-43 percent) and aid to local governments (-50 percent). Other expenditures were reduced an average of 12 percent; however, some of the cuts, though minor in magnitude, were painful: the Employment Fund (-34 percent); the Innovation Fund (-38 percent); health care (-25 percent); culture and arts (-39 percent); environmental protection (-38 percent). Expenditures on social protection of the population were left relatively unchanged. See Fiscal Analysis Office, Verkhovna Rada, "New Presidential Decree on 1998 State Budget," *Second Quarter 1998 Budget & Fiscal Report,* August 21, 1998, pp. 11–17.
74. "Ukraine's Currency Bond Rating Downgraded," Moscow Interfax 06:24 GMT, 10 September 1998. FBIS-SOV-98–253. Original in English.
75. Olena Bereslavska, "July's Market for Bonds of Internal Government Loan (BIGL)," *The Ukrainian Economic Monitor,* no. 8 (37) (August 1998): 11–13.
76. With the blessing of the IMF, which sought to avoid another major default like Russia's, some of the debt service costs were to be "eaten" by Ukraine's creditors.
77. Katya Gorchinskaya, "Kuchma Veers from West's Reform Path," *Kyiv Post,* 20 November 1998.
78. "Ukraine: Deputy Premier Outlines Ukrainian Anticrisis Program," Kiev, UT-1 Television Network, 0855 GMT, 10 September 1998. FBIS-SOV-98–253. Original in Ukrainian. See also "Ukraine, Finances Ailing, May Print More Money," *The New York Times,* 22 November 1998, p. 14.
79. "Kuchma Addresses Parliament on Crisis," transcript of November 19, 1998 Extraordinary Address to Parliament, "On Measures for Stabilizing the Economy and Stimulating Production," Kyiv, *Uryadoviy Kur'er,* 21 November 1998, pp. 3–5. FBIS-SOV-98–336. Original in Ukrainian.
80. Katya Gorchinskaya, "IMF, World Bank Freeze Ukraine Loans," *Kyiv Post,* 8 December 1998.
81. Roman Woronowycz, "Kuchma Tells Verkhovna Rada to get Moving on Economic Reform," *The Ukrainian Weekly,* 31 December 1998, p. 1.
82. "Ukraine: Strategic Development Program Outlined," Kiev, *Uryadoviy K'urer,* 16 January 1999, pp. 5–6. FBIS-SOV-99–027. Original in Ukrainian.
83. See "Pustovoiktenko Presents Reform Program," Kiev, *Uryadoviy K'urer,* 4 March 1999, pp. 2, 4. FBIS-SOV-1999–0316. Original in Ukrainian.
84. "Pustovoitenko Presents Reform Program," Kiev, *Uryadoviy K'urer,* 4 March 1999, pp. 2–4. FBIS-SOV-1999–0316. Original in Ukrainian.
85. Pavel Polityuk, "Government Presents 'Ukraine-2010' Program," *The Ukrainian Weekly,* 21 March 1998, p. 1.
86. See, for instance, Volodymyr Zviglianich, "Kuchma and the 'Ukraine-2010' Program: Remnants of Soviet-Era Planning Policy," *The Ukrainian Weekly,* 28 March 1999, p. 2.
87. Ibid. To be fair, Zviglianich admits this.
88. Roman Woronowycz, "Kuchma, Citing Parliament's Paralysis, Issues 39 Decrees on the Economy," *The Ukrainian Weekly,* 4 July 1999, p. 1.

89. Ibid. On authority conferred under the transitional regulations of chapter 11, paragraph 4 of the constitution of Ukraine, the president had by July 17 issued a total of 83 economic decrees not regulated by other laws. These included decrees on such important matters as a 1 percent tax on real estate; a 5 percent tax on tobacco; and a 6 percent tax on mobile telephones—all earmarked to satisfy the pension and wage arrears.
90. "Kuchma's Speech on Independence Day," Kiev, *Holos Ukrayiny,* 26 August 1999, pp. 3–4. FBIS-SOV-1999–0901. Original in Ukrainian.
91. "Presidential Package," *Eastern Economist,* 6 September 1999, p. 18.
92. Roman Woronowycz, "Communists Fail to Oust Pustovoitenko Government," *The Ukrainian Weekly,* 11 July 1999, p. 1. An attempt also had been fought back in October 1998. See Roman Woronowycz, "Pustovoitenko Government Survives Verkhovna Rada Vote," *The Ukrainian Weekly,* 18 October 1998, p. 1; and Katya Gorchinskaya, "Opposition Prepares to Sack Cabinet," *Kyiv Post,* 6 October 1998, p. 1.
93. Roman Vysotskiy, "Kuratchenko: The Market Will Never Regulate Anything on Its Own," *Eastern Economist,* 16 August 1999, pp. 5–6. See also, "Ukraine: Kuratchenko Disagrees with Government Methods," Moscow Interfax News Service, 1430 GMT, 30 July 1999. FBIS-SOV-1999–0730. Original in English.
94. Inna Pidluska, Ukrainian Center for Independent Political Research, "Research Update" 5, no. 137, August 2, 1999.
95. Kinakh was viewed at the time as a possible replacement for Pustovoitenko. He would rise to the premiership in 2001, succeeding Viktor Yushchenko.
96. "Ukrainian Government Loyal to Economic, Social Reform," Moscow Interfax News Service, 1557 GMT, 30 July 1999. FBIS-SOV-1999–0730. Original in English.
97. Roman Woronowycz, "Kuchma and Symonenko to Face Off on November 14," *The Ukrainian Weekly,* 7 November 1999, p. 1.
98. Roman Woronowycz, "Kuchma Re-Elected By a Landslide," *The Ukrainian Weekly,* 21 November 1999, p. 1.
99. Roman Woronowycz, "Kuchma Says Ukraine Must Sweep Aside Its Communist Past," *The Ukrainian Weekly,* 5 December 1999, p. 1.
100. The vote was 206 to 44, with 21 abstentions and 10 not voting. See "Parliament Rejects Putovoitenko's Nomination as PM," *The Ukrainian Weekly,* 19 December 1999, p. 1.
101. Pustovoitenko's demise was orchestrated by the three most pro-presidential factions: the United Social Democrats, the Vidrodzhennya Rehioniv (Regional Renaissance), and the Working Party. This lends credence to suspicions that the IMF and World Bank pressed Kuchma to appoint "suitable" candidates in order to renew the flow of loan funds. See Inna Pidluska, Ukrainian Center for Independent Political Research, "Research Update," 5, no. 153, December 20, 1999.
102. Ibid. According to some sources, the IMF had insisted on Yushchenko's candidacy for the premiership during President Kuchma's fall 1999 visit to Washington, D.C.
103. "Ukraine Bank Chief Uncertain about Taking Premiership," Moscow Interfax News Service, 1139 GMT, 17 December 1999. FBIS-SOV-1999–1217. Original in English.
104. "Ukraine: Yushchenko Urges Rada to Help Set Up Government," Moscow Interfax News Service, 1839 GMT, 20 December 1999. FBIS-SOV-1999–1220. (Original in English.)

105. "Ukraine: Reformist Ukrainian Premier Appointed," *Jamestown Monitor*, 12 January 2000.
106. In retrospect, it seems clear that Kuchma was more interested in the formation of a presidential majority in parliament rather than in the pursuit of reforms per se.
107. The ten factions in the parliamentary majority were: Motherland, Green party, United Social Democrats, Reforms-Congress, Labor Ukraine, Regional Renaissance, both Rukh wings, the Independents, and—in a break with the Left—Hromada.
108. Roman Woronowycz, "Kuchma Approves Appointment of Reformist Cabinet," *The Ukrainian Weekly*, 9 January 2000, p. 1.
109. "Yushchenko Promises Results Beginning on the 101st Day," *The Ukrainian Weekly*, 23 January 2000, p. 3.
110. German Advisory Group, *The Next 1000 Days: An Economic Reform Agenda for Ukraine* (Kyiv: German Advisory Group, 1999).
111. The draft Law of Ukraine, "On the Cabinet of Ministers," under parliamentary consideration at this time, also would prohibit ministries from exercising direct control over enterprises.
112. "Yushchenko Promises Results Beginning on the 101st Day."
113. According to the decree, the Cabinet of Ministers was to determine and publish by March 1, 2000, a list of off-shore zones, and to submit to parliament by May 1, 2000, a draft bill to increase control over the activities of Ukrainian citizens that would benefit nonresidents of Ukraine. Further, the NBU was to develop a mechanism and procedures whereby commercial banks would inform tax authorities of resident clients' transactions with nonresidents located in designated off-shore zones. The State Customs Service was to do likewise. For its part, the State Tax Administration was ordered to take measures to "strengthen fiscal control" over residents' foreign economic operations. Decree of the President of Ukraine, "On Improving Control Over Foreign Economic Activity of Residents of Ukraine," February 21, 2000. The Cabinet and NUB jointly reacted with resolution no. 127 amending a previous joint resolution of December 12, 1998, "On Strengthening Control Over Transactions Performed by Residents and Non-Residents in the Course of Foreign Economic Operations," no. 1968, to prevent concealment of hard currency abroad.
114. This program was originally published on January 28, 2000, in the government's official newspaper, *Uryadoviy K'urer*. For the text of Kuchma's speech, see "Ukraine: Kuchma Address to Parliament, Nation," Ukrainian Television UT-1, 0835 GMT, 22 February 2000. FBIS-SOV-2000–0033. Original in Ukrainian.
115. Decree of the President of Ukraine, "On Urgent Measures to Implement the Address of the President of Ukraine to the Verkhovna Rada, 'Ukraine Towards the XXIst Century: Strategy of Economic and Social Development for 2000–2001,'" February 23, 2000.
116. Roman Woronowycz, "Ukraine's Cabinet Submits New Plan for Economic Development to Parliament," *The Ukrainian Weekly*, 12 March 2000, p. 1.
117. Ibid.
118. This growth objective was, by early 2000, looking more feasible, insofar as the devaluation of the hryvnia had increased price competitiveness of Ukrainian goods, raising Ukraine's real GDP for the first time. See Roman Woronowycz, "Yushchenko Says Gains in Economy Indicate Beginning of Growth," *The Ukrainian Weekly*, 12 March 2000, p. 1.

119. Roman Woronowycz, "Government Threatens to Resign if Rada Does Not Approve Economic Revival Program," *The Ukrainian Weekly*, 26 March 2000, p. 1.
120. Roman Woronowycz, "Verkhovna Rada Overwhelmingly Passes Government's Economic Revival Program," *The Ukrainian Weekly*, 9 April 2000, p. 1.
121. Volkov's parliamentary faction was subsequently renamed "Democratic Union," apparently in order to avoid confusion after Azarov created the "Ukraine's Regions" faction and party.
122. Inna Pidluska, Ukrainian Center for Independent Political Research, "Research Update," 6, no. 166, March 27, 2000.
123. Inna Pidluska, Ukrainian Center for Independent Political Research, "Research Report," 6, no. 170, April 24, 2000.
124. Ibid.
125. It was common knowledge in Kyiv that Yushchenko's anticorruption and energy policies had incurred the ire of certain energy sector oligarchs, particularly Oleksandr Volkov, Viktor Pinchuk, and Hryhoriy Surkis. For a news report that actually names the perpetrators, see Roman Woronowycz, "Yushchenko Expresses Frustration Over Continuing Conflicts with Opponents," *The Ukrainian Weekly*, 12 November 2000, p. 3.
126. Ibid.
127. Deputies voicing support for Yushchenko came from such disparate ideological poles as Borys Oliyk of the Communist Party, Stepan Khmara of the Conservative Republican Party, Viktor Pynzenyk of the Reforms and Order Party, and Myhailo Syrota of the National Democratic Party, a centrist who is considered by many to be the "father of the constitution." See Roman Woronowycz, "Politicians of Various Stripes Voice Support for Yushchenko," *The Ukrainian Weekly*, 19 November 2000, p. 1.
128. Ibid.
129. "Ukrainian Premier Appeals to People to Support Economic Reforms," Kiev, IntelNews, 1100 GMT, 5 March 2001. FBIS-SOV-2001–0305. Original in English.
130. "Ukraine: Prime Minister Defends Government in Parliament, Calls for Accord." Kiev, *Uryadoviy K'urer*, 19 April 2001. FBIS-SOV-2001–0419. Original in Ukrainian.
131. Roman Woronowycz, "Yushchenko Government Hangs On, for Now," *The Ukrainian Weekly*, 22 April 2001, p. 1.
132. Ibid.
133. The president was apparently betrayed by a former SBU bodyguard, who released several hundred hours of audio tapes implicating Kuchma in the disappearance and apparent murder of Heorhiy Gongadze, a popular journalist who had been sharply critical of the president. Kuchma denies the allegations, claiming that the tapes are a fabrication. Known in the West as "Kuchmagate," the scandal precipitated demonstrations (some of which have turned violent), calls for Kuchma's resignation or impeachment, and stiffening opposition from his rivals in parliament. At this writing, it is still unknown whether Kuchma will survive the scandal. See the series of stories by Roman Woronowycz, especially: "Moroz Accuses Kuchma Administration of Plotting Gongadze's Disappearance," *The Ukrainian Weekly*, 3 December 2000, p. 1; "'Ukraine Without Kuchma' Protests Intensify," *The Ukrainian Weekly*, 11 February 2001, p. 1; "Anti-Kuchma Protests Continue in Ukrainian Capital," *The Ukrainian Weekly*, 18 February 2001, p. 1; and, "Protesters and Police Clash in Kyiv," *The Ukrainian Weekly*, 18 March 2001, p. 1.

134. Yuliya Mostova, "Ukrainian Newspaper Discusses Looming Government Dismissal," BBC Monitoring Service—United Kingdom, April 15, 2001, translated from: Kiev, *Zerkalo Nedeli,* in Russian, 14 April 2001, pp. 1, 2.
135. Giles Whittell, "Ukraine's Tycoons Unite with Communists," *The Times* (UK), 25 April 2001, p. 2. See also Askold Krushelnycky, "Vote of No Confidence Reflects Alliance between Communists and Oligarchs," *The Ukrainian Weekly,* 6 May 2001, p. 8.
136. The Communists accused Yushchenko of impoverishing Ukraine by pushing for land privatization and supporting other reforms called for by the IMF. "Ukraine Parliament Votes to Oust Yushchenko," Agence France Presse, 26 April 2001. See also Patrick E. Tyler, "Ukraine Parliament Dismisses Cabinet, in Blow to Reformists," *The New York Times,* 27 April 2001.
137. Roman Woronowycz, "Yushchenko Remains as Caretaker Only," *The Ukrainian Weekly,* 6 May 2001, p. 1.
138. Roman Woronowycz, "Verkhovna Rada Votes to Oust Yushchenko," *The Ukrainian Weekly,* 29 April 2001, p. 1.
139. Ibid.
140. Taras Kuzio, "Ukraine after Yushchenko," *The Ukrainian Weekly,* 20 May 2001, p. 2.
141. "Ukraine: President Pledges Adherence to Reforms in Speech to Outgoing Cabinet," Kiev, *Uryadoviy K'urer,* 4 May 2001. FBIS-SOV-2001–0504. Original in Ukrainian.
142. For a more thorough discussion, see Dominique Arel, "Ukraine: The Muddle Way," *Current History* (October 1998).
143. Åslund and de Ménil, *Economic Reform in Ukraine,* p. 9.
144. Arel, "Ukraine: The Muddle Way."

Chapter 5

1. Richard M. Bird, "The Adjustment Dimension of Tax Reform in Developing Countries," in Malcolm Gillis, ed., *Tax Reform in Developing Countries* (Durham, NC: Duke University Press, 1989); Jayati Datta-Misra, *Fiscal Management in Adjustment Lending* (Washington, D.C.: The World Bank, 1997); Grzegorz W. Kolodko, "Perverse Effect of Fiscal Adjustment in Transition Economies," *Economics of Transition* 1, no. 3 (1993): 345–55; Vito Tanzi, *Fiscal Policies in Economies in Transition* (Washington, D.C.: International Monetary Fund, 1992); Vito Tanzi, "Fiscal Policy and the Economic Restructuring of Economies in Transition," IMF Working Paper WP/93/22. (Washington, D.C.: International Monetary Fund, 1993); Vito Tanzi, *Transition to Market: Studies in Fiscal Reform* (Washington, D.C.: International Monetary Fund, 1993).
2. William Easterly, Carlos Alfredo Rodriguez, and Claus Schmidt-Hebbel, *Public Sector Deficits and Macroeconomic Performance* (New York and Washington, D.C.: Oxford University Press and The World Bank, 1994).
3. Michael Bruno and William Easterly, *Inflation Crises and Long-Run Growth,* NBER Working Paper no. 5209, August 1, 1995; Easterly, et al., *Public Sector Deficits;* and Datta-Misra, *Fiscal Management.*
4. International Monetary Fund (IMF), *Ukraine: Recent Economic Developments* (Washington,D.C.: IMF, 1993, 1994, 1995, 1996, 1997, 1999); International

Monetary Fund (IMF), *Ukraine: Statistical Appendix* (Washington,D.C.: IMF, 2001); Raphael Shen, *Ukraine's Economic Reform: Obstacles, Errors, Lessons* (Westport, CT and London: Praeger, 1996); Peter Cornelius and Patrick Lenain, eds., *Ukraine: Accelerating the Transition to Market* (Washington, D.C.: International Monetary Fund, 1997).

5. Jack Strauss, "The Role of Money and Credits in Explaining Inflation and Movements in the Karbovanets," *The Ukrainian Legal and Economic Bulletin* (June 1995): 6–16.
6. Sheetal K. Chand and Henri R. Lorie, "Fiscal Policy," in Vito Tanzi, ed., *Fiscal Policies in Economies in Transition* (Washington, D.C.: International Monetary Fund, 1992).
7. With the notable exception of the Fiscal Analysis Office of the Budget Committee of *Verkhovna Rada,* which—unfortunately—was closed during 2001 due to a reduction in U. S. Government financial support.
8. IMF, *Ukraine: Recent Economic Developments* (1997).
9. Ibid.
10. Including the Pension Fund, Chornobyl Fund, Employment Fund, Social Protection Fund, health expenditures, consumer and household subsidies, social support, education and the cultural sphere, sports, and like expenditures on the part of state enterprises. See Ulrich Thießen, with Tatyana Vakhnenko, Irina Antonyuk, Inna Lunina, and Oleksander Mertens, "Reforming the Social Security System," chapter 9 in Axel Siedenberg and Lutz Hoffmann, eds., *Ukraine at the Crossroads: Economic Reforms in International Perspective* (Heidelberg and New York: Physica-Verlag, 1999), pp. 161–188. These data are from table 9.1, p. 163.
11. In 1992, Ukraine devoted over 40 percent of GDP to social protection programs, a significant increase from the 1990 level of approximately 25 percent. This accounted for over two-thirds of total consolidated expenditures for all levels of government (including extrabudgetary funds). Almost no other government bears a burden of this magnitude, with most western countries spending well below 20 percent. IMF, *Ukraine: Recent Economic Developments* (1992, 1997); Ministry of Finance of Ukraine, *State Budget for 1992* and *State Budget for 1993*, documents in the author's possession.
12. Ukraine is a relatively aged society. In 1996, there were 14 million pensioners out of a total population of 50 million. At year-end 1996, the minimum eligibility age for pensions was 60 for men and 55 for women. IMF, *Ukraine: Recent Economic Developments* (1997), p. 45.
13. Ukraine issued its first government bonds ("T-bills") in the first quarter of 1995.
14. In early 1998, Parliament engaged in an election year "spending spree" that compromised its January 1998 Eurobond placement, causing Ukraine to pay 12 percentage points above German Eurobonds, the highest ever for a sovereign debt placement in that market. The NBU was also forced to stop defending the hryvnia on currency markets, as the willingness of both domestic and foreign investors to finance Ukraine's deficits sharply eroded.
15. Robert W. Campbell, *The Socialist Economies in Transition* (Bloomington, IN: Indiana University Press, 1991); Nicolas Spulber, *Restructuring the Soviet Economy:In Search of the Market* (Ann Arbor, MI: University of Michigan Press, 1991); and Tanzi *Fiscal Policies.*
16. Petr Aven, "Economic Policy and the Reforms of Mikhail Gorbachev: A Short History," in Merton J. Peck and Thomas J. Richardson, eds., *What Is to be Done? Proposals for the Soviet Transition to Market* (New Haven, CT: Yale University

Press, 1991); and Padma Desai, *Perestroika in Perspective* (London: I. B. Taurus, 1989).

17. IMF, *Ukraine: Recent Economic Developments* (1995).
18. IMF, *Ukraine: Recent Economic Developments* (1992).
19. On January 1, 1991, a sales tax of 5 percent succeeded the former tax on retail sales turnover, which had been in effect in the USSR since 1931. It has been estimated that the average turnover tax receipts amounted to some 26 percent of final sales, taking into account the numerous exemptions that applied. Dissatisfied with the yield of the sales tax and desperately in search of revenues, the government replaced it with a value-added tax (VAT) at a fixed rate of 22 percent, effective January 1, 1992. IMF, *Ukraine: Recent Economic Developments* (1992), p. 30
20. Ibid., p. 6; and IMF, *Ukraine: Recent Economic Developments* (1995), p. 98.
21. Parliament, in its concern over the impact of higher prices on incomes, passed a law on indexation of wages and social benefits in October 1991, providing for a sliding scale of automatic wage and benefits increases. Under the law, adjustments would be mandatory for budgetary organizations and for social benefits but indicative only for state sector enterprises. IMF, *Ukraine: Recent Economic Developments* (1993), pp. 21–2.
22. IMF, *Ukraine: Recent Economic Developments* (1992).
23. By the time the 1992 budget was adopted in June 1992, the VAT rate had been raised to 28 percent, which was projected to yield approximately 22 percent of GDP, up from the 9 percent raised in 1991 by the turnover and sales taxes that the VAT replaced. The bulk of the increase was to come from a broadening of the VAT tax base to include services. Nevertheless, the estimated VAT receipts were unrealistically high compared to other industrialized countries. IMF, *Ukraine: Recent Economic Developments* (1993), p. 27.
24. This measure was viewed as a solution to the problem that emerged throughout 1991–92, whereby the enterprise profits tax base tended to erode as enterprise directors expanded both gross income and wages—as opposed to net profits—as a means to avoid payment of taxes.
25. IMF, *Ukraine: Recent Economic Developments* (1992), p. 10; IMF, *Ukraine: Recent Economic Developments* (1993), p. 26.
26. The original 1992 budget estimates were based on the grossly invalid assumptions of price increases of no more than 2 to 3 times 1990 levels, and a nominal output increase for 1992. Further, the VAT was introduced with little investment in developing the administrative capacity required to levy and collect the VAT, which can involve significant administrative burdens. In retrospect, Ukraine's projected VAT receipts were unrealistically (even wildly) high by international standards. Most industrial countries collect VAT of between 10–12 percent, even those with highly efficient, modern tax administrations. According to IMF estimates, in order to collect the targeted 22 percent of GDP in VAT revenues, taking into account the structure of Ukraine's foreign trade and extensive VAT exemptions, the effective tax rate would have to be as high as 20 percent, which is almost double its actual yield from 1993–96. Alan A. Tait, ed., *Value Added Tax: Administration and Policy Issues* (Washington, D.C.: International Monetary Fund, 1991); IMF, *Ukraine: Recent Economic Developments* (1993).
27. IMF, *Ukraine: Recent Economic Developments* (1993).
28. Ibid.
29. Ibid., p. 27.
30. IMF, *Ukraine: Recent Economic Developments* (1995).

31. Ibid., p. 23.
32. Increased staffing levels were particularly sought in the Customs Service and State Tax Inspectorate, two key objects of institutional capacity-building.
33. IMF, *Ukraine: Recent Economic Developments* (1995).
34. The IMF reports that target levels were achieved largely because enterprises were required to "top up" tax payments in order to compensate for the impact of higher-than-expected inflation on their liabilities. In effect, the government sought to deprive debtors of any perceived "inflation windfalls." IMF, *Ukraine: Recent Economic Developments* (1995), p. 24.
35. Further, these loans were not repaid as it was originally announced they would be.
36. Agricultural income was to be the only significant exemption from enterprise income taxation.
37. In June, a presidential decree reintroduced VAT exemptions for imports of machine tools, raw materials, some production equipment, and imported goods intended for personal use.
38. IMF, *Ukraine: Recent Economic Developments* (1996), p. 18.
39. Local government arrears for household services subsidies continued to mount throughout 1995. Ibid.
40. "Kuchma Signs Ruling on Tighter Financial Discipline," Moscow Interfax, 3 May 1995, 19:03 GMT. FBIS-SOV-95–087. Original in English.
41. Parliament had discontinued an earlier version of this policy in February 1995. In contrast to the incomes policy of 1992, this one was enforced through intervention in the banking system, to tap directly enterprises' bank accounts.
42. The IMF estimates the 1996 cash deficit even lower, at 3.2 percent of GDP. IMF, *Ukraine: Recent Economic Developments* (1997).
43. Extended in April 1995, the total value of the Standby Loan with the IMF was approximately $1.5 billion.
44. In apparent anticipation of this eventuality, on December 22, 1995, parliament issued a decree, "On Procedures of Financing Expenditures for the Ukrainian State Budget in 1996 Prior to Passage of the Law of Ukraine, 'On the Ukrainian State Budget for 1996,'" no. 487–95-VR, which financed budget expenditures at late 1995 levels, adjusted for the CPI index. See "Ukraine: Economic Statistics for Jan-Feb 1996," *Uryadoviy Kur'er,* 28 March 1996, p. 2. FBIS-SOV-96–113-5. Original in Ukrainian.
45. Chrystyna Lapychak, "Ukrainian Government Cracks Down on Delinquent Energy Customers," *OMRI Daily Digest,* no. 152, part II, 7 August 1996. Available online at: http://www.omri.cz/Index.html. According to Energy Ministry officials, more than 50,000 enterprises—including small retail outlets as well as large factories—owed regional utilities some $1.1 billion in unpaid bills. See Chrystyna Lapychak, "Ukrainian Government Cuts Off Power to Thousands of Delinquent Customers," *OMRI Daily Digest,* no. 154, part II, 9 August 1996. Available online at: http://www.omri.cz/Index.html.
46. Leonid Brovchenko, "Nonpayments: A Companion of the Reforms or of the Difficulty of Their Implementation?" interview with Professor Vasiliy Feodorovich Besedin, *Golos Ukrainy* 6 May 1996, p. 12. FBIS-SOV-96–133-S. Original in Russian.
47. M. Romantsov, "Every Debt Should Be Repaid," *Vseukrainskiye Vedomosti* 7 May 1996, p. 6. FBIS-SOV-96–093. Original in Russian.

48. Hrant Bagratian and Emine Gürgen, *Payments Arrears in the Gas and Electric Power Sectors of the Russian Federation and Ukraine,* IMF Working Paper WP/97/162 (Washington, D.C.: International Monetary Fund, 1997).
49. Moscow Interfax, "Ukraine: Cabinet Examines Debt, Non-Payments Problems," 8 May 1996, 09:07 GMT. FBIS-SOV-96–092. Original in English.
50. IMF, *Ukraine: Recent Economic Developments* (1997), p. 43
51. Irina Titova, "Unpaid Back Wages Could Become External Debts," *Kievskie Vedomosti,* 20 January 1997, p. 3. FBIS-SOV-97–026. Original in Russian.
52. Decree of the President of Ukraine, "On Urgent Measures to Ensure the Timely Payment of Wages, Pensions, Stipends, and Other Social Payments," no. 33/96, May 12, 1996. See also Marta Kolomayets, "Presidential Decree Attempts to Counter Payments Crisis," *Ukrainian Weekly,* 26 May 1996, p. 3; and Chrystyna Lapychak, "Ukrainian President Issues Decree on Timely Wage Payment," *OMRI Daily Digest,* no. 92, part II, 13 May 1996. Available online at: http://www.omri.cz/Index.html.
53. Chrystyna Lapychak, "Ukrainian President Orders Austerity Measures." *OMRI Daily Digest,* no. 95, part II, 16 May 1996. Available online at: http://www.omri.cz/Index.html. IMF staff estimates suggest that the vast majority of wages arrears in 1996 were for health and education workers. IMF, *Ukraine: Recent Economic Developments* (1997), p. 44.
54. Roger Kargas, "IMF Loan to Pay Back Wages in Ukraine," *OMRI Daily Digest,* no. 101, part II, 24 May 1996. Available online at: http://www.omri.cz/Index.html.
55. Chrystyna Lapychak, "Ukrainian Teachers Hold Rally to Protest Unpaid Wages," *OMRI Daily Digest,* no. 194, part II, 7 October 1996. Available online at: http://www.omri.cz/Index.html.
56. For instance, see Roman Woronowycz, "85,000 Demonstrate in Ukraine for Back Pay and Pensions," *Ukrainian Weekly,* 23 March 1997, p. 1. It is estimated that, by December 1997, the government owed some UAH 20.2 billion (roughly, $10 billion) to: state enterprises and agricultural concerns (UAH 8.6 billion), state workers (UAH 6.4 billion), and pensioners (UAH 1.0 billion). Further, Kyiv was on the hook for UAH 4.2 billion in interenterprise arrears in payments for deliveries of goods arising from state orders placed with enterprises. From an interview with Viktor Lysnyckiy, Vice Rector, Kharkiv Branch of the Ukrainian Academy of Public Administration, December 2, 1997.
57. The acceptance by the public of issues having longer maturities depends directly upon the government's continued and credible commitment to anti-inflationary monetary policies.
58. Bond earnings in 1996 were subject to a 15 percent tax, if the profits were repatriated in Ukraine.
59. Natalia Gurushina, "The Trouble with T-Bills," *Transition,* 15 November 1996, p. 54.
60. Kuchma stated repeatedly in late 1996 and into 1997 that he would refuse to sign any budget that was not predicated on his tax reform proposals. See "A New 1997 Draft Government Budget Is Prepared," *The Ukrainian Economic Monitor,* III, no. 12 (19) (December 1996): 20. See also, "Kuchma Intends to Veto Law on Funding Outlay for 1997 Budget," Moscow Interfax, 26 December 1996, 16:20 GMT. FBIS-SOV-96–250. Original in English.
61. The seven draft laws were: "On the System of Taxation"; "On Taxation of Enterprise Profits"; "On Value-Added Tax"; "On Excise Taxes"; "On Public Domestic Debt"; "On Payments on the Territory of Ukraine"; and "On the

Write-Off and Restructuring of Taxpayers' Tax Liabilities as of 1 September 1996." See "Political Update on Ukraine," *Ukrainian Legal and Economic Bulletin* (December 1996): 51–53; and Roman Woronowycz, "Pynzenyk Leads Public Relations Campaign to Push Reforms," *The Ukrainian Weekly,* 15 December 1996, p. 1.

62. It is estimated that the shadow economy accounted for between 40 and 60 percent of total GDP by the end of 1996. Shadow activities cost an estimated UAH 3 billion in revenue losses to the state in the first nine months of 1996. Such lost revenues would increase in subsequent years.
63. Parliament apparently anticipated a long delay, having enacted legislation on December 11, 1996 to continue 1996 spending levels until April 1, 1997. See "Ukrainian Deputies Approve Legislation on Budget Expenditures," *OMRI Daily Digest,* no. 239, part II, 12 December 1996. Available online at: http://www.omri.cz/Publications/DD/Index.html. With no end in sight by April 8, 1997, President Kuchma asked parliament to extend the emergency budget based on 1996 expenditures from its original April 1 deadline, through June. See Roman Woronowycz, "Tax Reform Package Is Stalled, No Budget in Sight for Ukraine," *The Ukrainian Weekly,* 13 April 1997, p. 1.
64. "IMF Warns about Consequences of Delayed Budget Approval," Moscow Interfax, 28 January 1997, 17:04 GMT. FBIS-SOV-97–019. Original in English. After July 1, 1997, another $3 billion in economic reform loans would be withdrawn. See Roman Woronowycz, "Parliament Passes 1997 Budget after Seven Months of Wrangling," *The Ukrainian Weekly,* 6 July 1997, p. 1.
65. Roman Woronowycz, "Verkhovna Rada Oks 1998 Budget Thanks to Cooperation with Cabinet," *The Ukrainian Weekly,* 4 January 1998, p. 1.
66. VAT concessions amounted to an estimated 59.8 percent of the potential VAT revenues, amounting to around UAH 12 billion, or 40 percent of consolidated budget revenues. See "Ukraine: 98 Draft Budget Analyzed," text of a presentation to parliament by Valentyn Symonenko, head of the Ukrainian Audit Chamber, December 4, 1997, *Golos Ukrainy,* 9 December 1997, pp. 9–10. FBIS-SOV-97–365. Original in Russian.
67. See Fiscal Analysis Office of *Verkhovna Rada,* "Mid-Year and June 1998 Budget Report," *Second Quarter 1998 Budget & Fiscal Report,* August 21, 1998, pp. 3–10 and Appendix, pp. 47–54.
68. See Andrij Volchenko, "Budget's Obsession with Movables," *Biznes,* no. 28 (287), 13 July 1998, p. 11. Original in Ukrainian.
69. Specifically, Article 21.3 of the law of Ukraine, "On Taxation of Profits of Enterprises."
70. IMF, *Ukraine: Recent Economic Developments* (1999), p. 36.
71. Roman Woronowycz, "Kuchma Announces Austerity Program," *The Ukrainian Weekly,* 1 February 1998, p. 4.
72. The decree was issued pursuant to Article 33 of the "Law on Budget System," which permits the president to order proportional cuts in the event of revenue deficiencies. The decree does not explicitly identify a target deficit level. See Decree of the President of Ukraine, "On Cutting Expenditures for the State Budget of Ukraine for 1998," No. 860–98, August 8, 1998.
73. Other expenditures were reduced an average of 12 percent; however, some of the cuts, though minor in magnitude, were deep and painful: Employment Fund (-34 percent); Innovation Fund (-38 percent); health care (-25 percent); culture and arts

(-39 percent); environmental protection (-38 percent). Expenditures on social protection of the population were left relatively unchanged. See Fiscal Analysis Office of *Verkhovna Rada,* "New Presidential Decree on 1998 State Budget," *Second Quarter 1998 Budget & Fiscal Report,* August 21, 1998, pp 11–17.

74. See "Ukraine's Currency Bond Rating Downgraded," Moscow Interfax, 10 September 1998, 06:24 GMT. FBIS-SOV-98–253. Original in English.
75. Olena Bereslavska, "July's Market for Bonds of Internal Government Loan (BIGL)," *The Ukrainian Economic Monitor,* no. 8 (37) (August 1998): 11–13.
76. IMF, *Ukraine: Recent Economic Developments* (1999), p. 43.
77. See "Ukraine, Finances Ailing, May Print More Money," *The New York Times,* 22 November 1998, p. 14.
78. Roman Woronowycz, "Verkhovna Rada Passes Budget," *The Ukrainian Weekly,* 10 January 1999, p. 1.
79. Ibid.
80. Roman Woronowycz, "Budget Stalled as Rada Makes Its Modifications," *The Ukrainian Weekly,* 31 December 1998, p. 1.
81. Ibid.
82. Symonenko's official position is head of the Ukrainian Accounting Chamber. See "Ukraine: Accounting Official on 1999 draft Budget," Kiev, *Demokratychna Ukrayiny,* 10 December 1998, pp. 1, 3. FBIS-SOV-98–355. Original in Ukrainian.
83. "Ukraine: Tkachenko on Draft Budget for 1999," Kiev, *Holos Ukrayiny,* 6 December 1998, pp. 1, 3. FBIS-SOV-98–365. Original in Ukrainian.
84. "Ukraine: Lawmaker Discusses New *[sic]* Budget," Kiev, *Vechirniy Kyiv,* 29 September, 1998, pp. 1, 5. FBIA-SOV-98–279. Original in Ukrainian.
85. "Ukraine: 1999 Budget Law," Kiev, *Holos Ukrayiny,* 2 February 1999, pp. 5–8. FBIS-SOV-1999–0215. Original in Ukrainian.
86. "Interfax Provides Breakdown of 1999 Ukrainian Budget," Moscow Interfax News Service, 31 December 1998, 1729 GMT. FBIS-SOV-98–365. Original in English.
87. See the pertinent Resolutions of the Cabinet of Ministers of Ukraine, nos. 1 and 1755, of January 2 and September 23, respectively.
88. It is also a violation of the March 22, 2001 Budget Code of Ukraine.
89. Roman Woronowycz, "New Group to Begin Work on Ukraine's Budget," *The Ukrainian Weekly,* 13 June 1999, p. 1.
90. See the interview with Anatoliy Kinakh, in "Ukraine: Deputy Premier on Budget Passage, Gas Supply," Kiev, *Intelnews,* 25 October 1999, 0730 GMT. FBIS-SOV-1999–1025. Original in English.
91. Ukraine was then in technical default on some of its foreign debts and would attempt to restructure some of it during the coming year.
92. Law of Ukraine, "On the 2000 State Budget of Ukraine," no. 1458-III, February 17, 2000. Available online at http://www.rada.kiev.ua.
93. The special fund would also incorporate the new Social Security Fund, which was established by the Cabinet of Ministers in 2000.
94. Law of Ukraine, "On the 2000 State Budget of Ukraine," no. 1458-III, February 17, 2000, Article 67.
95. Ibid., Article 69.
96. Inna Pidluska, "Employment, Wage Arrears and Social Peace Are So Hard to Keep," Ukrainian Center for Independent Political Research, *Research Update* 6, no. 182 (July 17, 2000).
97. Ibid.

98. Resolution of the Cabinet of Ministers of Ukraine, "On Formation of the State Budget of Ukraine for 2001, Its Preliminary Indicators and Measures to Prepare the Draft Law on the State Budget of Ukraine for 2001," no. 937, June 9, 2000.
99. Cited in Piluska, "Employment, Wage Arrears and Social Peace."
100. Ibid.
101. Ibid.
102. Law of Ukraine, "On Introducing Changes to the Law of Ukraine 'On the State Budget of Ukraine for 2001,'" no. 1712-III, May 11, 2000.
103. Hahm, et al., in a study of deficit spending in nine industrialized parliamentary democracies, determined that the strength of a country's fiscal bureaucracy was negatively correlated with the size of its fiscal deficit. They found that strong, independent fiscal bureaucracies are both more fiscally conservative than other organs of government and more capable of achieving desired fiscal outcomes. See Sung Deuk Hahm, Mark S. Kamlet, and David C. Mowery, "The Political Economy of Deficit Spending in Nine Industrialized Parliamentary Democracies: The Role of Fiscal Institutions," *Comparative Political Studies* 29, no. 1 (1996): 52–77.
104. Tanzi notes that "Under the former USSR, to a great extent the monobank performed the function of a tax collection agency. The kind of separate tax administration, with clear legal powers over taxpayers, that exists in a market economy was largely nonexistent." *Fiscal Policies,* p. 16. Andic observes that "Revenues were designed and collected in a way that minimized the transactions costs within the context of the . . . communal economies which eliminated the need for a tax administration in the western sense." See Suphan Andic, "Organizational Dinmensions of Public Finance in Transition Economies: An Assessment of the Recent Literature," in Salvatore Schiavo-Campo, ed., *Institutional Change and the Public Sector in Transitional Economies,* World Bank Discussion Paper No. 241 (Washington, D.C.: The World Bank, 1994), pp. 53–96.
105. Carlos Silvani and Katherine Baer, *Designing a Tax Administration Reform Strategy: Experiences and Guidelines,* IMF Working Paper WP/97/30 (Washington, D.C.: International Monetary Fund, 1997); and Tanzi, *Fiscal Policies.*
106. Richard M. Bird, *Tax Policy and Economic Development* (Baltimore, MD: The Johns Hopkins University Press, 1992), pp. 189–90.
107. Datta-Misra, *Fiscal Management,* p. 68.
108. Law of Ukrainian SSR, "On the State Tax Inspectorate of Ukraine," no. 6–91-VR; revised in 1992 with law no. 39–92-VR, and again with law no. 3813–93-VR (December 24, 1993).
109. Decree of the President of Ukraine, "On Establishment of the State Tax Administration of Ukraine and Local State Tax Administrations," August 28, 1996. See *The Ukrainian Economic Monitor* III, no. 10(17) (October 1996): 20.
110. Andic, "Organizational Dimensions of Public Finance"; Milka Casanegra de Jantscher, Carlos Silvani, and Charles Vehorn, "Modernizing Tax Administration," in Tanzi, *Fiscal Policies,* pp. 120–141.
111. It is widely known that tax inspectors take considerable liberties in the interpretation of the tax laws as they apply to particular individuals and enterprises and their activities. Special "deals" are arranged by *rayon* (i.e., district) offices of the STA, including outright exemptions from tax. Sadly, there apparently is little uniformity in the application of tax law throughout the country.
112. The Taxpayer Services Division produced television and radio spots on the basics of the Ukrainian tax system, taxpayer rights and responsibilities, and other valuable

information. Further, hundreds of newspaper articles about Ukrainian taxes were submitted to the media during this period, and dozens of publications on various taxes were produced and distributed by the start of 1997.

113. Bird, *Tax Policy and Economic Development.*
114. David Newberry, "Taxation and Development," in David Newberry and Nicholas Stern, eds., *The Theory of Taxation for Developing Countries* (New York and Washington, D.C.: Oxford University Press and The World Bank, 1987), pp. 165–204. This citation appears on p. 201.
115. Stanley S. Surrey, "Tax Administration in Underdeveloped Countries," *University of Michigan Law Review* 12 (1958): 158–88.
116. The potential for improved collections may be enormous. Richupan reported that it is not uncommon for over one-half of potential income tax in developing countries to go uncollected. Bird reported similar proportions for other major taxes. Somchai Richupan, "Measuring Tax Evasion," *Finance and Development* 21, no. 4 (1984): 38–40; and Bird, *Tax Policy and Economic Development.*
117. Datta-Misra, *Fiscal Policies.*
118. Law of Ukrainian SSR, "On the Budget System of the Ukrainian SSR," no. 512-XII, December 5, 1990.
119. Law of Ukraine, "On Amendments and Additions to the Law of the Ukrainian SSR, 'On the Budget System of Ukraine,'" no. 253/95-VR, June 29, 1995.
120. Draft Law of Ukraine, "On the Budgetary System and Budget Process," text supplied by David Darby, U.S. Treasury Resident Budget Management Advisor to the Minister of Finance of Ukraine, October 31, 1997.
121. "Budget Process Codified," Kyiv, *DEN*, no. 10 (141), 27 March 2001, p. 1. In English.
122. "Executive Summary," *The Guide to the New Budget Code* (Kyiv: Fiscal Analysis Office of *Verkhovna Rada,* August 2000), as amended. Available online at http://www.fao.kiev.ua/Publications.
123. Law of Ukraine, "Budget Code of Ukraine," March 22, 2001, article 7. English language translation provided by the Office of Fiscal Analysis of *Verkhovna Rada* and summarized by the author.
124. The Budget Code stipulates that the main parameters of intergovernmental fiscal relations in any particular year must be fixed after the state budget law for that year is passed on its second reading. This should greatly enhance the process of regional and municipal fiscal planning.
125. Law of Ukraine, "Budget Code of Ukraine," March 22, 2001.
126. For detailed descriptions of the Soviet budgetary framework, see G. K. Shehovtsov, *Budjet Socialnisticheskogo Gosudarstva* (Moscow: Financiy I Statistika, 1983); and M. K. Shermeneva, *Gosudarstvenniy Budjet CCCP* (Moscow: Financiy, 1978).
127. That is, aside from a check for adherence to "per capita" spending norms developed by the Ministry of the Economy.
128. IMF, *Ukraine: Recent Economic Developments* (1997), p. 45.
129. Resolution of the Supreme Council, "On the Structure of the Budget Classification in Ukraine," July 12, 1996.
130. "Experimental IMF Report on Observance of Standards and Codes: Ukraine" (Washington, D.C.: International Monetary Fund, September 1999). Available online at: http://www.imf.org/external/np/rosc/ukr/INDEX.HTM.
131. Ibid.
132. Two notable instances were President Kravchuk's decree, "On the Procedure for the Fulfillment of the State Budget," no. 219–93, June 18, 1993, which ordered that

budget expenditures be made on the basis of actual revenue collections; and President Kuchma's later decree, "On Measures Aimed at Provision of Fulfilling the Budget and Improving Financial and Budget Discipline," August 28, 1997, which ordered prioritization of expenditures (to favor social payments), control of monopoly enterprises' wage bills, across-the-board 25 percent reductions in staffing of government ministries, and a reduction in the number of existing ministries and other bodies of state power.

133. The proposal was to have local branches of the Budget Bank set upon the premises of three former state banks that were converted to joint-stock companies: Prominvestbank, Ukrinbank, and Bank Ukrayiny, the former agro-industrial bank. The state would do so by increasing its share of the capital of these banks, as it had in 1995 (going from 1 to 30 percent that year, mainly by covering the unpaid loans of state enterprises with future dividends—a clever subterfuge. Commercial banks would then be forced to cede part of their premises, representing a proportional reduction in their share of authorized capital. See Nikolai Zakrevskiy, "Parliament Wants a Bank of Its Own," *Kyivskiye Vedomosti,* 27 May 1996, p. 7. FBIS-SOV-96–140-S. Original in Russian.
134. Decree of the President of Ukraine, "On the State Treasury of Ukraine," No. 335–95, April 27, 1995.
135. The treasury was to be implemented according to a joint resolution of the Cabinet of Ministers and the National Bank of Ukraine, dated January 12, 1997. See *The Ukrainian Economic Monitor* no. 3 (22) (March 1997): 21.
136. These are the State Security Service, Main Department of Government Communication, and the Presidential Committee on Intelligence Affairs. IMF, *Ukraine: Recent Economic Developments* (1999), p. 39.
137. Ibid.
138. To be fair, the number of state-funded agencies was reduced dramatically by Prime Minister Yushchenko, by nearly two-thirds. A January 8, 2000 resolution of the Cabinet of Ministers lowered the main budget managing agencies to 74. The Budget Code reduces the number further still.
139. Decree of the President of Crimea, "On Conclusion of a Treaty Between the Governments of Ukraine and the Republic of Crimea," No. 2–95, January 13, 1995, text of the treaty published in *Krymskiye Izvestiya* (Simferopol), 18 January 1995, p. 1. FBIS-SOV-95–115. Original in Russian.
140. The first auction was held on March 10, 1995, with two more held in April. In these initial auctions, demand greatly exceeded supply. But a two-month delay was taken before the third auction was held, so that preparations could be made for issuing bonds with maturities of 90, 180, and 270 days, having interest rates of 90 percent per annum. The third auction was finally held on June 16, 1995. No less than three auctions per month were held thereafter.
141. "NBU Trying to Legitimize Bonds in Ukraine; An Interview with NBU Securities Department Chairman Vitaliy Myhashko," *IntelNews,* 28 October 1994, p. 15.
142. IMF, *Ukraine: Recent Economic Developments* (1999), p.53.
143. Authorized initially under Resolution of the Cabinet of Ministers, no. 586–94, August 23, 1994. The main impetus was a requirement of the IMF that Ukraine issue and have outstanding by January 1, 1996, a minimum of KBV 17 trillion in government securities. Ukraine was to handily exceed this minimum.
144. Resolution of the Cabinet of Ministers, "On Main Provisions for Issue and Placement of Non-Interest Government Domestic Bonds for 1996," no. 469–96, April 29, 1996.

145. The savings bonds were first issued in June 1997, by Resolution of the Cabinet of Ministers, "On the Issuing of Bonds of 1997 Internal Government Savings Loan," no. 138–97, February 5, 1997.
146. "Foreign Investor's Guide to Ukrainian Investments," *IntelNews* 5 September 1996. Available online at http://www.osc.edu/ukraine_nonpubl/htmls/inewsecg.html.
147. *IntelNews,* 12 January 1996. FBIS-SOV-96–010. Original in English.
148. Matthew Kaminski, "Ukraine Embarks on Spending Spree, Hurting Currency," *Wall Street Journal,* 9 March 1998, p. 25.
149. Olena Bereslavska, "The Market for Bonds of Internal Government Loan in the Second Quarter 1997," *The Ukrainian Economic Monitor,* no. 7 (26) (July 1997): 11–13.
150. Resolution of the Cabinet of Ministers, "On the Issuance of Interest-Bearing Bonds of 1997 Internal Government Loan with Term of Circulation of 36 Months," no. 584–97, June 11, 1997.
151. Nonresidents were officially permitted to participate in primary and secondary markets by special resolution of the Cabinet of Ministers. See Olena Bereslavska, "Events in the Market of Government Securities," *The Ukrainian Economic Monitor* III, no. 11 (18) (November 1996): 9; and Olena Bereslavska, "Review of the Situation in the BIGL Market in January 1997," *The Ukrainian Economic Monitor,* IV, no. 3 (22) (March 1997): 14.
152. Telegram of the NBU to commercial banks registered to deal in bonds of internal government debt, dated February 19, 1997. Copy in the author's possession.
153. As part of this effort, in December 1997, the government issued UAH 750 million of 9- and 12-month T-bills denominated in hryvnia but linked to the U.S. dollar exchange rate so as to guarantee a minimum 22 percent yield in dollar terms. IMF, *Ukraine: Recent Economic Developments* (1999), p. 41.
154. In the United States, this practice is common and goes by the technical term "debt refunding."
155. Law of Ukraine, "On the National Bank of Ukraine," no. 679-XIV, May 20, 1999.
156. Until creation of the State Credit Investment Company, Ukrainian borrowing was regulated by Resolution of the Cabinet of Ministers, "On Exchange Control," no. 93–337, February 19, 1993, creating the Currency Crediting Council (CCC), which served as the highest debt decision-making body of the Cabinet. The CCC met twice a month to review loan proposals, which were presented jointly by the Ministry of the Economy, Ministry of Finance, and Eximbank. Projects were evaluated for technical feasibility by the Ministry of Economy, and for potential to generate foreign exchange by the Eximbank. The Unit for International Credits and Technical Assistance of the Department of International Relations in the Secretariat of the Cabinet of Ministers acted as the technical resource for the CCC. The role of the Ministry of Finance was limited until fall 1993, when a Debt Analysis Unit was created within the Foreign Exchange Department. Even after these developments, however, little consideration was paid until 1995 to the macroeconomic effects of borrowing or Ukraine's long-run ability to pay.
157. Law of Ukraine, "On State Credit Investment Company," December 19, 1995. Former Deputy Finance Minister Boris Sobolev, an extremely able, young, and articulate reformer with substantial experience in negotiating Ukraine's foreign debt obligations, was selected to lead the agency.
158. Lidiya Lyakh, "Ukraine's Foreign Debt," *The Ukrainian Economic Monitor* IV, no. 1–2 (20–21) (January-February, 1997): 6–9.
159. IMF, *Ukraine: Recent Economic Developments* (1997).

160. IMF, *Ukraine: Recent Economic Developments* (1999), p. 41.
161. V. Mykhaliov and I. Karpenko, "Afloat in Eurobonds," *Eastern Economist,* 21 July 1997, pp. 7–8; and Matthew Kaminski, "Ukraine Embarks on Spending Spree, Hurting Currency," *Wall Street Journal,* 9 March 1998, p. 25.
162. *OMRI Analytical Brief,* no. 455, November 11, 1996. Mitigating factors are Ukraine's relatively low external debt levels, as well as the conclusion in 1997 of a three-year, $3.1 billion agreement for an IMF Extended Fund Facility. It is also anticipated that Municipal Eurobonds would be issued early in the next century, primarily by Ukraine's largest industrial cities.
163. Cited in Inna Pidluska, "Chronology of a Potential Default," Ukrainian Center for Independent Political Research, *Research Update* 6, no. 164 (March 13, 2000).
164. "ING Barings Talks Pass Deadline," *Kyiv Post,* 17 June 1999, p. 3B.
165. "Ukraine Business Panorama 4–10 January 2000," Moscow Interfax News Service, 9 January 2000, 15:55 GMT. FBIS-SOV-2000–0109. Original in English.
166. "Ukraine Business Panorama 21 February 2000," Moscow Interfax News Service, 22 February 2000, 0901 GMT. FBIS-SOV-2000–0222. Original in English.
167. Tetiana Vakhnenko, "State Debt of Ukraine: Situation, Problems, and Solutions," *Ukrainian Economic Trends,* May 2001, pp. 4–11.
168. Tanzi even points to a potentially perverse circumstance that can develop, where the government raises state enterprises' profits taxes while directing the extension of bank credits or soft loans to the enterprise sector. This would reduce budget deficits without necessarily reducing monetary expansion, which in the instance of both Poland and the former Yugoslavia, resulted in both high inflation and budget surpluses. Vito Tanzi, "Inflation, Lags in Collection and the Real Value of Tax Revenues," *International Monetary Fund Staff Papers* 24 (1977): 154–67.
169. János Kornai, "Hard and Soft Budget Constraint," in *Contradictions and Dilemmas: Studies on the Socialist Economy and Society* (Cambridge, Massachusetts: MIT Press, 1986), pp. 33–51; and "The Soft Budget Constraint," in *Vision and Reality, Market and State* (New York: Routledge, 1990), pp. 20–46.
170. Of the vast and expanding literature on central bank behavior, two prominent works are: Alberto Alesina and Lawrence Summers," Central Bank Independence and Macroeconomic Performance: Some Comparative Evidence," *Journal of Money, Credit and Banking* 25, no. 2 (1993): 151–162; and Stanley Fisher, "Why Are Central Banks Pursuing Long-Run Price Stability?", working paper, prepared for "Achieving Price Stability," the 1996 Federal Reserve Bank of Kansas City Symposium, Jackson Hole, WY, August 29–31, 1996.
171. Law of Ukraine, "On the National Bank of Ukraine," no. 679-XIV, May 20, 1999.
172. Nathan Hodge, "Kuchma Signs Watered-Down National Bank Law," *Kyiv Post,* 17 June 1999, p. 3.
173. Viktor M.Pyzenyk, "How to Find a Path for Ukrainian Reforms," in Anders Åslund and Georges de Ménil, eds., *Economic Reform in Ukraine: The Unfinished Agenda* (Armonk, NY and London: M. E. Sharpe, 2000), pp. 78–93. The citation appears on p. 90.

Chapter 6

1. See Mancur Olson, *The Rise and Decline of Nations* (New Haven, CT: Yale University Press, 1982); and David Seddon and Tim Belton-Jones, "The Political

Determinants of Economic Flexibility, with Special Reference to the East Asian NICS," in Tony Killick, ed., *The Flexible Economy: Causes and Consequences of the Adaptability of National Economies* (London and New York: Routledge and Overseas Development Institute, 1995).

2. Jayati Datta-Misra, *Fiscal Management in Adjustment Lending* (Washington, D.C.: The World Bank, 1997).
3. M. G. Allingham and A. Sandmo, "Income Tax Evasion: A Theoretical Analysis," *Journal of Public Economics* 1, nos. 3–4 (November 1972): 323–38; D. Usher, "Tax Evasion and Marginal Cost of Public Funds," *Economic Inquiry,* no. 24 (1986): 563–86; Somchai Richupan, "Measuring Tax Evasion," *Finance and Development* 24, no. 4 (1987): 38–40; Somchai Richupan, "Determinants of Income Tax Evasion: Role of Tax Rates, Shape of Tax Schedule, and Other Factors," in Ved P. Ghandi, ed., *Supply-Side Tax Policy: Its Relevance to Developing Countries* (Washington, D.C.: The World Bank, 1987); F. A. Cowell, *Cheating the Government: The Economics of Tax Evasion* (Cambridge, MA: MIT Press, 1990); P. Webley, H. Robben, H. Elffers, and D. Hessing, *Tax Evasion: An Experimental Approach* (Cambridge, England: Cambridge University Press, 1991); Vito Tanzi, "Fiscal Policy and the Economic Restructuring of Economies in Transition," IMF Working Paper WP/93/22 (Washington, D.C.: International Monetary Fund, 1993); Vito Tanzi and Parthasarathi Shome, "A Primer on Tax Evasion," IMF Working Paper WP/93/21 (Washington, D.C.: International Monetary Fund, 1993).
4. This includes educating taxpayers, providing taxpayer advisory services, and developing targeted audit capabilities, withholding procedures, and management information systems.
5. Richard Musgrave, "Tax Reform in Developing Countries," in David Newberry and Nicholas Stern, eds., *The Theory of Taxation for Developing Countries* (New York and Washington, D.C.: Oxford University Press and The World Bank, 1987).
6. According to Newberry and Stern, the average share of central government revenue in GDP was 14 percent in 1960, 18 percent in 1970, and 24 percent in 1980 for developing countries for which data are available. Newberry and Stern, eds., *The Theory of Taxation for Developing Countries,* p. 3.
7. International Monetary Fund (IMF), *Ukraine: Recent Economic Developments* (Washington, D.C.: International Monetary Fund, 1999), table 35, pp. 100–101.
8. Ved P. Gandhi and Dubravko Mihaljek, "Scope for Reform of Socialist Tax Systems," in Vito Tanzi, ed., *Fiscal Policies in Economies in Transition* (Washington, D.C.: International Monetary Fund, 1992), pp. 142–165.
9. Tanzi, ed., *Fiscal Policies;* Vito Tanzi, ed., *Transition to Market: Studies in Fiscal Reform* (Washington, D.C.: International Monetary Fund, 1993).
10. See "Basic Provisions of Tax Policy in Ukraine," *Golos Ukrainy,* 26 December 1996, p. 5. FBIS-SOV-97–101. Original in Russian.
11. Law of Ukraine, "On the Introduction of Amendments to the Law of Ukraine on the System of Taxation," no. 77–97-VR, February 18, 1997.
12. See, for example, Richard Bird, *Tax Policy and Economic Development* (Baltimore, MD: The Johns Hopkins University Press, 1992).
13. Law of Ukraine, "On the Introduction of Amendments to the Law of Ukraine on the System of Taxation," Article 3. See also *Golos Ukrainy,* 25 March 1997, pp. 6–7. FBIS-97–070. Original in Russian.

14. Payroll taxes in 1997 were paid in hryvnia by the employer on a monthly basis, broken down as follows. Elimination of the Chornobyl Fund component in 1998 reduced the total employer contribution to 38 percent.

• Social Security Fund	4.44%
• State Pension Fund	32.56%
• Chornobyl Fund (Raised from 7.0% in July 1996.)	12.00%
• State Employment Fund	2.00%
TOTAL	51.00%

15. IMF, *Ukraine: Recent Economic Developments* (1999), table 43, p. 111.
16. OECD is the Organization for Economic Cooperation and Development, essentially the wealthy industrialized countries of the West, plus Japan.
17. International Monetary Fund (IMF), *IMF Economic Reviews: Ukraine* (Washington, D.C.: IMF, April 1992); International Monetary Fund (IMF), *IMF Economic Reviews: Ukraine* (Washington, D.C.: IMF, September 1993); Larisa Lozynskyj-Kyj, "The New Tax Program in Ukraine," *The Ukrainian Quarterly* LI, no. 4 (winter 1995): 369–382.
18. George Holland, "Planning for VAT," in Alan A. Tait, ed., *Value Added Tax: Administration and Policy Issues* (Washington, D.C.: International Monetary Fund, 1991); Lidia Lyakh, "The Value-Added Tax (VAT)," *The Ukrainian Economic Monitor* III, no. 8–9 (August-September 1996): 15–17.
19. IMF, *IMF Economic Reviews: Ukraine* (1992).
20. The usual required VAT preparations include forecasts of the economic and social consequences of VAT introduction (especially the redistributional effects); reorganization of the system of record keeping and national accounts; specification of necessary computation and collection procedures; design of forms and filing procedures; taxpayer education; the hiring and training of tax inspectors, etc.
21. From an address before Parliament by State Accounting Chamber Chairman Valentyn Symonenko, December 4, 1997. *Golos Ukrainy*, 9 December 1997. FBIS-SOV-97–365. Original in Russian.
22. Lyakh, "The Value-Added Tax (VAT)."
23. Ibid.
24. The Law of Ukraine, "On Value-Added Tax," no. 168–97-VR, was passed on April 3, 1997, and effective July 1, 1997. This new law was a watered-down version of a more comprehensive VAT reform that was proposed as part of President Kuchma's "Economic Growth '97" tax reform package, only pieces of which were enacted. The amended law introduced new reporting requirements, registration of taxpayers, and extended exemptions to include financial transactions (i.e., interest on mortgages, insurance, reinsurance, and other purely financial transactions). However, the VAT in Ukraine remains a somewhat modified tax on turnover, rather than a Western European-style VAT.
25. Decree of the President of Ukraine, "On Some Changes in Taxation," no. 857–98, August 7, 1998.
26. "Ukrainian Parliament Intends to Abolish the VAT in 2003," Moscow Interfax News Service, 12 July 2001, 11:36 GMT. FBIS-SOV-2001–0712. Original in English.

27. Kevin Manninen and David Snelbecker, "Obstacles to Doing Western Business in Ukraine," *The Ukrainian Legal and Economic Bulletin* (April 1993): 20–30; Larisa Melnychuk, "Small and Medium Business Development in Ukraine," *The Ukrainian Legal and Economic Bulletin* (November 1995): 20–36; Myron Rabij, "Top Twenty Legal Impediments to Doing Business in Ukraine," *The Ukrainian Legal and Economic Bulletin* (August-September 1996): 19–20; Patrizia Bernardini, "New Entrepreneurs in Kyiv," *The Ukrainian Legal and Economic Bulletin* (June 1996): 37–45.
28. International Centre for Policy Studies, "What Limits Production Growth?" *Business Opinion Review* (March 2000): 6–8.
29. The "Law on Taxation of Profits of Enterprises and Organizations' Income" was adopted February 21, 1992, establishing the legality of a tax on enterprise income. It was amended twice before being temporarily suspended by decree. It was finally replaced by a new "Law on the Taxation of Enterprise Incomes," on December 29, 1994. The 1994 law itself was subsequently amended on November 12, 1996.
30. International Monetary Fund (IMF), *Ukraine: Recent Economic Developments* (Washington, D.C.: IMF, 1997).
31. Tanzi, *Fiscal Policies,* p. 16.
32. IMF, *IMF Economic Reviews: Ukraine* (1992, 1993); IMF, *Ukraine: Recent Economic Developments* (1995, 1996).
33. However, wages and salaries remained subject to heavy employer payroll taxes of 51 percent until 1998, when the rate was reduced to 38 percent.
34. Law of Ukraine, "On Income Taxation for Enterprises and Organizations," no. 334–94-VR, December 28, 1994; revised by law no. 283–97-VR, May 22, 1997.
35. This measure was intended to encourage technological investment.
36. Including local agricultural production and food processing, fishing and fish products, rural construction, and (in principle) profits of enterprises with foreign investments registered before January 1, 1995, during the five-year period following the date of registration. (*Note*: Privileges for foreign investors were revoked in 1997.)
37. The State Tax Inspectorate required that the following financial and operational statements be submitted to an enterprises' rayon tax office: Balance Sheet; Explanatory Notes to the Balance Sheet; Income Statement; Tax Return; copy of the Payment Order for the Enterprise Income Tax; calculations of the Tax on Enterprise Income; VAT Declaration; Statement of import and export activities; copy of the Payment Order for the VAT; Excise Duty Certificate; Statement of bank accounts; Statement of land and water taxes; Declaration of the firm's hard currency holdings; Declaration on the firm's property outside of Ukraine; calculation of the Tax on Motor Vehicles; copy of the Payment Order for the Tax on Motor Vehicles; Certificate of inspection of firm-owned motor vehicles; Statement of hotels and hostels owned by the firm; and a statement of advertising expenses.
38. Tatyana Chernyak and Vadim Semjanovski, "Microeconomic Changes in Ukraine," *The Ukrainian Legal and Economic Bulletin* (March 1997): 45–47.
39. János Kornai, *The Socialist System: The Political Economy of Communism* (Princeton, NJ: Princeton University Press, 1992).
40. Bird, *Tax Policy and Economic Development,* p. 198.
41. Vito Tanzi, "Inflation Lags in Collection and the Real Value of Tax Revenues," *IMF Staff Papers,* no. 24 (1977): 154–167.
42. George Sharpe, "Taxes: Dealing with Uncertainty," *The Ukrainian Legal and Economic Bulletin* (January-February 1996): 7–8.

43. Ibid., p. 8.
44. Lidia Lyakh and Vanda Potij, "Income Taxes on Foreign Juridical Persons," *The Ukrainian Economic Monitor* III, no. 5 (May 1996): 15–17.
45. Law of Ukraine, "On Eliminating Discriminatory Taxation Against Enterprises Created Using Domestic Funds," no. 1457–00-XIV, February 17, 2000.
46. Lozynskyj-Kyj, "The New Tax Program in Ukraine," p. 378.
47. Maurice Downey, "Structural Problems of the Ukrainian Tax System," Ukrainian-European Policy and Legal Advice Centre (Kyiv: no date given, but presumed 2000).
48. Serhiy Yurhelevych and Maurice Downey, "Taxing Problems," *Ukrainian Economic Trends* (December 2000): 42–49.
49. Maurice Downey, "Tax Breaks in Ukraine: The Case for and against Their Withdrawal," *Ukrainian Economic Trends* (December 1999).
50. Marek Dabrowski, Marcin Luczynski, and Malgorzata Markiewicz, "The Phases of Budget Reform," in Anders Åslund and Georges de Ménil, eds., *Economic Reform in Ukraine: The Unfinished Agenda* (Armonk, NY and London: M.E. Sharpe, 2000), pp. 113–143.
51. Address of candidate for prime minister Viktor Yushchenko before parliament, December 22, 1999. Cited in Downey, "Tax Breaks in Ukraine."
52. Law of Ukraine, "On Fixed Agrarian Tax," no. 320–98-XIV, December 17, 1998.
53. Downey, "Tax Breaks in Ukraine."
54. Ibid.
55. Dabrowski, et al., "The Phases of Budget Reform."
56. "Mutual Settlements in 1999," Fiscal Analysis Office of the Budget Committee of *Verkhovna Rada* (December 1999). Available online at http://www.fao.kiev.ua/Publications/Monthly_report/December 1999/MS_e/MS_e.html.
57. Decree of the President of Ukraine, "On Enacting a Regime to Strictly Limit Budgetary Expenditures and Other Costs in Order to Preserve the Flow of Budget Revenues and Overcome the Financial Crisis," no. 41/98, January 21, 1998.
58. Leonid Samsonenko, "Budgetary Chickens Are Counted in Spring." Interview with First Deputy Finance Minister Stanislav Bukovynskiy, Kyiv, *Uryadoviy K'urer,* 14 November 1996, p. 10. FBIS-SOV-96–226. Original in Ukrainian.
59. State Tax Administration of Ukraine, "Tax Arrears Repayment Program" (Kyiv: State Tax Administration, 2000).
60. John Hansen and Vira Nanivska, eds., *Economic Growth with Equity: Ukrainian Perspectives* (Washington, D.C.: The World Bank, 1999), p. 68.
61. Ibid., p. 70.
62. IMF, *Ukraine: Recent Economic Developments* (1999), table 67, p. 152.
63. Hansen and Nanivska, *Economic Growth with Equity,* pp. 123–140.
64. Resolution of the Cabinet of Ministers of Ukraine, "On Certain Issues of VAT Refund and on Putting into Order the Settlements with Budget," no. 2215.
65. On June 5, 1997, parliament wrote off enterprise liabilities for the VAT, enterprise income tax, land tax, deductions to the State Innovations Fund, Chornobyl Fund, fine arrears, and related penalties and sanctions, including all payables to the Pension Fund and Social Insurance Fund. Law of Ukraine, "On Writing Off and Restructuring Tax Arrears as of 31 March 1997," no. 314–97-VR, June 5, 1997.
66. Law of Ukraine, "On the Suspension of the Decline of Agricultural Production and Foodstuff Provision of the Country in 1997–1998," no. 288–97-VR, May 23, 1997.
67. Hansen and Nanivska, *Economic Growth with Equity,* p. 71.
68. Ibid.

69. Specifically, tax debts were cancelled for firms in the following industries: coal mining, energy generating facilities, gas and oil extraction, transportation of energy products, thermal power plants, heat and water supply, and the fuel and energy complex. Law of Ukraine, "On the State Budget for 2001," no. 2120–00-XIV, December 7, 2000.
70. Law of Ukraine, "On Order of Clearing Obligations of Taxpayers to the Budgets and Target Funds," no. 2181–00-XIV, December 21, 2000. This law also repealed the infamous "*kartoteka* no. 2" regulation, which had permitted the unchallengeable seizure by the STA of funds in debtors' bank accounts.
71. Law of Ukraine, "On State Tax Administration in Ukraine," no. 509-XII, December 4, 1990; revised under law no. 3813-XII, December 24, 1993.
72. The following list is an expanded version of that provided in Downey, "Tax Breaks in Ukraine."
73. "Ukraine Leader Orders Crackdown on Tax Evasion," *Russia Today,* 24 June 2000 (Reuters). Available online at http://www.russiatoday.com/news.
74. Ibid.
75. "Ukrainian Tax Police Root Out Tax Dodgers, Recover 600m Dollars." Kiev, *IntelNews,* 22 November 2000, 0700 GMT. FBIS-SOV-2000–1122. Original in English.
76. Private communication with Ihor Shpak, Director of the Fiscal Analysis Office of the Budget Committee of *Verkhovna Rada,* July 11, 2000.
77. Colin Clark, "Public Finance and Changes in the Value of Money," *Economic Journal,* 60 (1945).
78. Robert Skidelsky, *The Road From Serfdom* (New York: The Free Press, 1995), p. 192.
79. The World Bank, *Lessons of Tax Reform* (Washington, D.C.: The World Bank, 1991), pp. 20–1.
80. Ibid., p. 5.
81. Tanzi, ed., *Transition to Market,* p. 21.
82. Ibid.
83. Tanzi further observes that "It would be an illusion to assume that these countries can become efficient market economies while maintaining their former level of taxation since that level would be a major obstacle to the efficiency of the economy. But it would equally be folly to let the level of taxation fall well ahead of the fall in public spending . . . Reducing tax rates when the tax base is shrinking and the need for some new public expenditure is increasing due to the output collapse, would be out of touch with reality." Ibid., p. 17.
84. The World Bank, *Lessons of Tax Reform,* p. 56.
85. Ibid., p. 21.
86. "Law on Value-Added Tax," no. 168–97-VR, April 3, 1997, effective July 1, 1997. The VAT reform was one of only two of the original seven tax reform bills of the "Economic Growth '97" package to be enacted. For more on the 1996 tax reform proposals, see Roman Woronowycz, "Pynzenyk Leads Public Relations Campaign to Push Reforms," *The Ukrainian Weekly,* 15 December 1996, p. 1; and "Tax Reform Package Is Stalled, No Budget in Sight for Ukraine," *The Ukrainian Weekly,* 13 April 1997, p. 1.
87. The "Law on Charging Tax on Profits of Enterprises," enacted May 22, 1997, amended sections 18 and 24 of the December 17, 1993, "Law on the State Program for Encouragement of Foreign Investment" to abolish the privileged tax treatment of enterprises with foreign investment registered before January 1, 1995, with at least $100 thousand in foreign investment. This move further called into question

Ukraine's commitment to maintaining guarantees made to foreign investors. Also, the new law immediately contradicted the "Law on Tax System," which stipulated that no amendments to current tax legislation may be made later than six months preceding the beginning of the fiscal year of its enactment. This law, and especially the revocation of foreign tax privileges, has been roundly criticized by such prominent reformers in the Cabinet of Ministers as Deputy Prime Minister Serhiy Tyhypko. See, "The New Law on Profit Taxation Adopted," *The Ukrainian Economic Monitor,* no. 6 (25) (June 1997): 23; and "Privileges Enjoyed by Enterprises with Foreign Investments Abolished," *The Ukrainian Economic Monitor,* no. 5 (24) (May 1997): p. 28.

88. Jorge Martinez-Vazquez, Charles E. McClure, Jr., and Sally Wallace, "Subnational Fiscal Decentralization in Ukraine," in Richard M. Bird, Robert D. Ebel, and Christine Wallich, eds., *Decentralization of the Socialist State: Intergovernmental Finance in Transition Countries* (Washington, D.C.: The World Bank, 1995), pp. 281–319. This citation appears on p. 290.
89. While the central government sets maximum rates that can be charged, public utility pricing has been a complex undertaking. Governments at all levels are able to provide exceptions, exemptions, and special deals for certain customers, apparently irrespective of the revenue impact on service providers. No specific data concerning regional disparities was available to the author, but interviews with finance officials at all levels indicate the presence of enormous regional variation.
90. Martinez-Vazquez, et al., "Subnational Fiscal Decentralization in Ukraine." This citation is on p. 289.
91. Ibid.
92. In 1994, the cost recovery rate for heat and hot water was a mere 12 percent; gas, 3 percent; water, 15 percent. None of these services was metered. Electrical consumption by industry is metered, but consumption by households is not. Cost recovery for electric power consumption—mostly by industry—averaged about 50 percent. In the prevailing fiscal environment, these rates became unsustainably low. At the urging of Anatoliy Dron, Chairman of the State Committee on Housing and Communal Services, in 1994 the Cabinet of Ministers issued a decree calling for long-term, progressive tariff increases to achieve cost recovery levels of 20 percent in 1994; 40 percent in 1995; and 60 percent in 1996. These targets were largely achieved on schedule. In October 1994, tariffs were raised to recover costs for heat, hot water, sewage, and gas at a rate of 15 percent. Tariffs were raised again in February 1995 (to 20 percent cost recovery), June 1995 (to 30 percent), and September 1995 (to 40–50 percent). IMF, *Ukraine: Recent Economic Developments,* p. 97.
93. See the interview with Hryniov in *Kyivska Pravda,* translated as "Kuchma Aide Outlines Regional Policy Concept," 7 September 1995, pp. 1–2, FBIS-SOV-95–176. Original in Ukrainian.
94. Law of Ukraine, "On State Budget for 1994," February 1, 1994. Original document in the author's possession. (Also published in *Uradoviy Kur'er,* 19 February 1994, pp. 6–8.)
95. Law of Ukraine, "On State Budget for 1995," April 6, 1995. See the translated text of the 1995 Budget Law from *Holos Ukrayiny,* 21 April 1995, pp. 3–5, in FBIS-SOV-95–102-S. Original in Ukrainian.
96. It should be noted that the Law on Local Self-Government and the Law on the Budget System also contradicted each other in several crucial respects. See Law of

Ukraine, "On Local Radas of Peoples' Deputies and Local and Regional Self-Government," February 7, 1992; and Law of the Ukrainian SSR, "Law on the Budget System," no. VR-513–12, December 5, 1990. Both laws have subsequently been amended several times (and since July 1996 are a matter of constitutional governance). Most recently, after much haranguing between President Kuchma and parliament, a new "Law on Local Self-Government in Ukraine," no. 280–97-VR, was enacted on May 21, 1997.

97. IMF, *Ukraine: Recent Economic Developments* (1997), p. 42.
98. In the case of the Personal Income Tax, the taxpayer's "tax home" is their place of employment, as opposed to one's place of residence.
99. Other significant factors contributing to the regions' fiscal planning difficulties have been the wildly swinging basic tax rates, frequent redefinition of the tax base, devolution of expenditure responsibilities from the center to the subnational level (see below), and parliament's consistent failure to pass the state budget until well after the start of the fiscal year.
100. In 1994, the Law on State Budget formalized a previously ad hoc practice, whereby some oblasts were periodically required to pay additional exactions to the central government, even though such transfers lacked a legal basis. Martinez-Vazquez, et al., "Subnational Fiscal Decentralization in Ukraine."
101. In the interests of full disclosure, the author confesses that he had pressed the Ministry of Finance for the 1994 approach during his 1993–94 tour in Kyiv as the U.S. Treasury's Budget Management Advisor to Ukraine. However, rampant inflation severely depressed the real value of the budgeted subventions, making frequent reappropriation a necessary feature of budget execution throughout 1994. The regions correctly understood that this placed them at a severe disadvantage to the center; consequently, they pressed for a return to the pre-1994 variable retention rate regime in the 1995 fiscal year.
102. Martinez-Vazquez, et al., "Subnational Fiscal Decentralization in Ukraine."
103. Ibid., p. 300.
104. The author has rather more extensive data on intergovernmental revenues than was possible to reproduce here. Interested parties may obtain such data by contacting the author.
105. The set of formulas for calculation of transfers is given in Resolution of the Cabinet of Ministers of Ukraine, "Procedure for the Calculation of Intergovernmental Transfer Volume," no. 1932, December 29, 2000.
106. For more detail on the weaknesses of the initial set of formulas, see Fiscal Analysis Office of the Budget Committee of *Verkhovna Rada,* "Intergovernmental Reform in Ukraine: Promising Start in 2001," *Budget and Fiscal Review* (June 2001): 1–38.

Chapter 7

1. In 1995–96, Ukraine's inflation slowed, and its record high price increase of 10,558 percent in 1993 was surpassed by Georgia and Armenia, among the central Asian republics of the former USSR.
2. Phillip Cagan, "The Monetary Dynamics of Hyperinflation," in Milton Friedman, ed., *Studies in the Quantity Theory of Money* (Chicago: University of Chicago Press, 1956).

3. An eighth occurrence, technically, took place in January 1992, but the 435 percent leap in prices that month was largely due to the partial price liberalization that took place at that time.
4. Robert Skidelsky, *The Road from Serfdom* (New York: The Free Press, 1996), p. 160.
5. Russia, under Premier Yegor Gaidar, took the lead on January 2, liberalizing 80 percent of wholesale prices and 90 percent of retail prices. Ukraine really had no choice but to reciprocate or suffer a severe disruption in trade, as goods would be diverted en masse to Russia. Ultimately to the benefit of all CIS countries, credit for this courageous step goes to Gaidar.
6. Johnson, Simon, and Oleg Ustenko, "Ukraine on the Brink of Hyperinflation," *RFE/RL Research Report* (1) 50 (December 18, 1992): 51–59.
7. International Monetary Fund (IMF), "Comments on the System of Multi-Use Coupons in the *[sic]* Ukraine," a note prepared by the staff of the International Monetary Fund, Kyiv, Ukraine, January 17, 1992. Copy in the author's possession.
8. Black market (i.e., street) exchange rates cited in Michael Zienchuk, "Ukraine in Numbers: No. 10, Year-End Review—1993," mimeograph published by the Ukrainian Ministry of the Economy and the International Centre for Advanced Studies, Kyiv, Ukraine, April 1, 1993.
9. IMF, *Ukraine: Economic Review* (1992).
10. John Williamson, *Trade and Payments after Disintegration,* Policy Analysis in International Economics, no. 37 (Washington, D.C.: Institute for International Economics, 1992); F. Desmond McCarthy, Chandra Pant, Kangbin Zeng, and Giovanni Zanalda, "External Shocks and Performance Responses During Systematic Transition: The Case of Ukraine," *Ukrainian Economic Review* I, no. 1–2 (1995): 27–48. Gijsbertus Van Selm, "The Economics of the Soviet Breakup," *Ukrainian Economic Review* I, no. 1–2 (1995): 80–95.
11. P. M. Garber and M. G. Spencer, "The Dissolution of the Austro-Hungarian Empire: Lessons for Currency Reform," *Princeton Essays in International Finance* (Princeton: Princeton University Press, 1994).
12. Petr Aven, "Discussion," *Economic Policy* (October 1994): 376–377. This citation is on p. 377.
13. Williamson, *Trade and Payments after Disintegration.*
14. Oleh Havrylyshyn, Marcus Miller, and William Perraudin, "Deficits, Inflation and the Political Economy of Ukraine," *Economic Policy* (October 1994): 354–401.
15. It was Gerashchenko whom *The Economist* in 1993 dubbed "the world's worst central banker." 16 October 1993, p. 78.
16. For a discussion of the Central Bank of Russia's monetary policy in 1992, see "O Godovom Otchete Banka Rossii," *Dengi I Kredit* 8 (1993): 3–29.
17. According to the IMF, stocks of rubles supplied by the Central Bank of Russia to Ukraine during this period were:

	Blln. Rubles	% of Total Circulating in Ukraine
1991-4Q	+31	11
1992-1Q	+32	9
2Q	+32	5
3Q	+32	3

See International Monetary Fund, *Ukraine: Economic Review* (Washington, D.C.: International Monetary Fund, September 1993).

18. This was not only a critical concern for energy-dependent states, like Ukraine. Russian crude oil export prices in March 1993 were but 17 percent of world market levels. Importing Russian oil at such price levels would obviously be of enormous benefit to any country.
19. Calculated at a rate of 420 rubles per U.S. dollar, with a term of 6 years, at interest of LIBOR + 1 percent. (*Note*: "LIBOR" stands for the "London Interbank Offer Rate."). IMF, *Ukraine: Economic Review* (1993).
20. Jeffrey Sachs and David Lipton, "Remaining Steps to Achieve a Market-Based Monetary System," mimeograph, 1992. Copy in the author's possession.
21. Decree of the President of Ukraine, "On Reform of the Monetary System of Ukraine," November 7, 1992.
22. Resolution of the Cabinet of Ministers of Ukraine and the National Bank of Ukraine, no. 610–2, November 8, 1992.
23. Viktor Zubaniuk, "Economic Specialists Examine Beginning of Monetary Reform," *The Ukrainian Weekly*, 22 November 1992, p. 3.
24. See Chrystyna Lapychak, "Prospects for the Karbovanets," *The Ukrainian Weekly*, 29 November 1992, p. 2.
25. One significant casualty of Ukraine's exit from the ruble area was NBU governor Vadim Hetman, who was dismissed on November 23, 1992, for calling for Ukraine to remain in the ruble zone and for proposing to apply payments to Russia for imported goods toward fulfillment of Ukraine's foreign debt obligations. He was succeeded by his able deputy, 39-year-old Viktor Yushchenko. Hetman's dismissal was a clear indication of the ascendancy in the government of a circle of reformers centered around Deputy Prime Minister Viktor Pynzenyk. (*Note*: Hetman was to reemerge some months later as chairman of the Ukrainian Interbank Currency Exchange. While serving in that position, Hetman was brutally murdered in the lobby of his apartment building in Kyiv in 1998. Speculation at the time centered on Hetman's close ties with Yushchenko, who has become one of Ukraine's most popular politicians, and a likely future candidate for president. To date, Hetman's murderers have eluded apprehension.)
26. At this time, the IMF was recommending to Russia that its energy export prices be raised rapidly to world market levels, a goal that was facilitated by Ukraine's exit from the ruble area.
27. Yushchenko succeeded Hetman as NBU governor on January 26, 1993.
28. For the interview with Pynzenyk, see *The Ukrainian Weekly*, 3 January 1993, p. 12.
29. Havrylyshyn, et al., "Deficits, Inflation, and the Political Economy of Ukraine," p. 358.
30. Ibid.; Olexander Babanin, "Inflationary Processes in the Ukrainian Economy," *The Ukrainian Legal and Economic Bulletin* (June 1994): 14–21; Jack Strauss, "The Role of Money and Credits in Explaining Inflation and Movements in the Karbovanets," *The Ukrainian Legal and Economic Bulletin* no. 3 (March 1995): 6–16; Georges de Ménil, "Ukraine, and the 'Ancient Sin' of Deficits," paper presented at the conference "Ukrainian Economics: Problems, Policies and Prospects," Yale University, New Haven, CT, May 16–17, 1996.
31. Growth rates are exponential growth rates, such that, for example, $g=\ln(CPI_t/CPI_{t-1})$. The continuously compounded rate varies in proportion to the length of the period, so that the quarterly rate is three times the monthly rate. The advantages are that a quick "eyeball" comparison is straightforward, and econometric analysis is facilitated.
32. There is a possibility of strong collinearity between the growth in M2 and that of enterprise and government credits. However, the coefficients on the M2 and credit

variables in the models suggest that the collinearity that is present does not confound the estimates. Obviously, M2 growth remains an intermediate variable in the inflation "transmission belt" process, albeit of lesser significance. For more on the methodology on which the analysis in this chapter is based, see Robert S. Kravchuk, "Budget Deficits, Hyperinflation, and Stabilization in Ukraine, 1991–98," *Public Budgeting & Finance* 18, no. 4 (winter 1998): 45–70.

33. Babanin, "Inflationary Processes in the Ukrainian Economy."
34. Brigitte Granville, *The Success of Russian Economic Reforms* (London: Royal Institute of International Affairs, 1995).
35. An advisor to the NBU, Georgés de Ménil examined two seeming paradoxes of Ukrainian money. First, if the peak year of monetary emissions was 1992, then why was 1993 the year of hyperinflation? The rate of monetary emission declined by about a third from 1992 to 1993. If so, then why did inflation accelerate so dramatically in 1993? Second, in 1992–96 actual inflation exceeded the calculated "equilibrium" rate of inflation (computed as the rate of inflation consistent with the observed average annual rates of seigniorage, velocity, and real GDP growth). Why did actual inflation seemingly exceed levels consistent with the simple logic of equilibrium inflation? Significant for present purposes, de Ménil resolves these paradoxes by relating inflation to money growth, with a lag of three months. See de Ménil, "Ukraine, and the 'Ancient Sin' of Deficits."
36. Strauss, "The Role of Money and Credits."
37. Ibid.
38. Ibid.
39. Recall that for present purposes M3 = M2 + foreign currency deposits.
40. John Maynard Keynes, *A Tract on Monetary Reform* (London: Macmillan, 1923; London: Royal Economic Society, 1971).
41. See Chapter 5 for a detailed discussion of the weakness of Ukraine's fledgling fiscal management institutions.
42. "Base money" is defined as currency in circulation plus banks' reserves (including cash in vaults).
43. Rudiger Dornbusch, "Lessons from the German Inflation Experience of the 1920s," in Rudiger Dornbusch and Stanley Fischer, eds., *Essays in Honor of Franco Modigliani* (Cambridge, MA: MIT Press, 1987), pp. 337–366.; Michael Bruno and Stanley Fischer, "Seigniorage, Operating Rules, and the High Inflation Trap," *The Quarterly Journal of Economics* (May 1990): 353–374.
44. M. A. Roberts, "Equilibrium Selection in a Seigniorage Model: Low Inflation or Repudiation of Money?" University of Keele Working Paper No. 93/17 (November 1993). Cited in Havrylyshyn, et al., "Deficits, Inflation, and the Political Economy of Ukraine."
45. Bruno and Fischer, "Seigniorage, Operating Rules, and the High Inflation Trap."
46. That is, it depends upon the sensitivity of the demand for money to marginal changes in its purchasing power. At base, this is a matter of both the public's confidence in the currency and the credibility of the government's commitment to defend it.
47. Havrylyshyn, et al., "Deficits, Inflation, and the Political Economy of Ukraine."
48. G. Cheikbossian, "Hyperinflation et Seigneurage en Ukraine: 1992–1993," memoire pour le diplome d'études approfondies, Ecole des Hautes Etudes en Sciences Sociales, 1994. Cited in de Ménil, "Ukraine, and the 'Ancient Sin' of Deficits."
49. Unpublished estimates referenced in de Ménil, "Ukraine, and the 'Ancient Sin' of Deficits."

50. Further tests were made of the effects of changes in real balances, changes in real balances expressed as a quadratic term, the "deposit money banks" deposit interest rate, on the M2 inflation tax, and also on enterprise sector money holdings. The interest rate was included as an independent regressor for control purposes, because for most of this period interest rates were subject to an administratively controlled ceiling set independently of the inflation rate. The conclusion is the same: The inflation tax in 1992–96 was a nonlinear function of the demand for real balances. These tests were omitted from this chapter in the interest of economizing on page length but can be found in Robert S. Kravchuk, "Budget Deficits, Hyperinflation, and Stabilization in Ukraine, 1991–98."
51. See de Ménil, "Ukraine, and the 'Ancient Sin' of Deficits," p. 10.
52. Havrylyshyn, et al., "Deficits, Inflation, and the Political Economy of Ukraine," p. 360.
53. In 1993, for instance, *Nova Ukrayina* (New Ukraine) faction leader Volodymyr Scherban, people's deputy from Donetsk, filed a suit against the government with the procurator general's office to prevent such "asset stripping." Deputy Premier Pynzenyk has also been a staunch opponent of such confiscatory policies. See "Government Accused of Confiscating Property," *IntelNews,* 1 December 1993, p. 3.
54. Indeed, the IMF attributes to households nearly 100 percent of the average annual increase in currency in circulation. See IMF, *Ukraine: Recent Economic Developments* (Washington, D.C.: International Monetary Fund, March 1996), table 12, p. 40.
55. If anything, these percentages are overstated just a bit, since enterprise cash holdings have not been excluded from the household money series. In any case, along with the IMF, the author believes that enterprise cash holdings were minimal.
56. Indeed, the relative power of enterprise directors within their concerns appears as a critical issue in formulating enterprise governance and privatization policy. See Padma Desai, *Perestroika in Perspective: The Design and Dilemmas of Soviet Reform* (London: I. B. Tauris & Co., 1989); Paul R. Lawrence and Charalambos A. Vlachoutsicos, eds., *Behind the Factory Walls: Decision Making in Soviet and U.S. Enterprises* (Boston, MA: Harvard Business School Press, 1990); Anders Åslund, *Gorbachev's Struggle for Economic Reform,* revised and expanded edition (Ithaca, NY: Cornell University Press, 1991); Anders Åslund, *How Russia Became a Market Economy* (Washington, D.C.: The Brookings Institution, 1995); E. S. Savas, "Privatization in Post-Socialist Countries," *Public Administration Review* 52, no. 6 (November/December 1992): 573–581; Yali Peng, "Privatization in Eastern European Countries," *East European Quarterly* XXVI, no. 4 (1993): 471–484; Peter Rutland, "Privatization in Russia: One Step Forward, Two Steps Back?" paper prepared as part of a project on "The Russian Construction Industry: From Plan to Market," funded by the National Council for Soviet and East European Research, contract no. 808–27; Alan Smith, ed., *Challenges for Russian Economic Reform* (London and Washington, D.C.: The Royal Institute of International Affairs and The Brookings Institution, 1995); Joseph R. Blasi, Maya Kroumova, and Douglas Kruse, *Kremlin Capitalism: Privatizing the Russian Economy* (Ithaca, NY: Cornell University Press, 1997).
57. It was the author's observation, while a resident advisor to the Minister of Finance of Ukraine from 1993–94, that enterprises in the energy, defense, and extractive industries had privileged access to the Cabinet of Ministers, largely due to their superior potential for earning scarce foreign exchange. Additionally, prior to ratification of the new Ukrainian constitution in 1996, many officials "moonlighted" in positions with industrial concerns, or in oblast administrations, a gross conflict

of interest. In a typical business day, many less-fortunate enterprise and sectoral representatives would spend long hours awaiting an opportunity to meet with officials, if they were even able to get an audience. Many came bearing gifts of one kind or another.

58. Ben Slay, "Ukraine Finally Introduces the Hryvna," *OMRI Analytical Brief*, no. 303, August 27, 1996. Available online at omripub@omri.cz.
59. Prompted by Yushchenko's repeated affirmations that the new currency would be introduced by the end of 1996, the Kyiv Universal Exchange reported trading futures contracts in the hryvnia. Trading began at a rate of KBV 100,000 to UAH 1, rising marginally to 101,604, a remarkable forecast of the conversion ratio announced three days later. See: "Ukrainian Exchange Begins Futures Trading in the Hryvna," *OMRI Daily Digest*, no. 163, part II, August 22, 1996. Available online at omripub@omri.cz.
60. The National Bank of Ukraine issued successively larger denominations of karbovantsi over the years in order to meet the demand for cash currency. Issues by year included:
    - 1991: 1-, 3-, 5-, 10-, 25-, 50-, and 100-coupon banknotes;
    - 1992: 100 (new series); 200-, 500-, and 1,000-coupon notes;
    - 1993: 2,000-, 5,000-, 10,000-, 20,000-, and 50,000-coupon notes;
    - 1994: 100,000-, 200,000-, and 500,000-coupon notes; and,
    - 1995: a 1,000,000-coupon note.
61. Based on the author's interviews on October 7, 1993, with NBU officials Mr. Oleg Rybachuk, head of the international department, and Mr. Vitaliy Myhashko, deputy head. (*Note*: The well-respected Mr. Myhashko in 1995 became head of the Department of Government Securities at the NBU, responsible for the issuance of Ukraine's state bonds, popularly known as "T-bills" in Ukraine.)
62. Natalia Zabolotna, "Currency Reform," *The Ukrainian Economic Monitor* III, no. 10(17) (1996): 8–9.
63. Ben Slay, "Ukraine Dodges a Bullet with the Hryvnya," *OMRI Analytical Brief*, no. 373, October 8, 1996. Available online at omripub@omri.cz.
64. For news coverage of the press conference, see *The Ukrainian Weekly*, 1 September 1996, p. 1.
65. Victor Yushchenko, "Monetary Reform in Ukraine," *The Ukrainian Legal & Economic Bulletin* (November 1996): 11–13.
66. "Ukraine to Lift Price Freeze Two Weeks Early," *OMRI Daily Digest*, no. 175, part II, September 10, 1996. Available online at omripub@omri.cz.
67. "Ukraine Extends Currency Exchange Deadline," *OMRI Daily Digest*, no. 181, part II, September 18, 1996. Available online at omripub@omri.cz.
68. Ibid.
69. Victor Yushchenko, "Monetary Reform in Ukraine," pp.11–13.
70. For the results of the poll, see Roman Woronowycz, "Public Upbeat about New Currency," *The Ukrainian Weekly*, 15 September 1996, p. 1.
71. Rudiger Dornbusch, "Lessons from Experiences with High Inflation," *The World Bank Economic Review* 6, no. 1 (1992): 13–31.
72. William Easterly, Carlos Alfredo Rodriguez, and Klaus Schmidt-Hebbel, eds., *Public Sector Deficits and Macroeconomic Performance* (New York: Oxford University Press and The World Bank, 1994).
73. Thomas J. Sargent and Neil Wallace, "Some Unpleasant Monetarist Arithmetic," *Federal Reserve Bank of Minneapolis Quarterly Review* (fall 1981): 1–17.

74. The argument of Sargent and Wallace is that monetary policy to check inflation fails in the long run because the real stock of bonds grows faster than the rate of growth of the economy as a whole. For some period, such supernormal growth is possible; however, a limit will be reached where the demand for bonds grows no further. Once that point is reached, debt service on bonds already issued would have to be financed through additional money creation. Knowing that they are to be repaid with cheaper currency, bond investors simply stop buying the government's paper. Thus, in the long run, Sargent and Wallace conclude that tight money must yield to additional inflation. The alternative, of course, is for the government to stabilize immediately.
75. The institutional placement of the NBU did not change under the new Constitution of Ukraine. However, under the constitutional appointments process, the NBU Governor became more difficult to remove, which provided a measure of increased central bank independence. However, under the 1999 "Law on the National Bank," the operations of the bank were formally subordinated to a 14-member council comprised of executive and legislative appointees. Only time will tell if this arrangement proves sufficient for the NBU to steer an independent course in the monetary realm.
76. Willem H. Buiter, "A Fiscal Theory of Hyperdeflations? Some Surprising Monetarist Arithmetic," *Oxford Economic Papers,* no. 39 (1987): 111–118.
77. Buiter essentially argues that, with rational expectations, "hyperinflation is impossible, but hyperdeflation may get under way" (Ibid., p. 112). The reason is that people will be on their money demand function in a rational expectations equilibrium. If we assume that the demand for real balances is a function only of expected inflation, then seigniorage equals the sum of the inflation tax plus the change in real balances. Where lax fiscal policy is accommodated through money issuance, seigniorage will cover government deficits. However, in a steady-state equilibrium, with constant real balances, seigniorage equals the inflation tax, and the rate of inflation is constant (that is, inflation is stable from period to period). If the fiscal deficit grows to be too large to be financed by the revenue-maximizing steady-state equilibrium rate of inflation, then real balances must grow to provide additional seigniorage. That is, real money demand has to increase. And here's the rub: This would require that inflation actually *fall*. Hence, Buiter concludes that, under rational expectations, unsustainable government deficits will give rise not to hyperinflation but to declining inflation. A further inference Buiter draws is that the monetarist's recommendation that governments pursue currency stabilization through fiscal austerity is unwarranted.
78. Havrylyshyn, et al., "Deficits, Inflation, and the Political Economy of Ukraine."
79. Von Hagen essentially argues that, even in a rational expectations regime, if expected inflation is below current inflation, a deficit larger than that which can be financed using the maximum steady-state seigniorage level can still be covered through an increase in real balances. Jürgen von Hagen, "Discussion," *Economic Policy* (October): 377–380.
80. Bruno and Fischer, "Seigniorage, Operating Rules, and the High Inflation Trap."
81. Partial price liberalizations occurred in Ukraine in January 1992, coinciding with Gaidar's moves in Russia; January 1993, when oil prices were raised by several times their previous level; and November 1994, when the state drastically reduced consumer subsidies and raised prices on many consumer items several times their previous level. According to de Ménil, these repeated liberalizations had the effect of "disturbing whatever underlying equilibrium relationship between deficits and

inflation may be at work." de Ménil, "Ukraine, and the 'Ancient Sin' of Deficits," p. 10.

82. Even the otherwise economically savvy former Economics Minister Roman Shpek was not immune from the impulse to blame external forces, indicated by his statements to the effect that Russian fuel price increases were to blame for Ukraine's 1993 hyperinflation. See Marta Kolomayets, "Government Announces Price Hikes for Food, Transportation, Electricity," *The Ukrainian Weekly,* 12 December 1993, p. 1.
83. On the topic of adaptive expectations, see Thomas J. Sargent, *Bounded Rationality in Economics* (Oxford, England: Oxford University Press, 1993).
84. Dornbusch, "Lessons from Experiences with High Inflation."
85. Ibid., p. 24.
86. Somewhat ironically, Ukraine was to largely meet its IMF-imposed deficit reduction targets by *failing* to meet some of its most basic obligations, by incurring large amounts of wages, pensions, and payables arrears. It is estimated that, by December 1997, the government owed some UAH 20.2 billion (roughly, $10 billion) to: state enterprises and agricultural concerns (UAH 8.6 billion), state workers (UAH 6.4 billion), and pensioners (UAH 1.0 billion). Further, Kyiv was on the hook for UAH 4.2 billion in interenterprise arrears in payments for deliveries of goods arising from state orders placed with enterprises. (From an interview with Viktor Lysnyckiy, vice rector, Kharkiv branch of the Ukrainian Academy of Public Administration, December 2, 1997.) These sums represent "suppressed inflation" to the extent that their immediate release would certainly raise prices dramatically in the near term. There is thus the real possibility that Ukraine may once again, in the not-too-distant future, suffer from the ravages of inflation. For more on the use of arrears as a form of "surrogate money," see chapter 8 of the present volume.

Appendix 7.1

1. Sales were so slow that the Ministry of Finance was repaying former T-bill debt faster than it was able to raise new funds. The new reserve requirements were expected to raise an additional UAH 100 to 150 million on the T-bill market. See Stefan Korshak, "National Bank Moves to Increase T-bill Sales," *Kyiv Post,* 25 November 1997, p. 16.
2. "New Hard Currency Trading Regulations Firm Up Treasury Bill Sales," *Kyiv Post,* 13 November 1997, p. 30.
3. Steve Gutterman and Irene Marushko, "Markets Turn Against Hryvnia; NBU Vows to Defend Currency," *Kyiv Post,* 21 November 1997, p.1.
4. The official exchange rate corridor had widened during the summer months, to 6.0 to 9.5 RUR/USD. However, even the 9.5 RUR/USD level proved to be difficult to defend; the CBR paid down $2.4 billion of its reserves from August 14–27 in the attempt. Official trading was suspended for a week, starting on August 26, but the first stirrings of a new black market in foreign currency was already showing itself. Consequently, the CBR floated the ruble against the dollar on September 1, and the exchange rate plunged below 20 RUR/USD within a week, before reversing to 8.67 on September 15. This proved to be a temporary reversal, however, when the rate stabilized at around 16 RUR/USD through early November 1998. See Marek

Jarociski, "Inflationary Consequences of the Russian crisis of August 17," analytical papers, Center for Social and Economic Analysis and the Harvard Institute for International Development, Kyiv, January 14, 1999.

5. Henceforth, all hard currency trades were restricted to the Ukrainian Currency Exchange and the Currency Exchange of the Crimean Autonomous Republic. Commissions for executing such trades were reduced from 0.15 to 0.05 percent. See "Ukraine's Economy in January-August 1998," *The Ukrainian Economic Monitor,* no. 9–10 (39–40) (September-October 1998): 6–7. See also Pavel Politiuk, "Ukraine Holds Steady Amid Financial Crisis," *The Ukrainian Weekly,* 6 September 1998,p. 1.
6. Resolution of the Cabinet of Ministers of Ukraine and the National Bank of Ukraine, "On Adopting Anticrisis Measures for Financial Stabilization," no. 1413, September 10, 1998; as amended by the Resolution of the Cabinet of Ministers of Ukraine and the National Bank of Ukraine, no. 1425, September 14, 1998.
7. "Ukrainian Banks to Set New Corridor at UAH 3.4 to 4.6 per dollar," Kiev, *Intelnews,* 0005 GMT, 10 February 1999. FBIS-SOV-1999–0210. Original in English. For additional analysis, see Pavel Politiuk, "National Bank of Ukraine Sets New Currency Corridor for Hryvnia," *The Ukrainian Weekly,* 14 February 1999, p. 1.
8. Roman Vysitskiy, "Short Hard Life—Part 1: The Hryvnia Turns Three," *Eastern Economist,* 6 September 1999, p. 19.
9. Ibid.
10. Roman Woronowycz, "Hryvnia Drops in Value by 20 Percent; Gas Shortage Seen as Cause of Destabilization," *The Ukrainian Weekly,* 15 August 1999, p. 1.
11. "Ukrainian Currency Rate Not to Change Until Election," Moscow Interfax News Service, 1517 GMT, 12 August 1999. FBIS-SOV-1999–0812. Original in English. Tyhypko's projection appears to have been based upon the fact that Ukrainian commercial banks at this time were strengthening their hryvnia reserves in order to meet their compulsory reserve requirements by the end of the month. See "Minister on Hryvnya Return to Corridor," Kiev, *Kiyevskiye Vedomosti,* 13 August 1999, p. 20. FBIS-SOV-1999–0822. Original in Russian.
12. *UICE Newsletter, 26(73)'99,* Kyiv, September 20, 1999. English edition.
13. "Ukraine: National Bank Not to Stop Currency Fall," Kiev, *Intelnews,* 9 December 1999, 0730 GMT. FBIS-SOV-1999–1209. Original in English.
14. The one proviso was that only T-bills purchased after mid-November 1997 and held to maturity were qualified "reserves."
15. Banks participating in auctions were required to meet all reserve requirements on a timely basis and have no other debts outstanding with the NBU.

Chapter 8

1. William Easterly, Carlos Alfredo Rodriguez, and Klaus Schmidt-Hebbel, eds., *Public Sector Deficits and Macroeconomic Performance* (New York: Oxford University Press and the World Bank, 1994); and Vito Tanzi, ed., *Transition to Market: Studies in Fiscal Reform* (Washington, D.C.: International Monetary Fund, 1993).
2. Ronald McKinnon, *The Order of Economic Liberalization* (Baltimore: The Johns Hopkins University Press, 1990).

3. Nouriel Roubinin and Xavier Sala-I-Martin, "Financial Repression and Economic Growth," *Journal of Development Economics* 39, no. 1 (1992): 5–30; McKinnon, *The Order of Economic Liberalization*; John Sheahan, "Market-Oriented Economic Policies and Political Repression in Latin America," *Economic Development and Cultural Change* 28, no. 2 (1980): 267–291.
4. James Tobin, "Money and Economic Growth," *Econometrica* 33, no. 4 (1965): 671–684.
5. Ronald I. McKinnon, *Money and Capital in Economic Development* (Washington, D.C.: The Brookings Institution, 1973); and Edward S. Shaw, *Financial Deepening in Economic Development* (New York: Oxford University Press, 1973).
6. Easterly, et al., *Public Sector Deficits.*
7. Lance Taylor, *Structuralist Macroeconomics: Applicable Models for the Third World* (New York: Basic Books, 1983); Sweder Van Wijnbergen, "Credit Policy, Inflation, and Growth in a Financially Repressed Economy," *Journal of Development Economics*: 13, nos. 1–2 (1983): 45–65, and "Interest Rate Management in LDCs," *Journal of Monetary Economics* 12, no. 3 (1983): 433–452, and "Macroeconomic Effects of Changes in Bank Rates: Simulation Results for South Korea," *Journal of Development Economics* 18, nos. 2–3 (1985): 541–554; Edward F. Buffie, "Financial Repression, the New Structuralists, and Stabilization Policy in Semi-Industrialized Economies," *Journal of Development Economics* 14, no. 3 (1984): 305–322; Sebastian Edwards, "The Order of Liberalization of the External Sector in Developing Countries," Princeton Essays in International Finance, no. 156 (Princeton, NJ: Princeton University Press, 1984); Carlos Diaz-Alejandro, "Goodbye Financial Repression, Hello Financial Crash," *Journal of Development Economics* 19, nos. 1–2 (1985): 1–24; Alice H. Amsden, *Asia's Next Giant: South Korea and Late Industrialization* (New York: Oxford University Press, 1989); Robert Wade, *Governing the Market: Economic Theory and the Role of Government in East Asian Industrialization* (Princeton, NJ: Princeton University Press, 1990); Laura Hastings, "Regulatory Revenge: The Politics of Free-Market Financial Reform in Chile," in Stephen Haggard, Chung H. Lee, and Sylvia Maxfield, eds., *The Politics of Finance in Developing Countries* (Ithaca, NY: Cornell University Press, 1993).
8. See Anthony Lanyi and Rusdu Saracoglu, "Interest Rate Policies in Developing Countries," IMF Occasional Paper No. 22 (Washington, D.C.: International Monetary Fund, 1983); The World Bank, *World Development Report: Financial Systems in Developing Countries* (Washington, D.C.: The World Bank, 1989); Nouriel Roubinin and Xavier Sala-I-Martin, "A Growth Model of Inflation, Tax Evasion, and Financial Repression," *Journal of Monetary Economics* 35, no. 2 (1992): 275–301; William Easterly, "How Much Do Distortions Affect Growth?" *Journal of Monetary Economics* 32, no. 4 (1993): 187–212; Ross Levine, "Financial Structures and Economic Development," *Revista de Analisis Economico* 8, no. 1 (1993): 67–89; and, "Financial Development and Economic Growth," Policy Research Working Paper No. 1678 (Washington, D.C.: The World Bank, 1996); and Robert G. King and Ross Levine, "Finance and Growth: Schumpeter Might Be Right," *Quarterly Journal of Economics* 108, no. 3 (1993): 717–738; and, "Finance, Entrepreneurship, and Growth: Theory and Evidence," *Journal of Monetary Economics* 32, no. 3 (1993): 513–542.
9. Philip L. Brock, "Reserve Requirements and the Inflation Tax," *Journal of Money, Credit, and Banking* 21, no. 1 (1989): 106–121; Valerie Bencivenga and Bruce D. Smith, "Deficits, Inflation, and the Banking System in Developing Countries: The

Optimal Degree of Financial Repression," *Oxford Economic Papers* 44, no. 4 (1992): 767–790; Alberto Giovanni and Martha de Melo, "Government Revenue from Financial Repression," *American Economic Review* 83, no. 4 (1993): 953–963; Easterly, et al., *Public Sector Deficits*; and Maxwell J. Fry, *Money, Interest, and Banking in Economic Development*, 2d. ed. (Baltimore, MD: The Johns Hopkins University Press, 1995).

10. Roubinin and Sala-I-Martin, "Financial Repression and Economic Growth."
11. Alberto Alesina and Howard Rosenthal, *Partisan Politics, Divided Government, and the Economy* (Cambridge, England: Cambridge University Press, 1995); Dennis P. Quinn and Carla Inclán, "The Origins of Financial Openness: A Study of Current and Capital Account Liberalization," *American Journal of Political Science* 41, no. 3 (1997): 771–813.
12. Fry, *Money, Interest, and Banking in Economic Development.*
13. Resolution of the National Bank of Ukraine, "On Formation of Mandatory Reserves for the Ukrainian Banking System," December 31, 1996.
14. Fry, *Money, Interest, and Banking in Economic Development.*
15. Robert J. Barro, "Economic Growth in a Cross-Section of Countries," *Quarterly Journal of Economics* 106 (1991): 407–443; King and Levine, "Finance and Growth: Schumpeter Might Be Right," and "Finance, Entrepreneurship, and Growth: Theory and Evidence."
16. Viktor A. Yushchenko, "Monetary Policy in the Transition to a Market Economy," in Anders Åslund and Georgés de Ménil, eds., *Economic Reform in Ukraine: The Unfinished Agenda* (Armonk, NY and London: M. E. Sharpe, 2000), pp. 94–110.
17. Subsidized crediting distorts factor prices and does not discriminate against inefficient investment projects.
18. Haggard, et al., *The Politics of Finance in Developing Countries*; Arvid J. Lukauskas, "The Political Economy of Financial Restriction: The Case of Spain," *Comparative Politics* 27, no. 1 (1994): 67–89.
19. Of course, direct budget subsidies are the ultimate zero-interest means of capital-rationing to enterprises.
20. Viktor Yushchenko and Viktor Lysytsky, "Excessive State Consumption: The Main Instability Factor for Ukraine," *Ukrainian Economic Trends* (June 1998): 122–131.
21. Ibid., p. 122.
22. This observation is based on the author's meetings and interviews with, among others, former minister of finance Hryhoriy Piatachenko, First Deputy Finance Minister Mykola Syvulskiy, and Deputy Minister of the Economy Volodymyr Naumenko. National Bank of Ukraine officials were not immune to the persistence of Soviet-era thinking about the role of money in the economy. For instance, the author attended a conference on "The Economy of Ukraine: Today and Tomorrow," hosted by Deputy Premier Viktor Pynzenyk in August 1993, where Ms. Galina Kuznetsova, head of the Department of Monetary Policy of the NBU, stated flatly that the Ukrainian inflation was not a monetary phenomenon but the result of distortions in retail pricing brought about by monopoly enterprises.
23. Gavin Peebles, *A Short History of Socialist Money* (Sydney, Australia: Allen & Unwin, 1991) p. 29.
24. Ibid.
25. I. Fogaras, "The Population's Savings Deposits in the European CMEA Countries," *Acta Oeconomica* 21, nos. 1–2 (1978): 141–150; Igor Birman and Roger A. Clarke, "Inflation and the Money Supply in the Soviet Economy," *Soviet Studies* 37, no. 4

(1985): 494–504; Jan Winiecki, "Portes Ante Portas: A Critique of the Revisionist Interpretation of Inflation Under Central Planning," *Comparative Economic Studies* 27, no. 2 (summer 1985): 25–51; Jan Winiecki, *The Distorted World of Soviet-Type Economies* (London and New York: Routledge, 1988); Gavin Peebles, "On the Importance of Establishing the Inverse Relationship Between Open Inflation and Household Liquidity Growth Under Socialism: A Critique of Jan Winiecki's Savings Deposit Data," *Comparative Economic Studies* 28, no. 4 (1986): 85–91.

26. See, for instance, Qixian Zeng, "Comments on Consumption and Savings," *Social Sciences in China* 4, no. 4 (1983): 137–163.
27. Richard Portes, "The Theory and Measurement of Macroeconomic Disequilibrium in Centrally Planned Economies," in Christopher Davis and Wojciech Charemza, eds., *Models of Disequilibrium and Shortage in Centrally Planned Economies* (London: Chapman and Hall, 1989).
28. For instance, former finance minister Hryhoriy Piatachenko persisted in arguing, as late as March 1994, that Ukraine's monetary problems were an instance of the "goods-money-goods" formula described in detail by Karl Marx in *Das Kapital.* Indeed, he stated that this "applies to [Ukraine] straight out of the book." A further indication of the government's attitudes at the time were provided by Piatachenko's rather telling assertion that "there is nothing bad about the fact that in 1993 the National Bank of Ukraine issued KBV 25 trillion in cash." See Serhiy Borysenko, "Piatachenko Defends 1994 Budget," *IntelNews,* 2 March 1994, p. 4.
29. Peebles, *A Short History of Socialist Money.*
30. It is exceedingly difficult to measure the quantity of foreign currency held by households. Almost none of it is deposited in banks. According to officials at the NBU, foreign currency deposits "on the record," as it were, are almost entirely in enterprise accounts.
31. Maxwell J. Fry, "Flexibility in Finance," in Tony Killick, ed., *The Flexible Economy* (London and New York: Routledge, 1995), pp. 297–324. This citation appears on p. 306.
32. McKinnon, *The Order of Economic Liberalization,* ch. 7, pp. 84–91.
33. Fry, "Flexibility in Finance," p. 306.
34. The World Bank, "Financial Intermediation Policy Paper" (Washington, D.C.: The World Bank, industry department, July 1985); David L. Gordon, "Development Finance Companies, State and Privately Owned: A Review," World Bank Staff Working Paper No. 578 (Washington, D.C.: The World Bank, 1993); Fry, "Flexibility in Finance."
35. World Bank, "Financial Intermediation Policy Paper."
36. Raj M. Desai and Katharina Pistor, "Financial Institutions and Corporate Governance," in Ira W. Lieberman, Stilpon S. Nestor, and Raj M. Desai, eds., *Between State and Market: Mass Privatization in Transition Economies* (Washington, D.C., The World Bank, 1997).
37. J. A. Poser, "Monetary Disruptions and the Emergence of Barter in FSU Economies," *Communist Economies and Economic Transformation* 10, no. 2 (1998): 157–77.
38. Ihor Zhyliaev, "Surrogate Money in the Ukrainian Economy: The Scale and the Dynamics," *Ukrainian Economic Trends* (March 1999): 50–67.
39. Mario Gara, "The Emergence of Non-Monetary Means of Payment in the Russian Economy," *Research Papers in Russian and East European Studies*, no. REES99/2, the University of Birmingham, December 1999, pp. 19–23.
40. Ibid.

41. Zhyliaev, "Surrogate Money in the Ukrainian Economy."
42. Gara, "The Emergence of Non-Monetary Means of Payment in the Russian Economy."
43. Simon Commander and C. Mumssen, "Understanding Barter in Russia," *Working Papers*, no. 37 (London: European Bank for Reconstruction and Development, 1999).
44. S. Williamson and R. Wright, "Barter and Monetary Exchange under Private Information," *American Economic Review* 84, no. 1 (March 1994): 104–123; Y. S. Kim, "Money, Barter, and Costly Information Acquisition," *Journal of Monetary Economics* 37, no. 1 (February 1996): 119–142.
45. S. Aukutsionek, "Some Characteristics of Transition Economies (II)," *Communist Economies and Economic Transformation*, no. 3 (September 1997): 289–336. This citation appears on p. 312.

Appendix 8.1

1. These small banks and cooperatives were formed in the late 1990s by perestroika-era legislation that authorized establishment of cooperative banks to serve workers' collectives, permitting enterprises to own and operate financial institutions.
2. Law of Ukraine, "On Banks and Banking Activity," no. 872-XII, March 20, 1991.
3. Started with authorized capital of ECU 3 million, and owned jointly by Credit Lyonnais Global Banking (35.0 percent), Credit Europ (35.0 percent), and Notolion BV (30.0 percent).
4. Natalia Zabolotna, "The Banking System of Ukraine," *The Ukrainian Economic Monitor* 4, no. 2 (1995): 10–12.
5. Natalia Zabolotna, "Review of the Monetary Sphere," *The Ukrainian Economic Monitor* 3, no. 2 (March 1997): 9–12. These data appear on p. 10.
6. Daniel Gros and Alfred Steinherr, "Banking Reforms in Eastern Europe with Special Reference to Ukraine," in Axel Siedenberg and Lutz Hoffmann, eds., *Ukraine at the Crossroads* (Heidelberg and New York: Physica-Verlag, 1999), pp. 193–216. This citation appears on p. 205.
7. National Bank of Ukraine, *Bulletin of the National Bank of Ukraine (Visnyk NBU)* 1, no. 1 (November 1997).
8. Law of Ukraine, "On the National Bank of Ukraine," no. 679-XIV, May 20, 1999.
9. See http://www.bank.gov.ua.
10. "National Bank to Select Potential Bankrupt Banks," Moscow Interfax News Service, 13 March 1995, 15:49 GMT. FBIS-SOV-95–049. Original in English.
11. For the ratios, see Natalia Samilova, "Banking in Ukraine," *Ukrainian Legal and Economic Bulletin* (July 1997): 10–13.
12. The following new departments were established at NBU: Banking Supervision Department, Bank Registration and Licensing Department, Off-Site Inspection Department, and the Bank Supervision Coordination Unit. Further, in 1998 an off-site Monitoring Department for Large Banks was created.
13. National Bank of Ukraine Regulation No. 315, "Means of Reforming of Accounting and Financial Statements of Commercial Banks," November 29, 1996.
14. Resolution of the National Bank of Ukraine, "On Creating Necessary Conditions for the State Tax Administration of Ukraine to Control Taxation, Provision of Supply of Cash Funds to the State Budget of Ukraine, and Improvement of the

Information Exchange Among the National Bank of Ukraine, Commercial Banks and Their Institutions and Bodies of State Tax Administration of Ukraine," December 14, 1999.

15. Decree of the President of Ukraine, "On Measures to Protect Rights of Individual Depositors to the Commercial Banks of Ukraine," no. 996–98, September 10, 1998.

Appendix 8.2

1. Attributed to a western economist. See *IntelNews,* 3 January 1995, p. 3.
2. Chrystia Freeland, "Ukraine Tries to Salvage Reform," *The Financial Times,* 6 April 1993, p. 1.
3. Marta Kolomayets, "Kravchuk Appoints Zviahilskiy Acting Prime Minister," *The Ukrainian Weekly,* 26 September 1993, p. 4.
4. In addition to fueling inflation, the ongoing credit emissions also had the effect of wiping out existing interenterprise debts as well as tax liabilities to the government, making it all but impossible to distinguish the loss-making enterprises from among the others.
5. *Bankivska Gazeta,* 24 September—2 October, 1993, p. 6. For Zviahilskiy's remark, which editors at *The Economist* humorously termed "a breakthrough in economic thinking," see the October 16, 1993 issue of that journal, p. 33.
6. For instance, in a December 15, 1993, NBU Memorandum to Acting Prime Minister Zviahilskiy, First Deputy Chairman of the NBU Oleh Veselovskiy stated flatly that, "the major source of inflation is the excessive credit and monetary emission . . . , the practice of directed crediting initiated upon the consensus between the Supreme Council and the President . . . , and the soft credit policy of the National Bank." Memorandum Regarding The Anti-Inflation Measures, December 15, 1993. (A copy of this memorandum is in the author's possession.)
7. Decree of the President of Ukraine, "On Additional Measures Concerning the Currency Regulations," no. 502–93, November 2, 1993.
8. Decree of the Cabinet of Ministers of Ukraine, "On the System of Currency Regulation and Currency Control," no. 15–93, February 19, 1993. The Ukrainian Interbank Currency Exchange (UICE) actually was started in fall 1992 by a consortium of 48 member banks. The cabinet's decree merely formalized its role. At the UICE, banks would buy and/or sell foreign currency on account of their clients, who were involved in import-export trade. Four days a week, the exchange held managed auctions between four different foreign currencies and the karbovanets (now, the hryvnia). Dollars were traded on Thursdays, Belarus rubles on Mondays, Deustche marks on Tuesdays, and Russian rubles on Wednesdays. By November 1993, the UICE-based auction had established itself as an important barometer of economic progress in Ukraine. Essentially, it provided an ongoing referendum on the government's economic policies, which the president found increasingly to his embarrassment.
9. Decree of the Cabinet of Ministers of Ukraine, "On the Temporary Procedure for the Use of Foreign Currency Earnings," no. 93–016, February 19, 1993.
10. Viktor M. Pynzenyk quoted in Alex Frishberg, "Ukrainian Currency Regulations: Yesterday and Today," *The Ukrainian Legal and Economic Bulletin* 3, no. 5 (January-February 1994): 9–11.

11. Resolution of the Cabinet of Ministers of Ukraine, "On Cancellation of Exemptions Granted to Enterprises and Organizations Regarding Mandatory Sale of Hard Currency Revenues," no. 961, November 26, 1993.
12. The 80 percent estimate was reported by Acting Prime Minister Zviahilskiy. See "Parliamentary Update," *IntelNews,* 26 November 1993, p. 1.
13. Resolution of the Supreme Council of Ukraine, "On a Procedure for Implementing the Law of Ukraine, 'On Amendments to the Decrees of the Cabinet of Ministers of Ukraine on Currency Regulation," November 25, 1993.
14. At the time, Ministry of Finance officials indicated to the author that the November 30 rate of 7,090 KBV per dollar was set based on a thorough examination of recent foreign trade transactions, which yielded a "weighted average" exchange rate of 7,090.
15. Law of Ukraine, "On Amendments to the Decrees of the Cabinet of Ministers of Ukraine on Currency Regulation," November 25, 1993.
16. Joint Resolution of the Cabinet of Ministers of Ukraine and National Bank of Ukraine, "On Implementation of the Decree of the President of Ukraine of November 2, 1993, 'On Additional Measures Concerning Currency Regulation'," no. 954, November 24, 1993.
17. The customary definition of "hyperinflation" is monthly inflation in excess of 50 percent. See Philip Cagan, "The Monetary Dynamics of Hyperinflation," in Milton Friedman, ed., *Studies in the Quantity Theory of Money* (Chicago: University of Chicago Press, 1956).
18. Serhiy Dmytrychenko, "Parliamentary Week in Review," *IntelNews,* 20 December 1993, p. 3.
19. Without controls on credit emissions, policies designed to "insulate" the public from the necessary price adjustment would be doomed to fail. Indeed, in the last four months of 1993, credit emissions accelerated to a level 1.4 times faster than the rate of price increase, pushing Ukraine over the threshold of hyperinflation.
20. Remarks of Volodymyr Naumenko, Deputy Minister of the Economy, before the American Chamber of Commerce in Ukraine, Kyiv, November 17, 1993. From the author's notes taken at the meeting.
21. Government telegram to Crimean, republican, and oblast departments of the National Bank of Ukraine, and commercial banks, November 11, 1993. (In the author's possession.) The telegram, signed by Acting Premier Zviahilskiy and NBU Governor Yushchenko, is telling in two respects. First, the government had virtually no control over the credit activities of NBU branches in the regions of Ukraine. In any case, the NBU felt compelled to maintain liquidity in the banking system by covering shortfalls in credit accounts of commercial banks that were ordered by parliament to extend enterprise credits. Second, with over three weeks before its implementation, the subtext of the telegram was that all previously authorized credits would have to be extended by December 2 or they would be "lost" to the potential recipients, who could not repay them in any event. Needless to say, the measure was of little effect. By December 22, Yushchenko would admit that the crackdown on credits was a failure and that the government had saved "a ridiculously small amount, 15 billion KBV. (See *IntelNews,* 23 December 1993, p. 3.
22. This amounted to approximately $80 million at December 1993 exchange rates. See "Finance Ministry Ready to Pay Out KBV 23 tn.," *IntelNews,* 5 December 1993, p. 2.
23. "Parliamentary Update," *IntelNews,* 26 November 1993, p. 1.
24. "Government Promises to Repay Farmers," *IntelNews,* 27 December 1993, p. 2.

25. The classic definition of "hyperinflation" posits a threshold average monthly price increase of 50 percent. See Philip Cagan, "The Monetary Dynamics of Hyperinflation."
26. Members of the committee charged with determining the priorities for hard currency use were Landyk (chair), UICE chairman Hetman, and representatives of the NBU, Ukraine's Security Service, Foreign Ministry, Cabinet of Ministers, and (interestingly) INKO Bank.
27. Alex Frishberg, "Review of Ukrainian Currency Reforms," *The Ukrainian Legal and Economic Bulletin* 3, no. 5 (May 1995): 1–5.
28. "Finance Ministry Ready to Pay Out KBV 23tn," *IntelNews,* 5 December 1993, p. 2.
29. "More Credit Emissions On the Way," *IntelNews,* 9 February 1994, p. 1.
30. A critical problem with this method, of course, was that in the hyperinflationary environment of late 1993, it was extremely difficult, if not impossible, to estimate the true value-added of production.
31. The three banks involved were ProminvestBank, Agrobank Ukrayina, and Ukrsotsbank. See "Banks Set Up Credit Fund," IntelNews, 10 February 1994, p. 3.
32. See "Government Heads May Role," *IntelNews,* 18 February 1994, p. 1; and "Government Emits Credit 'For Debt-Clearing Only,'" *IntelNews,* 25 February 1994.
33. "Payments Crisis Cure Announced," *IntelNews,* 23 February 1994, p. 1.
34. Yanina Sokolovskaya, "Kurs Domara Vrastet v Piatnitsu," Kyiv, *Nezavisimost,* 25 February 1994, p. 1.
35. "Currency Exchange Reopens," *IntelNews,* 11 February 1994, p. 3; See also: "Ukraine's Hard Cash Making Its Way to Moscow Auction," *IntelNews,* 4 December 1993, p. 3.
36. Ibid.
37. Oleh Borsuk, "Yushchenko Criticizes Fixed Rate," *IntelNews,* 15 April 1994.
38. Decree of the President of Ukraine, "On Perfecting Currency Regulations," August 22, 1994. See also Marta Kolomayets, "First of Presidential Decrees on Economy Covers Currency," *The Ukrainian Weekly,* 28 August 1994, p. 2.
39. See *Delovie Novosti,* no. 33 (August 1994): 2.
40. National Bank of Ukraine, Instruction No. 174, October 24, 1994.
41. Oleh Borsuk and Oleksandr Shtolko, "KBV Depreciates Amid Hard Currency Trade Expectations," *IntelNews,* 7 October 1994.
42. "Exchange Rate Rises as NBU Launches Tough Measures," *IntelNews,* 28 October 1994, p. 5.
43. "Prime Minister Declares Return of Ukrainian Money Successful," *IntelNews,* 13 April 1994.
44. Independent estimates placed the figure in the $25–50 billion range by November 1995. See: Ukrainian Press Agency, *UpressA,* 27 November 1995, p. 3. See also, Interfax—Ukraine, "Excess of $20 Billion Transferred Abroad Over Four Years," 22 November 1996. FBIS-TDD-97–001-L. Original in English.
45. Ibid.
46. Marta Kolomayets, "National Bank of Ukraine Rescinds Ban on Use of Hard Currency," *The Ukrainian Weekly,* 26 February 1995.
47. Victor Tkachuk, "What Pushed Karbovantsi Off Balance?" Ukrainian Press Agency, *UPressA,* 21 August 1995.
48. Decree of the President of Ukraine, "On Measures for Elimination of the Payments Crisis and for Support of National Producers," May 22, 1995.

49. For Kuchma's April 4, 1995, Address to Parliament on "The Economy of Ukraine in 1994," see "Zverennya Presidenta Ukrainy do Verkhovnoii Rady Ukrainy 4 Kvitnya 1995 Roku," *Holos Ukrainy*, 6 April 1995, pp. 3–4.
50. Yevhen Pivnev, "'Correction of Reforms,' Death Before Birth, and Life After Death," Ukrainian Press Agency, *UPressA*, 11 September 1995.
51. Ibid.
52. Anatoliy Galchinsky, "Ekonomicheskaya Politika Presidenta Nekotrye Itogi Pervogo Goda," *Kievskie Vedomosti*, 18 July 1995, p. 6.
53. "Government to Reduce Credits to Industry," *IntelNews*, 27 November 1995.
54. See *Moloda Ukrayina*, 5 May 1995, p. 2.
55. Decree of the President of Ukraine, "On Mutual Debt of Subjects of Entrepreneurial Activity," September 14, 1994.
56. Decree of the President of Ukraine, "On Measures to Normalize Payments Discipline," March 16, 1995.
57. Hreohoriy Larin, "Nonpayment Crisis Climaxes in a Chain Reaction of Bankruptcies," Ukrainian Press Agency, *UPressA*, 7 August 1995.
58. Marta Kolomayets, "Presidential Decree Attempts to Counter Payments Crisis," *The Ukrainian Weekly*, 26 May 1996, p. 3.
59. Irina Titova, "Unpaid Back Wages Could Become External Debts," *Kievskie Vedomosti*, 20 January 1997, p. 3. FBIS-SOV-97–026. Original in Russian.
60. Ibid. Indeed, on March 18, 1997, procommunist demonstrations where held in Kyiv, Dnipropetrovsk, Simferopol, and other cities to protest against nonpayment of wages. See Irene Marushko, Reuters News Service, March 18, 1997.

Index